THE CAMBRIDGE COMPANION TO
HEIDEGGER
2nd Edition

Martin Heidegger is now widely recognized alongside Wittgenstein as one of the greatest philosophers of the twentieth century. He transformed mainstream philosophy by defining its central task as asking the "question of being," and he has had a profound impact on fields such as literary theory, theology, psychotherapy, political theory, aesthetics, and environmental studies. His thought has contributed to the recent turn to hermeneutics in philosophy and the social sciences and to current postmodern and poststructuralist developments. Moreover, the disclosure of his deep involvement in the ideology of Nazism has provoked much debate about the relation of philosophy to politics. This new edition of *The Cambridge Companion to Heidegger* brings to the fore new works that appear in Heidegger's collected works, as well as new approaches to scholarship that have emerged since the original publication of the first edition. It presents new essays by distinguished Heidegger scholars Julian Young, William Blattner, Taylor Carman, and Mark Wrathall. Their essays cover topics such as Heidegger's conception of phenomenology, his relation to Kant and Husserl, his conception of the a priori, his account of truth, his stand on the realism/anti-realism debate, and his later conceptions of "dwelling," "place," and the "fourfold." This edition includes a new preface by the editor, revised versions of several essays from the first edition, and an exhaustive and up-to-date bibliography, providing guidance for both newcomers and established scholars to the most recent sources on Heidegger's work.

Charles B. Guignon is professor of philosophy at the University of South Florida. He is the author of *Heidegger and the Problem of Knowledge* and *On Being Authentic* and editor of *The Good Life, The Existentialists,* and *Richard Rorty.*

CAMBRIDGE COMPANIONS TO PHILOSOPHY

(Continued after Index)

The Cambridge Companion to
HEIDEGGER

2nd Edition

Edited by Charles B. Guignon
University of South Florida

CAMBRIDGE
UNIVERSITY PRESS

CAMBRIDGE UNIVERSITY PRESS
Cambridge, New York, Melbourne, Madrid, Cape Town,
Singapore, São Paulo, Delhi, Tokyo, Mexico City

Cambridge University Press
32 Avenue of the Americas, New York, NY 10013-2473, USA

www.cambridge.org
Information on this title: www.cambridge.org/9780521528887

First edition published 1993
Second edition published 2006
Reprinted 2007, 2008, 2011

A catalog record for this publication is available from the British Library.

Library of Congress Cataloging in Publication Data

The Cambridge companion to Heidegger / edited by Charles
Guignon. – 2nd ed.
    p.   cm. – (Cambridge companions to philosophy)
Includes bibliographical references (p.   ) and index.
ISBN-13: 978-0-521-82136-0 (hardback)
ISBN-10: 0-521-82136-3 (hardback)
ISBN-13: 978-0-521-52888-7 (pbk.)
ISBN-10: 0-521-52888-7 (pbk.)
1. Heidegger, Martin, 1889–1976.   I. Guignon, Charles B., 1944–
II. Series.
B3279.H49C25   2006
193 – dc22   2006001151

ISBN 978-0-521-82136-0 Hardback
ISBN 978-0-521-52888-7 Paperback

CONTENTS

CONTRIBUTORS

WILLIAM BLATTNER, Associate Professor of Philosophy at Georgetown University, specializes in early Heidegger and the American pragmatists, especially John Dewey. Author of *Heidegger's Temporal Idealism* (1999) and *Heidegger's "Being and Time"* (forthcoming), he has also published papers on temporality, Heidegger, and Dewey.

JOHN D. CAPUTO, David R. Cook Professor of Philosophy at Villanova, is the author of *Radical Hermeneutics* (1987), *Heidegger and Aquinas* (1982), *The Mystical Element in Heidegger's Thought* (1978), and *Demythologizing Heidegger* (1993) as well as a number of articles on Heidegger. His more recent books include *More Radical Hermeneutics* (2000) and *On Religion* (2001).

TAYLOR CARMAN is Professor of Philosophy at Barnard and Columbia University, specializing in nineteenth- and twentieth-century continental philosophy. He is the author of *Heidegger's Analytic: Interpretation, Discourse, and Authenticity in "Being and Time"* (2003), has written on various topics in phenomenology, and is co-editor of the *Cambridge Companion to Merleau-Ponty* (2005).

ROBERT J. DOSTAL, Rufus M. Jones Professor of Philosophy at Byrn Mawr College, is the author of numerous articles on Kant, Heidegger, and hermeneutics. He is the editor of *The Cambridge Companion to Gadamer* (2002).

HUBERT L. DREYFUS is Professor of Philosophy at the University of California, Berkeley. He is the author of *Being-in-the-world: A Commentary on Heidegger's "Being and Time," Division I* (1991) and co-editor of *Heidegger: A Critical Reader* (1992), the Blackwell *Companion to Heidegger* (2005), the *Companion to Phenomenology*

ix

and Existentialism (forthcoming), and the four-volume collection of essays, *Heidegger Re-examined* (Routledge, 2002).

DOROTHEA FREDE is Professor of Philosophy at the University of Hamburg in Germany. Her main field is ancient philosophy, and she has published widely in classical and Hellenistic philosophy. She has also published essays on Heidegger, emphasizing his criticism of, and dependence on, the history of Western philosophy.

CHARLES B. GUIGNON, Professor of Philosophy at the University of South Florida, is the author of *Heidegger and the Problem of Knowledge* (1983) and *On Being Authentic* (1983). He is the editor or co-editor of a number of collections and readers such as *Existentialism: Basic Writings* (2nd edition, 2001) and *The Existentialists* (2004).

PIOTR HOFFMAN is Professor of Philosophy at the University of Nevada, Reno. His most recent books include *Violence in Modern Philosophy* (1989) and *Doubt, Time and Violence* (1987). He has also written a number of articles about time in Heidegger's early thought.

DAVID COUZENS HOY, Professor of Philosophy at the University of California, Santa Cruz, is the author of *The Critical Circle: Literature, History and Philosophical Hermeneutics* (1978), editor of *Foucault: A Critical Reader* (1986), and co-author with Thomas McCarthy of *Critical Theory* (1994). His most recent book is *Critical Resistance: From Poststructuralism to Post-Critique* (2005).

THOMAS SHEEHAN is Professor, Department of Religious Studies, at Stanford University. He is the editor of *Heidegger: The Man and the Thinker* (1981), the author of *Karl Rahner: The Philosophical Foundations* (1987), and co-editor of *Edmund Husserl, Psychological and Transcendental Phenomenology and the Confrontation with Heidegger (1927–1931)* (1997). He has written numerous articles on Heidegger.

CHARLES TAYLOR has taught at Oxford and McGill Universities and is currently Professor of Law and Philosophy at Northwestern University. His writings include the two-volume *Philosophical Papers* (1985), *Sources of the Self* (1989), and, more recently, *Varieties of Religion Today* (2002) and *Modern Social Imaginaries* (2004).

MARK A. WRATHALL, Professor of Philosophy at Brigham Young University, specializes in philosophy of mind and modern European philosophy. He is editor, with Hubert L. Dreyfus, of collections and companions on Heidegger and phenomenology, and he is editor of *Religion after Metaphysics* (2003). His forthcoming book from Granta is titled *How to Read Heidegger* (2005).

JULIAN YOUNG is Professor of Philosophy at the University of Auckland, New Zealand. He specializes in aesthetics and continental philosophy, especially Schopenhauer, Nietzsche, and Heidegger, and has collaborated in the translation of Heidegger's *Off the Beaten Track* (2002). He is the author of *Heidegger, Philosophy, Nazism* (1997), *Heidegger's Philosophy of Art* (2001), and *Heidegger's Later Philosophy* (2001).

MICHAEL E. ZIMMERMAN is Professor of Philosophy at Tulane University. He has published many scholarly works on Heidegger as well as two books: *Eclipse of the Self* (rev. ed., 1986) and *Heidegger's Confrontation with Modernity* (1990). He has also written on radical ecology and postmodernity.

ABBREVIATIONS: WORKS BY HEIDEGGER

BP   *The Basic Problems of Phenomenology*, Translated by
A. Hofstadter. Bloomington: Indiana University Press,
1982; rev. ed., 1988.

BQP   *Basic Questions of Philosophy: Selected "Problems" of
"Logic."* Translated by Richard Rojcewicz and André
Schuwer. Bloomington: Indiana University Press,
1994.

BT   *Being and Time.* Translated by John Macquarrie and
Edward Robinson. New York: Harper & Row, 1962.

BW   *Basic Writings.* Edited by David F. Krell. New York:
Harper & Row, 1977.

DT   *Discourse on Thinking.* Translated by John M.
Anderson and E. Hans Freund. New York: Harper &
Row, 1975.

EGT   *Early Greek Thinking.* Translated by David F. Krell and
Frank Capuzzi. New York: Harper & Row, 1975.

EP   *The End of Philosophy.* Translated by Joan Stambaugh.
New York: Harper & Row, 1973.

ER   *The Essence of Reasons.* Translated by Terence Malick.
Evanston, IL: Northwestern University Press, 1969.

FCM   *Fundamental Concepts of Metaphysics: World,
Finitude, Solitude.* Translated by William McNeill and
Nicholas Walker. Bloomington: Indiana University
Press, 1995.

G   *Gelassenheit.* Pfullingen: Neske, 1959.

GA 1   *Gasamtsusgabe*, Vol. 1: *Frühe Schrifte.* Edited by
Friedrich-Wilhelm von Hermann. Frankfurt am Main:
Klostermann, 1977.

GA 4   *Gesamtausgabe,* Vol. 4: *Erläuterungen zu Hölderlins Dichtung.* Edited by Friedrich-Wilhelm von Herrmann. Frankfurt am Main: Klostermann, 1991.

GA 5   *Gesamtausgabe,* Vol. 5: *Holzwege.* Edited by Friedrich-Wilhelm von Hermann. Frankfurt am Main: Klostermann, 1977.

GA 9   *Gesamtausgabe,* Vol. 9: *Wegmarken.* Edited by Friedrich-Wilhelm von Hermann. Frankfurt am Main: Klostermann, 1976.

GA 12   *Gesamtausgabe,* Vol. 12: *Unterwegs zur Sprache.* Edited by Friedrich-Wilhelm von Herrmann. Frankfurt am Main: Klostermann, 1985.

GA 13   *Gesamtausgabe,* Vol. 13: *Aus der Erfahrung des Denkens.* Edited by Hermann Heidegger. Frankfurt am Main: Klostermann, 1983.

GA 14   *Gesamtausgabe,* Vol. 14: *Zur Sache des Denkens.* Edited by Friedrich-Wilhelm von Herrmann. Frankfurt am Main: Klostermann, 1962.

GA 20   *Gesamtausgabe,* Vol. 20: *Geschichte des Zeitbegriffs. Prolegomena zur Phänomenologie von Geschichte und Natur.* Edited by Friedrich-Wilhelm von Herrmann. Frankfurt am Main: Klostermann, 1976.

GA 21   *Gesamtausgabe,* Vol. 21: *Logik: Die Frage nach der Wahrheit.* Edited by Friedrich-Wilhelm von Herrmann. Frankfurt am Main: Klostermann, 1976.

GA 24   *Gesamtausgabe,* Vol. 25: *Die Grundprobleme der Phänomenologie* (1927 lectures). Edited by Friedrich-Wilhelm von Herrmann. Frankfurt am Main. Klostermann, 1989.

GA 26   *Gesamtausgabe,* Vol. 26: *Logik. Metaphysische Anfangsgründe der Logik im Ausgang von Leibniz.* Edited by Friedrich-Wilhelm von Herrmann. Frankfurt am Main: Klostermann, 1990.

GA 29/30   *Gesamtausgabe* 29/30: *Die Grundbegriffe der Metaphysik: Welt, Endlichkeit, Einsamkeit* (1929–30 lectures). Edited by Friedrich-Wilhelm von Hermann. Frankfurt am Main, 1983.

GA 34   *Gesamtausgabe,* Vol. 34: *Vom Wesen der Wahrheit. Zu Platons Höhlengleichnis und Theätet.* Edited by

Friedrich-Wilhelm von Herrmann. Frankfurt am Main:
Klostermann, 1988.

GA 39   *Gesamtausgabe,* Vol. 39: *Hölderlins Hymnen*
"Germanien" und "Der Rhein." Edited by
Friedrich-Wilhelm von Herrmann. Frankfurt am Main:
Klostermann, 1989.

GA 40   *Gesamtausgabe,* Vol. 40: *Einführung in die Metaphysik*
(1935 lectures). Edited by Petra Jaeger. Frankfurt am
Main: Klostermann,1983.

GA 42   *Gesamtausgabe,* Vol. 42: *Schelling: Vom Wesen der*
menschlichen Freiheit. Edited by Ingrid Schlüssler.
Frankfurt am Main: Klostermann, 1988.

GA 52   *Hölderlins Hymn "Andenken."* Edited by Curd
Ochwadt. Frankfurt am Main: Klostermann, 1992.

GA 56/57   *Gesamtausgabe,* Vol. 56/57: *Zur Bestimmung der*
Philosophie (1919 Freiburg lectures). Edited by Bernd
Heimbüchel. Frankfurt am Main: Klostermann,
1987.

GA 59/60   *Gesamtausgabe,* Vol. 59/60: *Vorlesungen*
Sommersemester 1920 and 1921. I. Phänomenologie
der Anschauung und des Ausdrucks. Theorie der
Philosophischen Begriffbildung. 2. Augustinus und der
Neuplatonismus. Edited by Claudius Strube and Bernd
Heimbüchel. Frankfurt am Main: Klostermann,
1993/1995.

GA 61   *Gesamtausgabe,* Vol. 61: *Phänomenologische*
Interpretationen zu Aristoteles. Einführung in die
phänomenologische Forschung (1921–22 lectures).
Edited by Walter Bröcker and Käte Bröcker-Oltmanns.
Frankfurt am Main: Klostermann, 1985.

GA 65   *Gesamtausgabe,* Vol. 65: *Beiträge zur Philosophie*
(Vom Ereignis). Edited by Friedrich-Wilhelm von
Hermann. Frankfurt am Main: Klostermann, 1989.

HCT   *History of the Concept of Time: Prolegomena.*
Translated by Theodore Kisiel. Bloomington: Indiana
University Press.

HE   "Hölderlin and the Essence of Poetry." In *Existence*
and Being. Edited by Werner Brock. London: Vision,
1949: 291–315.

I	*Hölderlin's Hymn. "The Ister."* Translated by William McNeill and J. Davis. Bloomington: Indiana University Press, 1996.
ID	*Identity and Difference.* Translated by Joan Stambaugh. New York: Harper & Row, 1969.
IM	*An Introduction to Metaphysics.* Translated by Ralph Manheim. New Haven, Conn.: Yale University Press, 1959.
KPM	*Kant and the Problem of Metaphysics.* Translated by James Churchill. Bloomington: Indiana University Press, 1962.
KPM2	*Kant and the Problem of Metaphysics.* 5th ed. Translated by Richard Taft. Bloomington: Indiana University Press, 1997.
MFL	*The Metaphysical Foundations of Logic.* Translated by Michael Heim. Bloomington: Indiana University Press, 1984.
N1	*Nietzsche I: The Will to Power as Art.* Edited and translated by David E. Krell. New York: Harper & Row, 1979.
N2	*Nietzsche II: The Eternal Recurrence of the Same.* Edited and translated by David F. Krell. New York: Harper & Row, 1984.
N3	*Nietzsche III: The Will to Power as Knowledge and as Metaphysics.* Translated by Joan Stambaugh, David F. Krell, and Frank A. Capuzzi. New York: Harper & Row, 1987.
N4	*Nietzsche IV: Nihilism.* Edited by David F. Krell; translated by Frank A. Capuzzi. New York: Harper & Row, 1982.
OGSU	"Only a God Can Save Us: *Der Spiegel's* Interview with Martin Heidegger." Translated by Maria P. Alter and John D. Caputo. *Philosophy Today,* 20 (Winter 1976): 267–84.
OHF	*Ontology: The Hermeneutics of Faciticity.* Translated by John van Buren. Bloomington: Indiana University Press, 1999.
OWL	*On the Way to Language.* Translated by Peter D. Hertz. New York: Harper & Row, 1971.

P   *Pathmarks*. Edited by William McNeill. Cambridge:
           Cambridge University Press, 1998.
PIK   *Phenomenological Interpretation of Kant's* Critique of
           Pure Reason. Translated by Parvis Emad and Kenneth
           Maly. Bloomington: Indiana University Press, 1997.
PLT   *Poetry, Language, Thought*. Translated by Albert
           Hofstadter. New York: Harper & Row, 1971.
PT   *The Piety of Thinking*. Translated by James Hart and
           John Maraldo. Bloomington: Indiana University Press,
           1976.
QCT   *The Question Concerning Technology and Other
           Essays*. Translated by William Lovitt. New York:
           Harper & Row, 1977.
SD   *Zur Sache des Denkens*. Tübingen: Niemeyer, 1969.
SG   *Der Satz vom Grund*. Pfullingen: Neske, 1971.
Sp   *"Nur Noch ein Gott kann uns retten." Spiegel*-
           Gespräch mit Martin Heidegger am 23 September,
           1966. *Der Spiegel*, No. 26 (May 31, 1976): 193–219.
SZ   *Sein und Zeit*. 15th ed. Tübingen: Max Niemayer
           Verlag, 1979.
TB   *On Time and Being*. Translated by Joan Stambaugh.
           New York: Harper & Row, 1972.
TK   *Die Technik und die Kehre*. Pfullingen: Neske, 1962.
US   *Unterwegs zur Sprache*. Pfullingen: Neske, 1965.
VA   *Vorträge und Aufsätze*. Pfullingen: Neske, 1959.
WM   *Wegmarken*. Frankfurt am Main: Klostermann, 1967.

CHRONOLOGY

Sept. 26, 1889	Born in Messkirch, Baden-Württemburg
1903–11	Studies for the priesthood at the Seminary of the Archdiocese of Freiburg
1903–9	Concurrent high school studies: State Gymnasium, Constance (1903–6); Berthold Gymnasium, Freiburg (1906–9)
1907	Receives a copy of Franz Brentano's *On the Manifold Meaning of Being in Aristotle* (1862), the book that led him to formulate the "question of being"
1909	Spends two weeks in the Jesuit novitiate, Feldkirch, Austria; leaves because of poor health
1909–13	Studies at the University of Freiburg; theology until 1911, then mathematics and philosophy
1912	First philosophical publications: "The Problem of Reality in Modern Philosophy" and "New Research on Logic"
1913	Awarded Ph.D. under Arthur Schneider (chair); dissertation, "The Doctrine of Judgment in Psychologism"
1915	Habilitation (teaching qualification dissertation) under Heinrich Rickert, "The Doctrine of Categories and Signification in Duns Scotus"
1915–23	*Privatdozent* (lecturer) at the University of Freiburg
1915–18	Military service
1917	Married to Elfride Petri
1919–23	Assistant to Husserl at Freiburg
1919, 1920	Birth of sons Jörg and Hermann

1923–8	Associate professor, University of Marburg
1927	*Sein und Zeit (Being and Time)* published
1928	Appointed Husserl's successor, professor of philosophy, at the University of Freiburg
1929	Break with Husserl
1929	Publishes *Kant und das Problem der Metaphysik (Kant and the Problem of Metaphysics)*, "Was ist Metaphysik?" ("What Is Metaphysics?"), and "Vom Wesen des Grundes" ("The Essence of Reasons")
Apr. 22, 1933	Becomes rector of the University of Freiburg
May 1, 1933	Joins the National Socialist Party
Nov. 11, 1933	Radio address supporting Hitler's withdrawal of Germany from the League of Nations
Apr. 27, 1934	Resigns as rector
1934–42	Lectures on Hölderlin and Nietzsche
1935	Lectures: "Der Ursprung des Kunstwerkes" ("The Origin of the Work of Art") and *Einführung in die Metaphysik (Introduction to Metaphysics)*
1936–8	Composes *Beiträge zur Philosophie (Contributions to Philosophy)*
Nov. 1944	Drafted into the People's Militia (Volkssturm)
1945	Denazification hearings; banned from teaching
1946	Nervous breakdown
1947	"Brief über den Humanismus" ("Letter on Humanism") published
1950	Reinstated to teaching position
1951	Granted emeritus status
1953	*Einführung in die Metaphysik (Introduction to Metaphysics)* published
1957	*Der Satz vom Grund (The Principle of Reason)* published
1959	*Unterwegs zur Sprache (On the Way to Language)* published
1961	Two-volume *Nietzsche* published
May 26, 1976	Dies in Freiburg

PREFACE TO THE SECOND EDITION

Preparing the second edition of a volume that has become a sort of mainstay turns out to be more difficult than one might suspect. For one thing, it is hard to select from among the many fresh and intelligent new Heideggerians on the scene a limited number of authors who will write the newly commissioned essays. Much harder was satisfying the editor's demand that some of the original contributions be removed. All of the original essays have proven valuable over the years, so none of them seemed "dispensable." Then there was the need to revise the bibliography, cataloguing the "complete works" edition (*Gesamtausgabe*) now finally worked out and selecting representative works from the massive output on Heidegger over the past twelve years. Finally, there was the somewhat distressing task of rereading my own Introduction to the volume from the 1993 edition. So many new Heideggerian texts have become available since then, and so many interesting insights have appeared in the literature, that the original introduction is showing its age. In this preface to the second edition, I will limit myself to discussing each of these tasks in turn.

The brightest moment in compiling a second edition came from reading the essays contributed by relatively new scholars working on Heidegger. The first addition is Taylor Carman's "The Principle of Phenomenology," a detailed and informative study of Heidegger's relationship to the founder of phenomenology, Edmund Husserl. Carman's paper helps clarify Heidegger's understanding of the phenomenological method, while showing how this differed from Husserl's original conception. Over the years it has become increasingly clear that assessing the role and force of phenomenology is one of the crucial tasks for those who would make the Heideggerian outlook part of their own.

William Blattner's "Laying the Ground for Metaphysics: Heidegger's Appropriation of Kant" provides a much needed addition to the original volume. Though Heidegger drew on many sources in composing *Being and Time,* the most striking and philosophically interesting of these sources would seem to be Kant. With great care and precision Blattner examines the reasoning found in Heidegger's Marburg lectures of 1927/28, *Phenomenological Interpretation of Kant's "Critique of Pure Reason,"* delivered during the same time frame in which *Being and Time* appeared and shortly before the publication of the better known but notoriously difficult *Kant and the Problem of Metaphysics.*[1] The story is often told of Heidegger, uncomfortably ensconced among Marburg neo-Kantians, trying to "out-Kant the neoKantians" by interpreting the first *Critique* through the lens of his phenomenological "fundamental ontology." Given his solid grasp of both Kant and Heidegger, Blattner is able to show the advantages and shortcomings of Heidegger's short-lived attempt to appropriate Kant. With this interpretation of Heidegger's Kantianism we can get a better understanding of the Kantian vocabulary and moves made in *Being and Time* as well as a grasp of the vehement rejection of everything "transcendental" in Heidegger's self-criticisms in his later *Contributions to Philosophy (From Enowning).*[2] Among his other valuable contributions, Blattner gives us a clue as to why "time" seems to fall out of its privileged position in the writings after *Being and Time.*

No concept in Heidegger's life's work is more pivotal or more contentious than the notion of "truth." Finding roots for this concept in the ancient Greek concept of *aletheia,* a term that etymologically suggests "un-forgetfulness" or "un-concealment," Heidegger sought to show that the ordinary understanding of truth as correspondence between proposition and fact is dependent upon an older, more basic understanding of truth as disclosure, the interplay of unconcealing and concealing. Whatever one thinks of this bit of etymological derivation, the Heideggerian conception of truth raises a number of problems connected with the well-known "realism/anti-realism" debate. Most strikingly, the question arises of whether we can say, for example, "Water is H_2O" is *true* in the full-blooded, non-relativistic sense in which we tend to think it is true. Mark Wrathall, in his rigorous and textually grounded essay "Truth and the Essence of Truth in Heidegger's Thought," shows how carefully Heidegger thought through issues of this sort. The outcome is a plausible and philosophically astute account of Heidegger's views.

One of the limitations of the first edition of the *Cambridge Companion to Heidegger* was the paucity of studies of the "later" Heidegger, that is, the works produced by Heidegger after the mid-1930s. One reason for this shortcoming was the difficulty in finding the sort of clear, illuminating exegeses of these works accessible to the audience the companion was supposed to reach. This is why I am especially pleased to add Julian Young's remarkable essay, "The Fourfold," to this edition. Young has written a number of works on Heidegger in recent years, proving himself to be one of the clearest and most engaging scholars in this field.[3] His contribution to this volume reflects the mastery and insightfulness characteristic of all his writings. Using vivid examples drawn from familiar cultural practices and ways of thought (quite a few of them from his home in New Zealand), he illuminates such Heideggerian concepts as earth, sky, mortal, gods, and, above all, dwelling and place. In Young's hands, obscure Heideggerian texts come alive and display their contemporary relevance.

Adding new essays led me to reorganize the volume as a whole. In this new edition, the first eight chapters deal primarily with the sources and themes of Heidegger's work up to and including *Being and Time*. Chapters 9 through 13 deal with issues and topics that span Heidegger's life's work. And the final chapter focuses on themes from the later writings.

The most challenging task for me in rethinking the volume was determining which chapters to remove. I felt comfortable removing Richard Rorty's essay because it is readily available in his *Philosophical Papers*.[4] Harrison Hall's essay, "Intentionality and World: Division I of *Being and Time*," an essay I find especially helpful to students and nonspecialists, found a home in my recently published collection, *The Existentialists*, and so is still available.[5] Finally, Frederick A. Olafson has produced a large body of valuable works on Heidegger that is worth reading as a whole.[6]

Revising the bibliography required incorporating some of the many fine secondary sources that have appeared since 1993. That also meant deleting some of the works that had appeared in the earlier edition. In working on the bibliography, and in many other tasks connected with producing a second edition, I was aided by Kevin Aho, Indrani Bhattercharjee, Chris Kirby, and Richard Polt. My deep thanks to them for their help.

In addition to the new entries in the bibliography, I would like to acknowledge here some exceptionally good new works that have appeared in the past twelve years. These include Karin de Boer's *Thinking in the Light of Time: Heidegger's Encounter with Hegel* (Albany: State University of New York Press, 2000), Michael Friedman's *A Parting of the Ways: Carnap, Cassirer, and Heidegger* (Chicago: Open Court, 2000), Hans Ruin's *Enigmatic Origins: Tracing the Theme of Historicity through Heidegger's Works* (Stockholm: Almqvist & Wiksell International, 1994), two volumes by Theodore Kisiel: *The Genesis of Heidegger's "Being and Time"* (Berkeley: University of California Press, 1995) and *Heidegger's Way of Thought: Critical and Interpretative Signposts* (New York: Continuum, 2002), John van Buren's *The Young Heidegger: Rumor of the Hidden King* (Bloomington: Indiana University Press, 1994), and a number of essays by Thomas Sheehan. I have also benefited immensely from works by, and conversations with, Iain Thomson, Hubert Dreyfus, Julian Young, Taylor Carman, Stephen Crowell, Richard Polt, and Benjamin Crowe. These influences, together with the revelations in the new volumes of the *Gesamtausgabe* and their English translations, have done much to shift my ways of thinking about Heidegger in recent years. Despite these pressures to change my interpretation, I have chosen not to revise my Introduction to the first edition beyond some minor changes. I think I would stand by most of what I said back then, including my assessment of Heidegger's involvement with the Nazis. But if I were to write an introduction to the companion today, it would certainly be different from what I wrote then. Perhaps a few hints of how my views have changed might be of interest.

First, thanks to Michael Friedman's and Theodore Kisiel's writings on Lask and Heidegger, I am less inclined than ever to think of Heidegger as an anti-realist in a strong sense. What misled me in my earlier thinking about Heidegger was the tendency on the part of translators to read the technical term *Seiende* as "beings" or "entities." Such translations ignore the fact that *das Seiende* is singular and refers not to a collection of items or (even more misleadingly) "things" or "objects." I have become convinced that the best way to translate this term is the way it was translated in some of the earliest translations of Heidegger's writings: as "what-is."[7] In contrast to the constructivism of the Kantian tradition, which treats objects of experience as built up from a manifold of intuition, Heidegger holds that Dasein "always already" finds itself thrown into the midst of what-is, already conditioned by something it can never master or fully grasp. Seen in this light, then, the question Heidegger asks is not "How are objects constituted from raw data?" but rather, "What are the conditions that make it possible for us to apprehend what-is in the ways we do apprehend it?" In his earliest writings, this was thought of as *world*; later it came to be thought of more as *language*; and in the late appropriations of early Greek thought, it comes to be thought of in terms of the old and rich concept of *logos*.

When the guiding question of Heidegger's life's work is seen as asking about the possibility of apprehension, then it becomes clear that what is at issue in his thought is not "Being," where this is seen either in the traditional sense of *essentia* and *existentia* or as mystified into some crypto-theological invention. Instead, what is at issue is the possibility for anything to emerge into presence *as* such and such, that is, to be taken *as* something or other. What Heidegger is concerned with is the play of identity and difference, the schema of "this-and-not-that," which provides the "Opening," leeway or realm of free play by virtue of which things can be freed up and allowed to show forth in some distinctive way. On Heidegger's account, humans, as occupying a site in the midst of what-is (i.e., by "being there"), play a pivotal role in this event of coming-into-presence. But they do not *create* "entities" in the sense of making them. It is better to say that humans are participants in an event of emergence and that they are as much dependent on that event as the event is dependent on them.[8] On this reading of Heidegger's thought, it is impossible to regard his views as "idealist" or "anti-realist" in the sense of a metaphysical claim about where all extant beings come from. Dasein's finitude includes its thrownness into and conditionedness by what-is. This is why in the later writings human beings ("mortals") make up only one point in a field of force called "the fourfold."

This shift in emphasis in reading the Heideggerian corpus has important consequences for Heidegger scholarship. First, it is now possible to see the discussion of the "ready-to-hand" and "present-at-hand," which seemed so important in *Being and Time* but was never taken up again after that work, as an example of how what-is can show up and how one mode of manifestation can be derivative from another.[9] Second, we can see more clearly the import of Heidegger's claims that there are certain crucial ways of being for humans – early on he mentions anxiety and boredom, later it is "startled dismay" or "shock" (*Erschrecken*) – in which we are able to apprehend what-is in its raw "*that it is.*" So it seems that Heidegger also leaves room for a sort of realism according to which we can gain some access to what-is as it is in itself, independent of any human perspectives.[10]

Finally, the conception of what-is as apprehended in different ways given different stances of Dasein makes it possible to distinguish (a) modes of apprehension that conceal more than what they reveal from (b) modes of apprehension that free things up so they can come into their own *as* what they are. In terms of this distinction, we can get clearer about Heidegger's contrast between technology, which treats everything as part of a "standing reserve" on hand for our use, and "releasement" (*Gelassenheit*), a stance toward what-is that lets it be what it can and should be.[11] What is important in taking a stance toward things, Heidegger suggests, is to maintain the *questionableness* of all that is if we are to let things show up as what they are "properly" (one meaning of the German word *eigen*).[12]

It should be obvious that this reading of the overarching viewpoint of Heidegger's life's work generates a set of puzzles about relativism, truth, and the idea of a "thing-in-itself." These are the sorts of puzzles that Heidegger scholars will want to hammer out before they can assess the overall plausibility of Heidegger's thought. But the fact that Heidegger's thought leads to interesting questions of this sort shows why it has proven to be such a fertile ground for philosophical excavation.

NOTES

1. The 1927/28 lecture course, *Phenomenological Interpretation of Kant's "Critique of Pure Reason"* (Bloomington: Indiana University Press, 1997), was translated by Parvis Emad and Kenneth Maly. A fifth, revised edition of Heidegger's 1929 work, *Kant and the Problem of Metaphysics*, translated by Richard Taft (Bloomington: Indiana University Press) also appeared in 1997.

2. This translation of the major work, *Beiträge zur Philosophie (Vom Ereignis)*, by Parvis Emad and Kenneth Maly (Bloomington: Indiana University), appeared in 1999.

3. See the three books by Julian Young listed in the bibliography.

4. See the third chapter of Rorty's *Essays on Heidegger and Others*, volume 2 of his *Philosophical Papers* (Cambridge: Cambridge University Press, 1991).

5. Charles Guignon, ed., *The Existentialists: Critical Essays on Kierkegaard, Nietzsche, Heidegger and Sartre* (Lanham, MD: Rowman & Littlefield, 2004): 103–18.

6. Frederick A. Olafson, *What Is Human Being? A Heideggerian View* (Cambridge: Cambridge University Press, 1995), *Heidegger and the Ground of Ethics: A Study of Mitsein* (Cambridge: Cambridge University Press, 1998), and his masterly work, *Heidegger and the Philosophy of Mind* (New Haven, CT: Yale University Press, 1987).

7. This translation appears, for example, in R. F. C. Hull and Alan Crick's translations of "On the Essence of Truth" and "What Is Metaphysics?" in the volume *Existence and Being*, edited by Werner Brock (Chicago: Henry Regnery Co., 1949).

8. My sketchy overview of Heidegger's overarching vision is indebted to a number of Thomas Sheehan's essays, especially "Kehre and Ereignis: A Prolegomenon to *Introduction to Metaphysics*," in *A Companion to Heidegger's "Introduction to Metaphysics*," edited by Richard Polt and Gregory Fried (New Haven, CT: Yale University Press, 2001): 3–16, and "A Paradigm Shift in Heidegger Research," *Continental Philosophy Review*, 34 (2001): 183–202.

9. For this reason I would no longer say, as I did in footnote 10 of the Introduction to the first edition, that the ready-to-hand is "more real" than the present-at-hand. Certainly it is true that encountering what-is as ready-to-hand is "more primordial" than the encounter with the present-at-hand, and it is presumably also less constrictive and distortive. But from that we cannot conclude that the ready-to-hand is "the real." At the same time, however, I would still disagree with Dreyfus' "minimal hermeneutic realism about nature." There is no justification for equating what-is with nature in the "naturalistic" sense of that term.

10. Heidegger's commitment to realism in this sense has been defended by Piotr Hoffman in his introduction, titled "How Todes Rescues Phenomenology from the Threat of Idealism," to Samuel Todes' *Body and World* (Cambridge, MA: The MIT Press, 2001).

11. The term *Gelassenheit* appears in Heidegger's 1929/30 lectures, *The Fundamental Concepts of Metaphysics: World, Finitude, Solitude*, translated by William McNeill and Nicholas Walker (Bloomington:

Indiana University Press, 1995), p. 91, in a discussion of the proper method of phenomenology.

12. Iain Thomson, in his *Heidegger on Ontotheology: Technology and the Politics of Education* (Cambridge: Cambridge University Press, 2005), shows how important the ideal of maintaining questionableness is to Heidegger's philosophy of education. It is because of this role of open-ended questioning in all thinking that Heidegger calls his writings "paths, not works" (*Wege, nicht Werke*).

Introduction

As the twenty-first century begins, it is increasingly clear that Heidegger will stand out as one of the greatest philosophers of all times. His writings have had an immense impact not only in Europe and the English-speaking world but in Asia as well.[1] And his influence has been felt in areas as diverse as literary theory, psychoanalysis, rhetoric, ecology, and theology. The continuing explosion of interest in Heidegger has come as a surprise to even his most ardent admirers. In the fifties and sixties it was still possible to consign Heidegger to the "Phenomenology and Existentialism" bin of the philosophy curriculum, treating him as the student of Husserl and precursor of Sartre. His talk about angst, guilt, death, and the need to be authentic seemed to place his work well outside the range of topics making up the mainstream Anglo-American curriculum. Though he was read in France, he was largely ignored in the English-speaking world.

In the past decades, however, a number of events have brought about a wider appreciation of the achievement of this fertile and complex thinker. First, in North America, the writings of such influential figures as Richard Rorty, Charles Taylor, and H. L. Dreyfus have helped us to see Heidegger as the seminal figure in what David Hoy calls a "hermeneutic turn," a new orientation with profound repercussions for such issues as the nature of the human sciences, the possibility of artificial intelligence, and the prospects for a postfoundationalist culture. As such respected theorists as Clifford Geertz, Thomas Kuhn, Michael Walzer, and Roy Schafer come to describe their approaches as "hermeneutic," there is a greater tendency to go back to the seminal texts that shaped contemporary hermeneutics. Second, the growing interest in Continental philosophers who start

I

out from Heidegger – including Gadamer in his debates with Habermas, and "postmodern" thinkers like Derrida, Foucault, Irigaray, and Bourdieu – has provoked curiosity about the figure who is a constant presence in all their work.[2] Third, and most recently, the recent revelations concerning the extent of Heidegger's involvement with the Nazis has led to a flurry of reflections on the relation of his thought – and of philosophy in general – to politics and culture.[3]

Heidegger's lofty ambition was to rejuvenate philosophy (and, at the same time, Western culture) by clearing away the conceptual rubbish that has collected over our history in order to recover a clearer, richer understanding of what things are all about. Since this calls for appropriating the underlying ideas that have formed our culture, his thought weaves together many different historical strands. The essays written for this volume reveal the complex range of sources of Heidegger's thought. He draws on St. Paul, the pre-Socratics, Aristotle, Augustine, Aquinas, Duns Scotus, Meister Eckhart, Kant, Hegel, Schelling, Schleiermacher, Kierkegaard, Nietzsche, Dilthey, Bergson, Husserl, and Scheler, and he does so in order to formulate an alternative to the assumptions that make up the tradition extending from Plato to Descartes to contemporary scientific naturalism. What is most striking about Heidegger's appropriation of historical sources is the way he blends together points of view generally regarded as irreconcilably opposed. Thus, we find Kierkegaardian passion combined with a commitment to systematic rigor, a Romantic concern with individual fulfillment together with a Hegelian communitarianism, a deep respect for German Idealism along with a hard-headed realism, and an awareness of the historicity and finitude of life together with the search for a stable "ground."

These overlapping themes steadily evolve during a philosophical career spanning nearly seventy years. Considering the diversity and scope of Heidegger's writings, it is hardly surprising that his influence has been so extensive. His thought has contributed to phenomenology (Merleau-Ponty, Levinas), existentialism (Sartre, Ortega y Gasset), hermeneutics (Gadamer, Ricoeur), political theory (Hannah Arendt, the early Marcuse), psychotherapy theory (Medard Boss, Ludwig Binswanger, Rollo May), theology (Rudolph Bultmann, Paul Tillich), as well as postmodern and "new pragmatist" trends.

Heidegger explicitly rejected epigonism and pedantic scholarship, calling on thinkers to travel along the paths he traversed instead of pondering his words. As a result, the finest scholarly work done on his writings tends to reflect widely divergent readings of what he has to offer. In addition, his claim that what is most important in any thinker is what remains "unsaid," together with his belief that authentic interpretation always requires doing "violence" to the texts, further fans the flames of the conflict of interpretations surrounding his works today. The contributions to this volume, written by philosophers whose primary goal is enriching our understanding of ourselves and our world, show the very different ways of understanding what Heidegger has to say.

My aim in this introduction is to sketch out a broad picture of Heidegger's lifework in order to provide a background for the essays that follow. The first section deals with the account of "Dasein" (human existence) and of the worldhood of the world in *Being and Time*. The following two sections deal with the "turn" to the so-called later Heidegger and with his involvement in National Socialism in the thirties. I should say here that my account of Heidegger's complicity with the Nazis represents my own personal perspective concerning this issue and that its meliorative tone is at odds with the brilliant and insightful work of Sheehan and Caputo, as well as with the majority of other commentators on this topic.[4] My goal, however, is not to justify Heidegger's actions (I find them disgraceful and contemptible), but to try to understand how a bookish academic from the backwoods of Germany – a person admired throughout his life by decent people who regarded him as a friend – could have become involved in such horrors. In presenting one more take on this hotly debated affair, of course, I do not pretend to have said the last word on it.

FUNDAMENTAL ONTOLOGY IN *BEING AND TIME*

Being and Time (1927) remains Heidegger's best-known and most influential work. Despite its heavy Teutonic tone and tortuous style (especially in the English translation), it can seem to bring a breath of fresh air to traditional philosophical puzzles. Heidegger's insight is that many of the knots in thinking that characterize philosophy are due to a particular way of understanding the nature of reality, an outlook that arose at the dawn of Western history and dominates our thought to this day. This outlook is what Dorothea

Frede in her essay calls the "substance ontology": the view that what is ultimately real is that which underlies properties – what "stands under" (*sub-stantia*) and remains continuously present throughout all change. Because of its emphasis on enduring presence, this traditional ontology is also called the "metaphysics of presence." It is found, for example, in Plato's notion of the Forms, Aristotle's primary substances, the Creator of Christian belief, Descartes's *res extensa* and *res cogitans*, Kant's noumena, and the physical stuff presupposed by scientific naturalism. Ever since Descartes, this substance ontology has bred a covey of either/ors that generate the so-called problems of philosophy: either there is mind or everything is just matter; either our ideas do represent objects or nothing exists outside the mind; either something in me remains constant through change or there is no personal identity; either values have objective existence or everything is permitted. These either/ors lay out a grid of possible moves and countermoves in a philosophical game that eventually can begin to feel as predictable and tiresome as tic-tac-toe.

Heidegger's goal is to undercut the entire game by challenging the idea that reality must be thought of in terms of the idea of substance at all. His claim is not that mind and matter do not exist, but that they are derivative, regional ways of being for things, the detritus of some fairly high-level theorizing that is remote from concrete, lived existence. As Thomas Sheehan notes, Heidegger in 1919 already regarded the objectifying outlook as originating not so much from natural science as from the theoretical attitude itself: "It is not just naturalism, as [Husserl] thought, . . . but the general domination of the *theoretical* that is messing up the real problematic" (GA 56/57 87). It is therefore possible to see the history of philosophy from Plato to contemporary naturalism – and including Husserlian phenomenology itself – as one extended misinterpretation of the nature of reality. This misinterpretation is inevitable once one adopts the detached standpoint of theoretical reflection, for when we step back and try to get an impartial, objective view of things, the world, so to speak, goes dead for us – things lose the meaningfulness definitive of their being in the everyday life-world. Following the lead of the influential turn-of-the-century movement called "life philosophy" (then seen as including Nietzsche, Bergson, and Dilthey), Heidegger hoped to recover a more original sense of things by setting aside the view of reality we get from theorizing and focusing instead on the way things show up in the flux of our everyday, prereflective activities.

To pave the way to a new understanding of ourselves and the world, *Being and Time* begins by asking the question posed by traditional ontology: What is the being of entities? But Heidegger quickly notes that ontology as such, the question of being, "remains itself naive and opaque" if it fails to inquire first into the *meaning* of being (BT 31). In other words, since what things *are* (their being) is accessible only insofar as they become intelligible to us (insofar as they show up for us as relevant or as counting in some determinate way), we need a "fundamental ontology" that clarifies the meaning (i.e., conditions of intelligibility) of things in general. And since *our* existence or "being-there" (Dasein) is "the horizon in which something like being in general becomes intelligible," fundamental ontology must begin by "clarifying the possibility of having any understanding of being at all – an understanding which itself belongs to the constitution of the entity called Dasein" (BT 274). This inquiry into the conditions for the possibility of having any understanding whatsoever, the analytic of Dasein, makes up the published portion of *Being and Time*. The investigation starts, then, with an inquiry into our own being, insofar as we are the entities who have some understanding of being, and it does so in order to lay a basis for inquiring into the being of entities in general (rocks, hammers, squirrels, numbers, constellations, symphonies).[5]

The question of being is therefore reformulated as a question about the conditions for the accessibility or intelligibility of things. The constant references to Kant in the essays that follow (especially in those by Blattner, Hoy, Dostal, and Frede) show how this project can be seen as a continuation of Kant's "Copernican revolution," the shift from seeing the mind as trying to hook up with an antecedently given world to seeing the world as being made over in order to fit the demands of the mind. But Heidegger's analytic of Dasein also marks an important break from Kant and from German Idealism generally. For Heidegger brackets the assumption that there is such a thing as a mind or consciousness, something immediately presented to itself in introspection, which must be taken as the self-evident starting point for any account of reality. Instead, though it is true that the first-person standpoint is basic (as Carman and Hoffman clearly show), it is not the mental that is basic but rather what Taylor calls "engaged agency." We start out from a description of ourselves as we are in the midst of our day-to-day practical affairs, prior to any split between mind and matter. Our inquiry must begin from the "existentiell" (concrete, specific, local) sense we have of ourselves as caught up in the midst of a practical world (in the "life-world" sense of this term found in such expressions as "the world of academia" or the "business world").

In Heidegger's view, there is no pure, external vantage point to which we can retreat in order to get a disinterested, presupposition-less angle on things. So fundamental ontology begins with a description of the "phenomena" where this means what "shows itself," what "becomes manifest" or "shows forth" *for us*, in relation to our purposes as they are shaped by our forms of life.[6] But this need to start from an insider's perspective is not a restriction in any sense. On the contrary, as Taylor shows, it is only because we are "always already" in on a way of life, engaged in everyday dealings with things in a familiar life-world, that we have some "pre-understanding" of what things are all about. It is our being as participants in a shared practical world that first gives us a window onto ourselves and reality.

The existential analytic therefore starts out from a description of our average everydayness as agents in practical contexts. Heidegger's early writings are filled with descriptions of such mundane activities as hammering in a workshop, turning a doorknob, hearing motor-cycles, and operating the turn signal on a car. But the goal of the inquiry is to identify the "essential structures" that make up the "for-mal scaffolding (*Gerüst*)" of any Dasein whatsoever. For this reason the phenomenology of everydayness is coupled with a hermeneutic or interpretation designed to bring to light the hidden basis for the unity and intelligibility of the practical life-world. Because interpre-tation reveals that in virtue of which (*woraufhin*) everything hangs together, Heidegger says that it formulates "transcendental general-izations" concerning the conditions for any interpretations or world-views whatsoever (BT 244). It is, as Hoy points out, *Interpretierung* aimed at revealing the "primary understanding of world" that under-lies and makes possible our day-to-day existentiell interpretations (*Auslegungen*). Since the goal of the inquiry is not to give an account of entities but rather to grasp the being of entities (what lets things be what they are, what "determines entities as entities" in their various ways of being), phenomenology seeks what generally "does not show itself at all," the hidden "meaning and ground" of what does show up (BT 25, 59). In the course of this investigation, it becomes clear that the entities taken as basic by certain regional sciences – for example, the material objects in causal interactions of classical mechanics – are theoretical constructs with no privileged status in helping us grasp the nature of reality.

Insofar as our commonsense outlook is pervaded by past theorizing, and especially by the Cartesian ontology of modernity, fundamental ontology will involve *"doing violence"* to the complacent assumptions of common sense. Nowhere is this challenge to common sense more evident than in Heidegger's description of being human, or Dasein.[7] This description is sharply opposed to the picture of humans we have inherited from Descartes. According to the Cartesian view, we are at the most basic level minds located in bodies. And this is indeed the way we tend to think of ourselves when we step back and reflect on our being. The binary opposition between mind and matter colors all our thinking in the modern world, and it leads to a kind of Cartesian extortion which tells us that if we ever question the existence of mental substance, we will sink to the level of being crude materialists who can never account for human experience and agency.

Heidegger's way of dealing with this extortion is to subvert the binary opposition that sets up the narrow range of options in the first place. In my own essay (Chapter 10), I try to show that instead of defining Dasein as a thing or object of any sort, Heidegger describes human existence as a "happening," a life story unfolding "between birth and death" (BT 427). This conception of existence as the "historicity" or "temporalizing" of a life course arises quite naturally when we reflect on the nature of human agency. For what a person is *doing* at any moment can be regarded as action (and not just as inadvertent movement) only because of the way it is nested in the wider context of a life story. For instance, what I am doing now can be seen as writing a philosophy essay only because of the relation of my current activity to my background (my training, my academic career) and to my future-directedness (the outcome of this activity in relation to my undertakings in general). In fact, it seems that what is most important to an event being an action is not just the beliefs and desires going on in a mental substance, since all sorts of things might be going through my mind as I type away here. Rather, what is crucial to this movement being *action* is its rootedness in meaningful contexts of the past and its directedness toward some future end state (despite the fact that this is all probably far from my "mind" when I am busily engaged in everyday activities).

When we think of a human being as the temporal unfolding of a life course, we can identify three structural elements that make up human existence. First, Dasein always finds itself "thrown" into a concrete situation and attuned to a cultural and historical context where things already count in determinate ways in relation to a community's practices. This prior thrownness into the medium of shared intelligibility, disclosed in our moods, makes up Dasein's "facticity." Second, agency is "discursive" in the sense that in our activities we are articulating the world and interacting with situations along the guidelines of interpretations embodied in our public language. Third, Dasein is "understanding" in Heidegger's special use of this term: it has always taken some stand on its life insofar as it has undertaken (or drifted into) the vocations, roles, lifestyles, personal relationships, and so on that give content to its life. Because our familiar skilled activities embody a generally tacit "knowhow," a sense of what things are all about in relation to our practical concerns, taking a stand is said to be a "projection" of possibilities of meaningfulness for things and ourselves.

As having taken a stand, Dasein's existence is "futural" in the sense that it is under way toward realizing some outcome (though this goal-directedness might never expressly come into one's mind). Thus, agency is characterized as "coming-toward" (*zu-kommend*) the realization of one's undertakings, that is, as being-toward the future (*Zu-kunft*). I attend a parent-teacher conference, for example, as part of my "project" of being a concerned parent, and I do so even though this way of doing things is so deeply ingrained in me, so "automatic," that I never think about *why* I am doing it. According to Heidegger, the future has priority over both the past and the present in defining the being of the self. This is so, first of all, because what a person is shooting for in life determines both how the past can be encountered as providing assets for the present and how the present can show up as a situation demanding action. But the future also has priority because, insofar as my actions commit me to a range of possible ways of being in the future, their future-directedness defines what my life – that is, my "being" – is adding up to as a totality, "right up to the end."

According to this description, Dasein's "being" or personal identity is defined by the stands it takes in acting in day-to-day situations over the course of its lifetime. Heidegger expresses this by saying that Dasein is an "ability-to-be," which comes to realization only through the ways it is channeled into concrete "possibilities," that is, into specific roles, relationships, personality traits, lifestyles, and so on, as these have been made accessible in its cultural context.[8] Thus, when I hold a door open for a friend or get on line at the theater, I am constituting myself as a fairly well-behaved person as this is understood in my culture. Here I just *am* what I make of myself by slipping into familiar patterns of action and reaction throughout my life.

The conception of human existence as an emergence-into-presence provides an insight into the understanding of being that Heidegger is trying to work out, a conception Zimmerman calls "ontological phenomenalism." My being – who I am – is nothing other than what unfolds in the course of my interactions with the world over the course of my life. In saying that "the 'essence' of Dasein lies in its existence" (BT 67), Heidegger suggests that there is no role to be played by the notion of an underlying substance or a hidden essence allegedly needed to explain the outward phenomena. What makes agency possible is not some underlying substrate, not some mental substance, but is rather the way our life stories unfold against the backdrop of practices of a shared, meaningful world. From Heidegger's standpoint, then, the ability to think of ourselves as minds located in physical bodies is a highly specialized self-interpretation rooted in detached theorizing, an interpretation lacking any broader implications for understanding human existence.

The power of the Cartesian extortion lies in its ability to keep us in line by telling us that doubts about the mind lead inevitably to crude materialism. Heidegger sidesteps this move by suggesting that not only mind but matter as well is a theoretical construct with no indispensable role to play in making sense of the everyday life-world. To get this point across, he undertakes a description of how things show up for us most "primordially" in the course of our everyday dealings with the world. In his now well-known example of hammering in a workshop, he suggests that what we encounter when we are absorbed in such an activity is not a "hammer-thing" with properties to which we then assign a use value. On the contrary, what shows up for us initially is the hammering, which is "in order to" nail boards together, which is "for" building a bookcase, which is ultimately "for the sake of" being, say, a person with a neat study. In our everyday dealings with things, the work-world as a whole – the light in the room, the workbench, the saw, the glue – shows up in its interconnected functionality in relation to our projects.

It follows, then, that what is "given" in average everyday dealings with the world is a holistic "equipmental totality," a web of functional relationships in which things are encountered in their interdependent functions and in terms of their relevance to what we are doing. The hammer is what it is by virtue of its reference to these nails and boards in hammering on this workbench under this lighting for this purpose. In Heidegger's vocabulary, the world of average everydayness is not an aggregate of "present-at-hand" objects, things that just occur, but is a holistic contexture of relations, the "ready-to-hand," where what something is – its "ontological definition" – is determined by its role within the projects under way within the workshop.⁹ The totality of these functional relations – the general structure of "in order tos," "by doing whichs," "for whichs," and "for the sakes of" as laid out in our culture's practices – Heidegger calls the "worldhood" of the world. His claim, as I understand it, is that the present-at-hand items taken as basic by traditional theorizing (for instance, physical objects and their causal relations) are derivative from and parasitic on the world understood as a context of involvements directed toward accomplishing things. To think that there are "at first" mere present-at-hand things "in a space in general," which then get concatenated into equipmental relations, is an "illusion" (BT 421), according to Heidegger (though it may be useful to assume that such things exist for the purposes of certain regional inquiries).¹⁰

The description of average everydayness leads us to see that what is most basic is a world of "significance" in which things show up as *counting* or *mattering* in relation to our practical affairs. This meaningful life-world is inseparable from Dasein's future-directedness, its being "for the sake of itself" in the various self-interpretations and roles it picks up from the public "we-world" into which it is thrown. Dasein is said to be a "clearing" or a "lighting" through which entities can stand forth *as* such and such. In other words, it is because

we take a stand on our being in the world – because we are "understanding," in Heidegger's special use of this word – that we engage in
familiar, skillful practices in everday contexts, and we thereby open
a leeway or field of free play (*Spielraum*) where things can stand out
as counting or mattering in some determinate ways. Given my self-
understanding as a cook in the kitchen, for example, I handle things
there in such a way that the spatula and pan stand out as significant
while the linoleum and wainscotting recede into insignificance.

This projection of possibilities opened by understanding is realized
and made concrete in "interpretation" (*Auslegung*, literally "laying
out"). Interpretation is our way of "explicitly appropriating" the
world "in preparing, putting to rights, repairing, improving [and]
rounding out," that is, in our familiar activities within ordinary contexts. Interpretation seizes on the range of possibilities laid out in
advance by the "fore-structure" of understanding and works it over
into a concrete "as-structure" of uses – using the pan to boil an egg,
for instance, rather than to simmer a white sauce (BT §§ 31–2). Given
this description of everydayness, we can see why Heidegger claims
that the *being* of everyday equipment in use – its readiness-to-hand –
is defined by our ways of using things in the course of our prereflective activities.

It should now be clear why Heidegger tells us that being-in-the-
world is a "unitary phenomenon." On the one hand, the being of
everyday functional contexts is inseparable from the specific uses
we put things to in the course of our shared practical involvements
in the world. On the other hand, who *I am* as an agent is determined
by the equipmental contexts and familiar forms of life that make
up the worldly "dwelling" in which I find myself. Since there is no
ultimate ground or foundation for the holistic web of meaning that
makes up being-in-the-world, Heidegger suggests that the meaning
of being (i.e., the basis of all intelligibility) is an "absence of ground"
or "abyss" (*Abgrund*) (BT 194).[11]

What must be explained given such a picture of being-in-the-
world, as Hoy points out, is not how an initially worldless subject
can get hooked up with a pregiven collection of objects "out there"
in a neutral space–time coordinate system. Rather, what we need to
show is why the tradition has overlooked this unified phenomenon,
and how the disjunction of self and things ever arises in the first
place. To explain the appeal of the substance ontology, Heidegger

describes how the spectator attitude and the objectifying ontology result from a "breakdown" in average everydayness. When everything is running smoothly in the workplace, he suggests, the ready-to-hand and the surrounding work-world remain unobtrusive and unnoticed. The ready-to-hand must "withdraw" into its usability, Heidegger says, "in order to *be* ready-to-hand quite authentically" (BT 99). We see through it, so to speak, in zeroing in on what we are out to accomplish.

When something goes wrong in the workshop, however, there is a "changeover" in the way things show up for us. If the handle breaks off the pot or the spatula is missing, the whole project grinds to a standstill and we are put in the position of just looking around to see what to do next. It is when things are temporarily unready-to-hand in this way that we can catch a glimpse of the web of functional relations in which they played a part. Thus, a breakdown makes it possible to catch sight of the worldhood of the world. If the breakdown persists, however, items can begin to obtrude in their unusability, and we can look at things as brute present-at-hand objects to be investigated from a theoretical perspective. As we adopt a stance in which things are explicitly noticed, we can be led to believe that what have been there "all along" are value-free, meaningless objects whose usefulness was merely a product of our own subjective interests and needs. Heidegger's point, however, is that this conception of reality as consisting of essentially contextless objects can arise only derivatively from a more "primordial" way of being absorbed in a meaningful life-world.[12] Such contextless objects are by-products of the "disworlding of the world," and so cannot be thought of as the basic components from which the world is built up.

According to Heidegger's phenomenology of being-in-the-world, what is most primordial is neither humans nor objects, but rather the "clearing" in which specific forms of human existence along with particular sorts of equipmental context emerge-into-presence in their reciprocal interdependence. Entities in general – the tools in a workshop, the unknown chemical in the chemist's beaker, even the precise kinds of sensation and emotion we can have – these can show up *as* what they *are* (i.e., in their *being* such and such) only against the background of the interpretive practices of a particular historical culture. Yet it is also true that *we* can be the kinds of people we are in our everyday affairs only by virtue of the practical contexts of worldly involvement in which we find ourselves. In the kitchen I can be a culinary artist or a klutz, but not a world leader signing a treaty. Thus, "Self and world belong together in the single entity Dasein. Self and world are not two beings, like subject and object; . . . [instead,] self and world are the basic determination of Dasein in the unity of the structure of being-in-the-world" (BP 297).

With its emphasis on our facticity, thrownness, and embeddedness in a concrete world, we might think of Heidegger's fundamental ontology as moving toward something like a "Ptolemaic reaction" to Kant's Copernican revolution. Humans do not construct the world. Rather, humans *and* things are constituted by the totality of what Heidegger in his earliest writings called the "worlding of the world." And *being* is understood neither as an essential property of things, nor as the mere fact that they occur, nor as something cast onto things by humans. Instead, being comes to be thought of as a temporal event, a "movement into presence" inseparable from the understanding of being embodied in Dasein's forms of life. It is the event (*Ereignis*) of disclosedness in which entities come to be appropriated into intelligibility.[13]

It follows from Heidegger's account of average everydayness that there can be no presuppositionless knowledge, no access of the sort philosophers sought when they dreamed of getting in touch with "reality as it is in itself." We are always caught up in a "hermeneutic circle": though our general sense of things depends on what we encounter in the world, we can first discover something as significant in some determinate way only because we have soaked up a "preontological understanding" of how things in general can count through being initiated into the practices and language of our culture.

Of course, to say that we always encounter entities *as* counting in such and such ways does not entail that, in some sense, a veil has been pulled over things so that we can never make contact with the things themselves. On the contrary, since the ways things show up – the appearances – just are what those things really *are*, access to what appears just is access to those things. Heidegger tries to clarify this point by considering what is involved when a city "presents a magnificent view" from the vantage point of a particular scenic overlook. Here it is the city itself that offers itself "from this or that point of view" (IM 104). It remains true, needless to say, that the city can present *this* panorama only because *we* are viewing it from a particular position. But this relativity to a standpoint does not entail that we are cut off from the city, having access to, say, only a mental picture of the city. It is not, after all, a representation of the city we encounter, but a *presentation* of the city as it shows itself from this particular point of view.

This example shows how Heidegger tries to undercut traditional skepticism about the external world by undermining the representationalist model that gets it going in the first place. The perspectival modes of access to the city, far from being barriers between us and reality, are in fact the conditions making possible any access to things at all. They *place* the city before us, and they place *us* in the setting, letting us be the observers we are. Thus, we can make no sense of the idea of getting a "view of the city as it *really* is," independent of all points of view and perspectives. For even aerial photographs and street maps are just more points of view; they are not privileged, "purely objective" indicators of what the city is "really" like. The idea of a pure, colorless, objective geographic or geological locale, distinct from all possible modes of presentation, is an illusion bred by the dominance of representationalism in our thinking. As a result, Heidegger's recognition of the Dasein-relativity of the being of entities is consistent with a full-blooded realism that affirms the reality of what shows up for us. *The* world just is the human world in its various manifestations.[14]

THE TURN TO THE HISTORY OF BEING

In his writings after *Being and Time*, Heidegger's thought began to shift in important ways, moving toward the often baffling writings of the later period. Heidegger himself speaks of a "turn" (*Kehre*) in his thought, which begins with the 1930 essay "On the Essence of Truth." In order to try to get a handle on this turn, we might distinguish two tightly interwoven strands of the shift that took place in his outlook through the thirties. First, there are his attempts to answer charges that *Being and Time* is merely a new move in the tradition of transcendental philosophy stemming from Kant – that it is "anthropocentric" and treats Dasein as a detached, "standpoint-free" source from which "the entirety of non-Daseinal . . . being" can be derived (ER 99). Second, there are Heidegger's responses to the "conservative revolution" in Germany that swept the Nazis into power in 1933. As we shall see, these strands are interdependent and ultimately arrive at the same point.

The first source of change consists in the shift away from fundamental ontology, with its focus on Dasein as the source of the intelligibility of things, to the project of thinking the "history of being," where humans and their modes of understanding are themselves treated as offshoots of a wider historical unfolding. In the new *seynsgeschichtlich* approach that took shape in the mid-thirties, being is seen as a complex "happening" that, although it "needs" and "uses" humans, is not to be thought of as something humans create. As Caputo puts it in Chapter 12, being has to be thought of as "the event of manifestness, the happening of the truth of being, the coming to pass of the history of the epochal manifestations of being." And because being just *is* the history of unfolding epochs of self-manifestation, Heidegger says that "the history of being is being itself" (EP 82). Humans are then seen more as respondents who are "called" to the task of the "safekeeping" of being than they are creators who constitute being. In this respect, being is very similar to language. When we talk to one another we say things that are often quite original and inventive. But we can do this only by drawing on the linguistic resources of our language. What we can say, then, is always preshaped by the articulations and schematizations built into our historical language. In the same way, our actions and thoughts contribute to the transmission of history, but even our most original articulations and creations are always guided and regulated by the generally tacit understanding embodied in the practices of our historical culture. This formative understanding of being "happens behind our backs," as it were, leading us at times to recapitulate the very patterns we might hope to overcome.

To understand Heidegger's turn to the history of being, we need to sketch out the rough contours of his historical story. It starts with the assumption, based on a reading of pre-Socratic texts, that at the dawn of Western civilization there was a "first beginning," in which the Greeks brought to light the ontological difference – the difference between being and entities – by asking the question, What are entities? or What is the *being* of entities? This has been the "guiding question" (*Leitfrage*) of Western thought to this day. The first answer to the question was *physis*, or presence understood as "emerging and abiding," as "self-blossoming emergence ..., unfolding, that which manifests itself in such unfolding and perseveres and endures in it" (IM 14). Being, according to this earliest Greek experience, is "*appearance* as a definite mode of emerging self-manifestation" in which things emerge from concealment into "*truth* in the sense of unconcealment" (IM 109).

An analysis of Sophocles' "Ode to Man" suggests that the Greeks were aware, if only in a dim and confused way, of the role of human practices and language in articulating how things can count within a world. For the earliest Greeks, the more-than-human, the "over-powering surge," is "made manifest and made to stand" through the "gathering" and "collecting collectedness" brought about by the comportment of a historical people (IM 171). By means of the "cap-turing and subjugating that opens entities *as* sea, *as* earth, *as* animal," humans "undertake to govern and succeed in governing the power of the overpowering" (IM 157, 172). Heidegger regards this insight into the connection between the coming-into-presence of entities and the role of human practices in articulating what shows up as fundamental to understanding being. In its "historical, history-disclosing essence," he writes, "human-being is *logos*, the gathering and apprehending of the being of entities" (IM 171). The event of being – *that* things stand forth, for example, as holy or as natural resources – is made possible by the understanding of being embodied in the practices of a historical culture, for example, *that* there are people who worship or people who challenge forth the energies of nature.

The first beginning makes up what the unpublished "de-structuring of the history of ontology" in *Being and Time* proposed to find when it spoke of retrieving the "wellsprings" of our understand-ing of being, "those primordial experiences in which we achieved our first ways of determining the nature of being – the ways which have guided us ever since" (BT 44).[15] It is because those initial experi-ences have shaped how Western people understand being to this day that Heidegger can say that "the beginning, conceived in an originary way, is being itself" (*Der Anfang – anfänglich begriffen – ist das Seyn selbst*) (58).[16] Since the first beginning has predefined all subsequent ways of experiencing things, it follows that the historically shifting interpretations of being in our culture have all been permutations on the understanding that took shape at the dawn of our civiliza-tion. Thus, the early Greek understanding of being as *physis* is not one outlook among others. Rather, it is definitive of who we are as participants in Western history. As a result, any new beginning will involve recapturing the insights flowing from those initial "well-springs" of understanding that set our civilization on its course: the new beginning is "realizable only in a dialogue (*Auseinandersetzung*) with the *first*" (58).

Nevertheless, the unfolding of different "epochs" in the understanding of being over the past millennia – the "history of metaphysics" – has involved a progressive masking or concealing of what was revealed in that primordial experience. In asking about entities and experiencing entities as what comes to presence, the Greeks overlooked what makes this presence possible – that is, the "presencing" of what is present. Thus, according to Heidegger's story, *being* itself "remains forgotten" in the first beginning (IM 18). Instead of thinking of being (*Sein*, or as Heidegger begins to write it, *Seyn*), the Greeks focused on "beingness" (*Seiendheit*) understood as the essential property of actually existent entities.

The history of metaphysics is therefore a history of forgetfulness or "withdrawal," in which entities obtrude as actually existing and as having essential properties, while being – that which first makes it possible for anything to show up in its *existentia* and *essentia* – remains concealed. This withdrawal is evident in Plato's interpretation of the beingness of entities as the aspect (*idea*) or perfect prototype, knowable through pure rational contemplation, that produces those diverse material things that come to be in our visible world. Later developments lead to a conception of entities as "what has been produced" and of being as "being produced" (by nature or by God). In the modern age, this production is seen as what "stands before" (*vor-stellend*) a subject or a Will. To be, then, is to be the stably persisting outcome of a productive act – that which "lies before" the producer as his or her product.[17]

As a result of the first moves at the dawn of history, being comes to be thought of as what endures, what is permanent, what is always there. It is the continuous presence of a substance (*ousia*) – that which "remains" through all changes (as Descartes later puts it when reflecting on the essence of a piece of wax in the second *Meditation*). To the extent that metaphysics focuses on "beingness" and is blind to the conditions that let anything whatsoever show up, metaphysics has been dominated by "error" or "going astray." Because

Plato inaugurated this interpretation of beingness, the entire history of metaphysics can be called "Platonism." And since Nietzsche still operates within the range of oppositions opened by Plato, Heidegger can say that Nietzsche is "the most unbridled Platonist."[18] It follows, then, that the entire history of Western thought consists of variations on the initial answer to the question, What are entities?: "The first beginning and its end comprise the entire history of the guiding question from Anaximander up to Nietzsche" (232).

Nevertheless, it is important to keep in mind that the history of metaphysics, far from being something people have *done* over the centuries, is something that happens from out of being itself *to* humans, though their practices play a role in its realization. Epochs in the history of being are brought about through what Heidegger calls an *Ereignis*, a word meaning "event" but tied to the idea of "ownness" or "appropriation" (*eigen*), and so suggesting "an event of coming-into-its-own." If unconcealment results from an event within being and so is not something humans do, it follows that the concealment running through the history of metaphysics is *also* something that happens within being itself. Concealment inevitably accompanies every emerging-into-presence in this sense: just as the items in a room can become visible only if the lighting that illuminates them itself remains invisible, so things can become manifest only if this manifesting itself "stays away" or "withdraws." This first-order concealment is unavoidable and innocuous. But it becomes aggravated by a second-order concealment that occurs when the original concealment itself is concealed. That is, insofar as humans are oblivious to the fact that every disclosedness involves concealment, they fall into the illusion of thinking that nothing is hidden and that everything is totally out front. Thus, to take a familiar example, the emergence of modern individualism concealed the role of shared social practices in making possible such a mode of self-understanding as individualism. This initial concealment in turn leads to the complacent assurance that individualism is the final, incontrovertible truth about human reality, and that collectives and social practices of any sort must be explainable in terms of artificial aggregates of initially isolated individuals. This second-order forgetfulness then reinforces and sustains the initial concealment that opened up the individualist understanding of life in the first place.

Because concealment occurs when a particular form of presenting comes to be taken as the ultimate truth about things, Heidegger says that being (as appearing) "cloaks itself *as* appearance insofar as it shows itself *as* being" (IM 109, my emphasis). In other words, what shows up at a particular time presents itself as the last word about reality, as the "only game in town," with the result that the current epoch's interpretation of reality comes to be taken as self-evident and beyond discussion. When a totalizing, homogenized understanding of things comes to seem so obvious that there is no longer any room for reflection about the being of entities, nothing is any longer genuinely *at stake* or *at issue* for a people. All the significance of what shows up in the world is bleached out. As the world becomes more constricted and inflexible, all that presents itself is a collection of fixed items on hand for us to use or discard as we like. This near-sighted preoccupation with entities understood as fixed and antecedently given, just there on hand for our use, conceals both the "world" (defined as the open arena of possibilities in which a historical people dwells) and that which resists all human mastery, the "earth." Where everything is leveled down to the familiar and the commonplace – the "actual" – things are no longer "possible" and challenging for us.

The characteristic of our age is that being's inevitable withdrawal has been aggravated into complete "abandonment" in the form of modern technology. Heidegger's later diagnosis of technology, discussed in detail by Dreyfus (Chapter 13), first began to take shape in the *Beiträge zur Philosophie*. According to that work, our age is characterized by the fact that "nothing is any longer essentially impossible or inaccessible. Everything 'can be done' and 'lets itself be done' ['*wird gemacht*' *und* '*lässt sich machen*'] if one only has the will for it" (108). The stance toward things in the modern age is that of "machination" (*Machenschaft*), which interprets all entities as representable (*Vor-stellbar*) and capable of being brought forth in production (108–9). Technology, then, is "the *priority* of machination, of discipline, and of method over *what* it is that goes into them and is affected by them"; it is "the priority of ordering over what it is supposed to accomplish" (336, 397).

The domination of ordering takes the form of "enframing" or "configuring" (*Ge-stell*), which reduces all entities, including humans, to the homogenized level of resources on hand to be ordered and used with maximum efficiency. This fascination with ordering for its own sake colors all our ways of understanding things. As Heidegger says, "*Immediate* graspability and usefulness and serviceability... self-evidently constitute *what is in being* and what is not" (30). Entities "are presupposed as what can be arranged, produced, and fixed (*idea*)" (493). The understanding of entities as whatever is at our disposal reinforces the self-certainty of the "greatness of the subject" in modern subjectivism (441). We experience reality as a "world-picture" set before (*vor-gestellt*) us, and ourselves as subjects who can challenge and control whatever there is. The result of this abandonment of being is that "entities appear as objects merely on hand, as if being were not [*als ob Seyn nicht wese*]" (115). Being – that which imparts focus, coherence, belongingness, and a richness of possibilities to things – is blotted out of view. This withdrawal of being is evident in the objectifying procedure of modern natural science that conceals the "essential fullness [*Wesensfülle*] of nature" (QCT 174), that is, the rich possibilities for cohering and belonging together harbored within things. When entities are treated as interchangeable bits cut off from any proper place or "region" to which they belong, they are "un-beings," devoid of the kind of connectedness to contexts of meaning that could let them become manifest in their being.

Only by coming to experience fully the distress of this abandonment of being can we begin to move beyond the mode of understanding dominated by technology and metaphysics. Heidegger speaks of a "new" or an "other" beginning that stands as a possibility before us if we can hear the "echo" (*Anklang*) of being. This "other beginning" will bring about a transformed relationship of humans and being. By bringing us face to face with the concealment itself, the transition to a new beginning will lead us to experience exactly what was forgotten in metaphysics: the *truth* of being. In Heidegger's words, "The *first beginning* experience[d] and posit[ed] the *truth of entities* without asking about truth as such. ... The *other beginning* experiences the truth of being and asks about the being of *truth* in order to thereby ground the essencing of being" (179). Instead of the "guiding question" concerning the beingness of entities (What are entities?) there will be the "basic question" (*Grundfrage*) that asks "about being in respect to its ground" (IM 32) – What is the truth of being? What is being itself? Or, as Sheehan puts it, "How come truth?"

As was the case for the first beginning, this new beginning will be not something humans do, but something that happens within being itself. In Heidegger's writings of the thirties, humans are always participants in a wider event. Projection, for example, is no longer described as a structure of human agency, but instead is something that *happens* to humans in the "thrownness of a . . . clearing" (448). And *truth*, understood in the sense of the Greek word for truth, which means unhiddenness or unconcealment,[19] is what lets humans show up in the midst of things: "Truth contains and grants that which *is*, grants beings in the midst of which man himself is a being, in such a way that he relates to beings" (N 3 24). The new beginning, because it recognizes this embeddedness and indebtedness, will carry with it an intensified sense of humans as "thrown" into an open space (Dasein, or "there-being"), where their task is to preserve and protect the being in entities. In reply to the critics of *Being and Time* who saw that work as a continuation of traditional transcendental philosophy, Heidegger insists that human understanding is not to be thought of as a transcendental condition in any sense. It is necessary to "leap beyond *transcendence*," he says, "and ask in an original way about being and truth" (250–1). The "experience of thrownness and the belongingness to being" marks the "essential difference" of this form of thinking from "all *transcendental* ways of knowing" (239).

As Dreyfus shows, we can get a clue to what the new beginning will look like from Heidegger's essay "The Origin of the Work of Art." According to this essay, a great work of art is a world-transforming event that crystallizes an understanding of being for a people, giving them a coherent focus and direction for their lives. Heidegger's description of a Greek temple shows how a focal work, what Dreyfus calls a "cultural paradigm," defines how things can *count* for a community:

Standing there, the building holds its ground against the storm raging above it and so makes the storm itself manifest in its violence. The luster and gleam of the stone . . . first brings to light the light of the day. . . . Tree and grass, eagle and bull, snake and cricket first enter into their distinctive shapes and thus come to appear as what they are.   (PLT 42)

What Heidegger wants us to see in this description is the way a world-defining work first opens a clearing in which things become accessible and intelligible, and thereby brings to realization the *being* of entities in a world. What was initially only inchoate and partial is given a shape and allowed to stand forth *as* something or other.

"But men and animals, plants and things, are never [just] present and familiar as unchangeable objects, only to represent incidentally also a fitting environment for the temple, which one fine day is added to what is already there." On the contrary, the appearance of the temple lets things show up as having a definite articulation, and so as *belonging* in some determinate way within the totality of a world: "The temple, in its standing there, first gives to things their look and to men their outlook on themselves" (PLT 42–3).

The account of the working of the temple in the ancient Greek world shows how an "event of being" can bring to realization a world of a particular sort. Here it makes no sense to think of a world as something humans create, since it is this newly emergent world that first *lets humans be the kinds of beings they are* in this world. It is only in the light of the world opened by the temple that humans can understand themselves as – and so *be* – the builders and creators that they are. The world is described as "the self-disclosing openness of the broad paths of the simple and essential decisions in the destiny of an historical people" (PLT 48). In opening a world, the temple defines the "measure" (*Mass*) or standards that disclose how things are *at stake* for a people. At the same time, it brings into focus what is "measureless for that people," what is yet "not mastered, something concealed, confusing" and so in need of a decision (PLT 55).

Heidegger says that because truth always happens through being articulated or composed (*gedichtet*, literally "condensed" or "bound together"), all art is essentially "poetry" (*Dichtung*) in the broadest sense of this term (PLT 70). But poetry in the narrow sense as a linguistic art has a special position among the arts. Poetry draws on the background "saying" (*Sagen*) of a people – that is, their proverbs, anecdotes, and oral traditions, but also the tacit interpretations embodied in their customs, rituals, and festivals – and transforms that "saying" into a configuration that articulates for a people their understanding of reality. Poetry "transforms the people's saying so that now every living word fights the battle and puts up for decision what is holy and what unholy, what great and what small, what brave and what cowardly" (PLT 43). Thus, the epics of Homer, the psalms of David, or the Sermon on the Mount are not merely aesthetically pleasing embellishments tacked on to a previously existing prosaic form of life. Instead, they formulate and bring to realization what is definitive of a people's form of life.

A great work of art therefore can inaugurate a new beginning for a community. What before had been humdrum and self-evident suddenly stands forth as strange and challenging as a result of this reconfiguration of the world: the work contains "the undisclosed abundance of the unfamiliar and the extraordinary, which means that it also contains strife with the familiar and the ordinary" (PLT 76). Through the work, the "dawning world brings out what is as yet undecided and measureless, and thus discloses the hidden necessity of measure and decisiveness" (PLT 63).

In this way the great poetic works of a historical community play the role of "founding" the existence of that community. The artwork is founding first of all in the sense that it is an "endowment" defining the tasks for the future "preservers" whose world has been opened by the work. In the poetic work, "truth is thrown toward the coming preservers, that is, toward a historical human community." The work sketches out in advance "the concepts of a historial people's essence, i.e., of its belonging to world history," and it thereby transports "a people into [their] appointed task" (PLT 75, 77). We can see this in the way the Gospels, by opening up a new understanding of the point of life in the ancient world, thereby laid out in advance what is demanded of future Christians. But second, world-defining works are also founding in the sense that they establish a "beginning" (Anfang) understood not just as the first event in a sequence, but as an origin that, filled with promise, "already contains the end latent in itself." A "genuine beginning," Heidegger says, "is always a leap forward, in which everything to come is already leaped over, even if as something disguised" (PLT 76). In this way, the possibilities of being a Christian are already anticipated in its beginning, though it is up to future Christians to realize and define what was implicit and "disguised" in that origin.

By sketching out the endowment and tasks of a community, the work of art provides a people with a narrative schema that lets them weave their own lives into a wider, future-directed, and so life-orienting historical unfolding. For Heidegger, the founding beginning for the West occurred "for the first time in Greece. What was in the future to be called 'being' was set into work in a way which set the measure" for what was to come (PLT 76–7). Heidegger points out that insofar as the power of a beginning can never sustain itself, "decline" is inevitable,[20] so that the beginning needs to be "repeated" or "retrieved" (*wiederholt*) if its promise is to be brought to realization. It is "only by thoughtful repetition [*denkende Wiederholung*] that we can deal appropriately with the beginning" (IM 191), recovering what is always there though in a concealed form. This requires that we act as "preservers" who, carrying forward what was undertaken at the dawn of our civilization, work to realize its latent possibilities. And that in turn means overcoming the forgetfulness pervading modern existence. Since the technological understanding of being is rigid and calcified, more a source of concealment than of genuine disclosedness, what is needed now is a new poet who can poetize the background in the way the earliest Greek poets and thinkers did in the first beginning.

Such a repoetizing Heidegger finds in Hölderlin, and especially in the late hymns, which, he says, hit him and others "like an earthquake" when they were first published in an edition by Norbert von Hellingrath in 1914 (OWL 78). Frank H. W. Edler sees Heidegger's reading of Hölderlin as rooted in Hellingrath's interpretation of Hölderlin's later poetry as the attempt to bring to language a "hidden or secret Germany [*das geheime Deutschland*]" that, though it does not yet exist, defines the essence of the Germany yet to come.[21] Hölderlin's poetry provides a language that can find new names to invoke the gods of antiquity: "The old gods are dead [and] live on only in mythical language [*Sage*] but their shadows crowd around for a new birth."[22] Heidegger's own conception of language as a Saying (*Sage*) whose "soundless voice" has the power to summon forth what is forgotten or concealed (OWL 124) seems to be quite in tune with this reading of Hölderlin.

What is most striking about Heidegger's vision of the "history of being" in the thirties is the soteriological and apocalyptic "metanarrative" that seems to underlie it. History is seen as a monolithic "happening" that, springing from primordial origins, passes through a "dark night of the soul" of forgetfulness, yet embodies the prospects for a redemption in the final recovery of its concealed origins. Just as "futurity" is basic to human temporality, so the future is definitive of history. As Heidegger says, "History as a happening is an acting and being acted upon which, passing through the present, *is determined from out of the future* and takes over the past" (IM 44, my emphasis).

This conception of history was already articulated in *Being and Time*. There Heidegger claimed that historiography must begin by projecting "monumental" possibilities for the future to serve as a basis for formulating our sense of where history is headed as a totality. This futural moment is unavoidable, for it is only in terms of some anticipated vision of the end state of historical development that we have a basis for *selecting* the events that can be taken as historically relevant in formulating our account of what history is adding up to. That is, we can narrativize the confusing array of events of the past in order to find some significance in them only on the basis of some conception of the future outcome of history. The projected sense of the possible achievement of history lets us see what should be "reverently preserved" from the past as the historical record of our culture's achievements (BT 447–8). This is why Dasein must "choose its hero" if it is to identify what is worthy of being retrieved from the past (BT 437). And only on the basis of such a monumentalized understanding of the past can we then have a standpoint for criticizing the "today." Authentic historiography is necessarily a "critique of the present," "a way of painfully detaching oneself from the falling publicness of the 'today'" (BT 449). Heidegger's point, it seems, is that a critique of the present can be carried out only on the basis of a vision of alternative ways of living that are possible for us, a "utopian" vision that itself could be *drawn only from our understanding of the past*. In other words, we can criticize what we *are now* only in the name of a monumentalized picture of what, given our history, we *could be*.

The aim of philosophy is "to restore humanity's historical Dasein – and that always includes our own *future* Dasein in the totality of the history allotted to us – to the domain of being, which it was originally incumbent on humans to open up for themselves" (IM 41–2, my emphasis). Understanding the task set for us by the future throws us back onto the need to "win back our roots in history," to take "a creative view of [our] tradition," and to "repeat the beginning...in order to transform it into a new beginning" (IM 38–9). To ask the question of being, then, is not just to dabble in an abstract academic pursuit. On the contrary, the question opens the "happening" of human existence to "yet unquestioned possibilities, futures, and at the same time binds it back to its past beginning, so sharpening it and giving it weight in the present" (IM 44). Behind this thinking there seems to be a belief that the unfolding event of being is itself eschatological: it is because "being itself is inherently eschatological," Heidegger wrote in 1950, that "we must someday anticipate the former dawn in the dawn to come" (EGT 18). Yet it is also clear from these writings that there can never be anything like a final, conclusive account of being: "the essence of being is never conclusively sayable" (460). The most we can do is try to think along with the poet who, hearing what is said in the silent Saying (Sage) of language, can "compose" it into a poetry that awakens a renewed experience of the truth of being.

HEIDEGGER AND THE NAZIS

One strand of the "turn" in Heidegger's thought in the thirties, then, is found in his shift away from a Dasein-centered account of being to one that starts from the history of being. This first strand is closely bound up with a second aspect of the turn, the shift connected with his involvement with the Nazis. In the great outpouring of heated debate that followed the publication of Victor Farias's *Heidegger and Nazism* in 1987, what has often been missing is a reflection on Heidegger's place within the wider arena of events of the time.[23] Certainly it does not *excuse* his behavior to observe that he was in most ways a fairly minor, almost laughable, actor in a much wider wave of support for Hitler. Within the context of the so-called conservative revolution that swept the Nazis into power, the backlash against modernization and liberalism that was building steadily in Germany from the 1870s to 1933, Heidegger's own contributions seem relatively paltry.[24]

It is perhaps hard for us to imagine the shock and bewilderment that accompanied the unification of Germany and the sudden rush of industrialization and urbanization at the end of the nineteenth century. The time of Heidegger's youth was a period of sudden, wrenching change, a time when "Germany was transformed from a relatively backward and predominantly agricultural nation into one of the greatest industrial powers in the world."[25] Especially among disaffected intellectuals and those living in rural areas, the result was a mood of despair over the collapse of traditional culture. We can see this response in the correspondence between Wilhelm Dilthey and Count Yorck, which made such a strong impression on the young Heidegger.[26] Dilthey and Yorck both bemoan the secularization of everyday life, the loss of all sense of hierarchy, the ascendancy of the *Naturwissenschaften*, and the encroaching dangers of what they call "Nietzscheanism," a term referring primarily, it seems, to Nietzsche's skeptical reflections on history in his early work, *The Use and Abuse of History*. The reaction against modernization is also evident in that spontaneous uprising, the Youth Movement at the turn of the century. The quest for *Bunderlebnis*, or a "feeling of belonging," the emphasis on youth, nature, health, and the simple life, and above all the search for firm values and the "longing for a Caesar, for an ultimate authority"[27] – these were the ideals that the young *Wandervögel* (wandering birds) set against what they regarded as the decadence of their bourgeois parents. Running through these conservative movements was the theme of recovering the essence of the *Volk* (people or folk) – the unique "blood and soil" and ancient bonds of the German people – from the forces of Westernization.[28]

In the first decades of the twentieth century this undercurrent of distrust of modernity continued to spread through intellectual circles. Heidegger speaks of those "exciting years between 1910 and 1914" that brought the first complete edition of Nietzsche's *The Will to Power* and the translation of the works of Kierkegaard and Dostoyevski (FS x). It would be hard to overestimate the impact of Dostoyevski on German intellectuals generally and, I suspect, on Heidegger in particular.[29] As Stern observes, "No other modern writer save Nietzsche had as great an impact on German thought as Dostoevski." Part of this impact was due to the influence of the editor of Dostoyevski's complete works, Arthur Moeller van den Bruck. In his introductions to the translations, Moeller quoted Dostoyevski as saying, "We are revolutionaries out of conservatism," and he portrayed the Russian as offering an escape from the West "via the theology of Kierkegaard."[30] Dostoyevski's critique of both liberal individualism and secularized collectivism paved the way for Moeller's own vision of a "third way" between capitalism and Marxism (what he called *das dritte Reich* in his 1922 book of the same name), a truly national, German socialism.

The defeat in the Great War and the seemingly endless economic crises under the Weimar Republic intensified the smoldering resentment of the conservatives. Through the spiraling inflation of the twenties and the collapse of the early thirties, the Republic appeared divided, defenseless, shabby, and hopelessly unstable. In contrast, the conservative Cult of the Young – the "rebellion of the young *for* authority, not *against* authority" – seemed to promise community, rejuvenation, purity, vigor, and *Bodenständigkeit* (rootedness in the earth).³¹ By the thirties, parliamentary democracy appeared to be a failure, and extremists from both the Left and Right squeezed out the defenders of the Republic. In what most at the time saw as a face-off between the Bolsheviks and the conservatives, it was the conservatives who seemed to offer the more truly German option. The conservatives "sought a breakthrough to the past, and they longed for a new community in which old ideas and institutions would once again command universal allegiance." Their aim of "destroy[ing] the despised present in order to recapture an idealized past in an imaginary future"³² parallels Heidegger's own nostalgic and apocalyptic vision of history. In the words of a recent book title, their appeal was in "the new politics of old values."

Raised in a lower-middle-class household in an agrarian, primarily Catholic part of the Black Forest region, Heidegger was, not surprisingly, conservative and often quite provincial in his outlook. Like many other inhabitants of the rural backwaters of Germany, which had suffered the greatest economic losses from sudden industrialization, Heidegger voted for a conservative regional party, the party of Württemberg winegrowers, as late as the Reichstag election of 1932.³³ In the first decades of the twentieth century, his views were generally in step with the prevailing currents of cultural despair. His attacks on the theoretical attitude and his adoption of the vocabulary of life philosophy were motivated by a sense of the "loss of meaning" associated with the ascendancy of the natural sciences and modernization in general.

In 1919 Heidegger spoke to his students about the "de-vitalizing" (*Ent-lebnis*) of life in contemporary scientific pursuits and the "extinguishing of the situation" (*Situation*) in the current context of life (*Lebenszusammenhang*). A "situation" is what imparts unity and meaning to the natural flow of life experience. Heidegger speaks of three fundamental characteristics of a situation: (1) a situation is "an 'event' ['*Ereignis*'], not a 'process' ['*Vorgang*']"; (2) a situation is relatively closed (*Geschlossenheit*); and (3) in a situation the "I" is never "detached" or "disengaged" (*Unabgehobenheit*) – "The 'I' never needs to come into view, [for] it swims within the situation" (GA 56/57 205–6).

It is our being-in-a-situation, where things are clearly *at stake*, that gives our lives focus and direction. At the current time, however, the character of there being a situation is disappearing: "The unity of the situation explodes. Experiences possess no unity of meaning, no unity of content [*Sacheinheit*]; they lose the unity the situation gave them" (GA 56/57 206). Only where life is marked by genuine possibilities of motivation does it produce an "intensification of life." Such an intensification is found in the "Youth Movement for a Free Germany," though not in those (presumably internationalist) forms of "activism" (*Activismus*) that are nothing but "machination" (*Machenschaft*). When the situation collapses, however, the contents of experience present themselves as mere states of affairs detached from any clear relevance to our lives. Everything is leveled down to the indifferent, the familiar, the commonplace (GA 56/57 208–9).

It was during this period that Heidegger broke with the Catholic church and threw himself into the religious radicalism he found in Pauline eschatology, in Kierkegaard and Dostoyevski, and above all in Luther.[34] His writings of this period suggest that we can recover a sense of the weightiness of our "factical" existence in the secularized world only by recapturing something like the world-defining "venture of faith" of authentic, primitive Christianity. As Heidegger sees it, our "worldly" existence as "average everydayness" is characterized by "falling," the tendency to be engrossed in day-to-day preoccupations and to drift along with the fads and trends of the crowd – the anonymous "they" or "anyone" (*das Man*). In this humdrum everydayness, life is leveled down to the lowest common denominator of doing what "one" does in typical, familiar circumstances. We are, as Piotr Hoffman puts it, "replaceable," mere points of intersection of social roles and functions we share with others. As placeholders in the public world, we become caught up in the turbulence of mindless busy-ness, yet we are at the same time "tranquilized," complacently assured that everything has already been worked out and that nothing really calls for a decision.

In my essay (Chapter 10) I run through Heidegger's description of inauthentic existence. Heidegger tells us that the totalizing commonsense interpretation reduces all undertakings to the level of what is "fitting and proper" (BT 239). In contexts calling for action, the "they" knows only "rules and public norms," and it therefore "deprives the particular Dasein of its responsibility [*Verantwortlichkeit*]" for what it does (BT 165, 334). "This leveling

off of Dasein's possibilities to what is proximally at its everyday disposal also results in a *dimming down of the possible as such*" (BT
239, my emphasis). In other words, in the complacency of worldly
existence, we become so absorbed in the things that show up on the
current scene – taking them as the "last word" about what is real –
that we lose sight of our own contribution to opening the clearing of
possibilities in which things can stand forth *as* such and such in the
first place. Preoccupied with the entities that show up in the lighting,
we are blind to what makes it possible for there to be any lighting at
all. In average everydayness, Heidegger says, Dasein "becomes blind
to its possibilities, and tranquilizes itself with that which is merely
'actual'" (BT 239).

What is needed, then, is a way of recovering a sense of the openness
of the possible and of our own responsibility as individuals in articulating and bringing to realization the worldly contexts in which we
find ourselves. And that means being able to experience our predicament not as a mere set of "circumstances" (*Lage*) subsumable under
universally valid (and hence anonymous) principles; but as a "situation" where the choice demanded of us is defined by the concrete
characteristics of the context itself. To become an authentic individual is to achieve the kind of clear-sighted, committed resoluteness
that first "*gives* itself the situation, and *brings* itself into that situation" by defining how things are to count in relation to one's stance.
In contrast to the "they," which "knows only the '*general circumstances*,' [and] loses itself in those '*opportunities*' which are closest
to it," the resolute individual finds him- or herself already in a *situation* of "taking-action," and so directly sees what the situation
demands (BT 347, 355).

What kind of stand is one to take in the situation? Heidegger
answers, "*Only* the resolution itself can give the answer....*The
resolution is precisely the disclosive projection and determination
of what is factically possible at the time*" (BT 345). Resoluteness
lets us achieve clear-sightedness about what is possible and what
is demanded in the current situation because it totally immerses
us in that setting. No longer "losing *itself* in the object of its concern," authentic Dasein in a *moment of vision* "makes the situation
authentically present." This authentic presence holds on to both the
future and the past, and it thereby provides the kind of coherence,
continuity, and "*constancy* of the self" that gives one "time *for* what

the situation demands" (BT 463). Only such an intense and unified stance gives one's life story the "steadiness" it needs to let one grasp what is genuinely *at stake* in the situation, and so to take a stand "*for* what is world-historical in [one's] current situation" (BT 442).

What is demanded of us as individuals, according to Heidegger's early view, is the courage to "simplify" ourselves and to seize on our lives as our "fate." Authenticity "snatches one back from the endless multiplicity of possibilities which offer themselves as closest to one ... and brings Dasein into the simplicity of its *fate*" (BT 435). Fate in turn is always tied into a wider "struggle" (*Kampf*) that makes up one's *destiny* "in and with [one's] 'generation'" (BT 436). This struggle will most likely require "*doing violence* ... to the claims of the everyday interpretation, or to its complacency and its tranquilized obviousness" (BT 399). And as "The Origin of the Work of Art" makes clear, it runs the risk of "going astray" into "the indefeasible severity of error" (PLT 55). But it is only by overthrowing what is calcified and stale – the familiar, the commonplace, the ordinary – that a new "measure" (*Mass*) can be found, a new world order brought to pass.

For Heidegger in the early thirties, the Nazi movement seemed to promise the sort of rejuvenation through retrieval envisioned by his apocalyptic view of history. Like many other conservative Germans, Heidegger must have "shudderingly admired the terroristic idealism of Hitler's movement,"[35] convinced that conditions had reached such a desperate state that only an act of violence could lead to a breakthrough to a purer, more stable form of life. At least this seems to be what is implied by Heidegger's Rectoral Address, delivered in May 1933, when he speaks of "the German fate in its most extreme distress" and of the need to recover "the *beginning* of our spiritual-historical being," that "first beginning" inaugurated by the Greeks.[36] This beginning "still *is*," Heidegger says. "It does not lie *behind us*, as something that was long ago, but stands *before* us. As what is greatest, the beginning has passed in advance beyond all that is to come.... The beginning had invaded our future. There it awaits us, as a distant command bidding us catch up with its greatness." It is part of the "spiritual mission of the German *Volk*," then, to "resolutely submit to this distant command to recapture the greatness of the beginning."[37] What previously was treated as solely the task of the individual is now seen as the task of an entire nation.

Heidegger's constant references in his speeches and popular writings to the *Volk*, the ideal of a *völkische Wissenschaft* (people's science), and the protection of the *Volkstum* (character of the cultural group) reveal his commitment to the *völkische* ideology of Nazism and his belief in the unique destiny and essence of the German people.[38]

By 1936, however, Heidegger was pulling back from his involvement in the political arena. There are still apocalyptic tirades about the darkening of the world and the need for rejuvenation. Our task, according to the *Beiträge*, is "the renewal of the world through the salvation of the earth," and for this we need to prepare ourselves "for the appearance of the last god" (411–12).[39] Humans still have a central role in this recovery. The truth of being can happen, Heidegger claims, only if we make a decision to achieve *Inständigkeit*, that is, "insistence," a steadfast "standing-in-a-site" which lets that site be a situation where things can show up in the fullest way. The "*truth of being . . .* comes-to-pass [*west*] only in the steady standing-in-a-site [*Inständigkeit*] of Da-sein, in the experience of thrownness into the There out of the calling-forth [*Zuruf*] of the *Ereignis*" (233). Insistence establishes a "grounded relation" to being, a relation that makes possible the "safeguarding of being in that which . . . shows itself as an entity in the clearing of the There" (467). The idea here seems to be that a necessary condition of entities fully manifesting their being is that we do not treat things as bits in the mosaic of a world picture laid out before our detached representation (*Vorstellen*), but instead experience our thrownness into a setting where we are "called" to the task of letting things show up in their full significance and belongingness together. This mode of "insistent caring [*Besorgung*]" (71) Heidegger later calls "dwelling," a way of abiding on the earth that opens a clearing where things can "gather" the surrounding environment into a coherent whole (a "region" or "play of time-space" [*Zeit-Spiel-Raum*]). The essay "Building Dwelling Thinking," for example, speaks of how the dwelling of peasants, embodied in a farmhouse built centuries ago, contributed to "the power [that] let earth and heaven, divinities and mortals enter *in simple oneness* into things," and so ordered the house in the world of the Black Forest (PLT 160).

From this new point of view, however, the *Volk* (and humans generally) come to be treated more as facilitators and participants in the wider event of a "Fourfold" in which mortals, gods, earth, and heaven are gathered into the "belonging-together" of a world. The term "Da-sein" now refers not to humans but to "the self-opening medium of the interplay of calling-forth and belongingness;...the *between* between humans...and gods..." (311). Increasingly, it is *things* that play the central role in letting a world happen, while we humans "are *called by* the thing as thing" precisely because "we are bethinged [*be-dingt*], the conditioned ones" (PLT 181, my emphasis).

The *Beiträge* still speaks of the need for us to make a "decision." This need, however, is revealed not by reflecting on the current political situation, but by coming to terms with the history of being. "Certainly this basic 'fact' of our history [i.e., the need for a decision] becomes apparent not through an 'analysis' of the 'spiritual' or 'political' 'situation' of the time." Indeed, an absorption in intellectual and political currents conceals the need to experience "authentic history – the struggle [*Kampf*] of the appropriation [*Ereignung*] of humanity through being" (309). Political involvement – including National Socialism – now comes to be regarded as a symptom of abandonment and nihilism rather than as their potential cure.

By 1936 the concern with the *Volk* is treated as merely a continuation of the domination of subjectivism and humanism of Western metaphysics. The *Volk* can "never be the goal and purpose," Heidegger says. On the contrary, belief in the priority of the people is "only a '*völkische*' expansion of 'liberal,' 'me-centered' thinking and of the economic representation of the maintenance of 'life,'" (319). The Nazi slogan "Everything must be at the service of the people" trivializes entities to the level of what is useful and at our disposal (30). But this shows that the Nazi movement itself is nothing more than one more stage in the ongoing story of the abandonment of being in metaphysics. As being withdraws, there is an "*idolizing* of the *conditions* for historical being – the *Völkisch*, for example, with all its ambiguity – to the [level of the] *unconditional*" (117). Heidegger's anti-Humanism now comes to be formulated in sharp opposition to the core beliefs of the Nazis. In response to what is perceived as nihilism – the loss of life-defining goals – the Nazis have made the people into the highest goal. But in doing so, Heidegger says, they take what is in fact merely a *means* to achieving goals – the *Volk* – and treat that as if it were the *goal itself* (139). The futility of Nazism becomes evident, however, once we recognize that it is precisely this humanistic tendency to treat humans as the ultimate goal, rather than as a means to achieving the authentic goal, that has created the sense of the aimlessness and nihilism of modern existence. The concern with recovering goals by, for example, making culture available to all the people, or by providing rich, meaningful "experiences," actually engenders greater nihilism: the "noisy drunkenness with 'experiences'" – seen in the *"gigantic* meetings" organized to overcome the people's fears – "is the greatest nihilism, the organized blindness to the aimlessness of humanity" (139).

Heidegger is contemptuous of the idea of a "people's philosophy," the idea that philosophy is one cultural accomplishment among others, like a style of dress or a local cuisine. With his characteristic air of paradox he asserts that a people does not create a philosophy, but rather a philosophy creates a people (42–3). In the same way, the ideal of a *"völkische* science" is just another symptom of nihilism, as is the idea that "blood and race" are the agents and bearers of history – as if it were *"pre*history that gives history its validity" (493). Thus Heidegger's verdict: the Nazi "revolution" is rootless, unable to face its own lack of ground to stand on, its own *Bodenlosigkeit* (122).

The task set before us, as Heidegger sees it, is to "open up the simplicity and greatness" of entities and to secure "the truth of being in entities, in order thereby to give a *goal* to historical humanity: *to become the grounder and preserver of the truth of being*, to *be* the There as the ground that is used by the essence of being itself" (16). The point of this obscure passage seems to be that, since humans are at the deepest level participants in a wider scheme of things (what comes to be called the Fourfold of earth, sky, humans, and gods described by Young), their proper function is to articulate and preserve a clearing in which things can become manifest in their "simplicity" and "greatness." Humans have a genuine goal, then, to the extent that they abandon their quest for self-aggrandizement and instead realize their function by doing what they are called on to do by the "destining" (*Geschick*) of being. Genuine *care* (*Sorge*) is needed, then, in order "to be simply '*for the sake of being*,' not for the sake of man but for the sake of the being of entities in totality" (16, cf. 99).

To achieve this sense of purpose, according to Heidegger, we need to experience ourselves as recipients of the "gift" of being. What is suggested here is the idea of treasuring things for what they are rather than for what they can do for us. Perhaps the best examples of what Heidegger envisions as this impending "new beginning" are such non-Western experiences as the Hopi sense of the land as a gift to be cared for and returned at the end of our dwelling on earth or the Japanese experience of "national treasures" that people are charged with preserving. It is such experiences of receiving a gift that Heidegger tries to capture when he speaks of a kind of thinking that is thankfulness. Because Western metaphysics has been anthropocentric from the earliest misreading of *physis*, however, it is hard for us to conjure up comparable experiences from our own heritage. Heidegger's reminders of temples from the past or anticipations of new ways of encountering a jug in the future give us only intimations of what the new beginning might bring. The later writings, as the essays by Caputo and Zimmerman show, move toward an ideal mode of comportment called *Gelassenheit*, a nonmanipulative, non-imposing way of "letting things be" what they are.

In treating Heidegger as a product of his times, we run the risk of either trivializing his thought by reducing it to its sociohistorical causes or "explaining away" his actions as "what everyone did" at the time. It is certainly not true, of course, that "everyone did" what he did in the thirties. Heidegger's friends at the time felt his attempts to "work within the system" and to provide leadership to the chaotic political upheavals were at best naive and were quite possibly opportunistic and self-serving. The fact that he was largely ignored by the Nazis makes his dream of a life-transforming "national religion" almost pathetic. Yet at least one friend, Hans-Georg Gadamer, wonders whether his own way of dealing with the events – keeping a low profile and waiting for it all to blow over – was really any better.[40]

Given Heidegger's actions, and given his own firm belief that those actions followed quite naturally from his philosophy, there is no way to buy into his philosophy without reflecting deeply on its moral and political implications. We must keep in mind that, as is true with Nietzsche, there is no way to make Heidegger's thought consonant with our own deepest democratic sentiments without distorting it. His nonegalitarian outlook is evident, for example, even as late as his 1950 essay "The Thing," in which he says that from among "the measureless mass of men as living beings" there may be some "living beings [who can] first *become* mortals" and so can be in the right relation to being (PLT 179, 182). And his lifelong belief in the possibility of a new dispensation of being leaves innumerable questions about why we should think, once being is detached from Christian providence or Stoic rationality, that such an event will be *good* in any sense. Nevertheless, while there is no way to play down the moral worries raised by Heidegger's thought, there is also no way to deny that this at times mystifying man from the backwoods of Germany more than once redrew the philosophical map, laying out lines of questioning for generations to come.

NOTES

1. Zimmerman's essay (Chapter 11) details some of this influence. See especially Graham Parkes, ed., *Heidegger and Asian Thought* (Honolulu: University of Hawaii Press, 1987).

2. Hoy sums up some of this discussion in Chapter 6. For insight into how Heidegger can be treated as the wellspring of current movements, see John D. Caputo, *Radical Hermeneutics: Repetition, Deconstruction, and the Hermeneutic Project* (Bloomington: Indiana University Press, 1987).

3. The new wave of interest in Heidegger's involvement with the Nazis was sparked by the appearance in 1987 of Victor Farias's *Heidegger et le nazisme*, translated as *Heidegger and Nazism*, ed. J. Margolis and T. Rockmore (Philadelphia: Temple University Press, 1989). Thomas Sheehan provides an excellent review of Farias's book in *New York Review of Books*, June 16, 1988, pp. 38–47. For an overview of key texts on Heidegger and politics, see Michael Zimmerman, "The Thorn in Heidegger's Side: The Question of National Socialism," *Philosophical Forum*, 20 (Summer 1989): 326–65. Especially useful among the many works examining Heidegger as a man and his political involvements are Hugo Ott, *Martin Heidegger: A Political Life*, translated by Allan Blunden (New York: Basic Books, 1993) and Rüdiger Safranski, *Martin Heidegger: Between Good and Evil*, translated by Ewald Osers (Cambridge, MA: Harvard University Press, 1998).

4. In addition to Sheehan's review mentioned in note 3, see John D. Caputo, "Thinking, Poetry and Pain," in *Heidegger and Praxis*, ed. Thomas J. Nenon, 1989. Spindel Conference, supplement to *Southern Journal of Philosophy*, 28 (1990): 155–81.

5. The contributions to this volume by Frede, Zimmerman, and Caputo are especially helpful in showing how Heidegger's view of the connection between being and human understanding builds on medieval thought, and especially on the Scotist account of the connection between the *modus intelligendi* of things (how they are comprehended) and their *modus essendi* (type of objectivity).

6. It seems that Heidegger drew this conception of phenomena not so much from Husserl as from Aristotle. As Martha Nussbaum points out, Aristotle held that philosophy starts from phenomena defined as "the world *as it appears to*, as it is experienced by, observers of our kind." Phenomena are found in "interpretations, often revealed in linguistic usage." Philosophy's aim, in Aristotle's view, is not to get at something *beneath* the appearances, but to grasp that in virtue of which appearances are unified and intelligible. In this sense, "the appearances go all the way down." See Nussbaum, *The Fragility of Goodness: Luck and Ethics in Greek Tragedy and Philosophy* (New York: Cambridge University Press, 1986), pp. 24–45, 251. Heidegger more than once expressed his debt to Aristotle's phenomenological method (cf. BP 232; TB 79).

7. I fully agree with Dreyfus's definition of "Dasein" as the basic structure of humans: *that* each human's own way of being is an issue for it. Thus, when Heidegger says, *"More primordial than man is the finitude of the Dasein in him"* (KPM 237), I take that to mean that Dasein *qua* finitude, though instantiated in each (normal) human, is conceptually distinct from the anthropological entity, *Homo sapiens*. On my view, to say that Dasein makes possible the world where entities can show up is not to suggest that *each* Dasein has its own monadic world, but rather that it is *because* an "understanding of being as essentially existent finitude" (KPM 238) has emerged, and is now deposited and preserved in communal practices, monuments, libraries, and so forth, that there is a field of intelligibility in which various sorts of things show up (for all of us) in familiar ways.

8. Dasein's understanding is a "self-projective being toward its ownmost ability-to-be. This ability is that for the sake of which any Dasein is as it is. In each case Dasein has already put itself together, in its being, with a possibility of itself" (BT 236).

9. For detailed examinations of Heidegger's conception of worldhood, see Hubert L. Dreyfus, *Being-in-the-World: A Commentary on Heidegger's "Being and Time," Division I* (Cambridge, MA: MIT Press, 1991), and Mark Okrent, *Heidegger's Pragmatism: Understanding, Being, and the Critique of Metaphysics* (Ithaca, NY: Cornell University Press, 1988).

10. When I say that Heidegger is a "realist," then, I mean something different from what Dreyfus means in his *Being-in-the-World* (pp. 251–65) when he speaks of Heidegger's "minimal hermeneutic realism about nature." According to my interpretation, Heidegger's claim is that it is the ready-to-hand world of familiar things that is real (or is "as real as anything can get"), whereas the entities held to exist by the natural sciences are products of working over or redescribing those familiar equipmental entities for particular purposes. On my interpretation,

Heidegger seems quite close to what John Dewey is saying in his distinction between water and H_2O in the opening chapters of *The Quest for Certainty* (New York: Putnam's, 1960).

11. Hoffman's essay (Chapter 8) shows how we become aware of this ultimate lack of foundations in the experience of anxiety.

12. Taylor (Chapter 7) shows how this kind of "primordiality" claim is similar to the Kantian argument that experiencing particular sensations as sensations is derivative from and parasitic on a background in which we experience a world of real, concrete things.

13. Thomas Sheehan points out that, in his 1928 seminar on Aristotle's *Physics*, Heidegger already was thinking of being (or *physis*) as a "movement" or "event" (*Ereignis*), the "disclosive event" of "appropriatedness into intelligibility" from out of concealment. See Sheehan, "On Movement and the Destruction of Ontology," *Monist*, 64 (October 1981): 534–42.

14. Nevertheless, I am not convinced that Heidegger's attempt to pull the rug out from under the skeptic is the last word on skepticism. One might still ask, for instance, how we are to deal with cases of *conflicting* presentations or appearances – that is, with disputes involving incompatible perspectives – once we abjure the traditional notion of a final "truth of the matter." Moreover, Heidegger's repeated claims that there are entities independent of Dasein's understanding, together with the plausible assumption that they can enter into our intelligibility only because they have what Dorothea Frede in Chapter 1 calls a "fittingness" to our modes of understanding, seems to pave the way to questions about the nature of these entities. Once again the Kantian *Ding an sich* threatens to rear its ugly head.

15. As a matter of fact, it appears that in *Being and Time* the primordial sources were to be found in primal Christian experience, especially the Pauline experience of the *kairos*, and that Paramenides already represented an initial stage of forgetfulness (cf. BT 133). As Caputo shows, however, by the thirties this priority given to Christian experience had dropped away in favor of a notion of "primal experience," which is, in fact, a Christianized reading of pre-Socratic thought. The possibility that at the core of Western civilization there is essentially dissension, a *conflict* of cultures and traditions (Greek, Judeo-Christian, African, etc.), is something Heidegger never considered, perhaps because he assumed that history, which he once called "mythology" (IM 155), requires a unified beginning in order to have a coherent narrative structure.

16. All plain page citations in parentheses in this Introduction are from the *Beiträge zur Philosophie* (*Vom Ereignis*) Vol. 65 of the *Gesamtausgabe*. first published in 1989. For my interpretation of this work I am

deeply indebted to Richard Polt's excellent study, "Heidegger and the Place of Logic" (Ph.D. dissertation, University of Chicago, 1991). I have also made use of F. W. von Hermann's "Technology, Politics and Art in Heidegger's *Beiträge zur Philosophie*," in *Martin Heidegger: Politics, Art, and Technology*, edited by Karsten Harries and Christoph Jamme (New York: Holmes and Meier, 1994). Since this writing, the *Beiträge* has been translated as *Contributions to Philosophy (From Enowning)* by Parvis Emad and Kenneth Maly (Bloomington: Indiana University Press, 1999). In this second edition of the companion, I have retained my own translations. For an exhaustive study of the *Contributions*, see Richard Polt's *The Emergency of Being: On Heidegger's "Contributions to Philosophy"* (Ithaca, NY: Cornell University Press, 2006).

17. Zimmerman succinctly traces these developments in Chapter 11. For an illuminating account of Heidegger's thought as a sustained reflection on "productionist metaphysics," see his book, *Heidegger's Confrontation with Modernity: Technology, Politics, and Art* (Bloomington: Indiana University Press, 1990).

18. "Platons Lehre von der Wahrheit," *Wegmarken*, p. 133. Quoted in Robert J. Dostal, "Beyond Being: Heidegger's Plato," *Journal of the History of Philosophy*, 23 (January 1985): 71–98, p. 79.

19. In *The Fragility of Goodness*, Martha Nussbaum points out that the Greek word for truth, *a-letheia*, means etymologically "what is brought out from concealment" (p. 241).

20. This seems to be the point of the statement in *Being and Time* that "in the field of ontology, any 'springing from' is degeneration" (BT 383).

21. Norbert von Hellingrath, *Hölderlin: Zwei Vorträge*, 2d ed. (Munich: Hugo Bruckmann, 1922), pp. 41, 47. Quoted in Frank H. W. Edler, "Philosophy, Language, and Politics: Heidegger's Attempt to Steal the Language of the Revolution in 1933–34," *Social Research*, 57 (Spring 1990): 197–238, p. 208.

22. Hellingrath, *Hölderlin*, p. 44, quoted in Edler, "Philosophy, Language, and Politics," p. 214.

23. The essay by Sheehan (Chapter 2) is one exception. Other notable exceptions are Pierre Bourdieu's *The Political Ontology of Martin Heidegger*, trans. P. Collier (Stanford, CA: Stanford University Press, 1991), which first appeared in French in 1975, Zimmerman's *Heidegger's Confrontation with Modernity*, Hans Sluga's *Heidegger's Crisis: Philosophy and Politics in Nazi Germany* (Cambridge, MA: Harvard University Press, 1993), and Julian Young's *Heidegger, Philosophy, Nazism* (Cambridge: Cambridge University Press, 1997).

24. According to Hans Sluga, "The historical record shows...that [Heidegger] was of no central importance within the world of Nazi

philosophy, and that he was, if anything, an outsider to the philosophical establishment of the time." "Metadiscourse: German Philosophy and National Socialism," *Social Research*, 56 (Winter 1989): 795–818, p. 817.

25. Fritz K. Ringer, *The Decline of the German Mandarins: The German Academic Community*, 1890–1933 (Cambridge, MA: Harvard University Press, 1969), p. 43.

26. Heidegger devotes an entire section of *Being and Time* (§77) to a discussion of Count Yorck's thoughts on history as formulated in the *Briefwechsel zwischen Wilhelm Dilthey und dem Grafen Paul Yorck von Wartenburg*, 1877–1897 (Halle: Niemeyer, 1923).

27. Fritz Stern, *The Politics of Cultural Despair: A Study in the Rise of the Germanic Ideology* (Berkeley and Los Angeles: University of California Press, 1961), p. xxviii.

28. See George L. Mosse, *The Crisis of German Ideology: Intellectual Origins of the Third Reich* (New York: Schocken Books, 1981), for a study of how *völkische* ideology contributed to Nazi anti-Semitism.

29. According to Otto Pöggeler, Heidegger held that among all early critics of the European tradition, "the greatest importance then surely belonged to Dostoyevski." See Pöggeler, *Martin Heidegger's Path of Thinking*, trans. D. Magurshak and S. Barber (Atlantic Highlands, NJ: Humanities Press, 1987), p. 265. Karl Löwith recalls that of the two portraits Heidegger kept on the desk in his office, one was of Dostoyevski. "The Political Implications of Heidegger's Existentialism," *New German Critique*, 45 (Fall 1988): 117–134, p. 121.

30. Stern, *Politics of Cultural Despair*, pp. 209–10.

31. Ibid., pp. 224–25.

32. Ibid., p. xvi.

33. According to a letter from Heidegger's son, Dr. Hermann Heidegger, as reported by Edler in "Philosophy, Language, and Politics" (pp. 237–8). The record suggests that the Nazis drew most of their support from the small local parties. V. R. Berghahn shows that, in the 1930 Reichstag election, smaller regional and conservative parties accounted for about 21% of the electorate, whereas only 15% voted for the Nazis. By November 1932, support had shifted to 10% for local and right-wing parties as opposed to 27% for the Nazis. See V. R. Berghahn, *Modern Germany: Society, Economy and Politics in the Twentieth Century* (Cambridge: Cambridge University Press, 1982), p. 113.

34. In Chapter 12, Caputo describes this shift toward Protestantism as Heidegger's "first turn." It is interesting that, according to Hans-Georg Gadamer, Heidegger once said his life's goal was "to be a new Luther" (personal communication). The theologian Rudolf Bultmann, whose

seminar on St. Paul Heidegger attended in 1923, described Heidegger as "*the* Luther expert" and said of him, "He comes out of Catholicism, but he is totally Protestant." See Hugo Ott, *Martin Heidegger: Unterwegs zu einer Biographie* (Frankfurt: Campus, 1988), pp. 11, 123. Karl Löwith reports that Heidegger "knew Luther's works better than many a professional theologian" ("The Political Implications of Heidegger's Existentialism," p. 122). That Heidegger saw himself as in protest against mainstream Christendom is evident in such remarks as his 1928 reference to "the enormously phoney religiosity" of the times (MFL 165n).

35. Stern, *Politics of Cultural Despair*, p. xxx.
36. "The Self-Assertion of the German University," trans. K. Harries, *Review of Metaphysics*, 38 (March 1985): 467–502, p. 471.
37. Ibid., pp. 473, 476.
38. See, e.g., the "Declaration of Support for Adolph Hitler and the National Socialist State" of November 11, 1933, "A Word from the University" of January 6, 1934, or "National Socialist Education" of January 22, 1934, in Guido Schneeberger, *Nachlese zu Heidegger: Dokumente zu seinem Leben und Denken* (Bern: Suhr, 1962), translated by W. S. Lewis in Richard Wolin, "Martin Heidegger and Politics: A Dossier," *New German Critique*, 45 (Fall 1988): 91–114.
39. In Chapter 13 Dreyfus tries to clarify this important notion of the coming of a new "god." See also Young's discussion of the "gods" in chapter 14.
40. The comment was made as, with characteristic candor, Gadamer reminisced about the past with his former students at a conference in Heidelberg in 1989.

1   The question of being: Heidegger's project

An on-the-way in the field of paths for the changing questioning of the manifold question of Being.[1]

It may remain forever a matter of debate how much truth there is in the old claim that every important thinker has essentially one fundamental idea. In the case of famous philosophers, its vindication may oblige us to summarize the "one great idea" in such broad terms as to make it almost meaningless. What can probably be claimed with more justification is that for most great minds there has been *one question* that guided their thinking or research. This certainly applies to Martin Heidegger, and the question that fascinated him throughout his long philosophic life can be stated simply: what is the meaning of being? Ontology, in the widest possible sense, was his main concern throughout his life. This does not mean, of course, that he was forever looking for an answer to the same old question. As his thinking evolved, the meaning of the question changed; but Heidegger to the end of his life remained convinced that the "questionability" of the *Seinsfrage* was the main thrust of his life's work (cf. GA 1 438).

Impressive as such single-mindedness may seem, the phrase "meaning of being" on careful examination seems so vague that philosophers and nonphilosophers alike may wonder what kind of question this is. The meaning of being? Does this refer to all beings, to whatever we may say that it *is* – rocks, trees, clouds, colors, sounds, dreams, or irrational numbers alike? Or does the question presuppose some high-flying metaphysical concept like Being as such, as seems to be indicated by the fact that English translations usually capitalize the letter "B"? Heidegger made it his task to show that there is a meaningful concept of the being of all beings, a conception that underlies all our understanding of reality. As he saw it, this conception has been the aim of all metaphysical thinking, even if it was not always properly understood. The search for an answer remained a search for a clarification of the question, as Heidegger's reference to "the changing questioning" in the epigraph to this chapter shows.

It is not possible in one short essay to trace the meaning of this question throughout Heidegger's lifetime – why he continued to think it worth asking, and why it seemed so elusive. The discussion here will have to be confined to a clarification of the sense in which the "question of being" came to vex the young Heidegger, and why he treated its "neglect" after a promising start in early Greek philosophy as the most serious omission in the history of Western philosophy. Basing the origins of the problems he is dealing with in ancient Greek philosophy is more than the conventional homage paid to the Greeks by educated Germans of Heidegger's generation. Understanding Heidegger's reference to that tradition is indispensable for a proper understanding of the question of the meaning of being itself.[2] As he never tired of repeating, the problem of the meaning of being, the guiding star of his philosophical thought, started to concern him while he was still a high school student. It began when one of his teachers presented him with Franz Brentano's book *On the Several Senses of Being in Aristotle.*[3] A brief summary will provide a rough picture of the history of Aristotelian ontology, for in its traditional ramifications, this is the conception that Heidegger pits himself against with his claim that the meaning of the question of being must be revived. This chapter will therefore try to point out in a kind of dialectical discussion how Heidegger relates himself to the tradition.

THE QUESTION OF BEING IN HEIDEGGER'S EARLY WRITINGS

Certain peculiarities of the Greek language favored the development of ontology, the "science of being," as Aristotle called metaphysics. Even in prephilosophical Greek it was quite common to refer to "beings," to "what there is," both in the sense of "things" and in the sense of what we would call "states of affairs." The fact that there is a clear linguistic distinction between "beings," *ta onta*, referred to by the participle with the definite article, the verb "to be," *einai*, and the abstract noun "being," *ousia* (the nature of beings), makes the development of such a philosophical discipline much more natural than our contrived renderings in English (or in German for that matter) would suggest.[4] Once a certain level of abstraction and conceptual reflection was reached, it became only natural to raise the question whether there is a unified meaning of *being* that accrues to all beings (in contradistinction to "what is not") or whether *being* has irreducibly many different meanings that fall into different categories, depending on the kind of entity that is under investigation. It became natural to ask whether there is a unitary meaningful concept that demarcates the realm of being as such.

Plato was the first to raise this question explicitly in the *Sophist*; he calls the problem of being a *gigantomachia*, a "battle among giants," that has to be settled if there is to be any chance of solving problems about the meaning of not-being. Whether the conception of being as "what has the power to act or be acted on," offered as a compromise in the *Sophist* (242 ff.), is in effect Plato's own answer cannot be examined here.[5] Heidegger was well aware of Plato's struggle with this problem, since he used the passage in the *Sophist* as his point of departure in *Being and Time* (BT 19). Nevertheless, whatever Plato may have thought about the "unity of being," it was the *Aristotelian* doctrine of a *manifold* of meanings of being that came to dominate the history of Western metaphysics. It is Aristotle's doctrine of the *categories* of beings that Heidegger refers to when he presents his view of the historical development of Western thought that ended in complete "forgetfulness of the question of being." To understand Heidegger's reaction to this tradition that made the conception of "substance" its main focus, we have to take a closer look at Aristotle's theory.

Aristotle distinguished as many meanings of "being" as there are categories of entities. There is the primary category of *substance*, designating natural "things" that exist in their own right,[6] while all other entities are *attributes of substances* either inhering in them or standing in some other relation to them (quality, quantity, relation, place, time, action, affection, possession, position). Although it is not entirely clear how Aristotle arrived at his list of categories of all the things there are, it is fairly obvious that he used linguistic criteria as one of his guides. Thus, when we take a naturally existing independent object (e.g., a stone) and try to determine what predicates we assign to it, what characteristics it has, we get different types of answers about its nature in all its respects (its quantity, qualities, place, time, etc.). That the way we speak about entities provides the guideline for their classification does not imply, however, that Aristotle regarded his system of categories as a man-made conceptual scheme. He regarded the categories as distinctions contained in the nature of things; they are read off nature and are not schemas read into or imposed on nature by us.

Aristotle therefore remained a metaphysical realist with respect to his "discovery" of the natural structure of reality. This structure is based on the *primacy of substances*, naturally existing *independent* entities that form the building blocks of Aristotle's universe. Substances are the only entities that can exist in their own right, while all other entities are attributes that need substances as the substrate for their existence. "To be" then means either to be a substance or to be (one of the nine other kinds of) attributes of a substance. And since the being of a substance, a quality, a quantity, or other attributes are *irreducibly different*, there is no unified sense of "being" that could be predicated of items in all categories. There is only an "analogy of being" that has in recent years been dubbed "focal meaning" to indicate the centrality of the substance, without permitting a univocal definition of the term "being."

Since this focus of the conception of being on *substantiality* determined the future development of metaphysics, not only in later antiquity but through the Middle Ages into the modern age, "substance" remained the central term in traditional ontology, and substances or "things," natural entities with attributes and the capacities to interact causally with one another, remained the building blocks – and became Heidegger's main challenge.[7]

The young Heidegger's apparent unease at the "untidiness" of this allegedly natural order of things, with its resulting emptiness of the concept of being itself, increased when he immersed himself in medieval philosophy. He could see how heavily Christian doctrine was leaning on Aristotelian metaphysics, as neo-Thomism does to this day. In spite of all changes in the adaptation of Greek philosophy to Christian theology, the handmaiden exerted a decisive influence over her mistress: the substance-oriented ontology of the Aristotelians dominated the medieval discussion and determined what solutions were even considered viable.

It took Heidegger some time to find his own way and to overcome this tradition, founded by Aristotle and carried on by the Aristotelians, a tradition that continued to exert its influence even over Kantian and post-Kantian philosophy. We will have to follow some further steps in Heidegger's development to see what he found so pernicious in the "substance ontology" and how he arrived at the solution to the difficulties. His self-attested continued perplexity concerning the question of being helps to explain an otherwise rather surprising feature of his philosophical biography. A contemporary of the young Heidegger who had to evaluate his early published work (before *Being and Time*) could not have had an inkling that Heidegger would become one of the most important and influential philosophers of the twentieth century. His early work, if not actually dull, is at least rather conventional and must look at first blush as of historical interest at best. Neither his thesis, "The Doctrine of Judgment in Psychologism" (1913), nor his monograph, *The Theory of Categories and Meaning of Duns Scotous* (1915), would seem to promise great originality, let alone revolutionary thinking. Had Heidegger done no more, he would rightly have vanished without a trace in the archives.

A closer look at these early writings (which we can only touch on here) would show, however, that Heidegger had not been wasting his time. As early as his thesis, his critique of psychologism – at that time still a fashionable trend in the philosophy of mind in Germany – shows that he was firmly convinced that the key to *meaning* cannot lie in the empirical observation of the actual psychological processes that constitute our thoughts. This conviction formed the basis of his later allegiance to Husserlian phenomenology. The act of judging must not be confused with the meaning of what is judged (GA 1 110). If we want to know what our thoughts are *about* (what philosophers after Brentano call the "intentionality" of acts of consciousness), we must analyze the *content of thought* itself, as distinct from the psychic events that are at work.

Nevertheless, Heidegger gained valuable insights concerning the *Seinsfrage* from this discussion of a philosophy that he regarded as fundamentally mistaken. His reflections on the psychologistic philosophers' explanations of how psychological processes constitute the objects of our thoughts forced Heidegger to reflect more on the connection between the act of thinking in contradistinction to the *meaning* of the thought and on its relationship with the *language* in which it is expressed. Tentative results of these reflections are found in side remarks which indicate that Heidegger was moving toward a characterization of "being" that is rather different from the one generated in the Aristotelian naturalist ontology.

He envisages the future task of the theory of knowledge to be to "divide the whole realm of 'being' into its different *modes of reality* [*Wirklichkeitsweisen*]" and regards epistemology as crucial for such a division: "The characteristics of the different forms of reality must be sharply demarcated and determined, including the appropriate method of knowing [*Art ihrer Erkenntnis*] and its limitations" (GA 1 186). The "division of being" into the realms of the physical, psychic, metaphysical, and logical (GA 1 160)[8] makes no claims to being comprehensive, however; it is rather tentative, and it follows conventional lines. Heidegger is clearly still far from seeing any way to provide for the possibility of a unified meaning of being. But although he advocates a strict separation of the realm of the psychic and that of logical validity, what is important for him is the question of how *meaning* as a whole is embedded in the actual life of the person who entertains a thought; the distinction between the different "realms" is not as rigid as his adherence to the terminology might suggest.

A major step forward in the search for a clearer conception of the different meanings of being can be found in Heidegger's second monograph, the discussion of the theory of categories and meaning found in Duns Scotus. What intrigued him in particular was why Duns Scotus came to see the Aristotelian system of categories as only one of several such systems, a subclass that fits one special part or *specific realm* of being but does not exhaust reality as such. The need for a widening of the ontological categories seems to have occurred to Scotus first for theological reasons. If the most fundamental concepts apply to God at all, then they can do so only in an analogous sense. For God is not a substance like other substances, nor can the concepts of unity, truth, and goodness apply to him in the same sense that they do to other entities (GA 1 260, 263). But it was not just a widening and a diversification that separated Scotus's treatment of the problem of the categories of being from the traditional treatment by the Aristotelians. As Heidegger saw it, Scotus did not just assign different realms of reality to the different subject matters of different disciplines; rather he saw the need for a new conception of *reality* as such. Behind this revision stands the insight that if different disciplines import different (senses of the) categories, then the categories of reality cannot simply be *read off* nature, as they were for Aristotle, but they are obviously also read *into* nature by us, or rather into reality as a whole. The "question of being" becomes then the question of the givenness of the object to the subject. For Scotus, therefore, the conditions of *subjectivity* (how does the subject grasp or interpret its objects?) attain central importance. If all "objects" depend on the meaning that is bestowed on them by the subject, and if they are always part of a wider network of a referential totality, then it must be the philosopher's task to work out in what sense there is a *structure of meaning* that stands in relation to or conditions what one might call the *structure of reality.*

Scotus realized at the same time that all meanings find their expression in linguistic signs, and this explains the importance that he attributed to the reflection on language as the tool to work out the structure of meanings. The question whether language, particularly its grammatical structure, imposes a definite analyzable *form* on our thinking acquired special importance, since Scotus was aware of the fact that it provides the basic concepts that hold together the different realms of reality, of all that "can be experienced and thought."[9] The question is then how the meaning of linguistic terms (the *ratio significandi*) reflects and conditions the concepts of the mind (the *ratio intelligendi*), and how both of them are based on and constitute at the same time the mode of being of the actually existing object that is understood (the *ratio essendi*). To express it in less abstract and scholastic terms: the meaning of the name "Socrates" and the aspect under which Socrates is referred to by the speaker are interdependent (e.g., whether Socrates is being regarded as a living individual, a figure of history, or merely a stand-in exemplifying any man, as was common usage in medieval philosophy). The example makes clear why the "being" of the subject matter is in each case determined by the *mode* in which it is referred to in a judgment: only the whole statement determines in what sense and whether we are in fact referring to the individual Socrates at all. "Being" then means "object-givenness," the aspect under which the entity is understood ("It is the function of the form in the complex of meaning to give the

object its *being*" [GA 1 325; cf. 215, 266]). The meaning of the concepts employed, the formal structure of judgments as a functional
whole, reveals the givenness of objects.

The discovery of this structure of meaning also brought it home
to Scotus, according to Heidegger, that this "logical reality" that is
intended by the subject cannot be identical to or isomorphic with the
empirical reality of what lies outside the realm of meaning. Scotus
therefore distinguishes between the "*ens rationis*" and the "*ens nat-
urae*," the being of reason and the being of nature, and he comes
to realize that there cannot be any simple correspondence theory of
truth in the sense that our thoughts could be a mirror of reality. The
signs "stand for" but do not bear any similarity to what they signify,
just as the sign that advertises wine outside a tavern need not resem-
ble the wine itself (GA 1 265 ff., 271). Following Scotus, Heidegger
came to dismiss "mirror theories" of language and truth early on.
The categories of "all that is" become the categories of *our understanding of being*: the categories become the "elements and means
of the inter-pretation of the meaning of what is experienced" (GA 1
400). Aristotle's metaphysical realism has been challenged.

The subtlety of the scholastic philosopher Duns Scotus is not our
topic here. If we follow Heidegger's reception of Scotus's theory of
categories and meaning, it is because Scotus clearly realized that
objective reality is determined by the thinking *subject*'s understanding (cf. GA 1 318–19, 337). That there can be "objective subjectivity"
and that there is an overall order and structure underlying all "object-
givenness" is the most important principle in Scotus's structural
analysis of what the different parts of language signify. The importance of the interdependence between language, interpretation, and
"outside reality" that is to become so crucial in *Being and Time* may
have impressed Heidegger here for the first time. The interconnec-
tion between meaning and the intended object also drew Heidegger's
attention to the question of what constitutes the "fitting" between
the realm of meaning and the real object in the world. So we find here
several indications of seminal ideas that will gain major importance
in *Being and Time*, namely that it is *our* comprehension that assigns
a "significance" to the object and that the object in turn must be able
to bear such a significance, a significance that is determined by the
context of our understanding and our activities, whether they are of
a practical or a theoretical nature.[10]

Of particular importance is Scotus's doctrine of the *intentional-ity* of the nature of all objects – that all things have to be regarded as the intentional objects of acts of comprehension, and so depend on the general structure of our understanding (GA 1 281). Heidegger came to realize, however, that such an attempt to "fix" the different kinds of meanings once and for all in a purely formal way must remain sterile as long as it does not include the "living experience" of the speaker in whose understanding all intentionality must be grounded.[11] As he emphasizes, all understanding is at the same time historically conditioned understanding of the living spirit (GA 1 405, 407). Heidegger's most important critical qualification in his admiration of Duns Scotus's effort to overcome the "poverty of categorical systems" as such is the recognition that medieval thought, with its transcendent orientation toward the being of God and its rigid division of being into the two fundamental categories of "created being" and "uncreated being," was not flexible enough to accommodate historical and individual conditioning.

If his work on Duns Scotus represents a decisive advance toward the realization that the meaning of being must be sought in human understanding (i.e., that to be means "to be understood as something"), Heidegger still had a long way to go in the development of his own fundamental ontology. While he realized the sterility of an abstract search for categories of being that did not take into account the individual "living experience," in his book on Scotus Heidegger willingly follows the division of being into different "realms of being and reality" (*Seinsbereiche, Wirklichkeitsbereiche* [GA 1 211]) that exist more or less comfortably but *unconnected* side by side. Each of the realms of mathematical, natural, metaphysical, logical, and psychic reality has its own structure and order, which depend on a particular point of view (cf. *Scotus*, Chaps, 1 and 2). Even though Heidegger realized that there can be no isolated significance of any object because it is always part of a referential totality (GA 1 212, 202), he does not go beyond Scotus's compartmentalization of being into different realms with their separate meanings and systems of order.

There is as yet no sign of Heidegger's own holistic conception of human existence as "Dasein," that is, as being-in-a-world, or of "care" as the meaning of our existence, which comprises and unifies in its understanding all the different conceptions of what there is, let alone of temporality as the transcendental horizon of the overall meaning of being as such. What is clear, however, is that the research on Duns Scotus had not put to rest Heidegger's old concern with the manifold meanings of being but that it had rather sharpened his perception of its difficulties. The very fact that he found the Scotist schematization and formal structuring inadequate to capture living experience as a whole or to overcome what he calls the "impression of a deadly emptiness of all previous systems of categories" (GA 1 399, 408) shows that he was searching for a way of getting beyond abstract schemes of classification. His conclusion indicates that he was already aware of one major shortcoming underlying all such purely formal categorizations of beings: that they regard the *theoretical* attitude as the only one that gives shape to reality. He calls it a fateful error (GA 1 406). To remove that error will become one of the main tasks of Heidegger's mature philosophy.

THE QUESTION OF BEING IN *BEING AND TIME*

What made the difference? What led to the "breakthrough" that provided Heidegger with the clue for attacking the question of the meaning of being in a new way, so new that he found it necessary to invent an original philosophical language in order to prevent any confusion of his new approach with traditional lines of thought? It is often maintained that the "new Heidegger," who had not published anything for twelve years before he produced the monumental work *Being and Time*, owes the incentive for his own philosophy to the influence of Edmund Husserl, whom he met personally only after the completion of his early writings. But this is true only in a very limited sense. First of all, Husserl's phenomenology clearly (and with Heidegger's acknowledgment) already formed the background of Heidegger's critique of psychologism and had supplied him with the necessary conceptual framework for the discussion of Scotus's theory of language and meaning. Heidegger in fact reports that he had already been intrigued by Husserl's *Logical Investigations* when he was a student, but at that time he could not see how it would help him to solve his problem of *being*. Only when he came into personal contact with Husserl and the practice of the phenomenological method did he see more clearly what phenomenology could do – and, increasingly over the years, its shortcomings. As we shall see, it was these shortcomings that guided him on the way to the ideas he developed in *Being and Time*.

A short characterization of Husserl's phenomenology will be necessary to clarify the issue. Husserl had adopted Brentano's conception of the intentionality ("directedness toward") of all mental acts in order to give a comprehensive depiction of all phenomena as *objects of* – or, more precisely, the contents of – different types of acts of consciousness. Every object is to be interpreted as it is grasped by an act of comprehension in consciousness; it is something thought of, wished for, doubted, imagined, seen, heard, or known. If we want to understand the nature of all phenomena, we therefore have to work out the precise way in which consciousness intends its objects.

As Husserl saw it, such a precise description of the working of consciousness must furnish us with a proper understanding of all the *types* or ways of intending the objects of consciousness.[12] This claim is based on the notion, familiar since Descartes, that the content of consciousness is transparent and indubitable to the pure *I*, or *ego*, which forms the basis of consciousness, while facts about the world are at best probable. For Husserl the precise examination of the intended objects leads to a comprehension of their being or *essence*; if we want to know what phenomena really are, we have to look at consciousness itself rather than at the results of the empirical sciences. He therefore tried to establish philosophy as a strict *ego-centered* science that furnishes all other disciplines with the *a priori* conditions of their specific modes of cognition. Husserl can therefore be characterized as a "transcendental subjectivist"; that is, he held the view that it is the *subject* that provides the conditions of all determinations of the *objects* of experience and thought. Reflections on the acts of consciousness were supposed to render the essence not only of the acts of consciousness themselves, but also of the objects, while questions of actual external facts of experience were to be kept aside. The importance of the actual world that transcends consciousness was not denied by Husserl, but it was "bracketed," or kept out of consideration, for phenomenological purposes; only the experience of the subject and the *content* of the intentional acts of consciousness were to be studied.

Heidegger acknowledged with Husserl that the "being" of all entities lies in the sense we gain of them in our understanding. This much he shared with both Husserl's *transcendental subjectivism*

and modern *anthropocentrism*. What Heidegger saw as crucial difficulties in Husserl's approach (apart from the fact that Husserl's
phenomenology leaves him still with an unanalyzed multiplicity of
meanings of being) can be summed up as three interrelated points.
(1) He objected to treating the subject in whose understanding all
ontology must center as an impersonal and *transparent ego* that
is infallible in its intuitions about the activity and the content of
its consciousness. That the "I" is in a sense closest to me does
not mean that I comprehend it; we may be very far from possessing any such self-transparency. As Heidegger takes great pains to
show, our self-understanding in fact is usually not at all authentic.
(2) Heidegger questioned the feasibility or advisability of "bracketing" the *world*. He regarded Husserl's "immanentism" as mistaken,
since it came dangerously close to turning the objects of consciousness exclusively into objects *in* consciousness, and it made Husserl
dispense with the question of the ties there are to the actual world
that transcends consciousness. (3) In spite of Husserl's attempt to
capture all modes of consciousness including emotional attitudes, for
Heidegger the very fact that the objects of consciousness are assumed
as simply given in the stream of consciousness and to be studied in
a detached "viewing" or "intuition" showed that Husserl's ontology remained tied to the traditional theoretical stance and ontology
of the "occurrent." Since all three of these points are crucial issues
to Heidegger, they can be used as a key to understanding what is
characteristic of Heideggerian ontology in *Being and Time*.

(1) Heidegger's realization that the picture we form of ourselves
may be influenced (and even distorted) by our personal interests and
propensities, and that it is conditioned by the general historical situation, made it seem questionable whether there is such a neutral transcendental "I" that underlies all acts of consciousness. He therefore
adopted a policy one might call *systematic suspicion* (to be distinguished from Cartesian systematic doubt), which takes into account
that we may not be transparent to ourselves – that the "I" of the
intentional act may be rather far from any proper selfunderstanding
(for his critique of the givenness of the "I," see BT §25, 150 ff.). That
the phenomena may be familiar to us but not properly understood
leads to the special approach Heidegger takes in *Being and Time*,
that is, starting with a characterization of human beings in their
everydayness. His approach has a twofold advantage. First of all, he

can avoid "passing over" the peculiar nature of those ties we have with the world that get lost when we take the armchair philosopher's detached theoretical stance. Second, he can turn the distortions that we are prone to import in our "average everydayness" into the subject of his phenomenological investigation.

Since Heidegger disagreed with Husserl's assumption that there is an impersonal transcendental ego providing us with incontestable truths, he had to work out *who* that entity really is that in its very nature has a concern with the question of being. Because he did not want to foist yet another artificial construction on this entity in his own interpretation, Heidegger started his phenomenological investigation by capturing the phenomenon that all philosophers before him had "passed over" as trivial and not worth the theorist's attention, namely, everyday existence. The vocabulary he introduced to characterize the various features of everyday existence and its structure was designed to avoid all associations with common philosophical terminology; it was not designed to turn it into a secret doctrine open only to the initiate. His terminology, though often unusual in German, is much easier to understand than its English counterpart, because Heidegger plays with easily comprehensible etymological family relationships that often do not exist in English.

This method of suspicion explains the special methodological twist Heidegger gives to his phenomenology. While acknowledging his debt to Husserl (his teacher's painstaking analyses seem to have greatly sharpened his sensitivity to the importance of precision in phenomenological description), he did not think that phenomena can simply be read off from the way they are given in acts of consciousness. Rather, they have to be unearthed as that which might be only implicitly contained in our understanding. So Heidegger was looking at the phenomena behind the surface appearances – at what lies hidden behind what we find familiar and regard as natural "in the first approach and for the most part," as he expresses it. This method of suspicion explains Heidegger's predilection for an archaeological vocabulary in his depiction of the phenomenological method: that it is the task of his analysis to "uncover" the phenomena that have been covered up, buried, or hidden, so that they have to be "freed" or "laid bare." The same conception forms the background of his famous theory of truth as "unhiddenness" and of understanding as a form of "disclosedness" in general. Heidegger's method of "uncovering" proceeds on two levels. He distinguishes between (a) the "ontic" level of the factual (for human existence Heidegger introduces the special term "existentie*ll*") that is open to observation, the level of field studies for the phenomenologist, and (b) the "ontological" level, the phenomenological description of the deep structures that underlie and explain the ontic (for the structure of human existence Heidegger introduced the term "*existentiale*"). Although Heidegger himself gives few examples on the ontic or existentiell level, he always stresses that all ontological claims must find their "ontic confirmation."

In spite of our tendencies to "cover up" the phenomena, Heidegger saw it as necessary to start with the analysis of human existence, since human understanding is the only entrance and key to the nature of being. For we are always already concerned with both ourselves and our whereabouts ("the world") and have always already an at least implicit understanding of the being of both ourselves and the world. Because of this self-awareness and world awareness, he introduced the technical term "Dasein" for human beings. Although the term "Da-sein" has become so customary in English that it needs no further introduction, it is useful to keep the literal meaning of the German "being-there" in mind, since it is designed to signify that the "disclosedness" of our whereabouts, and therefore a natural tendency to form at least a preontological understanding, is the most decisive characteristic of humans for Heidegger.

The aim of Heidegger's phenomenological description of our everydayness is to make explicit what basic structures underlie this preunderstanding. If the key to all understanding of being lies in Dasein's disclosedness of the world, then an analysis of Dasein must precede a general "fundamental ontology." As Heidegger indicates, it had been his original plan for *Being and Time* to proceed through a "preparatory fundamental analysis" of Dasein's being to an explication of how time provides a "transcendental horizon" for the question of being as such. He never finished this task (for the original outline, see BT 63–4); that is, he never got beyond the analysis of Dasein, for reasons to which we will have to return later. The publication of *Being and Time*, with its focus on the analysis of the conditions of human existence, made Heidegger instantly famous after 1927. It is this focus that justifies, within limits, calling him an *existentialist* philosopher, a label he always rejected since he regarded fundamental ontology as his real task.

(2) If the pure "I" is, then, an abstraction that permits a proper comprehension neither of Dasein nor of the embeddedness of all meaning and understanding in everydayness, it is also clear why Heidegger came to the conclusion that any *bracketing* of the factual *world* in phenomenology must be a crucial mistake. For Heidegger, who was concerned with a penetrating analysis of how we are related to the world and to ourselves as beings with a world, all abstraction from the way Dasein actually experiences the world must destroy the phenomenon of "having a world." For the world is precisely the context in which we encounter beings and *ourselves*, and it is this encounter that determines what they *are* for our understanding.

Heidegger's analysis of the *a priori* structure of our having a world therefore consists in displaying the way we deal with the world, with the entities in it, as we encounter them in our actual existence. As Heidegger saw it, we are not "thinking things" that may on different occasions entertain different relationships to different items in different intentional acts. Instead, our very being is defined by the fact that we are beings-in-a-world. This existential analysis consists of a two-pronged investigation that elucidates not only in what sense we encounter entities in the world and what makes them fit for such encounters, but also what *in us* constitutes such encounterings, what in our understanding makes it possible to disclose the entities to ourselves in this way. The analysis is transcendental in the Kantian sense that it unearths the conditions that make it possible for us to encounter whatever we do encounter in the way we make "sense" of the phenomena, because all such encounterings are ways of determining the being of the entities in the world. There is no other "sense" or "meaning of being" than the one we bestow on entities in our understanding. This is how Heidegger time and again defines how he understands "the *meaning* [or sense] of being": "Meaning is that wherein the intelligibility of something maintains itself" (BT 193).

This transcendental investigation is not supposed to supply us with new insights about the world, but to retrace and articulate the way in which we "always already" understand what we are dealing with. If "to be" means "to be already understood as," then a thorough investigation of all different kinds of *understanding* that underlie our dealing with the world is called for. This explains the importance that *interpretation* has for Heidegger, for in all interpretations we give in our activities, we draw on the implicit understanding of the meaning things have without being fully aware of it. The phenomenologist has to trace the different ways in which we deal with the "given" and bring them to articulation. So Heidegger is merely trying to bring to light what we always in a sense know "in our bones," as Ryle phrased it in his review of *Being and Time*.[13]

(3) Since our implicit understanding of being is not only the basis of Heidegger's own interpretation but, as he saw it, the all-pervasive feature that characterizes humankind in general, there has always been an at least dim understanding of the "question of being." Heidegger makes no claims to originality here. What needs an explanation is, rather, why this dim understanding was never fully developed before, and a good deal of Heidegger's originality consists in his explanation of what he calls our "forgetfulness" of being.

The forgetfulness is twofold. There is the forgetfulness of our everyday understanding, which does not even try to gain any authentic comprehension but takes over the ready-made interpretations that it finds in its environment, the explanations and evaluations of one's own society and time. For the most part, we simply adopt our mode of living and self-understanding in compliance with the general standards: we behave, speak, and value as "one" speaks, behaves, and values. Heidegger's depiction of the all-embracing influence of the anonymous public "one" (the impersonal pronoun, not the numeral) is one of the most colorful sections of *Being and Time* (Div. I, Chap. 4). The English translation of *das Man* as "the They" is misleading, since it does not show that there is not usually any detachment from this basic mode of existence that "anyone" shares. It takes a special effort to shake off the yoke of this public interpretation in order to gain an authentic understanding; for Heidegger, the experience of coming to terms with our finitude in the *anxiety* of facing up to death is the crucial situation that forces us to wrench ourselves away from domination by the anonymous public understanding (Div. II, Chap. 1). As he repeatedly affirms, there is no way to live permanently in authenticity, since we have to take the everyday world and its routine for granted in all our practical concerns.

If the "forgetfulness of being" in our everyday absorption in the world seems natural, the special forgetfulness that Heidegger ascribes to philosophers seems much less so, since it is their task to reflect explicitly on this question, and they in fact have reflected on it ever since the Greeks first raised the question, What is being? If philosophers up to Heidegger's time missed the crucial point, there must be a definite reason for this monumental misunderstanding. And Heidegger thought indeed that he could put his finger on the crucial mistake: the mistake lies in the *theoretical* approach as such.

As mentioned earlier, the stance taken in theorizing allows the thinker to have a detached point of view. The thinker can treat the objects of his investigation as "indifferently occurring"[14] things that exist independent of observation, just as the observer in his turn is at liberty to fasten on any object. So observer and observed, thinker and the object of his thought, are regarded as "indifferently occurring" alongside one another. And this theoretical stance, according to Heidegger, was not overcome by the subject-centered ontology in the Kantian tradition; it was not even overcome by Husserl's insistence that all objects be treated as intentional objects, that is, as objects represented in consciousness. As Heidegger sees it, in Husserl's phenomenological analysis the objects in consciousness retain the status of mere occurrence, just as consciousness itself remains in an ontologically uninterpreted state, for it is treated as an entity that simply occurs. *Being* in Husserl would therefore have to be defined as the "occurrent" correlate of the series of meanings as they are determined separately by each act of intuiting an essence revealed by phenomenological analysis.

That the theoretical stance does have its justification for the theoretician himself Heidegger does not deny. It would in fact be quite innocuous if scientists, and particularly philosophers, had recognized it for what it is: a *derivative* mode of being, constituted by their special way of viewing the objects of their research. By mistaking it for *the* significant mode of being that underlies all entities, however, they become guilty of suppressing the discovery of the other modes of being that Heidegger takes great pains to work out. Besides the "mere occurrence" ("presence-at-hand") of theoretical understanding, there is also "readiness-at-hand" constituting our practical understanding of dealing with equipment, "being-with" other human beings, and "in-each-case-mineness," the relation to and concern for our own selves that we are and have to be.

For Heidegger, our everyday life is determined largely by our understanding of all entities in terms of our practical concerns, purposes, and designs, and this includes our dealings with other human beings and with ourselves. Among the four modes of being, therefore, the theoretical stance fastens on the least characteristic one, the one Heidegger calls "founded" or "derivative" because it comes into focus only when we disregard what he calls the "referential totality" of those practical and personal concerns that make up the everyday world (cf. BT § 13).

The mode of being that we assign to different entities is not always fixed, at least not on the "ontic" level. One and the same "thing" can be treated as a piece of equipment with a practical meaning, or as a piece of art, or as the object of scientific investigation. Other human beings can be treated as "scientific objects" (as ciphers in statistics) or as mere tools (something ready-to-hand) instead of as "Dasein-withs." The context therefore determines their "being." There can even be (ontically) a certain indeterminacy as to which of the ontological possibilities will be seized upon in such treatments under a specific aspect. What is not open for decision in the particular context is the preexisting *structure* of these different possibilities, since it forms the ontological structure of our very nature.

HEIDEGGER'S TWOFOLD TASK

If Heidegger has found important supplementary modes of being that determine our existence in the world, one may wonder why he regards the age-old commitment to the ontology of *Vorhandenheit* (occurrence) as so fateful a mistake that he comes back to it again and again. If his predecessors omitted something of importance, is it not enough to supply what is omitted, without harping so much on the omission? The point, however, is that simply supplying what is omitted will not do. What is needed is rather a complete revision in two respects. The first concerns the intepretation of the history of philosophy; the second concerns the proper search for the conception of "being" itself, that is, Heidegger's actual enterprise. This is in fact the *twofold task* that Heidegger has set for himself in *Being and Time,* the task he calls the "Ontological Analytic of Dasein as Laying Bare the Horizon for an Interpretation of the Meaning of Being in General" and the task of "Destroying the History of Ontology" (see BT 36–49).

A clarification of this twofold task, even if sketchy, will provide a better understanding of Heidegger's project as such. Let us start with the second task, the task of destroying the history of ontology. Heidegger is not out to do violence to history or to badger his predecessors for their blindness. The German word "*Destruktion*" is not as violent as its English counterpart. This "destruction" is not a *deconstruction,* as some people would have it nowadays, but an analysis intended to show where the decisive steps of the derailment took place in Kant, Descartes, and Aristotle. Heidegger does not have the deconstructionists' detachment from tradition: he thinks it can be mastered and rectified even while acknowledging that the "missteps" were inevitable. His emphasis on continuity in the history of being (through all historical vicissitudes) also speaks against recruiting him for the now fashionable "historicist" camp. A historicist Heidegger could not regard himself as the rightful heir of Parmenides, the discoverer of the tie between being and thinking; he could not look for any continued problems through different periods of history, but would only notice curious doxographical coincidences that are as external and as accidental as the resemblance between a triceratops and a rhinoceros.

Heidegger's concern is rather with "unravelling" the history of ontology to show the decisive steps that lead to the dominance of the ontology of *Vorhandenheit* and to the forgetfulness of "being," that is, to the prejudice that being has no concrete meaning because it is the "most general of generalities" (BT 29). If in the past this prejudice was derived in one way or another from Aristotelian ontology's view that *being* transcends the categories and can therefore have no "real" content, today it rests on the view that "being" applies indifferently to whatever we may introduce by the existential operator or include in our universe of discourse.

What Heidegger finds most fateful in the development of Western philosophy is, to repeat, the orientation toward being as "*reality*" or "thinghood" (BT 96), for this makes the world a sum total of *independently* existing entities that exist for observing subjects insofar as those subjects manage to make contact with them. He blames this ontology for all the difficulties philosophers have been unable to solve through the many turns that philosophy has taken since its origin with the Greeks, difficulties that did not end when philosophy became "subject-centered" in the Cartesian-Kantian tradition. If there are basically two separate entities, subject and object, that occur side by side, the question of how contact is possible between the thinking subject and independently existing objects remains an insoluble problem, even if one grants that the subject somehow bestows the "form" or the "meaning" on the objects. For the question remains: How can there be truth if it is conceived of as the *correspondence* between our thoughts (or the content of our consciousness) and the outside world? In other words, what guarantees the objectivity of our subjective impressions? Even the critical realist remains saddled with the question of what we can know about the world and, most of all, with the problem of how we can even be sure of the existence of the "world outside us." In spite of his "Copernican turn" toward subjectivity, Kant left the main feature of ancient ontology intact: the centrality of substance, the *thinghood* of the thing, remained uncontested. That is to say, for Kant the independent substance that persists through time remains the fundamental building block of all reality. The independent "thing" that is dealt with and categorized in all our experience and determined by scientific thought remains in its very *being* separate from the subject. In particular, the attempt to prove the existence of the external world is treated by Heidegger as a clear indication that Kant had not questioned the basis of traditional ontology rigorously enough.[15]

The idealist, in turn, seems to be condemned to *immanentism*, the problem of explaining the "transcendence" of objects in relation to our minds such that it makes sense even to talk about the natural world outside us. All these problems arise, Heidegger tells us, only if one posits a fundamental *rift* between the isolated subject or "mind" and an independently existing realm of objects. Such a rift for Heidegger is not a necessary presupposition; it is rather the result of the philosopher's mistaken "theoretical stance" and leads to what Heidegger calls a "splitting asunder of the phenomena" (BT 170). There is no way to get beyond the split between what occurs inside us and what occurs outside so long as "occurrence alongside" is the only available ontological category.

Because in *theoria* we merely "gaze" at what appears as an isolated object, we are led to take this "reification" as the natural way of being of that "object." Such a dissociated perspective is quite justified for

the "theoretical view" so long as we do not forget that it is an artificial isolating perspective and we fully realize that it is neither the
only perspective nor one that is even capable of doing justice to the
other ways in which things are "given" to us. Because for centuries
the theoretical stance had been regarded as the only one worthy of
the philosopher-scientist, no other way of understanding, and at the
same time, therefore, no other way of *being* of objects, was ever
taken into consideration. The ontology of "merely occurring things"
is therefore cut back by Heidegger and relegated to the scientists' special point of view as a "founded mode" or derivative understanding
of being. This derivative point of view, which treats us as initially
worldless subjects who somehow establish cognitive contact with
separate objects, ought rather to be understood as a special version
of the more original way of understanding ourselves as beings *with
a world* that is characterized as a "being-among" or involvement in
the world of the ready-to-hand.

The promised "destruction" of the history of ontology, as
Heidegger had initially planned it, was never carried out (see BT 64).
Part II of *Being and Time*, which was to contain a discussion of
"Kant's doctrine of schematism and time," "the ontological foundation of the 'cogito sum' of Descartes," and "Aristotle's essay on
time, as providing a way of discriminating the phenomenal basis
and limits of ancient ontology," never appeared and can be, at best,
reconstructed from some of his later publications. It seems clear
that the treatment of history itself was not the stumbling block.
Heidegger found himself increasingly at a loss as to how to complete his first task, the "laying bare of the horizon for an interpretation of the meaning of being as such," for he never published the
missing Division III of Part I of *Being and Time*, the division he
claimed he had merely "held back" (BT 17) when he was forced to
publish his manuscript sooner than planned. This division was to
bring the "reversal" of *Being and Time*, that is, "Time and Being."
Why Heidegger was so dissatisfied with this last part perhaps will
never be known, since he did not consent to have it included in his
posthumous edition. We will not try to enter into any speculations
here, but will try to follow Heidegger in his initial project as far as he
took it.

The gravest consequence of the omission of a proper understanding of "being" in the ontology of occurrence is that it does not permit

the development of what one might call a *dynamic* rather than a *static* ontology. It cannot lead to a proper development of the conception of time or temporality as Heidegger envisages it. To work out this concept is the ultimate task of *Being and Time* as we have it. We have seen that for Heidegger a human being is never an isolated, worldless subject, but is an entity that in its very essence is constituted by its *world*. We have to see what is meant by this. So far, the modes of being of the occurrent, the ready-to-hand, being-with, and being-oneself do not seem to form a meaningful whole. Nor do they form a unity if one looks at the corresponding kinds of understanding in which they are grounded: theoretical understanding, practical concern, solicitude, and the many ways of comportment toward one's own self. All these modes of comportment are, as Heidegger explains, different kinds of "-sights," different kinds of "enlightenment" about the world.[16] Up to this point in his analysis they do not form any unity that would constitute anything like *the* meaning of being. We seem to have only different ways of understanding *beings*, just as in Husserl's phenomenological analysis. If Heidegger had gone no further, the only difference between him and Husserl would be that Heidegger fastened on different "root types" of understanding, with an emphasis on our direct involvement in the world rather than on "intuiting" the essences of beings in consciousness.

But Heidegger did not leave matters here. First of all, he introduced a unifying term – "care" – to designate the basic feature in us that constitutes all our involvements in the world (BT Div. I, Chap. 6). It is the analysis of the structure of care that allows him to claim that our being is at the same time "being-in-the-world" as an organic whole. This holistic conception of "care" must take account of the overall *sense* we give to our existence as being-in-the-world by virtue of which it is an integrated whole. The decisive characteristic in our relation to the world as such, which includes ourselves as our ultimate point of reference, is conditioned by the care that allows us to treat everything as part of our *project* in the largest sense of the word. This feature leads to the temporal interpretation of the structure of our being-in-the-world. We project ourselves, our whole existence, into the world and understand ourselves as well as everything in the world in terms of the *possibilities* within the design or "projection" that we make of ourselves. (Since the translation of *Entwurf* as "projection" [see BT 184] may suggest wrong associations with psychological projection, "design" in the sense of an architect's blueprint is perhaps a less misleading synonym.)

Everything we are dealing with finds its meaning within this projection, and things have a meaning only insofar as they form part of it. Within this "project" we make of ourselves, everything has its meaning and thereby its *being*. The design is, as the term suggests, directed into the future: we project ourselves into an anticipated future as the ultimate aim of our endeavors. But this is not the only temporal dimension that is at work in our projection, because our projection is not a free choice of the future. According to Heidegger, we cannot make any such projections without an existing understanding of the world and ourselves in it, an understanding determined by the past we have been and still are. Therefore, not only do we carry our past with us, as one carries weighty memories, but we always already understand ourselves and our projects in terms of the past and out of the past. Finally, in all our enterprises, whatever they may be, we are tied to the present, because we are in and with the world that absorbs us and ties us down to our everyday endeavors. The absorption by the here and now constitutes our (for the most part) inescapable involvement in the inauthentic, or "falling," way of understanding the world in terms of the One (BT §§27, 71).

This, in a nutshell, is the structure Heidegger calls our "temporality." By temporality he does not mean that we are, as are all other things, confined to time, nor that we have a sense of time, but rather that we exist as three temporal dimensions at once: it is being ahead of ourselves in the future, drawing on our past, while being concerned with the present that constitutes our being. The way we project ourselves into the future (*ahead of ourselves*) while taking with us our past (*being already in*) in our immersion into the present (*being at home with*) is what Heidegger designates as the "*ekstases*" of temporality. There is nothing "ecstatic" about this. All it means is that we are already "extended" outward in temporal dimensions and so are never contained in a "punctual" here and now (see BT 370 ff.).

Since we are neither static points in a preexisting indifferent universe nor confined to a segment of an infinite arrow of time, but are instead entities whose very understanding makes up the temporal dimensions of our existence, this temporality is the transcendental condition of Dasein's having a universe of meaningful beings. The "meaning of being" as it is constituted by our understanding is thus grounded in the temporal structure that underlies our under-standing. Temporality in this sense was to provide the foundation for Heidegger's further analysis of the "transcendental horizon" of being as such, that is to say, of the being that goes beyond Dasein itself. Dasein provides access to being in understanding insofar as we disclose it, but our understanding neither is identical to being as such nor does it *create* it. How Heidegger had planned to complete this step toward an analysis of being as such is not clear. The pub-lished portion of *Being and Time* breaks off after the repetition of the analysis of everydayness in terms of temporality, the explanation of our concern with history, and the accounts of our "historicality" and of the everyday conception of time.

It would require a survey of Heidegger's later work, sailing out on the high sea of speculation, to find out why he did not take the last step from Dasein's temporality to being when he wrote *Being and Time*. At one point, he mentioned the difficulties language presented.[17] This would be a genuine problem, because the language and concepts that describe the "horizon of intelligibility" would nec-essarily be derived from the language and concepts we use to describe the realms of the beings that are contained within that horizon. We would have to describe the conditions of all understanding – of being as such – in terms of what is conditioned by the horizon, that is, the foundations in terms of what is founded on them. It is doubtful that this can be done in a nonmetaphoric way.

In later years, Heidegger seems to have become increasingly skep-tical about the enterprise of a fundamental ontology that "lays bare" the structures of being as such, since this now seems to him a kind of "foundational" enterprise that reeks of metaphysics, the project of establishing an ultimate basis for all things. To make human under-standing the key to such a transcendental investigation carries such dangers in itself, for it somehow suggests that we are in *control* of the "being" of all beings, if the sense of whatever is given depends on our understanding.

If Heidegger seems to develop a kind of transcendental anthro-pocentrism in *Being and Time*, as I have tried to show, we must also emphasize the fact that, for him, this can be only half the story. For it is only in a limited sense *up to us* how we understand the "being" of all beings. Heidegger's "light" and "sight-metaphors," and such terminology as "disclosedness" and "unhiddenness," show that we do not create our own universe, not even its meaning. The intelligibility resides as much in the "things" encountered themselves as in the understanding residing in us, and this "fittingness" is not due to any merit of ours. *Enlightenment* (*Lichtung*) is something that simply *happens* to us, and in this sense "being" is quite out of our control. It is an "opening," a "free gift," as Heidegger liked to say later in his life; all we can try to do is "appropriate it" in an authentic understanding. Heidegger always insisted that there is "being" only as long as there is the understanding of being in Dasein, but that the entities themselves do not depend on that understanding (BT 269 ff.). That we are passive recipients of "being" seems to be a strong argument against recent attempts to interpret Heidegger as a predecessor of the "new pragmatism" that would make "being" a matter of social construction. Heidegger would agree that *ontically* every epoch articulates (constructs) its own interpretations, but that does not justify a pragmatist conception of *ontology* itself. He in fact warned against our present-day submission to the spirit of technology. What sense can such warnings and the wistful claim that "only a God can save us" make in the mouth of a pragmatist?[18]

Why we are enlightened entities, why being "speaks to us," is shrouded in mystery for Heidegger, a mystery he tended to express in increasingly mystifying terms in his later years. It is undeniable that his increasing skepticism about the feasibility of transcendental reasoning as such, and his conviction that Dasein is confined to the "receiving end" of being, represents a major shift in Heidegger's thinking after *Being and Time*. That this "turn" is a radical shift away from the project of *Being and Time* can nevertheless be doubted with good reasons. In his preface to the edition of 1953, Heidegger reaffirmed that "the road it has taken remains even today a necessary one, if our Dasein is to be stirred by the question of being" (BT 17). Who is to contradict this testimony?

NOTES

1. Heidegger's last comments on his lifework, found in his unfinished notes for a preface to the edition of his collected writings (*Gesamtausgabe letzter Hand*) written shortly before his death in 1976, in *Frühe Schriften* (GA I 437). All translations or paraphrases are my own.

2. Since space is limited, this essay gives only a very rough sketch of Heidegger's development without any detailed discussion of the formative influence on him of the pre-Socratics, Plato, Aristotle, the Scholastics, Descartes, Kant, or Husserl. Nor does it deal with the question of whether his reading of these philosophers does justice to them.

3. *Von der mannigfachen Bedeutung des Seienden nach Aristoteles* (Freiburg: Herder, 1862), trans. Rolf George (Berkeley and Los Angeles: University of California Press, 1975). Brentano's book has remained a classic (he was the first in modern times to stress the importance of the special relationship of the "focal meaning" of being as centered around substantiality; see 56 ff.), and Heidegger was fully aware of its importance. He could not have come across a better introduction to Aristotle's metaphysics. For Heidegger's acknowledgment, see GA I 56: "The question of the unity of the manifold of being that stirred then, darkly, unsteadily, helplessly, remained throughout many reversals, wanderings and indecisions, the persistent source leading up to *Being and Time*, which appeared two decades later." His early admiration for Brentano's work on Aristotle was not diminished by his critical stance toward Brentano's later work in the tradition of psychologism (see GA I 155 ff.).

4. For a comprehensive discussion of the different meanings of "being" and the importance of the distinction between the copulative, existential, and veridical senses of "is" for the development of philosophy, see C. H. Kahn, *The Verb 'Be' in Ancient Greek* (Dordrecht: Reidel, 1973).

5. What Plato meant by his claim that "being" is the "kind that pervades everything or combines with everything" (*Sophist*, esp. 25rd ff.) is still very much a matter of debate, so it is difficult to say whether the being that accrues to all that is has *one* definable meaning for Plato.

6. "So we say that not only animals and plants and their parts are substances, but also natural bodies such as fire and water and earth and everything of the sort" (*Metaphysics* Z 2, 1028b9 ff.). By the latter Aristotle does not mean "stuff" but individual "pieces" that actually exist and display their own characteristic functions.

7. The unreflected identification of "being" with "thinghood" or "reality" – derived from the Latin word *"res"* (the same etymology applies to the German term *"Realität"*) designating "thing" as an indifferently occurring independent entity or a carrier of attributes – is the main point of criticism of traditional ontology in *Being and Time* (see BT 245, passim). It is in this sense only that Heidegger refused to be called a "realist."

8. By "logical" Heidegger usually means *conceptual analysis*, in accordance with the German tradition that goes back to the scholastics; the same meaning is to be found in Kant and Hegel and is still presupposed

by Husserl. Formal logic is usually called "logistic" or "mathematical logic."

9. The theory itself can be called "Scotist" only in a qualified sense, for Heidegger (following the distinguished linguist H. Steinthal, *Einleitung in die Psychologie und Sprachwissenschaft;* see GA 1 303–4) uses as one of his main sources the *Grammatica speculativa,* now by common consent regarded as the work of Thomas of Erfurt, as well as the equally spurious *De rerum principio.* But Heidegger's interpretation is also based on genuine writings by Duns Scotus: extensive references are given to the *Quaestiones subtilissimae super libros Metaphysicorum Aristotelis,* the *Reportata,* and the *Ordinatio.* Heidegger is aware of the fact that his attempt to demarcate reality may go beyond the scope of what Scotus clearly saw and worked out systematically himself, but he claims that he is following at least Scotus's intentions (GA 1 211).

10. We find here already some of the terminology that Heidegger used later in *Being and Time,* e.g., "*Bewandtnis*" for "significance" (see GA 1 223, 346, 387).

11. He stresses the need to allow for "the peculiar mobility of meaning that is constituted through live speech and assertion" – "*eine durch die lebendige Rede und Aussage gegebene eigentümliche Beweglichkeit der Bedeutung*" (GA 1 336). This emphasis may have made Heidegger skeptical about Husserl's rather abstract phenomenological approach from early on.

12. Since Husserl worked and reworked his conception of phenomenology throughout his long life, there are quite differing accounts of it. For the uninitiated, the most accessible depiction is a short article that appeared in the *Encyclopaedia Britannica* in 1927. Husserl had prepared no less than four German versions, three of which are reprinted, with comments by Heidegger, at Husserl's request, in *Phänomenologische Psychologie, Husserliana,* Vol. 9, ed. W. Biemel (The Hague: Nijhoff, 1962), pp. 237–301.

13. "Review of *Sein und Zeit,*" *Mind* 38 (1929): 355–70. Rpt. in G. Ryle, *Collected Papers* (New York: Hutchinson, 1971), Vol. I, pp. 197–214.

14. I prefer to translate "*Vorhandenheit*" as "occurrence", even though "presence-at-hand" (see BT 67) has become customary and preserves the etymological connotations as well as the parallel with the "readiness-at-hand" of equipment. But the parallel between "Vor*handen*heit" and "Zu*handen*heit" cannot be imitated in English. In German, "*Vorhandenheit,*" though originally signifying being "on hand," has lost all connotation of nearness (one can say of any distant star in the Milky Way that it is "*vorhanden*"), hence my preference for "occurrence." In contrast, "*Zuhandenheit*" signifies the "handiness" of equipment for use.

"Extant" has replaced "present-at-hand" in some recent translations (e.g., *Basic Problems of Phenomenology*), but it might wrongly suggest a contrast to what has become extinct.

15. For a more extensive discussion of this problem, see my "Heidegger and the Scandal of Philosophy," *Human Nature and Natural Knowledge*, ed. A. Donagan, A. Perovich, and M. Wedin (Dordrecht: Reidel, 1986), pp. 129–51.

16. It is impossible to render adequately in English all the terms Heidegger derives from the German roots "*Licht*" and "*Sicht.*" There is the "sight" by which we deal with equipment (*Umsicht* = circumspection), or with others (*Rücksicht*), and the perspective of our projection into the future in foresight (*Vorsicht*). Light metaphors are used when Dasein is compared to a "clearing" (*Lichtung*) or is "lit up" (*gelichtet*). Heidegger sees himself in an old tradition, for he refers to the ancient *lumen naturale* theory as an anticipation of his own view of our natural disclosedness (see BT 171).

17. A revised later version of his lectures in 1927, *The Basic Problems of Phenomenology*, supplements *Being and Time* but does not carry the promised "reversal" or "turn" much further. Heidegger's late remarks, *On Time and Being*, trans. J. Stambaugh (New York: Harper & Row, 1972), contain some comments by the later Heidegger on the difficulties of the younger one: "(it) must still in a way speak the language of metaphysics."

18. "Nur noch ein Gott kann uns retten." Interview in *Der Spiegel* (May 1976): 193–219.

2 Reading a life: Heidegger and hard times

THE END OF A CATHOLIC PHILOSOPHER

It was just before Christmas Eve – Monday, December 23, 1918 – when the young Mrs. Heidegger, eight months pregnant, decided to brave Freiburg's bitterly cold weather, travel across town, and break the bad news to Father Krebs. Engelbert Krebs, a Catholic priest and professor of theology at Freiburg University, was a close friend of her husband, the philosophy lecturer Martin Heidegger. In fact, Krebs had officiated at the Heideggers' Catholic wedding in Freiburg Cathedral on March 21, 1917.

At the time of that wedding, Father Krebs had already been skeptical. It was a confessionally "mixed" marriage – Elfride Petri was a Lutheran, Martin Heidegger a Catholic – and even though the bride had solemnly declared her intention to convert to Catholicism and raise her children in the Roman faith, Father Krebs had had his doubts. Therefore, he was not entirely surprised when, a year and a half later, the 24-year-old mother-to-be sat across from him in his office and poured out her feelings:

My husband has lost his church faith, and I have not found mine. At the time of our marriage, his faith was already undermined by doubts. But I insisted on the Catholic wedding, hoping that with his help I would find faith. We have read, spoken, thought, and prayed a great deal together, and the result is that both of us now think only as Protestants – that is: we believe in a personal God and pray to Him, but without any dogmatic ties and apart from Protestant or Catholic orthodoxy. Under these circumstances, we would consider it dishonest to let our child be baptized in the Catholic church. But I felt it was my duty to tell you this beforehand.[1]

70

Two weeks later, on January 9, 1919, Martin Heidegger himself decided to write to Father Krebs and explain the personal and philosophical transformation he had undergone in the past two years.

What had caused these changes in Heidegger? Was it the cataclysmic Great War, which had ended a few weeks earlier at a cost of 16 million lives? Or his own disastrous four months on the Western Front, which ended, as if symbolically, with his promotion to lance corporal on the day the German generals petitioned for an armistice? Or the role he played as a weatherman in preparing poison gas attacks on U.S. soldiers during their final push from Verdun to Sedan in early October?[2] Edmund Husserl would think so. "The war and ensuing difficulties drive men into mysticism," he said a dozen years later (August 13, 1931), after his bitter falling out with Heidegger.[3]

But in his 1919 letter to Father Krebs, Martin Heidegger did not refer at all to the world-shattering events that had transpired over the past two years – the war, for example, or the Bolshevik Revolution, or the end of the Hohenzollern dynasty and the proclamation of a socialist republic in Germany, or the outbreak in January 1919 of a virtual civil war between the left-wing Spartacus League and the reactionary Free Corps with their shadowy death squads, the Feme.

Yes, these were hard times for Germany, but in his letter Heidegger mentioned none of that. After all he was a philosopher, even something of a theologian – in any case, a deeply religious man – and in writing to Father Krebs he addressed what was presumably most important to him. Since 1916 Heidegger had been teaching Catholic philosophy at Freiburg University, occasionally in tandem with Krebs, and had built something of a reputation as a Catholic philosopher of the future. But now he had to tell Krebs that he had abandoned dogmatic Catholicism both in philosophy and in his personal life:

Freiburg
January 9, 1919

Esteemed Professor,

Over the last two years I have set aside all scientific work of a specialized nature and have struggled instead for a basic clarification of my philosophical position. This has led me to results that I could not be free to hold and teach if I were tied to positions that come from outside of philosophy.

Epistemological insights that pass over into the theory of historical knowledge have made the *system* of Catholicism problematic and unacceptable to me – but not Christianity and metaphysics, although I take the latter in a new sense.

I believe that I – perhaps more than those who work on the subject officially – have perceived the values that the Catholic Middle Ages bears within itself, values that we are still far from really exploiting. My investigations into the phenomenology of religion, which will draw heavily on the Middle Ages, should prove beyond dispute that in transforming my basic standpoint I have not let myself be dragged into abandoning my objective, high judgment of and esteem for the Catholic life-world, in favor of the empty polemics of an embittered apostate.

Therefore, it is especially important to me – and I wish to extend you my heartfelt thanks for this – that I not lose the benefit of your invaluable friendship. My wife, who first told you about this, and I too would like to preserve the very special confidence we share with you. It is hard to live as a philosopher – inner truthfulness toward oneself and those one is supposed to teach, demands sacrifice, renunciation and struggles that remain forever foreign to the academic "tradesman."

I believe that I have an inner call to philosophy and, by fulfilling it in research and teaching, a call to the eternal vocation of the inner man – *and for that alone* do I feel called to achieve what is in my powers and thus to justify, before God, my very existence and activity.

With cordial thanks,   Yours,

Martin Heidegger

P. S. My wife sends her warmest greetings.[4]

We note that Heidegger does not say he has lost his religious faith or broken with the Catholic worldview and the values he perceives in it. Nor does he say he has abandoned the Catholic church, taken as a community of people with shared traditions and rituals. (Later in life he would tell a confidant that he had never left the Catholic church: "Ich bin niemals aus der Kirche getretten.")

Rather, Heidegger is announcing his break with the *system of dogmatic Catholicism* and in particular with its way of policing its members' freedom to research and teach as they see fit. Once liberated from ecclesiastical restrictions, Heidegger intends to continue working to retrieve the meaning he has found latent in Christianity and traditional metaphysics, although he says he now understands metaphysics in a different sense than before. And he proposes to present the positive results of his research in a study devoted to the phenomenology of religion.

This letter is a watershed in the philosophical and religious development of the 29-year-old Martin Heidegger. Firmly and decisively it marks the end of his budding career as the up-and-coming "Catholic philosopher," a reputation he had been carefully cultivating around Freiburg University ever since he took his doctorate in philosophy there in 1913.[5]

Martin Heidegger was born on September 26, 1889, in Messkirch, southwest Germany, the first child of a relatively poor Catholic couple, simple village people who had lived through the hard times of Bismarck's *Kulturkampf*. After grammar school, he spent seven and a half years of his academic curriculum studying for the Roman Catholic priesthood: six years as a high school seminarian (1903–9), two weeks in a Jesuit novitiate (September 30 to October 13, 1909; he was dismissed for reasons of health), followed by a year and a half of theology studies at Freiburg University.

However, in February 1911 a deteriorating heart condition forced Heidegger to leave the seminary and abandon all plans to become a priest. In October 1911 he took up studies in mathematics and, under the strong influence of Professor Heinrich Rickert, in philosophy. On July 26, 1913, Heidegger received the doctorate in philosophy with a dissertation entitled "The Doctrine of Judgment in Psychologism."

A few weeks later members of the Philosophy Faculty, particularly philosophy professor Arthur Schneider and history professor Heinrich Finke, began grooming the promising young scholar, then 23 years of age, to take over Freiburg University's Chair of Catholic Philosophy. A grant from the Catholic church was arranged to tide Heidegger over for two years while he wrote the requisite "qualifying dissertation" (*Habilitationsschrift*) that would win him a license to teach at the university as a *Privatdozent*, or unsalaried lecturer. The terms of the grant stipulated that in order to receive the stipend of 1,000 marks per year Heidegger had to promise to follow the church's line and "remain true to the spirit of Thomistic philosophy."

Moreover, Heidegger's mentors suggested that if he wanted the chair in Catholic philosophy, he should change the topic of his qualifying dissertation from his chosen subject, titled "The Logical Essence of the Concept of Number" (which reflected his interest in the philosophy of mathematics, inspired by reading Edmund Husserl and Heinrich Rickert), to a topic in medieval philosophy. Heidegger decided to write on Duns Scotus's doctrine of categories and meaning, basing himself on the *Tractatus de modis significandi*, which was later found to have been written not by Scotus (1266–1308) but by his follower, Thomas of Erfurt, around the year 1379.

These were hard times for Catholic intellectuals. For the better part of the preceding century, the traditional Catholic worldview – especially but not exclusively its fundamentalist interpretation of the Bible – had been on the ropes, severely buffeted by the revolution in religious and philosophical thinking that the Vatican, tarring with a very broad brush, denounced as "Modernism." Launching his counterattack in the summer and fall of 1907, Pope Pius X lashed out against alleged Modernist tendencies in Catholic university circles, and in the process plunged the church into one of its darkest, most repressive periods. Among other things, the Vatican demanded (September 1910) that certain Catholic professors swear an anti-Modernist oath of fidelity to traditional formulations of doctrine on such things as miracles, the founding of the church, and the nature of faith.

Even Heidegger, when he was 20 years old and still a seminary student, had thrown in his lot with the Vatican on this one. He publicly condemned Modernism and defended the church's teaching authority both in a speech he gave in Hausen im Tal, near Messkirch, on September 6, 1909 (three weeks before entering the Jesuits), and in an article he published in the conservative Catholic weekly *Der Akademiker* in May 1910.[6]

Four years later, however, while in the throes of writing his qualifying dissertation, Heidegger apparently began to feel the pinch of the church's anti-Modernist crusade and changed his mind. In a letter to his friend Father Krebs (July 19, 1914, just two weeks before the Great War broke out), he remarked ironically how the Vatican might guarantee conformity among Catholic intellectuals: "Philosophical demand could be met by setting up vending machines in the train station (free of charge for the poor)" and "all who succumb to having independent thoughts could have their brains taken out and replaced with spaghetti."[7]

Nonetheless, Heidegger, in hot pursuit of the chair of Catholic philosophy, continued to assure the administrative offices of Freiburg's
Catholic archdiocese, in writing and presumably with conviction,
that his academic work would be devoted to "researching and teaching Christian-Scholastic philosophy" (September 20, 1914), that he
saw himself as standing "in the service of Christian-Scholastic philosophy and the Catholic worldview" (November 23, 1914), and
that his philosophical career would be dedicated to "making the
intellectual riches stored up in Scholasticism available and usable
for the spiritual battle of the future over the Christian-Catholic
ideal of life" (December 13, 1915). Moreover, in a handwritten curriculum vitae that he presented to the philosophy department on
July 2, 1915, he declared that his "basic philosophical convictions
[remain] those of Aristotelian-Scholastic philosophy" and that his
lifework would be taken up with (here we find a slight twist away
from neo-Scholasticism and toward Husserl) "a comprehensive presentation of medieval logic and psychology in the light of modem
phenomenology."[8]

Therefore, a year after he had successfully completed his dissertation on medieval philosophy, and after being told for three years that
he was the inside favorite for Freiburg University's chair of Catholic
philosophy, it came as a great shock and a bitter disappointment
when in June 1916 Martin Heidegger saw the philosophy department
give the chair to Josef Geyser, a second-rate neo-Scholastic professor
from the University of Münster.

It seems that between June 1916 and March 1917 Heidegger underwent the personal and philosophical conversion that culminated in
his abandonment of dogmatic Catholicism. Several factors, including a personal crisis of faith, contributed to this Protestantizing
turn.

For one thing (and probably bound up with his disappointment at
being passed over for the Catholic chair) there was the increasing tension that Heidegger felt between, on the one hand, the conformity to
ecclesiastical authority that the Vatican's anti-Modernist campaign
demanded and, on the other, the "inner truthfulness towards oneself and those one is supposed to teach" (as he would later put it
to Father Krebs) that was demanded by his vocation to philosophy.
It is significant that Privatdozent Heidegger, after a year of giving
courses in Catholic philosophy, spent the summer of 1917 reading

the Protestant theologian Friedrich Schleiermacher (1768–1834) and would soon be studying Martin Luther.

Another factor was Heidegger's encounter with Edmund Husserl, who had come to Freiburg University in April 1916 to take over the chair of non-Catholic philosophy. Heidegger's first personal meetings with Husserl, from late July 1916 through the fall of 1917, were disappointing. To be sure, Husserl was happy to help the young man get some part-time teaching at the university. However, he gave Heidegger's qualifying dissertation only a desultory reading and, in October 1917, sent to Professor Natorp of Marburg University an at best lackluster evaluation of Heidegger's promise as a scholar.[9]

Again, one of the major issues was religion. Husserl, who called himself a "free Christian" and a "non-dogmatic Protestant" and who once denounced what he termed the "Catholic International," vigorously opposed ecclesiastical interference with philosophical research. "Scientific work would be deprived of its freedom," he said on January 16, 1920, with explicit reference to the Vatican, "if one had to fear being censured by some learned commission." The point is that up through October 1917 Husserl, being unfamiliar with the religious transformation Heidegger was undergoing, thought that the young lecturer was still passing himself off around Freiburg as a Catholic philosopher.[10]

Only in November – December 1917 did Husserl learn from his student, Heinrich Ochsner, who was a close personal friend of Heidegger, how radically Heidegger's views on Catholicism had changed. That was the turning point. Husserl now began to open up to Heidegger both personally and professionally. However, after only a few weeks, their direct personal contacts were broken off when Heidegger was called up, on January 17, 1918, for active military duty and eventually, at the end of August, 1918, was sent to the Western Front.[11]

In any case, Husserl was clearly pleased when he could finally announce to Professor Natorp that by 1917 the young Dr. Heidegger had "freed himself from dogmatic Catholicism" and had "cut himself off – clearly, energetically, and yet tactfully – from the sure and easy career of a 'philosopher of the Catholic worldview.'" But the change had not come easily. In a letter to Professor Rudolf Otto, also of Marburg University, Husserl would recall – as if describing the conversion of a modern St. Augustine – the hard times Heidegger had gone through and the "difficult inner struggles" that had led him to "radical changes in [his] basic religious convictions." But the outcome, Husserl wrote, had been happy: Heidegger had "migrated over to the ground of Protestantism."[12]

No doubt aiding the troubled young scholar to chart his course through the crisis was his romantic encounter during the summer of 1916 with his Protestant student Thea Elfride Petri. An economics major, she had been following his philosophy courses since the fall of 1915. By the late summer of 1916 they were vacationing together at Reichenau, by Christmas they were engaged; and three months later – both of them in deep religious crisis – they were married.

THE RADICAL PHENOMENOLOGIST

On February 7, 1919, amid the social and political chaos of Germany's collapse and regeneration, Heidegger began his first lecture course after the war, and he hit the ground running. "Today we are not ready for *real* reform of the university," he announced to his students. "And just getting mature enough for the task will take a *whole generation*" (GA 56/57, 4).[13]

These were hard times for Germany, both economically and politically. Right-wing death squads had just murdered Rosa Luxemburg and Karl Liebknecht, and the bodies of other leftist victims were turning up by the scores. The reichsmark was falling in value and by November 1923 would exchange at 4.4 trillion to the dollar. The Versailles Peace Conference was busily paring away 10 percent of Germany's population, 13 percent of its national territory, and 100 percent of its colonies, as well as imposing (over and above Germany's war debt, which had set the national wealth back by 25 percent) a war reparations bill that was worth, in today's exchange rates, $220 billion.[14]

Renewing the nation in general and the university in particular, said Privatdozent Heidegger on the first day of class, would require a "return to the authentic origins of the spirit," and that meant not flights of rarified theory but a concrete immersion in the practical experiences of real life in order to get to the core of what it means to be authentically human. "Man, become essential!" he exclaimed, citing the German mystic Angelus Silesius (1624–77). And quoting a somewhat better known figure: "He who can grasp it, let him grasp it!" (5).

What was going on? Certainly the passionate intensity of Heidegger's lecture style announced that there was a new force to be reckoned with at Freiburg University. But something else was afoot. Just two weeks before, fresh from his "letter of resignation" to Father Krebs, Heidegger had been appointed Edmund Husserl's new teaching assistant, taking the place vacated by Edith Stein. And yet virtually everything the young lecturer had to say in his first course, "The Idea of Philosophy and the Problem of Worldview," seemed to undercut, or at least to reinterpret radically, Husserl's own positions on phenomenology.

Heidegger's main attack was on the primacy that Husserl attributed to theory over lived experience and to the pure transcendental ego over what Heidegger at this point called the "historical ego" and the "ego of the situation" (205–6) and that he would later term "Dasein." "We find ourselves at a methodological crossroads," he said on March 14, "where it will be decided whether philosophy shall live or die" (63). And everything depends on first getting clear what philosophy's true issue is. "What is messing up the real problematic is not just naturalism as some people think," he said with explicit reference to Husserl, "but the overall dominance and primacy of the *theoretical*" (87).

For Heidegger the theoretical orientation of the pure ego of Husserlian phenomenology sucks the blood out of the richly textured *Umwelt*, the firsthand world of lived experience (*Erleben*) in which one primarily exists and carries out practical tasks. In this firsthand world, things are not just "there," and they do not primarily have "value." They are not even just "things." They are "*the meaningful* – that's what's primary. . . . When you live in the firsthand world, everything comes at you loaded with meaning, all over the place and all the time, everything is enworlded, '*world happens.*'" (73). Here we do not know ourselves as egos who observe the entities lying around us. Rather (this was Heidegger's rereading of intentionality), we are the act of experientially "*living out unto something*," which has "absolutely nothing to do with an *ego*" (68–9). And this primary level of experience is intensely personal: "Only in the resonances of one's own individual 'I' does a firsthand thing get experienced, only there does 'world happen,' and wherever and whenever world does happen for me, *I* am somehow entirely there" (73; for Heidegger's discussion of sociality, see 210).

But this richly textured firsthand world gets drained of all life, meaning, and history when it becomes infected by theory (89; *ent-lebt, ent-deutet, ent-geschichtlicht,* and *Infizierung*). The dynamic, personal, and historical "happening" of world (*Er-eignis*), which is intimately bound up with the living and appropriating of one's own life, gets flattened out to a "process" (*Vor-gang*) of objective knowledge. Ultimately the human being is reduced to a level of experience that is "absolutely without world, world-alien, a sphere where the breath is knocked out of you and you cannot live" (75, 78, 112; cf. 205). "In theoretical acts I leave my lived experience behind. To be sure, something of the experiential still comes along with me – but no one knows what to do with it, so they invent the convenient label of the 'irrational' for it" (117).

To preserve the firsthand world of lived experience, including the world of religious experience (207, 211), from the ravages of theorizing, Heidegger radically reinterpreted the "principle of all principles" that Husserl had laid down for phenomenology in Section 24 of his *Ideas for a Pure Phenomenology and a Phenomenological Philosophy* (1913). If, according to the Master, firsthand intuition is the starting point of phenomenology, that intuition ("even though Husserl doesn't say this in so many words") is not some theoretical comportment but an "understanding intuition, a *hermeneutic intuition,*" from which theory is but a precipitate (117). This hermeneutic intuition, which already understands the world prior to any theorizing and which is the basis of all the rigor that phenomenology claims for itself, is

the aboriginal intention of authentic living, the aboriginal comportment of lived experience and of life as such, the absolute *sympathy with life* that is identical with lived experience. Prior to anything else – that is, if we take this path away from theory and more and more free ourselves from theory – we *see* this basic comportment all the time, we have an orientation *to* it. This basic comportment is absolute, but only if we live in it directly. And no conceptual system, no matter how elaborately constructed, can reach it. Only phenomenological living, as it continually intensifies itself, can get to it. (110)

But this *Urhabitus,* or basic way-of-being, that Heidegger calls phenomenological living "cannot be acquired from one day to the next, like putting on a uniform." It is not a method and has nothing to do with adopting "standpoints" (that, he says, would be the "mortal sin" that ruins everything). Rather, phenomenology, like lived experience, "can authenticate and prove itself only through itself," that is, only in the *living* of it (110).

This was pretty gutsy stuff, but it did not promise a faithful adherence to traditional Husserlian phenomenology. In any case, Heidegger not only continued the attack during the following semester in his course "Phenomenology and the Transcendental Philosophy of Value" (May 9 to July 25, 1919), but even let Husserl in on what he was saying. In the middle of June in one of the Saturday morning discussions that Husserl used to hold at his Freiburg home with his close associates, Heidegger told Husserl publicly that the much vaunted pure ego of Husserlian phenomenology was "derived" from the historical ego by the "repression" of historicity and concretion, and that the pure ego was limited to the role of being the "subject" only of "theoretical acts."[15]

A dozen years later Husserl would say that in those early years he thought Heidegger actually did agree with him (Husserl used to tell Heidegger, "You and I are phenomenology") and that the only problem was that he did not understand Heidegger's language.[16] But clearly the game was up from the beginning, even though it took Husserl ten more years (until the summer of 1929) to realize how much Heidegger had gone off on his own.

Which way had Heidegger taken? From his doctoral studies onward, Heidegger had been captivated not by Husserl's *Ideas* with its neo-Kantian turn toward transcendental subjectivity, and even less so by his Cartesian turn in the twenties, but rather by the Master's earlier, groundbreaking work, *Logical Investigations* (1900–1). There Husserl had advanced Franz Brentano's notion of intentionality – the idea that all mental acts are characterized by directedness to a meant object – and solidified it into the fundamental problematic of the *phenomenological correlation* between intentional acts and the mental objects they reveal. And Husserl did so specifically with reference to acts of logical-theoretical intentionality and their logical-theoretical correlates. Heidegger, however, took at least seven important steps both behind and beneath Husserl's early work and its theoretical interests.

First, Heidegger went back to the ancient Greeks and came to see the intentional relatedness-to-the-meant of Husserlian phenomenology as only an imperfect carry-over of what Aristotle had already worked out in terms of human acts of "disclosing" entities (Greek: *aletheuein*). Thus, "What phenomenological investigations had recently discovered to be the underlying posture of thinking turns out to be the basic trait of Greek thinking, indeed of philosophy as such" (SD 87; TB 79).

Moreover, whereas Husserl's interests in intentionality remained focused primarily on theoretical comportment, Heidegger began probing the *pretheoretical* intentional acts operative in such everyday lived experience as work, talk, self-concern, and faith. He argued that we first encounter things within historical contexts of meaningfulness that first of all are bound up with our pretheoretical concerns and practical interests. And there a more primordial "hermeneutic" *logos* is at work: we know the present objects of practical concern by reaching "beyond" them to antecedently grasped purposes and goals. Heidegger claimed to find clues for this firsthand "hermeneutic" understanding in Aristotle's discussions of self-referential acting (*praxis–phronesis*) and creative making (*poiesis–techne*) in *Nicomachean Ethics* VI.[17]

Second, Husserl had already argued in *Logical Investigations* VI, 6, that intentionality or disclosive comportment reveals not just entities but also and primarily the *essence* of entities, their "being." Following Husserl, Heidegger interpreted this "being" (*Sein* or *Seiendheit*) no longer objectivistically as the whatness and thatness of entities, the way much of traditional metaphysics had done. Rather, he read it phenomenologically, that is, in correlation with acts of disclosive intentionality, as referring to the howness (*das Wie*) or hadness (*die Habe*) of entities: the way in which, at any given moment, they are disclosed to and "had" in the human acts that coperform that disclosure. But since practical activity entails prior anticipation of a goal or purpose, the primary modes of the being of an entity are not the presential modes of "being there" before a static subject but rather the future-oriented modes of "being for" the purposes posited by self-exceeding human existence.

Third, Heidegger's intense rereading of Greek philosophy in general and of *Metaphysics* IX 10 in particular led him to the major if implicit tenet of Greek thinking, namely, that entities, to the degree that they are "natural" (*physei on*), are intrinsically self-presentative, that is, accessible and intelligible – *on hos alethes* – even if that accessibility and intelligibility is always shot through with finitude.

Fourth, Heidegger conjugated this "aletheiological" insight of the Greeks with the phenomenological insights he had learned from Husserl and Aristotle: entities are self-disclosive (*alethes*) only insofar as they are in *correlation* with the various modes of the human co-performance of disclosure (*aletheuein*), primarily the practical ones. Thus, the phenomenological correlation became the "aletheiological" correlation, and Heidegger found it already named in Heraclitus as *logos* (Frag. 50) and *physis* (Frag. 123), and in Parmenides as the "togetherness" (*to auto*) of thinking and being (Frag. 3). This "event" of intelligibility in its facticity became, for Heidegger, the "thing itself" that philosophy had to interrogate. It was, he thought, the ultimate *a priori*, the "first" of everything about the human world, and thus (for those with the sensitivity for it) the most obvious fact of all.[18] Yet it is generally overlooked, not primarily because of some human defect but above all because it "prefers to hide" (Heraclitus, Frag. 53) in the sense of being ultimately unfathomable. In any case, the "happening" of this correlation – the always-already operative empowering of the essential togetherness of disclosive human comportment and of entities *qua* accessible – is what Heidegger, both tentatively in his early courses and boldly in his final writings, called *Ereignis*.

Fifth, insofar as intentionality reveals the being of entities, phenomenology became for Heidegger only a method for probing more deeply metaphysics' unresolved question about the essence or meaning of being, that is, about the analogical unity underlying all the various modes of the being of entities. However, given his phenomenologizing reading of the tradition, Heidegger now reshaped the question about the meaning of being into the question about the essence of the phenomenological correlation, that is, about the analogical unity underlying all possible ways in which entities can present themselves and thus be humanly appropriated. If the human "world" is at bottom a matter of the disclosive correlation, or *aletheia*, then how come *aletheia*? What is the essence, provenance, and "cause" of the disclosure of entities that happens in and with human nature?

Sixth, in working out the essence of this phenomenological – aletheiological correlation from the side of human nature and its pretheoretical "hermeneutic" understanding of things (as he mainly did in the twenties), Heidegger burrowed beneath the Husserlian structures of pure intentional consciousness with its alleged immanence, self-transparency, and apodictic self-givenness and spelled out the more primordial elements of fallenness and finitude, mortality and temporality, which he saw as the *a priori* or "fated" essence of human existence and its hermeneutic understandings.

Seventh, in working out the question about the essence of the disclosive correlation with emphasis on how it happens at all (the question of *Ereignis,* which he took up explicitly in the thirties), Heidegger came to see that the *a priori,* factical, and inexplicable *givenness* of the correlation – its "fatedness," back behind which one cannot go – was itself bound up with the *a priori,* factical, and inexplicable finitude that is the essence of human existence. This state of affairs – the unfathomable fatedness of the phenomenological correlation in conjunction with the inexplicable fatedness of human finitude – he called the *lethe* at the heart of *aletheia.*

Heidegger gestated these issues for a period of seven years, first at Freiburg, where he continued as a *Privatdozent* and as Husserl's assistant from 1919 until 1923, and thereafter at Marburg, where he was appointed associate professor in the fall of 1923 and taught until the summer of 1928. Between 1916 and 1927 Heidegger published absolutely nothing, and in the eyes of some colleagues this stood in the way of his being appointed to the chair of philosophy that Nicolai Hartmann was about to vacate at Marburg University in the fall of 1925.

But Edmund Husserl came to Heidegger's defense. In a letter to Professor Jaensch of Marburg's Philosophy Faculty (June 30, 1925), he said that "in the new generation [Heidegger] is the only philosophical personality of such creative, resourceful originality." "In my eyes," Husserl wrote, "Heidegger is without a doubt the most significant of those on their way up" and is "predestined to be a philosopher of great style. . . . He has kept silent for years so as to be able to publish only what is completely mature and definitively compelling. His publications that are soon coming out will show just how much he has to say and how original it is."[19]

Despite Husserl's rousing recommendation, Heidegger failed to get the appointment. Nonetheless, his reputation as a radical phenomenologist continued to grow. In late April 1927 Heidegger's question about the essence of the phenomenological–aletheiological correlation came to birth – a bit prematurely, as he himself later admitted – in his most famous work, *Being and Time*. The fame of that book won him the appointment first to Hartmann's chair at Marburg in the fall of 1927 and then, in the fall of 1928, to the position he most coveted: Husserl's successor in the chair of philosophy at Freiburg University.

It would take two years before Husserl got around to reading *Being and Time*, and only then would he realize how much Heidegger's path had split off from his own. But even before that, personal tensions were building up between these two very different phenomenologists, now bottled up in the same provincial town of Freiburg, the one in retirement, the other at the height of his career. Husserl began to suspect his protégé; Heidegger began to avoid his old master; and, to make matters worse, their wives no longer seemed to get along.

But they kept up appearances. April 8, 1929, marked Husserl's seventieth birthday, and Heidegger, in the name of Husserl's closest collaborators, publicly presented him with a *Festschrift*, a collection of essays in his honor. But the brief speech Heidegger gave on this festive occasion was fraught with ambiguity and gave strong hints that Heidegger thought he was leaving the Master in the dust. He said in part:

The works we are presenting to you are only a testimony that we *want* to follow your guidance, not a proof that we have succeeded in doing so. For is it not the case that your research has, in the first instance, created an entirely new space for philosophical inquiry, one with new demands, transformed assessments, a fresh regard for the hidden powers of the great tradition of Western philosophy? Yes, precisely that![20]

Heidegger's message was clear, and Husserl finally got it. Two months later, having at long last read through *Being and Time* while on vacation at Lago Como (July–August 1929), Husserl took a pencil and scrawled on the title page, no doubt sadly, "Amicus Plato, magis amica veritas": "Plato is my friend, but truth a greater friend."[21]

THE POLITICAL ACTIVIST

Four years later Germany was in revolution, and not for the better. On January 30, 1933, President Paul von Hindenburg had appointed

Adolf Hitler chancellor of the German Republic. A month later, following the burning of the Reichstag building on February 27, 1933, Hitler got the Parliament to suspend the German Constitution and replace it with a permanent state of emergency, under which fundamental civil liberties such as freedom of speech and assembly and privacy of the mails were canceled. Within a week of that (March 7) Hitler arrested all eighty-one of the Communist deputies who had been duly elected to the Reichstag the day before and confined them to the newly opened concentration camps. On March 23, the Reichstag passed the Enabling Act, giving Hitler plenipotentiary lawmaking powers, and with that the Nazi dictatorship was born. This was followed on April 5 by the Nazi "cleansing laws" aimed at excluding Jews and Marxists from the civil service.

Then on Monday, May 1 – one day before Hitler would arrest hundreds of labor leaders and throw them into concentration camps – Martin Heidegger, the newly elected rector of Freiburg University, very ostentatiously joined the National Socialist German Workers Party.

That same day, Professor Emeritus Edmund Husserl and his wife Malvine, who were vacationing near Locarno, received a letter from Mrs. Elfride Heidegger, dated April 28. These were hard times for Jews. Because of the "cleansing laws," Husserl, who was born a Jew and converted to Protestantism in his youth, had been forced to resign from Freiburg University two weeks earlier. In these difficult times, Mrs. Heidegger wrote, she and her husband wanted to assure the Husserls of their continuing gratitude for all the help in the past.

Husserl was close to rage. On May 4 he wrote his old friend Professor Dietrick Mahnke of Marburg University to tell him what he felt. Many of his students and colleagues over the years had been a consolation to him, he wrote, but

with others I have had to suffer the worst experiences – the final case (and it hit me the hardest) being Heidegger: hardest, because I had come to place a trust (which I can no longer understand) not just in his talent but in his character as well. The loveliest conclusion to this supposed bosom friendship between philosophers was his publicly enacted entrance into the Nazi party (very theatrical, indeed) on May 1. Before that there was his self-initiated break in relations with me (in fact, soon after his appointment [at Freiburg]) and, over the last few years, his anti-Semitism, which he came to express with increasing vigor – even against the coterie of his most enthusiastic students, as well as around the department. That was a hard thing to get over.[22]

Heidegger had been supporting the Nazi party at the ballot box at least since the spring of 1932, and in 1936 he told his former student Karl Löwith that the basis for his political engagement with the Nazis was his very central philosophical concept of "historicity" (Geschichtlichkeit).[23] Although it seems he did not accept the party ideology in its entirety, Heidegger strongly supported its anticommunism. He saw Nazism as a force for crushing Marxism and as a vehicle for realizing the ultraconservative vision of one of his favorite political theorists, Friedrich Naumann (1860–1919), that of a strong nationalism combined with a militantly anticommunist "socialism" under the guidance of a charismatic leader. The goal was to fashion a middle European empire that preserved the spirit and traditions of Wilhelmian Germany against what Heidegger saw as the onslaught of global technology.[24]

From April 1933 through April 1934, Heidegger served as the heavy-handed and controversial rector of Freiburg University, and in the early months of his tenure he not only lent his name and efforts to the Nazi revolution but also became an outspoken propagandist for Hitler's foreign and domestic policies. During this period he rushed to establish the Führer principle at the university (October 1, 1933), thereby making himself the virtual dictator of the campus. He applied the Nazi "cleansing laws" to the Freiburg University student body (November 3) and thus ended financial aid for "Jewish or Marxist students" or anyone who fit the description of a "non-Aryan" in Nazi law. On the same day he told the assembled students that "the Führer himself and he alone is German reality and its law, today and for the future," and a week later (November 10) he took to the radio to urge ratification of Hitler's withdrawal of Germany from the League of Nations.[25]

In private he engaged in the more despicable work of a Nazi informer. On September 29, 1933, he secretly denounced a colleague, Professor Hermann Staudinger, for having been a pacifist during the Great War, and when the Gestapo confirmed his tip, Heidegger quietly urged the government to fire the man without a pension

(February 10, 1934). He also wrote a secret and damning letter to the head of a Nazi organization against a former friend and colleague, Professor Eduard Baumgarten (who, he said, had "very actively frequented the Jew Fränkel"), and thereby helped get the man suspended from a teaching job (December 16, 1933). As late as 1938 he prevented the young Max Müller from getting an academic position by informing the administration of Freiburg University that Müller was "unfavorably disposed" to the Nazi regime.[26]

And always just under the surface, there was the odor of anti-Semitism. On October 2, 1929, some three years before Hitler came to power, he wrote a letter to the Society for the Support of German Science recommending his assistant, the same Eduard Baumgarten (when they still were friends), and he offered his reasons why the Society should give financial aid to this young scholar who was not a Jew:

I would like to say more clearly in this letter what I could only hint at indirectly in my report: It is nothing less than the urgent consideration that we are faced with a choice, either to provide our *German* intellectual life once more with real talents and educators rooted in our own soil or to hand over that intellectual life once and for all to the growing influence of the Jews [*Verjudung*] in the broad and narrow sense. We will find our way back only if we are able, without baiting and without useless arguments, to assist budding talents in their development.

Regarding this important objective I would be especially grateful if Mr. Baumgarten, whom I have selected to be my assistant, could be helped with a grant.[27]

And on July 1, 1933, in what would seem to be a typical expression of his mind, Heidegger announced his belief that "there is a dangerous international alliance of Jews" – this to Karl Jaspers, whose wife was Jewish.[28] Moreover, from 1934 on, Heidegger declined to direct the doctoral dissertations of Jewish students. Fifty years later Heidegger's close friend Heinrich Petzet wrote (as if no further explanation were needed) that Heidegger felt ill at ease with big-city life,

and this was especially true of that mundane spirit of Jewish circles, which is at home in the metropolitan centers of the West. But this attitude of his should not be misunderstood as anti-Semitism, although it has often been interpreted that way.[29]

After Heidegger resigned the rectorate in April 1934, he continued to support the Nazi regime, though more quietly and perhaps more critically. In the spring and summer of 1936, he still thought that Hitler and National Socialism were the right path for Germany (although he did criticize some forms of Nazi bureaucracy), and he spoke positively of the achievements of both Mussolini and Hitler in the battle against nihilism (GA 42 40–1). And to judge from his public lectures, he apparently supported Hitler's war aims at least until the inevitability of an Allied victory became obvious.[30]

After the war the State Committee for Political Purification declared Heidegger a Nazi "fellow traveler" and prohibited him from teaching. But Freiburg University came to his defense, and in 1951 he was granted emeritus status and was allowed to teach and lecture again at the university.

In posthumously published texts – some prepared in 1946 for the denazification committee, one for eventual publication in *Der Spiegel*[31] – Heidegger tried to explain what he called his political "error." Otherwise he maintained a hermetic silence about the motives, responsibility, and particular forms of his involvement with National Socialism. But in 1953 he published the text of a 1935 lecture course in which he had attempted briefly to distinguish between, on the one hand, vulgar Nazism and, on the other, the "inner truth and greatness" of the Nazi movement, namely, its alleged effort to mediate between human beings and global technology. However, the paragraph was so shot through with ambiguity and even subterfuge that Heidegger himself tried, unsuccessfully, to get Yale University Press to drop it from the eventual English translation, *Introduction to Metaphysics*.[32]

In general, Heidegger put the blame (if we can call it that) for the tragedy of World War II and the Holocaust not on any individuals or political movement but on an impersonal planetary force, the Will to Power, which he thought lay beyond anyone's responsibility or control. This force had brought about a new and unfortunate form of human nature: the "worker" taken as technology-oriented, world-dominating subjectivity. Heidegger frequently affirmed that in the thirties and forties Ernst Jünger's book *Der Arbeiter* (The Worker, 1932) had opened his eyes to a suprametaphysical vision of the true meaning of the modern social, political, and economic order: "From the standpoint of the reality of the Will to Power I saw even then (in 1939–40) what *is*," Heidegger wrote.[33] And he tried to capture that vision in a handwritten text, dating from the late thirties, which has recently been found among his papers at the Marbach Archives:

The "form of the worker" is not *any one man* – not even primarily a type of man. Rather, as a type, it is only a form of *subjectivity*, whose essence consists in the *certitude* of calculation. As the Will to Power it is one form, the *last* form, *of the "truth" of beings as a whole*. Therefore, in essence it is *techne*, but a deeper essence than Jünger sees: he keeps turning around in a superficial circle but does not sense the whirlwind.

The "worker" is the unconditional *menial* who has been expanded into the limitless *master*, i.e., the modern "free" enactor of *techne*, the latter taken as the planning, cultivating, calculating and finally the securing of entities as a whole (including human beings) within its own power to fabricate – a complete actualization of what lies at hand, but an actualization of its essence. The "worker" and the limitless subjectivity of such complete anthropomorphism consists in this: Being happens as power-to-make.[34]

It was this power to dominate everything that Heidegger, in his role as political philosopher, saw as infecting all modern political forms without differentiation. "Today everything stands within this reality, whether it is called communism or fascism or world democracy."[35]

To put it minimally, Heidegger was never a very strong supporter of democracy, whether before or after the war. He excoriated the "democratized decay" of Germany's postwar institutions and declared himself unconvinced that democracy was the best political system for the modern age.[36] He used to like to cite Homer (*Iliad* II 204): "The rule of the many is not good; let there be one ruler, one king," and at least for a while, whether he was finally happy with it or not, he apparently got his wish.

WHAT WILL HEIDEGGER HAVE BEEN?

The period after the war saw the spread of Heidegger's writings throughout the intellectual world in an explosion of interest that crossed lines of language, culture, and academic disciplines. By the time of his death on May 26, 1976, at the age of 86, his books and essays had been translated into all Western languages, as well as into Chinese, Japanese, and Arabic, and the voluminous *Collected Edition* of his works was already under way.

Yet throughout all those works Heidegger claimed to be the thinker of "one thought only," which took many forms of expression: What is the provenance of disclosure? What is the essence of "world?" What is the "cause" of the correlation that lets human beings have meaningful access to entities? In a word, How come *aletheia*?

Over the half-century of his philosophical career Heidegger largely succeeded in establishing the structures of human existence that are essential to this event-of-intelligibility, and he worked out as well the general lines of its historical forms and epochs. However, he insisted that the question about the originating source of this disclosive correlation – the "how-and-why-it-comes-about" – was finally unanswerable. We cannot say why, whence, or to what end there is disclosure (i.e., why *es gibt Sein*) without already presuming the fact of disclosure and thereby moving in a circle. Thus, the essence of *aletheia* is *lethe*; the provenance of disclosure is unfathomable.

Unfathomable, yes, but something can be said about this correlation insofar as it always affects human existence and remains its chief, if largely unheeded, concern. First, Heidegger calls the "origin" of disclosure *das Er-eignis*, which we can translate as "empropriation": the event that brings disclosive comportment and disclosible entities together into their asymptotic "own" (*proprius*, *eigen*), that is, into the openness of disclosure.

Second, he speaks of the "origin" of disclosure as *difference* (Greek *diaphora*, German *Unterschied*), that is, that which is responsible for the fact that human existence and the human world are always nonimmediate and not self-coincident – right down to the non-self-coincidence that is dramatically registered in human mortality and that condemns us to ineluctably finite meanings derived from endless mediation.

Third, regarding the "origin" of disclosure, Heidegger insists on the simple fact that *es gibt Sein*, "disclosure just happens to happen." In this context there seems to be no real room for history in the usual sense. Instead, Heidegger calls the *a priori* happening of the correlation *das Geschick des Seins*, disclosure's inherent "fatedness" or givenness to human nature, on the basis of which alone entities are accessible. And when he considered this *a priori* givenness in its various epochal forms, he called it *die Geschichte des Seins*, the "dispensations" of disclosure.[37]

Fourth, the facticity of human existence is its condition of being ineluctably bound up with this *a priori* givenness of disclosure. Facticity is the human fate of being "thrown" into the endless, finite mediation necessitated by difference, without being able to know why this endless mediation is necessary.

And fifth, because disclosure is always-already operative everywhere in the human world, all entities are, in principle, open to human appropriation. That is, everything is endlessly accessible, except the *fact that* everything is endlessly accessible. This now achieved state of affairs, which is the gift of the intrinsic unfathomability of the aletheiological correlation, Heidegger termed "nihilism," and he suggested that human beings be not less nihilistic but more.[38]

Heidegger thought that the archaic Greek poets and thinkers implicitly understood the fact of this endless but finite accessibility of things, and he set it against all theological traditions that would root the comprehensibility of entities in the *full* comprehensibility of God. Yes, "the belonging-together of subject and object [arises] from something that first imports their nature to both ... and hence is prior to the realm of their reciprocity." But no, this "wellspring" of the aletheiological reciprocity "does not want ... to be called by the name Zeus" (Heraclitus, Frag. 32); that is,

it does *not* properly admit of being named Zeus, and of being thereby degraded to the level of existing as one entity present among others – even if the "among" has the character of "above all other present entities."[39]

Heidegger thought that the "hiddenness" or "oblivion" of the disclosive correlation led to its being increasingly overlooked throughout Western history, to the point that in our own day it has become completely forgotten and counts for nothing. He took it as his mission to reawaken a new sense of the unfathomable mystery that, whether attended to or not, yawns like an abyss under the tidy little world of bourgeois certitude – all of this in the interests of helping to bring about a revolutionary transformation of human nature.

And somehow, he said, he came to see Hitler's National Socialism as a movement that might help with that reawakening, at least in Germany.

The degree to which Heidegger's political convictions and actions were a faithful reflection of his philosophy – and vice versa – is a matter of much debate today. Many of his most devoted followers believe that his intellectual work is in no way significantly related to, much less contaminated by, his support for Nazism, even though Heidegger himself rooted that support in his own very central notion of historicity. Other Heideggerians claim that "metaphysics made him do it"; that is, they explain his political "error" as the result of his being victimized by the intrinsic hiddenness of disclosure, which, in the form of "errancy" (*Irre*), inevitably tends to lead people astray, almost like a secularized form of Original Sin. Still others claim that Heidegger got trapped for a period of time in the nightmare of metaphysical "humanism" from which he was struggling to awake – with the corollaries, first, that Heidegger's political blunder is in fact very concrete proof of everything he had to say about the dark side of the forgottenness of disclosure and, second, that the alleged "overcoming" of metaphysics in his later thought is a guarantee that such an error would not happen again.

Others, however, argue that the reasons for Heidegger's support of Hitler and the Nazis were much more simple – and much more base – than these rather high-flown explanations would have it, and that in order to understand his political motives and despicable actions during the Third Reich one must start by investigating the hard times he lived through and specifically the concrete economic and social factors that conditioned his decisions.

If Heidegger himself insisted that his engagement with Nazism came from the very essence of his philosophy, perhaps his followers should believe him on this point. If Heidegger himself felt free, even for a while, to put not just his person but also the major categories of his philosophical thought at the service of Nazi foreign and domestic policy, then one would do well to ask whether those categories are really as free of economic, social, and political interests as most Heideggerians contend.[40]

The point is not to condemn a man for his past but to learn something about oneself in the present, not to dismiss Heidegger's philosophical work out of hand but likewise not to join the Perpetual Adoration Societies that currently thrive among the Heideggerian faithful in Europe and America. The task, for those who care to take something from Heidegger, is to learn how to read him critically, both his life and his works, not to swallow his philosophy whole but to sift it for what is still of value and what not.

That would entail asking whether Heidegger's dogged pursuit of the *essence* of disclosure did not blind him to crucial problems bound up with *specific modes* of disclosure, particularly in the economic, social, and political orders. It would entail asking whether one risks perpetuating that same blindness to the very degree that one remains faithful to Heidegger's metaontological line of questioning. Maybe it is not wise – whether the times are hard or easy – to be the thinker of "one thought only."

As Derrida puts it, the task of critically rereading Heidegger requires "showing – without limit, if possible – the profound attachment of Heidegger's texts (both writings and deeds) to the possibility and actuality of all nazisms,"[41] even, one might suggest, those that pass themselves off in the guise of furthering "Western democracy," preserving the "American way of life," or instituting various kinds of "World Order," whether old or new.

Heidegger has been dead for some years now, and it is still not entirely clear who he was or what he meant to say. His works lie there, some seventy-odd volumes of them, and it is not entirely clear what they mean either. The hermeneutic principle that Heidegger himself suggested for reading texts, be they books or lives, was: "Possibility is higher than actuality." The way we read his life and his works in our own hard times can help determine, in some far-distant future, who and what Heidegger will have been.

NOTES

1. Hugo Ott, *Martin Heidegger: Unterwegs zu seiner Biographie* (Frankfurt: Campus, 1988), p. 108.
2. Ibid., pp. 104–5. For anecdotal accounts of the effects of these gas attacks on U.S. soldiers, see Elaine George Collins, ed., *If Not for War* (Redwood City, Calif.: Collins, 1989), pp. 86–7, 123–4.
3. Dorion Cairns, *Conversations with Husserl and Fink* (The Hague: Nijhoff, 1976), p. 9.
4. Ott, *Martin Heidegger*, 106–7.
5. On Heidegger's education and career up to July 1915, see Thomas Sheehan, "Heidegger's *Lehrjahre*," in *The Collegium Phaenomenologicum: The First Ten Years*, ed. John Sallis, Giuseppina Moneta, and Jacques Taminiaux (Amsterdam: Kluwer, 1988): 77–137.

6. Victor Farias, *Heidegger et le nazisme,* trans. Myriam Benarroch and Jean-Baptiste Grasset (Lagrasse: Verdier, 1987), pp. 51–2. Also see Ott, *Martin Heidegger,* pp. 63–4.

7. The entire letter is translated in Sheehan, "Heidegger's *Lehrjahre,*" p. 113.

8. Ibid., pp. 114, 137 n. 178, and 80–1.

9. See Thomas Sheehan, ed., *Heidegger, the Man and the Thinker* (Chicago: Precedent, 1981), pp. 7–8.

10. For the quotations in this paragraph, see Thomas Sheehan, "Heidegger's 'Introduction to the Phenomenology of Religion,' 1920–1921," *Personalist* 60 (July 1979): 312–24, p. 314, and Ott, *Martin Heidegger,* pp. 113, 110.

11. According to written statements he made in 1915 and 1928, Heidegger had already been in the army three times before, once as a volunteer (August 2–10, 1914) and twice as a draftee (October 2–10, 1914, and August 18 to October 16, 1915), and each time had been dismissed for reasons of health. See the documentation in Sheehan, "Heidegger's *Lehrjahre,*" pp. 119, n. 2, 121 n. 13.

12. See Sheehan, "Heidegger's 'Introduction to the Phenomenology of Religion,'" pp. 313–14.

13. Unless otherwise noted, in this section all page references within parentheses are to GA 56/57.

14. V. R. Berghahn, *Modern Germany: Society, Economy and Politics in the Twentieth Century,* 2d ed. (Cambridge: Cambridge University Press, 1987), p. 72.

15. See Gerda Walther's letter to Alexander Pfänder, June 20, 1919, Husserl Archives, Leuven, cited in "Introductory Note" to Martin Heidegger, "The Understanding of Time in Phenomenology and in the Thinking of the Being-Question," *Southwestern Journal of Philosophy,* 10 (Summer 1979): 199–200, p. 199.

16. Cairns, *Conversations with Husserl and Fink,* pp. 9, 106.

17. Heidegger treated the issue at length in the first half of his course "Interpretation platonischer Dialoge (Sophistes, Philebus)," winter semester, 1924–5, and summarized it in his lecture "Dasein und Wahrsein nach Aristoteles: Interpretationen von Buch VI der Nikomachischen Ethik" delivered at Cologne University on December 2, 1924, at the invitation of Max Scheler.

18. See *Physics* B 1 193 b 3–6, and *Metaphysics* 1006 a 5–11. See also the quote from GA 56/57 110, cited above on page 79, where Heidegger says that "we *see* this basic comportment all the time...."

19. Husserl's handwritten letter from Freiburg, dated Tuesday, June 30, 1925, in response to Jaensch's letter of June 24, was intended to answer the question Professor Wedekind had raised at the Marburg Philosophy

Faculty meeting of June 24 about how little Heidegger had published. Husserl's letter and other documentation relating to Heidegger's application for Hartmann's chair are found in the Staatsarchiv Marburg, "Akten der Philipps-Universität Marburg: Philosophie und Pädagogik, 1922–1943" (Bestand 307d: Acc. 1966/10, No. 28) and "Akten Universität Marburg betreffend die Professoren der philosophischen Fakultät..." (305a: Acc. 1950/9, No. 646). See Thomas Sheehan, "'Time and Being,' 1925–1927," in *Thinking about Being: Aspects of Heidegger's Thought,* ed. Robert W. Shahan and J. N. Mohanty (Norman: University of Oklahoma Press, 1984), pp. 180–3, and Theodore Kisiel, "Why the First Draft of *Being and Time* Was Never Published," *Journal of the British Society for Phenomenology,* 20 (January 1989): 3–22, p. 31.

20. Martin Heidegger, "Edmund Husserl zum 70. Geburtstag," *Akademische Mitteilung: Organ für die gesamten Interessen der Studentschaft an der Albert-Ludwigs-Universität in Freiburg/Br.,* 4. Folge, 9. Semester, No. 4 (May 14, 1929): 46–7, p. 46.

21. Cf. *Nichomachean Ethics,* A 6 1096 a 14–17.

22. The German text appears in Bernd Martin, ed., *Martin Heidegger und das "Dritte Reich": Ein Kompendium* (Darmstadt: Wissenschaftliche Buchgesellschaft, 1989), p. 149.

23. Karl Löwith, *Mein Leben in Deutschland vor und nach 1933* (Stuttgart: Metzler, 1986), p. 57.

24. See Thomas Sheehan, "Heidegger and the Nazis," *New York Review of Books,* June 16, 1988, p. 44.

25. These texts are printed in Guido Schneeberger, *Nachlese zur Heidegger: Dokumente zu seinem Leben und Denken* (Bern: Suhr, 1962), pp. 136–7, 144–6.

26. Bernd Martin and Gottfried Schramm, "Ein Gespräch mit Max Müller," *Freiburger Universitätsblätter,* 92 (June 1986): 13–31, pp. 27–9.

27. The German text appears in Ulrich Sieg, "Die Verjudung des deutschen Geistes," *Die Zeit,* "Feuilleton," December 22, 1989, p. 50. The term *"Verjudung"* became a Nazi term of contempt ("Jewification") in the thirties.

28. Karl Jaspers, *Philosophische Biographie,* expanded ed. (Munich: Piper, 1977), p. 101; also his *Notizien zu Martin Heidegger,* ed. Hans Saner (Munich: Piper, 1978), pp. 15, 257, 284.

29. Heinrich Wiegand Petzet, *Auf einen Stern zugehen* (Frankfurt: Societät, 1983), p. 40.

30. Heidegger's criticism of the Nazi bureaucracy is mentioned in Löwith, *Mein Leben in Deutschland,* p. 57. Heidegger's positive statement about Hitler and Mussolini was intentionally omitted from the first German edition of his 1936 course *Schellings Abhandlung "Über das Wesen der menschlichen Freiheit"* (1809) (Tübingen: Niemeyer, 1971), and

therefore is absent from the English translation by Joan Stambaugh, *Schelling's Treatise on the Essence of Human Freedom* (Athens: Ohio University Press, 1985). It has been restored in the *Gesamtausgabe* edition of the work, GA 42 40–1.

31. The *Der Spiegel* interview appears in English translation by William J. Richardson: "Only a God Can Save Us," in Sheehan, ed., *Heidegger, the Man and the Thinker*, pp. 45–67.

32. The disputed text appears in Martin Heidegger, *Einführung in die Metaphysik* (originally published in 1953), republished in 1983 as GA 40 208; English translation by Ralph Manheim, *Introduction to Metaphysics* (New Haven, Conn.: Yale University Press, 1959), p. 199; it is discussed in Sheehan, "Heidegger and the Nazis," pp. 42–3. Regarding the Yale incident see Elisabeth Young-Bruehl, *Hannah Arendt: For Love of the World* (New Haven, Conn.: Yale University Press, 1982), p. 443.

33. Martin Heidegger, "The Rectorate 1933/34: Facts and Thoughts," trans. Karsten Harries, *Review of Metaphysics*, 38 (March 1985): 481–502, p. 485.

34. The transcribed text, with a photograph of the original, appears in Heimo Schwilk, ed., *Ernst Jünger: Leben und Werk in Bildern und Texten* (Stuttgart: Klett Cotta, 1988), p. 131.

35. Heidegger, "The Rectorate," p. 485.

36. Petzet, *Auf einen Stern zugehen*, p. 82; cf. p. 232.

37. The German verb *schicken*, as transitive, means to send or dispatch and, as reflexive, to happen. From the transitive sense comes the noun *das Geschick*: destiny, fate, fortune. From the reflexive sense comes the noun *die Geschichte*: event or happening; history; story. The Latin deponent verb *fari* means to say or speak something to someone. The past participle *fatum*, taken as a substantive, means that which is "spoken" (destined, fated) to someone.

38. See Thomas Sheehan, "Nihilism, Facticity, and the Economized *Lethe*," in *Heidegger: A Centenary Appraisal*, ed. Edward S. Casey, Samuel IJsseling, Thomas Sheehan, and Jacques Taminiaux (Pittsburgh, PA: Duquesne University, Simon Silverman Center, 1990), pp. 28–61.

39. Martin Heidegger, *Early Greek Thinking*, trans. David Krell and Frank Capuzzi (New York: Harper & Row, 1984): finite comprehensibility, pp. 107–8; "belonging-together," p. 103; "wellspring," p. 102; Zeus, p. 74.

40. See, e.g., the text from November 11, 1933, in Schneeberger, *Nachlese*, pp. 148–50.

41. Jacques Derrida, "Heidegger, l'enfer des philosophes," *Nouvel Observateur*, November 6–12, 1987, p. 173.

3 The principle of phenomenology

Heidegger was remarkable not just for his philosophical originality, but also for the breadth and depth of his response to the tradition. He learned an enormous amount from, and engaged in provocative ways with, figures spanning the entire history of ancient, medieval, and modern philosophy from the Presocratics to Nietzsche. And yet, perhaps inevitably, to other important thinkers he remained either indifferent or hostile – for example, Spinoza, Rousseau, Fichte, Schopenhauer, Marx, Freud, Frege, Wittgenstein, Carnap, not to mention practically the entire Anglo-American tradition from Hobbes to Dewey.

In which of the two groups would the founder of phenomenology, Edmund Husserl, have found himself, had he not accepted the appointment as chair at the University of Freiburg in 1916 and become a kind of professional mentor to his younger colleague? Heidegger assumed the Freiburg chair himself upon Husserl's retirement in 1928; indeed, the association of their names had already become a fact of history even before the publication of *Being and Time* in Husserl's *Jahrbuch*, complete with its dedication to him "in admiration and friendship." And yet the philosophical significance of the affiliation remains obscure. Apart from the circumstances that brought them together, was there really any deep affinity between their questions, their values, their methods, their ambitions? As early as 1916, before they met, Heidegger wrote to a friend lamenting Husserl's appointment at Freiburg, describing him as "lacking the necessary breadth of vision."[1] In 1923 he wrote to Karl Löwith, with characteristic harshness, "I am now convinced that Husserl was never a philosopher, not even for one second in his life."[2] Finally, to

Jaspers in 1926, as he was completing *Being and Time*, he announced, "If the treatise is written 'against' anyone, it's against Husserl."[3]

Would Husserl's phenomenology have inspired Heidegger's fundamental ontology, as it seems to have done, had they never crossed paths in Freiburg, as they did? Or would it not have, though it did in fact? Or did it only seem to? The counterfactual question is unanswerable, and the precise breadth and depth of Husserl's influence on Heidegger may also be impossible to determine. In any event, a lengthy investigation would be needed to untangle all the threads running through this peculiar chapter in the history of ideas.[4] What I want to discuss here instead are the broad outlines of Husserl's influence, set over against the particular ways in which, philosophically speaking, the two thinkers remained so deeply at odds. What I want to suggest is that while Husserl's phenomenology was a crucial formative influence on *Being and Time*, it was an influence that exerted itself only at a rather abstract and programmatic level, touching neither the core nor the details of Heidegger's project.

THE THINGS THEMSELVES

What *was* phenomenology for Husserl and Heidegger? In his oft-cited letter to William Richardson, Heidegger explicitly distances the hermeneutic phenomenology of *Being and Time* from Husserl's ahistorical perspective: "'phenomenology' in Husserl's sense," he writes, "was elaborated into a particular philosophical position already anticipated by Descartes, Kant, and Fichte. The historicity of thinking remained utterly foreign to it." Husserl inherited from rationalism and idealism a conception of philosophy as a rigorous discipline or science (*Wissenschaft*),[5] and that methodological ideal, Heidegger contends, clouded Husserl's view of the phenomena from the outset, contrary to his own stated aims. "The question of being developed in *Being and Time*," he continues, "set itself against this philosophical position and on the basis of what I still today believe to be a more faithful adherence to the principle of phenomenology."[6]

What was "the principle of phenomenology"? There are at least three versions of the principle worth distinguishing. In its most famous and least objectionable formulation, it was simply Husserl's memorable injunction to philosophers to return "To the things themselves!" What things? Not physical things (*Dinge*) or empirical facts (*Tatsachen*) in contrast to ideal types or essences (*Wesen*), but any immediately accessible matters (*Sachen*) susceptible to concrete description, as opposed to hypothesis or explanation. What Husserl meant was that philosophy had for too long failed to take seriously the form and content of appearance or opinion (*doxa*) themselves as phenomena worthy of description in their own right, rather than as so much surface or illusion to be explained away by a fully objective metaphysics or theory of knowledge.

Although philosophical contempt for *doxa* is at least as old as Plato, Husserl's slogan was above all an indictment of the creeping naturalism of modern thought since the Scientific Revolution. A fully objective physical world of blind mechanical causes and effects, after all, seems to leave no room for mind, meaning, value, normativity. Yet those categories are indispensable to our understanding of ourselves and the world, including our theoretical understanding of physical nature. Philosophers and psychologists often find themselves trying to explain how it is possible for such phenomena to emerge, or even *seem* to emerge, from the colorless, mindless material world described by the natural sciences. Husserl thought such naturalistic presuppositions got the order of philosophical inquiry all wrong, and Heidegger agreed, at least up to a point. So, when Husserl wrote in 1911, "The impulse to research must proceed not from philosophies but from things and from the problems connected with them," Heidegger wrote in the margin, "We take Husserl at his word."[7] Heidegger remained faithful, indeed he later insisted "more faithful" than Husserl himself, to the idea of philosophizing from a direct acquaintance with the phenomena, rather than advancing hypotheses and constructing explanations.

Of course, as we have already seen, the very general, programmatic watchword "To the things themselves!" stands in need of interpretation. What exactly *are* "the things themselves"? What understanding of phenomena must we already have in order to know them when we see them? Not surprisingly perhaps, Husserl's conception of phenomena proves on closer inspection to rest on presuppositions that Heidegger could never accept. For the principle of phenomenology – or perhaps we should now say a second, more refined version of the principle – identifies phenomena with appearances (*Erscheinungen*). Husserl points out that the term "phenomenon" is ambiguous "between *appearing* and *that which appears*." But phenomenology is not interested in transcendent objects as such, only with our immanent awareness of them. So, although "*phainomenon* (phenomenon) in its proper sense means that which appears," Husserl writes, "it is used primarily for the appearance itself, the subjective phenomenon."[8] Phenomena are, for Husserl, appearances, which is to say the contents *of* or *in* consciousness, not the things themselves appearing *to* consciousness. Phenomena are subjective, and phenomenology is essentially an inquiry into the nature of subjectivity in its own right, in strict distinction from the objective entities and structures studied by the empirical and formal sciences, in abstraction from our experience of them.

But what about the distinction between subjectivity and objectivity itself? Is it given phenomenologically? If so, in what way? Is it a self-evident fact, or an unexamined theoretical prejudice underwriting Husserl's notions of phenomena and phenomenology? Like Nietzsche before and Wittgenstein after, Heidegger rejected all global metaphysical distinctions between appearance and reality, for any notion of seeming presupposes some notion of being.[9] Appearances cannot coherently be detached from our primitive understanding of things showing up in some way, manifesting themselves, which is to say *being* somehow: "appearance is only possible *on the basis of* something showing itself," Heidegger writes. "If one then says that with the word 'appearance' we refer to something wherein something appears without itself being an appearance, the concept of phenomenon is not thereby defined, but *presupposed*" (SZ 29).[10]

In Heideggerian phenomenology, then, a phenomenon is not an appearance in contrast to something that appears, but rather "that which shows itself, the manifest" (SZ 28), a primitive notion that, he insists, "has in the first instance nothing whatever to do with what one calls 'appearance,' or indeed 'mere appearance'" (SZ 29).[11] More to the point, phenomena are not, for Heidegger, anything essentially subjective; they are not, as they are for Husserl, the inner contents of conscious experience standing in representational or referential relations to the outer objects making their appearance in or through them. Of course, the phrase "that which shows itself, the manifest" is what Heidegger calls a "formal indicator," a mere placeholder, which he then supplements with a more substantive or "phenomenological" concept of phenomena. And phenomena in the robust phenomenological sense are not what is self-evidently accessible to conscious reflection, but the hidden aspects of what lies open to view, hidden aspects in need of evocation and interpretation. A phenomenon in the Heideggerian sense is

> something that first and foremost precisely does *not* show itself, something that, in contrast to what first and foremost shows itself, is *hidden*, but is at the same time something that essentially belongs to that which first and foremost shows itself, and belongs to it in such a way as to constitute its meaning and ground.   (SZ 35)

The proper task of phenomenology, then, is not the kind of "pure" description urged by Husserl, but an attempt to draw out and highlight obscure but fundamental aspects of what shows itself. Moreover, fittingly, Heidegger construes the Greek *logos* as "letting something be seen" (SZ 33), so that phenomenology consists precisely in letting the ordinarily *unseen* dimensions of what is seen *be seen*. And such *letting be seen* is an ineluctably interpretive or *hermeneutic* effort.

For both Husserl and Heidegger, then, phenomenology is essentially a descriptive, not a hypothetical or explanatory, enterprise. Heidegger even insists that the expression "descriptive phenomenology" is a tautology.[12] But whereas Husserl aspires to what he calls "a systematic and eidetic morphology" of intentional attitudes,[13] Heidegger explicitly renounces any purely observational conception of description. Indeed, as if with Husserl's metaphor specifically in mind, he writes, "Description here does not mean a procedure in the manner of, say, botanical morphology" (SZ 35). Rather, "the meaning of phenomenological description as a method is *interpretation*." In a word, "The phenomenology of Dasein is a *hermeneutic*" (SZ 37).

But Heidegger's hermeneutic conception of phenomenology as interpretation, as opposed to mere observational description, is even more obviously inconsistent with a third version of the principle of phenomenology, what the title of §24 of Husserl's *Ideas I* deems "the principle of all principles," namely,

> that every primordially presenting intuition (*Anschauung*) is a source of legitimacy for cognition, that everything that presents itself to us primordially in "intuition" (so to speak, in its incarnate actuality) is to be accepted simply as what it presents itself to be, but also only within the constraints in which it presents itself. (Id I 43–4)[14]

This principle of resting one's findings on primal, self-evident intuitions is a methodological application of a broader, systematic doctrine central to Husserl's phenomenology, early and late. It appears in *Logical Investigations* as the concept of "categorial intuition"; in *Ideas I* it becomes "essential intuition" (*Wesenserschauung*), or simply the "seeing" (*Sehen*) of essences. According to Husserl, "immediate 'seeing,' not merely sensuous, experiential seeing, but seeing in general as primordially presenting consciousness of whatever kind, is the ultimate source of legitimacy of all rational assertions" (Id I 36). Since it is widely assumed that Heidegger inherits this notion of intuition from Husserl and simply takes it for granted, with or without trying to render it consistent with his own hermeneutic approach, it is worth recalling what he actually says about it, and where he stands with respect to this, the third and strongest version of Husserl's cardinal principle.

CATEGORIAL INTUITION

As he himself tells it, Heidegger was fascinated early on by the theory and practice of phenomenological seeing, particularly as Husserl describes it in the Sixth of the *Logical Investigations*. Husserl's early magnum opus seemed to emanate a "magic," a "spell" that captivated the young Heidegger, owing in part to its promise to offer insights into intentionality by carving a middle way between logic and psychology, between the purely formal and the empirically concrete (GA 14 81–6; TB 74–8).

But Husserl felt he could justify his own intuitive claims about intentionality only by showing intuition itself to be a legitimate source of philosophical evidence, capable of delivering general, intelligible contents, not just brute particulars. He therefore insisted that we enjoy not just sensuous, but also categorial, or logically structured, intuitions. We see objects (such as dogs) and their properties (such as black), but we also see – and not just in a metaphorical sense – that the dog *is* (or *is not*) black. Similarly, without having to see the pen and see the paper (in two distinct acts of seeing), we see the pen *and* the paper together on the desk; we literally see their conjunction or togetherness. So too, we see that *if* the glass falls, *then* the wine will spill onto the carpet, or that *either* the glass will *not* fall *or* the wine will spill.[15] According to Husserl, that is, we have concrete intuitions satisfying or fulfilling anticipations whose contents include formal elements such as *is* and *not*, the logical connectives *if*, *then*, *and*, and *or*, and quantifiers like *all*, *some*, *many*, *few*, *a*, and *none*. Contrary to the empiricists, we cannot derive logical or conceptual content from sensations simply through a process of abstraction. Instead, we must have insight into the logically structured states of affairs that render our higher-order judgments true or false.[16]

Heidegger was intrigued and impressed by this notion of a concrete acquaintance with the structure of intelligibility, in particular Husserl's idea that we have a direct intuition not just of entities, but of *being* (and nonbeing). Understandably, then, he found himself drawn especially to the account of "the origin of the concept of being" in §44 of the Sixth Investigation. There Husserl argues that we do not derive a notion of being from reflection on our own mental states, as if our understanding that something is (or is not) rested on an introspective observation of our own minds. Rather, more simply, we understand what is contained in the *is* precisely by being aware of states of affairs themselves. Not reflections on our experiences, then, but intuitions of things in the world are the source of our understanding that things *are*.

Husserl's theory of categorial intuition in *Logical Investigations* is crucial to understanding Heidegger's philosophical development. Not only did it resonate with his long-standing fascination with the question of the meaning of being, it also offered a powerful antidote to the intellectualism of contemporary neo-Kantian theories of mind, according to which all experience must be mediated by concepts and judgments. Indeed, the real attraction of Husserl's view for Heidegger lay not so much in its claim for the primacy of intuition as in its suggestion that our fundamental understanding of being is something preconceptual, prior not just to reflection and introspection, but to conceptual and propositional attitudes as such. This is why Heidegger would later remark that, for all its importance, Husserl's essential insight had already been "more primordially thought by Aristotle and in the whole of Greek thinking," which was moreover free of the Cartesian prejudices still alive in Husserl's work. Heidegger continues:

The more decisively this insight became clear to me, the more pressing became the question, Whence and how is it determined what is to be experienced as "the thing itself" (*die Sache selbst*) in accordance with the principle

of phenomenology? Is it consciousness and its objectivity or is it the being
of entities in its unconcealedness and concealment?   (GA 14 87; TB 79)

If Heidegger remained true to the spirit of the principle of phenomenology, then, it was only by repudiating the letter of Husserl's
theory of categorial intuition, and with it Husserl's location of "the
things themselves" in the contents of consciousness. In *Being and
Time* Heidegger insists that Husserl's emphasis on intuition is itself
part of an ongoing Cartesian obsession with the mind understood
as a self-contained region of being, abstracted from the practical
embeddedness of moods and understandings in the natural and social
world:

> Under the unbroken hegemony of traditional ontology, the genuine mode
> of registering what truly is has been decided in advance. It lies in *noein*,
> "intuition" in the widest sense, from which *dianoein*, "thinking" (*Denken*),
> is simply derived as a founded form. And it is from this fundamental onto-
> logical orientation that Descartes gives his "critique" of the still possible
> intuitively apprehending mode of access to what is, *sensatio* (*aisthēsis*) as
> opposed to *intellectio*.   (SZ 96)

Heidegger goes on to argue, moreover, that the restriction of intentionality to intuition and thought is part and parcel of the ontological
prejudice he is most concerned to overturn, namely, the assumption that all entities *are* in virtue of being object-like or "occurrent"
(*vorhanden*), hence ideally accessible to theoretical attitudes such as
observation and judgment. Notwithstanding its laudable injunction
to return to a concrete description of the phenomena, Husserl's phenomenology is, in Heidegger's eyes, just another case of the Western
intellectual tradition's fixation on intuition, presence, and the temporal present:

> The thesis that all cognition has its goal in "intuition" has the temporal
> meaning that all cognition is a making present (*Gegenwärtigen*). Whether
> every science, or even philosophical thought, aims at a making present shall
> remain undecided here. Husserl uses the expression "making present" to
> characterize sense perception. . . . It was no doubt the *intentional* analysis of
> perception and intuition in general that suggested this "temporal" charac-
> terization of the phenomenon. The following division will show that and
> how the intentionality of "consciousness" is *grounded* in the ecstatic tem-
> porality of Dasein.   (SZ 363n)

In *Being and Time*, that is, Heidegger attempts to supplant long-standing metaphysical and epistemological prejudices, including those still in force in Husserl's phenomenology, with a hermeneutic account of understanding as situated projection into future possibilities. Such an account is meant to reveal the untenability of the idea that all understanding rests on thoughts and intuitions directed to objects and objective states of affairs. The allusion to Husserl is unmistakable:

> By showing how all sight is grounded primarily in understanding... we have robbed pure intuition of its privilege, which corresponds noetically to the privileging of the occurrent in traditional ontology. "Intuition" (*Anschauung*) and "thought" are both derivatives of understanding, indeed rather remote ones. Even the phenomenological "intuition of essences" (*Wesensschau*) is grounded in existential understanding.   (SZ 147)

Like his later notion of "essential intuition" (*Wesenserschauung*), then, Husserl's theory of categorial intuition finds no home in Heidegger's hermeneutic phenomenology. Taken simply as a commitment to philosophize by attending to concretely describable phenomena, the principle of phenomenology was and remained a source of inspiration for the fundamental ontology of *Being and Time*. As a thesis concerning the primacy of intuition in everyday experience and in our understanding of being, it did not.

THE PHENOMENOLOGICAL REDUCTIONS

Husserl's claim that the human mind intuits not just objects and properties, but also logical structures constituting intelligible states of affairs, resurfaces in the chief methodological innovations of his middle and later works, the famous phenomenological "reductions." Heidegger's departure from Husserl is most striking in his repudiation of the reductions, particularly the two that figure most prominently in *Ideas I*, the transcendental and the eidetic.[17]

The most familiar of the reductions is the phenomenological *epochē*, or transcendental reduction (Id I §§31–34, §§56–64), which consists in a bracketing, or methodically setting aside from consideration, everything transcendent or external to consciousness in favor of the immanent, or transparently accessible, content of consciousness itself, content available to the mind upon reflection.[18] There is, Husserl believes, an "essential difference," indeed a phenomeno-logically self-evident difference, "between *being qua experience* and *being qua thing*" (Id I 76). Indeed, here "the fundamental distinc-tion among modes of being, the most cardinal that there is, reveals itself: that between *consciousness* and *reality*" (Id I 77). Conscious-ness and the world are radically distinct: "Between consciousness and reality there yawns a veritable abyss of meaning" (Id I 93). Tran-scendental subjectivity is fundamentally discontinuous with any-thing natural or positive: "Everything that is purely immanent to experience . . . is separated from all nature and physics, and no less from all psychology, by abysses – and even this image, as naturalis-tic, is not strong enough to indicate the difference" (Id I 184). The transcendental reduction consists in turning away from everything worldly, or external to consciousness, and focusing instead on what is internal to it. The reduction amounts to a special kind of reflec-tion in which we concern ourselves not with the ordinary objects of our intentional attitudes, but with the immanent contents of those attitudes themselves. Pure consciousness, then, is where the phe-nomena of Husserlian phenomenology reside.

For Heidegger, by contrast, intentionality must be understood as a distinguishing feature of human beings, entities whose very being is being-in-the-world. Unlike Husserl, who takes for granted the "diver-sity between consciousness and reality" (Id I 77), and for whom sub-jects and objects are separated by an "abyss," Heidegger insists that "For Dasein there is no outside, which is why it is also nonsensical to talk about an inside" (GA 24 93; BP 66). Heidegger does not deny that there is something like an abyss separating human beings from other entities in the sense that they cannot all be assimilated into the same ontological categories. Husserl's argument, however, is that human beings themselves are divided internally between the immanence of their consciousness and the transcendence of their bodies.[19] For Husserl, that is, the salient ontological distinction runs not between human and nonhuman entities, but between consciousness and *the world*. Intentionality is internal, the world is external, and the tran-scendental reduction focuses on the former to the exclusion of the latter.

Taken by itself, however, the inward turn of the transcenden-tal reduction would not be enough to distinguish phenomenology from introspective psychology. What is needed in addition is a turn from the empirical facts of consciousness to its essential structures, from the material or stuff of experience to the intelligible forms that, Husserl argues, render our awareness genuinely intentional, or object-directed.[20] This reduction from content to form, or from fact to essence, is what Husserl calls the "eidetic" reduction (from the Greek *eidos*), an abstraction from contingent facts to the types or essences and the necessities they entail (Id I 4, passim). The eidetic reduction thus turns our attention away from "real" mental events (occurring in time) toward "ideal" (abstract, atemporal) aspects of subjectivity. What matters to phenomenology is not concrete experiential episodes, but the essences those particulars instantiate. Husserl can therefore write that

a phenomenological doctrine of essence is no more interested in the methods by which the phenomenologist might ascertain the *existence* of some experiences...than geometry is interested in how the existence of the figures on the board or the models on the shelf might be methodically confirmed.   (Id I 153)

That intentional phenomena are is strictly speaking a matter of indifference to Husserl; the sole concern of phenomenology under the eidetic reduction lies with *what* they are.

But this bracketing of existence in favor of essence is precisely what Heidegger thinks blinds Husserl to the distinctive ontological character of Dasein, whose very essence, Heidegger insists, "*lies in its existence*" (SZ 42). The point is not, as Sartre would later argue, that human existence somehow precedes or determines its own essence by means of a radically free choice.[21] Rather, as Heidegger says in his 1925 lectures, the traditional concepts of *essentia* and *existentia*, whatness and thatness, precisely by admitting of a sharp conceptual distinction, fail to capture the way in which the very *being* of human beings is inextricably bound up with *what* they take themselves to be. Husserl's eidetic method in effect buries the phenomenon in obscurity from the outset:

in the contemplation and elaboration of pure consciousness, only the *what-content* is brought out, without inquiring into the being of the acts, in the sense of their existence. In the reductions, the transcendental as well as the eidetic, not only is this question not posed, but *it gets lost precisely through them*. From the what, I never experience anything about the meaning and the manner of the that.   (GA 20 151–2; HCT 110)

If the very fact of our existence is constitutive of our self-understanding, then the eidetic reduction suppresses what is *most essential* to intentionality, namely its *existential* moment. Since "The point of the reduction is precisely to make no use of the reality of the intentional . . . to dismiss the reality of consciousness as such," it cannot comprehend intentionality in its being. Indeed, "The sense of the reduction is precisely to give up the ground on which alone the being of the intentional could be asked about" (GA 20 150; HCT 109). Husserl's

notion of ideation as disregarding real individuation thrives on the belief that the what of any entity is to be defined by disregarding its existence. But if there were an entity *whose what is precisely to be and nothing but to be*, then this ideative contemplation of such an entity would on the contrary amount to a fundamental misunderstanding. It will turn out that this misunderstanding is dominant in phenomenology, and moreover dominates because of the dominance of the tradition.   (GA 20 152; HCT 110)

The identity of Dasein, whose being is precisely to-be-in-the-world, and whose essence "lies in its *to be*" (SZ 42), is simply not amenable to analytically distinct concepts of *essentia* and *existentia*.

Heidegger's argument, then, is not that the eidetic reduction fails because we cannot help positing ourselves as objectively present things alongside other things. Rather, precisely because Husserl mistakes human existence for mere objective presence, he wrongly infers that the essence of intentionality can be grasped apart from any interest in its existence. In what he calls the "natural attitude," Husserl writes, the world "is continually 'occurrent' (*vorhanden*) for me, and I myself am a member of it" (Id I 50). "As something occurrent, I continually find the one spatiotemporal actuality to which I belong like all other human beings who are to be found in it and who are related to it as I am" (Id I 52). In short, "I, the actual human being, am a real object like others in the natural world" (Id I 58). Tellingly, Husserl himself calls the natural standpoint a "theoretical attitude" (Id I 7), not a practical stance or orientation. Indeed, the attitude Husserl has in mind is not so much natural as naturalistic, fixated on entities generally as mere parts of nature, discrete chunks of a homogeneous objective world. For Husserl, moreover, the "positive sciences" are

mere extensions of the "general positing that characterizes the natural attitude" (Id I 53).

But how "natural" is such an attitude? Do we ordinarily understand ourselves as just so many pieces of objective nature? Or
is Husserl's description of everyday experience a theoretically
motivated distortion of the phenomena? Quoting Husserl directly,
Heidegger comments in his 1925 lectures, "How am I given in the
natural attitude in Husserl's description? I am 'a real object like others in the natural world,' that is, like houses, tables, trees, mountains. Human beings thus occur *realiter* in the world, among them
I myself" (GA 20 131; HCT 96). At a primitive level, Heidegger is
suggesting, we do not understand things, least of all ourselves, in
this blandly objective way. Instead, we make use of things, we rely
on them, we avail ourselves of them, we take them for granted by
manipulating, adjusting, wearing, stepping on, and ignoring them.
Only rarely do they stand over against us as mere objects. In short,
we do not simply *intuit* them as "occurrent" (*vorhanden*), we *treat*
them as "available" (*zuhanden*).

Husserl's account of the natural attitude, then, is at best a description of a kind of reflective standpoint we can adopt by stepping back
from our ordinary involvements with things and coming to regard
them as mere objects. Only by taking such an object-oriented construal of ordinary understanding for granted is he able to describe
the transcendental and eidetic reductions as plausible abstractions
from mundane objectivity to pure consciousness. Conversely, it is
only by rejecting the phenomenology underlying Husserl's theory
that Heidegger is able to reject the reductions themselves as incoherent methodological devices for uncovering the essential structures
of intentionality.

HEIDEGGER'S IMMANENT CRITIQUE OF HUSSERL

Heidegger's deep dissatisfaction with Husserl's phenomenology
comes into especially sharp focus in the "immanent critique" he
advances in his 1925 lectures. What Husserl's theory of intentionality lacks, Heidegger insists, is a proper appreciation of the *being*
of intentional phenomena. Pursuing "a more radical definition of
the task of phenomenological research," he therefore says, "The

immanent critique of the course of phenomenological research itself allows the question of being to arise" (GA 20 124; HCT 91).

Heidegger asks, "How is the fundamental and explicit elaboration of the thematic field of phenomenology carried out by Husserl?" (GA 20 129; HCT 94). The question concerns

the concrete individuation of intentionality, of comportments, of experiences; it now has to do with a determination of the field in which comportments become accessible in the first place. . . . The question is: How do comportments, from which the structure of intentionality is to be read off, become accessible? How is anything like intentionality, the structure of experience, experience [itself] initially given? Initially given, that means: given for the so-called *natural attitude*.   (GA 20 130–31; HCT 95)

The question is a transcendental question. Heidegger asks, What allows us to understand intentional phenomena *as* intentional? And how does intentionality become intelligible in the reflective attitude of the phenomenologist? Heidegger posed the same question to Husserl two years later in their collaboration on the *Encyclopaedia Britannica* article: "What is the mode of being of the entity in which the 'world' is constituted?" Heidegger calls this "the central problem of *Being and Time* – i.e. a fundamental ontology of Dasein."[22] For Heidegger, then, the question of being is not just a separate ontological problem, distinct from and irrelevant to phenomenology. Rather, just as "Ontology is possible only as phenomenology" (SZ 35), so too phenomenology inevitably expresses an understanding of the being of the phenomena it studies. Absent an acknowledgement of the question of being, Heidegger argues, Husserl's phenomenology will not just be incomplete, but "phenomenologically inadequate" (GA 20 140; HCT 102).

Husserl takes it for granted that intentionality is manifest solely in consciousness, as opposed to overt "comportment" (*Verhaltung*), or embodied activity. How then does he conceive of the mode of being of consciousness? Heidegger finds in Husserl's theory four central assumptions: (1) consciousness is "immanent," or transparent to itself; (2) it is given "absolutely," or nonperspectivally; (3) it is itself "absolute," or conceptually self-sufficient, intelligible to itself nonrelationally; and (4) it is "pure," its contents ideal. Do these "determinations of being," Heidegger asks, "emerge from a regard for the thing itself (*die Sache selbst*)? Are they determinations of being drawn from consciousness and from the entity intended by this term?" (GA 20 142; HCT 103). No. Instead, he maintains, Husserl has taken them over as part and parcel of a Cartesian notion of "absolute science," a methodical procedure meant to yield fully objective knowledge of the mind, bearing no trace of contextual relativity or interpretive indeterminacy.

To begin with, Husserl's concept of "immanence" simply means the inclusion or inherence of one thing inside another. It describes a relation among things, but says nothing about what kinds of things they *are*. It describes entities in relation to one another, but not in their mode of being as such, that is, not *as* entities: "This relation is characterized as a *real* [being-]*in-one-another*, but nothing at all is said about the being of this being-in-one-another, about realness (*Reellität*), about entities as a whole in this region. A relation of being among entities, not being as such, is defined here" (GA 20 142; HCT 103).

Similarly, the "absolute givenness" of consciousness merely describes the relation of one experience to another within the same immanent phenomenal domain, but says nothing about the mode of being of those experiences as such:

With the first characteristic, immanence, a relation of being between acts of the same region was identified, now it is the particular mode of being-an-object that one entity in the region of experience can have for another. Once again, not the entity in itself, but rather the entity insofar as it is a possible object of reflection, becomes the theme.   (GA 20 143; HCT 104)

All this says is that one experience affords complete and transparent access to another. It does not tell us what consciousness *is*, that is, how it is intelligible to us in the first place. Third, to say that consciousness is itself "absolute" or self-sufficient is to agree with Descartes that it presupposes nothing with respect to the world beyond it. Indeed, in his description of consciousness Husserl appeals explicitly to Descartes's definition of substance as that which depends on no other thing for its own existence: "Immanent being is therefore indubitably absolute being," Husserl writes, "in the sense that by essential necessity immanent being *nulla 're' indiget ad existendum*" (Id I 92). Consequently, "while the being of consciousness ... would indeed necessarily be modified by an annihilation of the world of physical things, its own existence would not be touched"

(Id I 91). For Husserl, Heidegger explains, "Consciousness is the earlier, the a priori, in the Cartesian and Kantian sense." The "absolute being" of consciousness is thus tantamount to "the priority of subjectivity over every objectivity":

> This third determination – absolute being – is once again not one that defines entities themselves in their being, but one that grasps the region of consciousness in the order of constitution and grants it a formal priority in that order before everything objective. This determination and conception of consciousness is at the same time the point where idealism and the idealistic problematic, more precisely idealism in the sense of neo-Kantianism, enter into phenomenology. Accordingly, this determination of being is also not an original one.   (GA 20 145; HCT 105–6)

Husserl's notion of the self-sufficiency of consciousness is drawn not from an open inquiry into "the things themselves," but from a philosophical tradition that took subjectivity to be the intrinsically intelligible starting point for all philosophical inquiry.

Finally, Heidegger considers the "purity" of consciousness, which is to say the ideality of intentional content as revealed by the eidetic reduction, over against the real flux of experience isolated by the transcendental reduction. In *Ideas I* Husserl defines intentional content in abstraction from the mental acts realizing it in order to draw "a distinction between two realms of being that are radically opposed and yet essentially related to one another," so that "consciousness taken universally must be accepted as a proper region of being." As a result, Husserl says, "we notice that while objects simpliciter (understood in the unmodified sense) stand under fundamentally different highest genera, all object-senses and all *noemata* taken completely, no matter how different they may be otherwise, are of essential necessity of one single highest genus" (Id I 265).[23] Psychological phenomena regarded as real events in time are multiple and various, but ideal meanings constitute a systematic whole and exhibit rational structure. Heidegger remarks, "With this characteristic of being, consciousness as pure, it becomes especially clear that it concerns ... not the determination of the entity that has the structure of intentionality, but the determination of the being of the structure itself as in itself detached" from that entity (GA 20 146; HCT 106). Similarly, in *Being and Time* Heidegger refers disparagingly to "the ontologically unclarified separation of the real and the ideal" (SZ 217; cf. 156, 229).

In Heidegger's estimation, then, Husserl's description of consciousness is not adequately grounded in the phenomena: "All four determinations of the being of the phenomenological region," he concludes, "are in no way drawn from the entity itself" (GA 20 146; HCT 106). The true source of Husserl's account is not the things themselves, but the Cartesian ideal of scientific certainty: "All of these determinations of being are in fact derived with a view to working out the *experiential context as a region of absolute scientific contemplation*." Heidegger continues:

Husserl's primary question is simply not concerned with the character of the being of consciousness, instead he is led by the following concern: *How can consciousness become the possible object of an absolute science?* The primary concern guiding him is the *idea of an absolute science*. This idea, *that consciousness should be the region of an absolute science*, is not simply invented, rather it is the idea that has occupied *modern* philosophy since Descartes. The elaboration of pure consciousness as the thematic field of phenomenology is *not derived phenomenologically by going back to the things themselves*, but by going back to a traditional idea of philosophy. For this reason, none of the defined characteristics put forward as determinations of the being of experiences is primordial . . . . the four characteristics of being that are given for consciousness are not derived from consciousness itself.   (GA 20 147; HCT 107)

"In the fundamental task of determining its proper field," Heidegger concludes, "phenomenology is *unphenomenological!*" (GA 20 178; HCT 128). Husserl was not sufficiently faithful to the principle of phenomenology he himself articulated in the rallying cry, "To the things themselves!" As Heidegger writes in *Being and Time*, "The idea of a '*pure I*' and a 'consciousness in general' contain so little of the a priori of 'actual' (*wirklich*) subjectivity that they pass over, or do not even recognize, the ontological characteristics of facticity and the constitution of the being of Dasein" (SZ 229).

THE WONDER OF WONDERS

While from the air, then, it might look as if Husserl and Heidegger stand shoulder to shoulder in a continuous philosophical tradition, on the ground the differences between them are striking. And yet there is also a way to see their respective projects as flowing from the same deep source: philosophical wonder. Both Plato and Aristotle said philosophy begins in wonder,[24] and for Husserl, "The wonder of all wonders is the pure I and pure consciousness."[25] Indeed, appreciating Husserl's contribution to philosophy, above all the impact his work had not just on Heidegger, but on Sartre and Merleau-Ponty as well, demands that we keep in mind the enigma of intentionality to which he applied himself throughout his career. How is it possible, after all – indeed, how is it even intelligible – that our perceptions, our thoughts, our expectations, our memories, our imaginations are able to reach out beyond themselves, as it were, and come into contact with things other than themselves, alien to them? And is it not simply incoherent to talk about something literally extending or reaching out "beyond itself"? What can that mean? The mystery of intentionality is one of those deep problems in philosophy that make us feel we are pressing up against the limits of thought.[26] What did Husserl make of this so strangely familiar miracle of awareness?

What distinguishes Husserl from his predecessors in modern philosophy, even including his mentor, Brentano, is precisely his willingness to confront intentionality as a genuine phenomenon, indeed as the defining feature of the mind itself. In describing, perhaps even purporting to explain, the relation between mind and world in terms of the mere presence of ideas or representations in consciousness, philosophers and psychologists had simply buried the question, or deferred it indefinitely. For if, contrary to common sense, the true objects of our immediate awareness are not things outside us, but ideas within us, then what is the mind's relation to its own ideas? Is it an intentional relation? If so, then we are back where we started. Or is it literally a kind of containment or presence of some real mental token in the head? Then the enigma of intentionality seems more obscure than ever.

Husserl made great strides in dismantling this epistemological picture by insisting on the *directness* of our awareness of things, and by refusing to evade the problem of intentionality by positing intermediary mental tokens or proxies, which only beg the question how our awareness manages to be an awareness *of* anything in the first place:

It is a serious error to draw any kind of real distinction between "merely immanent" or "intentional" objects on the one hand, and "actual" or "transcendent" objects possibly corresponding to them on the other. . . . One need only say it and everyone will acknowledge *that the intentional object of representation is the same as its actual, on occasion external, object, and that it is absurd to distinguish between the two.* The transcendent object would not be the object of *this* representation at all, if it were not *its* intentional object.[27]

Similarly, in §43 of *Ideas I* Husserl maintains that it is a "fundamental error to suppose that perception...does not arrive at the thing itself." For "perception does not present something not present, as if it were a memory or fantasy; it presents (*gegenwärtigt*), it seizes on a [thing it]self (*ein Selbst*) in its bodily presence" (Id I 78–79). If the concept of directness in perception is intelligible at all, then perception is direct, and Husserl is a direct realist if anyone is.[28]

What is peculiar about intentional attitudes, of course, is that they preserve their intentionality even in the absence of their (putative) objects. You can fear the devil or search for the fountain of youth, even though such things do not exist. This notion of the mind's indifference to the existence of its objects might seem to put the very idea of intentionality at odds with Heidegger's conception of human existence as being-in-the-world. And at one level, of course, it does, for Heidegger would insist that such occasional instances of indifference in no way warrant the global distinction Descartes and Husserl want to draw between subject and object, consciousness and world. And yet the possibility of intending nonexistent objects serves as a reminder of what is truly uncanny about intentionality, namely, that we *understand that entities are*, whether they are or not. We perceive things *as* existing, without having to *judge* that they do.

It should be no surprise, then, that Heidegger was so impressed with Husserl's work, in spite of his misgivings about the systematic direction it took. For although they would disagree immediately about how to proceed in the wake of that initial insight into the mystery of intentionality, they clearly begin with a shared fascination with the fact that it is indeed *we* who somehow register and acknowledge – rightly or wrongly in any particular case – *that* and *what* things *are*. Objects may exist independently of us, but only in experience and understanding is there anything like *truth* and *falsity*, convergence on and divergence from things, disclosedness and concealment.

Heidegger appeals to this, what might fairly be called their common philosophical inspiration, in his remarks on Husserl's second

draft of the *Encyclopaedia Britannica* article on which they tried in
vain to work together in 1927. Where Husserl struggles to pry transcendental subjectivity apart from all objective existence, including the de facto existence of consciousness itself, Heidegger urges
him instead to understand Dasein's worldly and world-constituting
dimensions as necessarily interconnected, as opposed to merely het-
erogeneous principles coinciding in what Husserl elsewhere calls the
"paradox of subjectivity."[29] Heidegger writes:

Transcendental constitution is a central possibility of existence of the factical self. This, the concrete human being as such – as an entity, is never
a "real worldly fact" because the human being is never merely occurrent
but exists. And what is "wondrous" is the fact that the existential constitution of Dasein makes possible the transcendental constitution of everything
positive.[30]

Heidegger's question of being is not the same as what he calls "the
fundamental question of metaphysics," namely, *Why is there something rather than nothing?*[31] That fact is astonishing enough. Even
more uncanny, however, is the fact that one existing entity among
others *knows* that there is something, and wonders *why*. What is
truly wondrous is the possibility of wonder, that is, our understanding of being and our ability to pose the questions of metaphysics.

Common to Husserl and Heidegger, then, there is hardly a "principle" of phenomenology worthy of the name, apart from their shared
commitment to a philosophical program of concrete description, as
opposed to hypothesis and explanation. And yet, beneath the substantive and methodological disagreements that drove them apart,
there is an abiding source of philosophical inspiration moving their
projects from the outset: the enigma of human experience and understanding.

NOTES

1.   Letter to Ernst Laslowski, January 1916. Quoted in Hugo Ott, *Martin
     Heidegger: A Political Life*. trans. A. Blunden (New York: Basic Books,
     1993), p. 90.
2.   Letter to Löwith, 20 February 1923. Quoted in Husserl, *Psychologi-
     cal and Transcendental Phenomenology and the Confrontation with
     Heidegger (1927–1931)*, ed. and trans. T. Sheehan and R. E. Palmer
     (Dordrecht: Kluwer, 1997), p. 17.

3. Letter to Jaspers, 26 December 1926. *Briefwechsel 1920–1963*. ed. W. Biemel and H. Saner (Munich: Piper, 1992). For more on Husserl and Heidegger's personal relations, see Hugo Ott, *Heidegger: A Political Life*, pp. 172–86, and Rüdiger Safranski, *Martin Heidegger: Between Good and Evil*, trans. E. Osers (Cambridge, MA: Harvard University Press, 1998), chapter 5, passim.

4. See *Psychological and Transcendental Phenomenology* for a comprehensive collection of documents pertaining to Husserl and Heidegger's intellectual relationship.

5. See Husserl, "Philosophy as Rigorous Science," in *Husserl: Shorter Works*, ed. F. Elliston and P. McCormick (Notre Dame: Notre Dame University Press, 1981).

6. Heidegger, Preface to Richardson, *Heidegger: Through Phenomenology to Thought* (The Hague: Nijhoff, 1963), p. xiv.

7. Quoted by Sheehan, *Psychological and Transcendental Phenomenology*, p. 4.

8. Husserl, *Die Idee der Phänomenologie: Fünf Vorlesungen*. ed. W. Biemel, 2nd ed. (The Hague: Martinus Nijhoff, 1958), p. 14.

9. In the page-long section of *Twilight of the Idols* entitled "How the 'True World' Finally Became a Fable," Nietzsche infers the incoherence of the metaphysical concept of appearance from the incoherence of metaphysical realism: *"with the true world we have also abolished the apparent one."* In a similar spirit Wittgenstein writes, "To begin by teaching someone 'That looks red' makes no sense. For that is what he must say spontaneously once he has learned what 'red' means. ... Why doesn't one teach a child the language-game 'It looks red to me' from the outset? Because it is not yet able to understand the more refined distinction between seeming and being?" *Zettel*, ed. G. E. M. Anscombe and G. H. von Wright (Oxford: Blackwell, 1967), §§418, 422 (my translation).

10. All translations of Heidegger in this paper are my own. For texts other than *Being and Time*, I also cite the corresponding page numbers of the English translations.

11. By "mere appearance" Heidegger means the appearance of "what is essentially *never* manifest" (SZ 30). What Kant calls a "phenomenon" is a mere appearance in this sense, since what appears through it is a thing in itself, or noumenon, which never shows itself as such.

12. See also his remark a few pages later that the term 'philosophy of life' (*Lebensphilosophie*) "says about as much as botany of plants" (SZ 46). The deeper substantive question, of course, is what *life* is, just as the deeper methodological question for phenomenology is precisely what *description* amounts to.

13. Husserl, *Ideen zu einer reinen Phänomenologie und phänomeno-logischen Philosophie: Allgemeine Einführung in die reine Phänomeno-logie* (Tübingen: Max Niemeyer Verlag, 1913; 5th ed., 1993), p. 302. Hereafter Id I, my translations.

14. Heidegger refers explicitly to this passage years some forty later, SD 69–70; TB 63.

15. Cf. Sartre's example of *seeing* that Pierre is not here in the café at four o'clock, as opposed to judging idly that the Duke of Wellington and Paul Valéry are not. *L'Être et le néant* (Paris: Éditions Gallimard, 1943), pp. 43ff. *Being and Nothingness: An Essay on Phenomenological Ontology*. trans. H. Barnes (New York: Washington Square Press, 1966), pp. 40ff.

16. Husserl, *Logische Untersuchungen*, II/2, 5th ed. (Tübingen: Niemeyer, 1980), §40.

17. Heidegger's account of "being-with" (*Mitsein*) in §26 of *Being and Time* also amounts to a repudiation of what in §44 of *Cartesian Meditations* Husserl calls the reduction to "the sphere of ownness." If Dasein is essentially worldly and social, then, a total abstraction from environmental and cultural significance of the sort Husserl envisions would leave nothing intelligible of ourselves remaining.

18. For several slightly different accounts of the reductions, see also Husserl's fourth version of the article he wrote for *Encyclopaedia Britannica*, §§3–5 and 9, and the reworking of that text in his 1928 Amsterdam Lectures on "Phenomenological Psychology," §§6, 8, 13. Both in *Psychological and Transcendental Phenomenology*.

19. For a discussion of Husserl's account of the body in the Second Book of *Ideas*, see my "The Body in Husserl and Merleau-Ponty," *Philosophical Topics* 27 (1999), 205–26.

20. This distinction between the real and the ideal aspects of mental phenomena had been Husserl's chief concern in *Logical Investigations*, prior to his elaboration of the *epochē* several years later, his subsequent emphasis on the "transcendental" status of subjectivity, and his eventual if only temporary self-identification as a "transcendental idealist," for example the 1929 *Cartesian Meditations: An Introduction to Phenomenology*, trans. D. Cairns (The Hague: Martin Nijhoff, 1960), §41.

21. Sartre, *L'Existentialisme est un humanisme* (Paris: Les Éditions Nagel, 1970), p. 17; *Existentialism and Humanism*, trans. P. Mairet (Brooklyn: Haskell House, 1977), p. 26. In the "Letter on 'Humanism,'" Heidegger rejects Sartre's pithy formulation as the mere reversal of a thesis couched in inappropriate metaphysical terms to begin with. Metaphysical thinking since Plato has maintained that essence precedes existence. Sartre says instead that, for human beings at least, existence precedes essence.

But "the reversal of a metaphysical proposition remains a metaphysical proposition" (GA 9 325; P 250). Neither thesis, that is, properly comprehends the peculiar ontology of the entity whose very being, in being constituted by an *understanding* of being, makes metaphysics possible.

22. See Husserl, *Phänomenologische Psychologie*, ed. W. Biemel *Husserliana* IX (The Hague: Nijhoff, 1968), p. 601; *Psychological and Transcendental Phenomenology*, p. 138.

23. Cf. *Logische Untersuchungen*, II/2, §§30–35, pp. 102–27.

24. Plato, *Theaetetus*, 155d. Aristotle, *Metaphysics*, A 2, 982b12.

25. Husserl, *Ideen zu einer reinen Phänomenologie und phänomenologischen Philosophie. Drittes Buch: Die Phänomenologie und die Fundamente der Wissenschaften*, M. Biemel, ed. *Husserliana* V (The Hague: Nijhoff, 1952), p. 75. Cf. *Erste Philosophie*, I: 27; *Phänomenologische Psychologie*, 174; *Analysen zur passiven Synthesis: Aus Vorlesungs- und Forschungsmanuskripten (1918–1926)*. M. Fleischer, ed. *Husserliana* XI (Dordrecht: Nijhoff, 1970), pp. 13, 21, 213.

26. In a similar spirit, Merleau-Ponty frequently resorts to describing the intentionality of perception and action as a kind of mundane "magic" or "miracle." *Phenomenology of Perception*, trans. C. Smith (London: Routledge, 1962), pp. 94, 112, 139n, passim; *Signs*, trans. R. McCleary (Evanston: Northwestern University Press, 1964), p. 66.

27. Husserl, *Logische Untersuchungen*, II/1, 424–5 (Appendix to §§11 and 20).

28. Notice that direct realism is compatible with the sharp distinction Husserl draws between the immanence of consciousness and the transcendence of the world. The point is not that we are worldly all the way down, as Heidegger would insist, but that intentionality is a feature of consciousness vis-à-vis the world, not an inner relation we stand in to the contents of our own minds.

29. Husserl, *The Crisis of European Sciences and Transcendental Phenomenology: An Introduction to Phenomenological Philosophy*, trans. D. Carr (Evanston: Northwestern University Press, 1970), §53.

30. In Husserl, *Phänomenologische Psychologie*, pp. 601–2; *Psychological and Transcendental Phenomenology*, p. 138.

31. See GA 40; *Introduction to Metaphysics*, trans. G. Fried and R. Polt (New Haven, CT: Yale University Press, 2000), chapter 1.

4   Time and phenomenology in Husserl and Heidegger

One common view of the history of twentieth-century Continental philosophy is as follows. At the beginning of the century, Edmund Husserl, disturbed by what he saw as the increasing relativism and historicism of Western culture, introduced the phenomenological method as a way to ensure that philosophy would arrive at final, incontrovertible truths. Phenomenology means primarily description – description of the things presented in our experience and description of our experience of them. The phenomenological movement was heralded by Husserl's cry, "Back to the things themselves!" Because phenomenology "brackets," or suspends belief in, all metaphysical constructs in order to focus solely on what shows up *as* it presents itself in our experience, its findings are supposed to be apodictic, beyond all possible doubt.

According to the standard story, the early Heidegger came along and raised questions about the viability of Husserlian phenomenology by taking an "interpretive" turn. What is most important about Heidegger's hermeneutic ontology, so the story goes, is his recognition of the significance of the finitude, worldliness, and historicity of our human predicament – the recognition that our access to things is always colored and preshaped by the sense of things circulating in our historical culture. The story then concludes with poststructuralists and various postmodern thinkers detecting a nostalgia for metaphysics even in such Heideggerian concepts as worldliness, finitude, and history. Jacques Derrida especially points out that Heidegger still seems to be trapped in essentialism and totalization, twin sins of the very "metaphysics of presence" that his hermeneutic approach was supposed to displace.

Critical to this story is the assumption that Heidegger's ontological hermeneutics succeeded in undercutting Husserl's phenomenology. Yet a closer look at Heidegger's early work suggests that the real story is not so simple. Thinkers such as Hans-Georg Gadamer and Paul Ricoeur, who build on Heideggerian hermeneutics, make it clear that their own thought presupposes phenomenology.[1] And Heidegger himself, who is supposed to have broken with Husserl, bases his hermeneutics on an account of time that not only parallels Husserl's account in many ways but seems to have been arrived at through the same phenomenological method as was used by Husserl. So important is the phenomenological account of time to recent Continental philosophy that even Derrida's well-known critique of the metaphysics of presence was initially formulated through a reflection on the Husserlian account of temporality.[2] The phenomenology of time, then, can serve as a key for understanding not only the relation of Husserl and Heidegger, but the development of Continental thought throughout this century as well. The differences between Husserl and Heidegger are significant, but if we do not see how much it is the case that Husserlian phenomenology provides the framework for Heidegger's approach, we will not be able to appreciate the exact nature of Heidegger's project in *Being and Time* or why he left it unfinished.

In this essay I will focus on Heidegger's early phenomenological account of time and its roots in the work of Husserl. It was Husserl himself who first undertook the project of phenomenological ontology – that is, the attempt to clarify the being of entities in general – and, as we shall see, he saw the phenomenological account of time as central to this project. Heidegger's *Being and Time*, with its explicit task of relating being to time, follows in the footsteps of Husserl's project. By showing the relation of Heidegger's thought to Husserl's, and by showing the similarities of both to the transcendental philosophy of Kant, I hope to show why time has such a central role in Continental thought. But it will also become clear that serious problems arise for the accounts of time in both Husserl and Heidegger. These problems can help us understand why *Being and Time* was never completed. But they also point to deep questions about the possibility of phenomenology generally, and they can clarify the motivation for some of the recent moves made by poststructuralists, postmodernists, and (to use Richard Rorty's self-descriptive oxymoron) postphilosophical philosophers.

HUSSERL AND TIME

Let us look first briefly at Husserl's project. Husserl hoped to provide a formal ontology linked with material ontologies of the various regions, or sorts, of entities. Ontology, as we have already noted, is the account of being in general and concerns essences and fundamental categories. A "formal" ontology treats the basic "forms" or structures of being in general, while a "material" ontology considers how these more general forms are filled out "materially," so to speak, in the various main types of entities. Husserl uses the geographic metaphor of "region" for these main divisions of entities – hence, the expression "regional" ontology, which is interchangeable with "material" ontology. In *Formal and Transcendental Logic* (1929) Husserl writes that the task of formal ontology is to "state what holds good for any objects whatever, any object-provinces whatever, with formal universality, in what forms they exist or merely can exist."[3] What the phenomenologist asserts in formal ontology must be true of any entity whatever. Sometimes Husserl speaks of formal ontology as treating the basic concepts (*Grundbegriffe*) or categories of objectivity as such. He thinks of being as objectivity. The notion of "object" and "objectivity" is a broad one, for "object" means more than the objects of perception. There are higher objectivities for Husserl such as those established in mathematics or the social sciences.

Husserl also refers to his project of phenomenological ontology as transcendental. We have just noted that phenomenology describes "objects" (in a broad sense). In order to justify these descriptions and in order to understand ourselves as describers, phenomenological description requires, in addition to careful and methodical description, a consideration of what description is and how it is made possible – that is, phenomenology considers the condition of the possibility not only of objects but of the description of objects. Thus, Husserlian phenomenology is "transcendental" in much the same sense as this term is defined in Immanuel Kant's introduction to the *Critique of Pure Reason*, the work that inaugurates the tradition of transcendental philosophy: "I entitle *transcendental* all knowledge which is occupied not so much with objects as with the mode of our knowledge of objects in so far as this mode of knowledge is to be possible a priori."[4] By *a priori* is meant knowledge gained of objects, as well as of the knower or subject, by way of rigorous philosophical reflection and not through the empirical sciences or generalization from everyday experience. *A priori* literally means "prior to experience." Such knowledge is said by Kant to be "necessary," while Husserl calls it "essential." According to the above citation, transcendental philosophy is particularly concerned with the self or subject who carries on this rigorous reflection. Kant was so much concerned with the subjective conditions of objective knowledge that he came to assert that we can never know things as they are in themselves, but only as they appear to us conditioned as we are by certain subjective cognitive structures. Here we find the most important disagreement of Husserl with Kant, for Husserl thinks we can know things as they are in themselves. How Husserl squares this commitment with his own version of "transcendental idealism" is something we cannot consider here. Many of his closest students did not think he could; others defended his attempt. In any case, it is important to note that not only objectivity, but also subjectivity must come under scrutiny for a fully justified philosophy. The bare rational self or ego considered only in terms of its basic cognitive structures (or forms) is called the "transcendental ego" by both Kant and Husserl.

Further comparison with Kant's *Critique of Pure Reason* might be helpful here. Formal ontology corresponds to what Kant attempted to accomplish in the Transcendental Analytic, that is, the *a priori* knowledge of an "object in general." For Husserl and Kant, the key to the discovery of the basic forms of objectivity is formal logic. Kant in the metaphysical deduction held that any formal logical law can be converted into an equivalent formal ontological law. Like Kant in the *Critique,* Husserl in *Formal and Transcendental Logic* begins with formal logic and moves on to "transcendental logic," which is formal ontology, though Husserl wants to avoid what he thinks is Kant's naive acceptance of traditional logic as a ground from which to derive the forms of objectivity. Formal logic for Husserl serves rather as a starting point and clue for the development of a formal ontology. For Kant, the regional or material ontology based on the "formal ontology" of the *Critique* would be the metaphysics of nature. According to Husserl's *Ideas II* and *Ideas III*, the task is somewhat more variegated since there are three primary regions: material nature, animate nature, and souls (or persons), and accordingly three regional ontologies: physics, somatology, and psychology.[5]

If we pursue the Kantian analogy further, we find that Husserl's *Formal and Transcendental Logic* also requires a supplementary transcendental aesthetic and a schematism, two other important components of Kant's *Critique.* The intelligible aspect of experience, treated in formal and transcendental logic, needs to be related to the sensible aspect of experience. In the conclusion of this work Husserl acknowledges this need. Recall that the Transcendental Analytic of the *Critique* is preceded by the Transcendental Aesthetic, which is an account of space and time. Recall further that after the argument of the metaphysical and transcendental deductions establishing the basic categories, there follows a section entitled "Schematism," which shows how each of the categories, initially presented independent of time, is in the end nothing other than a form or configuration of time. The categories are temporalized, though they are not "spatialized" because, for Kant, all experience is temporal but not all experience is spatial. Time has priority for Kant as it does for Husserl and, as we shall see, for Heidegger. Another way to express this is to say that the categories are nothing other than rules of temporal configuration (or schematization). To give two Kantian examples, the category "substance" is the "permanence of the real in time" and the category "cause" is "succession subject to a rule."[6]

Husserl had long been involved in the attempt to provide a phenomenological account of space and time, of the spatial and the temporal, but these accounts were never adequately integrated into the larger project.[7] As we have just noted, time has an important priority for reasons similar to those given by Kant. Husserl, however, never shows us how his formal objectivities or categories are temporalized. But he does return again and again throughout his life to the theme of time because he becomes convinced that time is the basic form of all experience. One might not infer the importance of this topic for Husserl from his publications, since his only publication in this regard is *The Phenomenology of Internal Time Consciousness*, lectures from 1905 with addenda. These lectures first appeared in 1928 (the year after the publication of *Being and Time*) under Heidegger's editorship. Husserl had asked Heidegger to publish his 1905 lectures some time earlier, and Heidegger agreed on the condition that he first complete *Being and Time.* It seems that this was Husserl's last attempt to remind Heidegger of Husserl's account of time and Heidegger's debt, as a phenomenologist, to this account. In the introduction to the first English translation of these lectures (1964), Calvin Schrag comments that the materials of the volume were "compiled and published" by Heidegger.[8] Though Heidegger did edit and publish them, it has become clear that he did not "compile" them. Husserl's assistant, Edith Stein, had compiled the manuscript, and Heidegger did relatively little but pass it on to the publisher. After 1928 the only further publication of Husserl's work on time was the republication of that edition together with extensive addenda that doubled the size of the volume.[9] But from approximately 1917 on Husserl returned in his writing again and again to time as his central and most basic theme. In the early twenties, Stein compiled another manuscript dedicated to the theme of time, and Husserl touted it at one point as his most important work. He attempted unsuccessfully to get first Roman Ingarden and then Eugen Fink to publish it.[10] This manuscript, usually referred to as the "Bernauer" or "L" manuscripts, remains unpublished, as does a later collection of manuscripts on the phenomenology of time from the late twenties and early thirties called the "C" manuscripts.

The phenomenology of time requires, of course, that we ignore our ordinary or scientific assumptions about time and attend rigorously to the lived experience of time. We must bracket "objective" time, as Husserl calls it in those lectures, to see how time is constituted immanently in experience – hence the title "inner time conscious-ness." On this account, we experience time primarily as the present "now." Yet it is important to see how fundamentally significant for Husserl is the rejection of the "objective" view of time as a puncti-linear row of "nows" that stretch both back and forward to infinity and constitute a one-dimensional line, the objective time line. In contrast with this one-dimensional view of time, Husserl offers us a three-dimensional view. The present, for him, is not the nondimen-sional point of the instantaneous now. Rather, we might say that the present is "thick" to the extent that, *within* the present, we find both the past and the future; that is, we find all three dimensions of time. Any present moment, according to Husserl, has what he calls "retentive" and "protentive" aspects. In other words, any moment is what it is in virtue of what it retains of the past (retention) and what it anticipates of the future (protention). Every present moment carries these two aspects as essential to its being what it is *as* present. Crudely expressed, they are part of the present. The past is retained *as* past in the present, and the future is anticipated *as* future in the present. Husserl says that these three dimensions constitute the present. As time passes, each present (this "thick" present with three dimensions internal to it) is retained in the succeeding moment – retentionally. This retention and anticipation is, in our everyday experience, unconscious, but philosophical reflection shows it to be constitutive of the structure of any moment. Husserl distinguishes retention from memory, for in memory the past moment is experienced simply as past and not as part of the present. In similar fashion, he distinguishes protention from hopes and expectations, the conscious focusing on some imagined future event as future and not as a constitutive aspect of the present. There is a certain symmetry in the constitution of the lived experience of time; both protention and retention are essential to the account and both are distinguished, respectively, from memory and hope. Yet there is at least one other important element of Husserl's account: the flow of time is directional. Time flows ineluctably toward the future; it is not reversible. This understanding of the present as constituted by retention and protention is the core of Husserl's contribution toward a philosophy of time.

The centrality of "the present" for this analysis has led to Derrida's criticism of Husserl's phenomenology as a "metaphysics of presence." The primary point of this critique is that the Husserlian account suppresses absence. Rudolf Bernet, who has developed Derrida's critique, writes, for example, that absence cannot so easily be disposed of and that it returns to haunt Husserl – in his words, "the repressed element returns."[11] I would suggest on the contrary that absence is not ignored in Husserl's account, but is considered an essential element of the present. Retention and protention are modes of the presence of the absent (the past and the future) as well as the absence of the present (the past as no longer present and the future as not yet present). Husserl's thickening of the moment is just the attempt, I would argue, to render the temporal character of human experience as the ineluctable interplay of presence and absence.

When, in his *Ideas I* of 1913, Husserl comes to reflect on the phenomenological approach of the time lectures and of his earlier ground-breaking work, *Logical Investigations* (1900–1), he defends his method in the problematic terms of "transcendental idealism." Here as before, Husserl distinguishes phenomenological time and objective (or cosmic) time. Phenomenological time, he writes, is "the unitary form of all lived experience (*Erlebnisse*) within *one* stream of lived experience (*Erlebnisstrom*), i.e., within *one* pure Ego."[12] "Phenomenological" or subjective inner time is given methodological precedence over "cosmic" or "objective" time, which is said to be constituted in inner time.

Husserl's form of idealism follows from the methodological precedence of subjectivity. In the words of *Formal and Transcendental Logic*, "The whole of phenomenology is nothing more than the self-examination on the part of transcendental subjectivity."[13] Only transcendental subjectivity, Husserl claims in the concluding sections of this book, exists "in and for itself." And so he writes that "the ultimate grounding of all truth is a branch of the universal self-examination that, when carried through radically, is absolute. In other words, it is a self-examination . . . which leads me to the grasping of my absolute self, my transcendental ego."[14] This egological self-interpretation of phenomenology Husserl calls the Cartesian way into phenomenology.[15]

When we turn to the question of time, we find that instead of time being just another object constituted in the thematic field of transcendental subjectivity, subjectivity is itself radically temporal. Frequently Husserl simply identifies time with subjectivity (much as Kant sometimes identifies "inner sense" with the subject). At other times it seems as though Husserl is arguing that the ego, as absolute, is not itself temporal but is the source of temporality. He speaks of the ego as the origin (*Ursprung*) and the source (*Quelle*) of time.[16] As the *Quelle,* which also means "spring," the ego is the spring of the stream of time. The spring itself does not flow but is constantly in the same place. Thus, in these same manuscripts Husserl often refers to the ego, which is this source or spring, as the *nunc stans,* or "standing now," a phrase that goes back to medieval scholasticism. It is the now that originates the flow of time but is not itself in time – hence its "standing" character. The standing now is the ego's primal form of being. As "standing," it constitutes the flow of time.

We have just noted how one approach of Husserl is to say that subjectivity (or the ego) is radically temporal. Taken this way, it is just
the flow of time. A second approach sees the ego as somehow outside
of time constituting time. But as Husserl develops his treatment of
time in the late C manuscripts, he comes to think of time in relation
to the subject in a third way – that is, neither (1) as subjective, nor
(2) as originating in atemporal subjectivity, but (3) as somehow prior
to the distinction between subject and object. In this third way time
itself comes to be understood as that primordial source (*Ursprung*)
out of which the ego and object poles emerge. The ground of the ego is
time; time itself is "radically pre-egological." It is "a temporalizing-
temporal primal occurring [*Urgeschehen*] which does not spring from
egological sources (*aus Quellen des Ichs*); it therefore occurs without participation of the ego."[17] Again and again Husserl here takes
up the notion of the "standing and perduring primal now," which
itself is not in time but temporalizes – which is to say that it is the
source of time. What is flowing and ephemeral is grounded in what is
permanent. The permanent standing now is the absolute, which has
its own ground in itself and is not grounded in anything else. It is,
he writes, without ground (*grundlos*); as constituting, it is not itself
constituted. We could say of time, seen in this way, what Heidegger
later comes to say: "Temporality temporalizes" (BT 377).[18]

Thus we can see that when Husserl develops his treatment of
time, he is ambivalent about the relation of transcendental subjectivity and temporality. Are subjectivity and temporality identical? Or
is temporality prior to subjectivity and its objective correlate, that
is, is it a pre-egological source out of which subjects and objects are
constituted in time? If it is, then it is no longer appropriate to characterize the most important level of phenomenological analysis as
egology. The egological project breaks down. The paradox of subjectivity (being both a subject for the world and an object in the world)
becomes the paradox of time (being both a nontemporal source of the
world and a temporal objective characteristic of the world). Further,
we are led to ask whether phenomenology can resolve these questions. Is Husserl still maintaining a phenomenological standpoint
when he discusses the primal ego as a monad or when he develops
the concept of the standing now? That is, is this still a description of
what is immanent in consciousness? Another way to see this difficulty is to recall the title of the early lectures on time: "Inner Time

Consciousness." Time on the later account just discussed is neither "inner" nor a function of "consciousness." These two closely related sorts of questions – the ontological and the methodological – are two aspects of what might be called Husserl's deep problem with time.

There is a second important complex of ontological problems with respect to time that we should note here, if only briefly. It concerns not the deep question of the nature of time itself, but the "higher-level" question of the temporal constitution of different sorts of entities. As we have seen, Husserl is committed to the thesis that human experience is radically temporal. All aspects of experience have a temporal genesis – hence the importance of *genetic* (as opposed to static) phenomenology. But what are the relations between (1) time as such, (2) natural time (which Husserl sometimes calls "space-time" [*Raum-Zeit*]), and (3) historical time? Husserl never treats this question extensively, though he does distinguish natural and historical time as different modes of time. Sometimes Husserl seems to be working toward a treatment of natural and historical time that would render them equally fundamental, each with its own basis in the temporality of transcendental subjectivity. More often he seems to be working toward the view that historical time is founded on natural time. That which mediates the two is human bodiliness. We historical beings are also natural and bodily beings.

To sum up, we have seen how the transcendental phenomenology of Husserl was confounded by the problem of time in at least two ways. The deeper ontological problem of time concerns the relation of temporality and subjectivity, and it leads us to the limits of an egological phenomenology. The higher-level difficulty concerns the relation of natural time and historical time to each other, and to time as such. We can find parallel problems concerning time in Heidegger's ontology, problems both methodological and substantive.

THE EARLY HEIDEGGER AND TIME

Some of the disagreements between Husserl and his protégé Heidegger result from a fundamental misunderstanding on the side of Husserl as to the nature of Heidegger's project. Husserl had established a phenomenological research program in the early twenties in Freiburg. Based on his method, this research program was to be a cooperative one. Husserl, as founder of the method, understood his own task as doing the ground-breaking work in formal ontology and methodology. He hoped his followers and students would develop the regional ontologies. His journal, theYearbook of Philosophy and Phenomenological Research, would publish the results of their research.[19] He hoped that Heidegger, whom he considered his most able follower, would provide the regional ontology for history and the historical sciences.[20] Sometimes Heidegger himself presented his own project in this way, but in fact what Heidegger chose to do instead was to pursue the ontology of time itself (what I have called the deeper ontological question) rather than the regional ontology of the historical realm. From Husserl's perspective, however, Heidegger asserts of time itself and being as such what might well be appropriate of the historical region. For Husserl, such a move historicizes being in such a way that we are left only with anthropology, historicism, and relativism. It seems that he understands Heidegger this way because Heidegger's starting point is Dasein, defined as being-in-the-world, a being-in-the-world that is thoroughly historical.

Whatever Husserl's assessment of Heidegger's attempt, a careful look at Heidegger's early project shows that he gets caught up in methodological and ontological problems similar to those of Husserl. Heidegger never completed this project and later abandoned it. We can find it developed in *Being and Time* (1927) and in the early published works that immediately follow it: *Kant and the Problem of Metaphysics* (1928) and *On the Essence of Reasons* (1928), as well as in the recently published lectures delivered when he was at Marburg from 1922 to 1928. Though we cannot here examine the problems and the parallels in detail, we can provide a short sketch.

Heidegger's early project: ontological, phenomenological, transcendental, and hermeneutic

The question for *Being and Time* is the question of being. In the Introduction, Heidegger tells us that he seeks to clarify the meaning of being (BT 31). This is his question, he tells us further, because it is the most basic question. All other questions presuppose that there is being, and all the sciences make assumptions about being. Since the work is about being and not about this or that sort of being or entity, his task is, in the first place, ontology. He calls the work "fundamental ontology" because it is concerned with the most basic question and because ontologies of the various sorts of entities necessarily presuppose it:

The question of Being aims therefore at ascertaining the a priori conditions not only for the possibility of the sciences, which examine entities as entities of such and such a type, and, in so doing, already operate with an understanding of Being, but also for the possibility of those ontologies themselves which are prior to the ontical sciences and which provide their foundations.   (BT 31)

We find here a clear parallel with Husserl's project. Fundamental ontology concerns the meaning of being as such. It establishes the basis for the ontologies of various regions of being, which, in turn, provide the philosophical basis for the sciences, clarifying the assumptions and basic concepts of the sciences. By "ontical" in the passage just quoted Heidegger means that which is concerned primarily with entities and not with being as such. The regions that Heidegger has in mind are those of history and nature. The regional ontology of each would provide the appropriate philosophical basis, respectively, for the human sciences and for the natural sciences. It is not clear whether Heidegger ever intended for himself to develop the regional ontologies, but it is clear that it is in relation to possible regional ontologies that Heidegger conceived of his task in *Being and Time* as fundamental ontology.[21]

Being and Time is also a work in transcendental phenomenology in much the same sense as the philosophy of Husserl. Phenomenology, Heidegger writes in the Introduction, "signifies primarily a *methodological conception.* This expression does not characterize the *what* of the objects of philosophical research as subject-matter, but rather the *how* of that research" (BT 50). It is a descriptive method that allows things to show themselves for what they are. To call it "transcendental" is to adopt terminology from Kant and Husserl, which means, as we saw earlier, "*a priori*" or necessary knowledge. As the preceding quotation states, fundamental ontology hopes to establish the *a priori* or necessary conditions for the regional ontologies and the sciences. In other words, fundamental ontology would develop the background required for the regional ontologies to proceed. It should establish the basic concepts and assumptions of these fields by making clear the basic or "formal" structures of being.

Heidegger expresses his debt to Husserl in a footnote about the *a priori*, in which he writes that "Husserl has given us the necessary tools" (i.e., a method) for discovering the *a priori*. Here Heidegger asserts, "A-priorism is the method of every scientific philosophy which understands itself" (BT 490).

Heidegger's phenomenological method is also transcendental in the further related sense discussed earlier that such a method is as much concerned with the structures of subjectivity as it is with the structure of objectivity. In the Introduction Heidegger, self-consciously using Kantian language, criticizes Kant for not adequately treating the "subjectivity of the subject" (BT 45). Heidegger sets out to deal with this aspect in a better way than his predecessors Kant and Husserl. Important to Heidegger's improved approach is to drop the language of subject and subjectivity, object and objectivity. When Heidegger uses these terms, they are almost always in quotation marks to indicate that he is referring to the way things have been discussed in the philosophical tradition. One of the chief reasons Heidegger is so keen on avoiding this language is that to start with this duality of subject and object seems inevitably to lead to an unbridgeable gap between them, so that the logical outcome is subjectivism in some form or other. One prominent form of subjectivism related to the question of knowledge is representationalism, the view that the subject makes the world available to itself by means of representations. Since these representations are inevitably of its own making, there is no way of knowing in the end whether the representations mirror nature truthfully or are "merely" useful fictions. Kant's denial of any knowledge of the way things are in themselves is a good example of one such view. For Kant, neither the transcendental ego nor things in themselves are in time. Rather, time is a function of our subjective capacity to represent things to ourselves, so that the things we experience are shaped by our activity of representing. Though Heidegger did not regard Husserlian phenomenology as a form of representationalism, he did think that Husserl's language, particularly the language of subjectivity and objectivity, often betrayed Husserl's best insights.

So Heidegger sets the stage for his own attempt to clarify the meaning of being by giving an account of what he calls *Dasein*, the "there" (*Da*) where being (*Sein*) shows itself. Before directly addressing the central theme, being, we are to consider first where it is that being shows itself. And this means examining ourselves, since being is "an issue" for us in a way that it is not for other entities. To consider this is to consider the conditions that hold for there to be meaning. *Being and Time* sets for itself the task of establishing the meaning of being, and it addresses the question of meaning before it directly addresses being. Much like Kantian transcendental philosophy, Heidegger's fundamental ontology asks about the conditions of the possibility of knowing the subject matter of the inquiry before it takes up the subject matter, though Heidegger focuses on "understanding" instead of "knowing" with its implied relation of a subject to an object.

It is important to note that Heidegger's study of Dasein is a study of us *insofar as* we can come to terms with being. Heidegger's study or phenomenological account is about Dasein, being-there, and not about human being or human nature. Thus, it is not an attempt to give a full account of what it means to be human. According to Heidegger, his account in *Being and Time* should provide the appropriate basis or background for such an account, but this work is intended to be fundamental ontology, not philosophical anthropology.

The most important single fact about *Being and Time* is that it is unfinished. This work, as envisaged at the end of its introduction (BT 63 – 4), was to have two parts, each with three sections. The published text provides only the first two sections of Part I, which means that only the preparatory treatment of Dasein is accomplished. The third section, which is entitled "Time and Being" and which was to elucidate directly the concept of being, was never satisfactorily completed. In the end we have only the account of Dasein.

Time and the analysis of Dasein

Let us look at what is accomplished in the published text, that is, the analysis of Dasein, and notice the centrality of the theme of time. In the Introduction Heidegger declares that

in contrast to all this [the history of philosophy], our treatment of the question of the meaning of Being must enable us to show that *the central problematic of all ontology is rooted in the phenomenon of time, if rightly seen and rightly explained,* and we must show *how* this is the case.   (BT 40)

Heidegger shows "how" time is central through the description, or "Interpretation," of Dasein. Because we are temporal beings, our ability to encounter things *as* such and such is also temporal. Dasein is thoroughly temporal, and thus Dasein's understanding is temporal. And so must be our understanding of being. Thus, to cite the Introduction once again, "the Interpretation of Dasein" is to be accomplished "in terms of temporality (*Zeitlichkeit*)" (BT 63). In this way time comes to serve "as the transcendental horizon [or context] for the question of Being" (BT 63). Accordingly, it is clear that the phenomenology of time is at the heart of Heidegger's ontological project.

The first half of the text ("Preparatory Fundamental Analysis of Dasein") provides what could be called a "static" structural or "formal" account of Dasein. The second half ("Dasein and Temporality") then shows how these structures must be understood as temporal structures. Heidegger himself calls the analysis formal but explicitly rejects calling it categorial. Categories, as we will see later, pertain to nature but not to Dasein. Heidegger names the formal structures and defining concepts of Dasein "existentialia." Dasein, as already noted, is defined as being-in-the-world. The hyphens, almost as awkward in German as they are in English, are indicative of the fact that, as Dasein, self and world are a unity. The world is not something external but is constitutive of Dasein. We are born into a world whose history and culture help make us who we are. The Christian view that "we are in the world, but not of the world" is transformed. We are both in and of the world. "Worldliness" is an ontological property of Dasein; it is our context of involvements.

The preparatory analysis of Dasein is concerned primarily with an explication of what it means to be in the world, of how we find ourselves in relation to things in the world in "average everydayness." This "being in relation" is our worldliness. Being-in is seen to have two principal structures: understanding and state of mind. We understand ourselves and our world in terms of our practical involvements and projects. In understanding, we are ahead of ourselves, writes Heidegger. State of mind is the way we find ourselves already disposed toward things in this way or that. ("Disposition" might be a better translation for *Befindlichkeit* than is "state of mind.") The analysis concludes with an attempt to show how both of these are aspects of care (*Sorge*), which best captures not just one aspect of Dasein but Dasein in its entirety. Heidegger defines care as "ahead-of-itself-Being-already-in-(the world)-as Being-alongside-(entities encountered within the world)" (BT 237). This is a tripartite definition which says that Dasein has the following structures: (1) ahead of itself (understanding), (2) already in (disposition), and (3) alongside. Heidegger often refers to these three structures as existentiality, facticity, and fallenness.

For our purposes here it is most important to note that these three aspects of Dasein are given a temporal interpretation in the second half of Being and Time: "The primordial unity of the structure of care lies in temporality" (BT 375). The three aspects of care correspond to the three dimensions of time: the future (ahead of itself), the past (facticity), and the present (fallenness). The unity of Dasein is founded on care, whose unity in turn is founded on temporality. Any moment of human experience has these three dimensions. Heidegger talks about this three-dimensionality of the lived experience of time as the "ecstatic" unity of time. By this he means how each of these three dimensions is distinctive and distinguishable from the other two, that is, how each dimension "stands out" from the others. "Standing out" is the literal meaning of "ecstasy." By the ecstatic character of time Heidegger also means to describe how any moment is a crossing point of past and future. The present bears within it the past and the future. Past and future make it up. This connectedness and ecstatic unity he sometimes refers to as the "transcendence" of time and the transcendence of Dasein, which is essentially temporal in just this way. The present moment goes beyond, or "transcends," the merely present in the way that it, as present, is at the same time future and past. In this way Heidegger recovers and maintains in the context of his own work the Husserlian insight about what I have called the thick unity of time. He follows Husserl as well in criticizing the view of time that thinks of it as an infinite series of points, of nows – what Heidegger calls "now-time" (Jetzt-Zeit; see BT §81).[22]

What most obviously distinguishes Heidegger's account from Husserl's is the way, on Heidegger's account, Dasein can live out its temporality as authentic or inauthentic. Thus, there are authentic and inauthentic modes of understanding and disposition.[23] For the most part, according to Heidegger, Dasein is inauthentic and fallen, caught up and lost in the present in a way that cuts it off from its authentic future (its "ownmost possibility") and its past. What the future holds for any and every Dasein is death. Another definition of Dasein is therefore provided: being-toward-death. In the authentic moment, we recognize and accept our mortality. Heidegger's story of Dasein is, in this regard, not so unlike the Christian story of fallen human nature (though Heidegger denies that his story is just another version of original sin). While the present has priority for the inauthentic, the future has priority for the authentic life. Notice that this gives priority to understanding over disposition, since Heidegger connects the understanding with the future and disposition with the past.

Time and the meaning of being

Being and Time, as we have already noted, never gets so far as to address directly the meaning of being, but instead concludes with the question: "Is there a way which leads from primordial *time* to the meaning of *Being?*" (BT 488). Approximately a year after his completion of the text of *Being and Time*, in the lectures of the summer semester of 1927, *Basic Problems of Phenomenology*, Heidegger explicitly sets for himself the task of finding this way from time to the meaning of being and so of completing Part I of *Being and Time* with a full-fledged ontology.[24] Yet the reader (and the student in the lecture hall) is disappointed, because the lectures break off just before the designated treatment.[25] We can find in these lectures, nonetheless, indications of the approach Heidegger was taking and the problems he faced. As required, he approaches the question of being through time. The shift from the analysis of the temporality of Dasein to the temporality of being is marked terminologically by the shift from the standard German *Zeitlichkeit* (temporality) to the Latinate *Temporalität* (temporality). The temporality of Dasein is *Zeitlichkeit*; the temporality of Being is *Temporalität*. A question the text does not answer concerns what the consequences of this shift might be. Is the analysis of the temporality of being merely an extension of the account of time in *Being and Time*, or are there important differences in the two accounts? Heidegger's comment in the *Letter on Humanism* makes us wonder about the shift when he says of the third section of Part I, "Time and Being": "Here everything is reversed" (BW 208). This comment, however, comes after the great turn in Heidegger's thought and his abandonment of the project of fundamental ontology. There is no talk of "reversal" in *Basic Problems.*

What we do find Heidegger doing in *Basic Problems* is giving an account of being in terms of its regions that is consistent with the stated project of developing a fundamental and regional ontology. The regions are divided according to their type of temporality. There are two main regions, each with two subdivisions: (1) that within time (*das Innerzeitige;* subdivisions: nature and history) and (2) the atemporal (*das Unzeitige;* subdivisions: extratemporal and supra-temporal). We might be inclined to object to these divisions of being and the notion of the atemporal, since Heidegger has rejected eternal truths and asserted that we are to understand being only through temporality. Yet the discussion here in *Basic Problems* does not deny the temporality of all understanding. It insists, rather, that the atemporal can be understood only in terms of temporality. Being and time are not simply equivalent, though the understood meaning of being must, in some way, be temporal.

Working out these divisions while at the same time maintaining the unity of being clearly posed serious problems for Heidegger. This is indicated directly in the title of the lecture series, *The Basic Problems of Phenomenology,* and by the introductory outline for the lectures, which indicates that Part II was to be concerned with thematic problems in laying out the basic structures of being, while Part III was to be concerned with the methodological problems of Heidegger's phenomenological approach to the question of being. Heidegger's designation of these problems for his fundamental ontology reminds us of what we have called Husserl's "deep" ontological problems of theme and method. Though we can distinguish the problems this way, that is, as thematic and methodological problems, they are closely related. Their close relationship can best be seen if we ask how the method allows us to make this thematic distinction of regions within being. Does the method take us outside both regions such that from the perspective of being we view these regions and differentiate them? In other words, is the distinction made "externally"? Yet if we are speaking from the perspective of Dasein, are we not making the distinction from "within time"?

In *Basic Problems* as well as in *The Metaphysical Foundations of Logic,* lectures of a year later (the last lectures at Marburg, summer

semester, 1928), Heidegger is clearly concerned with the methodology of phenomenology and its specifically scientific character. As
scientific, phenomenology according to Heidegger is necessarily neutral and indifferent with respect to its subject matter or themes.[26] In
other terms, phenomenological methodology is inevitably objectifying. In the context of his discussion of the regions of being according
to time as "in time," "out of time," and "above time," we must wonder about the justification of the distinctions and how it is that these
regions become objects of study. This is particularly problematic if
we recall Heidegger's oft-stated criticism of objectivism and his treatment of "indifference" in *Being and Time* as an inauthentic quality
of Dasein. Were we simply and straightforwardly to follow Heidegger's suggestion that indifference is inauthentic, it would seem that
phenomenology must be inauthentic. This is, of course, absurd in
the context of Heidegger's project. We are left to wonder if, in the
projected last part of *Basic Problems,* where Heidegger was to have
addressed these questions of methodology at length, he would not
have reinterpreted indifference for the philosophical attitude. Perhaps the indifference and neutrality of philosophy are significantly
different from the indifference of inauthentic everyday experience.
But nowhere in Heidegger's early work is a satisfying account to be
found.

The ontological difference between nature and history

Another major problem with the project of *Being and Time* that
becomes quite apparent in *Basic Problems* concerns the distinction
within the temporal region of being, the distinction we have referred
to as that between nature and history. Earlier we referred to Husserl's
treatment of this distinction as his "higher-level difficulty." Anyone
who has attended to Heidegger at all knows how important for his
work – early, middle, and late – is the ontological difference (*ontolo-
gische Differenz*), the difference between being and beings. But there
is another ontological difference that plays an equally significant but
systematically quite different role for the early Heidegger. In German
he calls this the ontological *Unterschied*, as opposed to the ontological *Differenz*. This less discussed difference, the *Unterschied*,
is the difference, just mentioned, between nature and history. Heidegger charges the philosophical tradition with indifference to this

ontological difference (*Unterschied*) and rests much of his own claim to philosophical originality on just this distinction.

He recognizes, of course, that something like this distinction has commonly been made in modern philosophy. Kant's distinction between persons and nature is the most pertinent example because of Kant's lasting influence in philosophy. Heidegger objects to the way that Kant handles the distinction, because, according to Heidegger, the distinction implicitly collapses inasmuch as persons (historical beings for Heidegger) are treated much like natural entities. Though Kant means to present the person as quite different from natural entities (most importantly different, since persons are free and morally responsible), he does not, according to Heidegger, adequately sustain the distinction. Ultimately, the person is treated as a different sort of natural entity. It is worth noting here that Heidegger is almost never critical of the Kantian treatment of nature. In fact, he sometimes affirms it. The mistake he sees being made is the dominance of the treatment of nature over the treatment of persons. Kant's first *Critique* is a regional ontology of nature for Heidegger, and it is within this frame that persons are presented. Thus, for Heidegger the Kantian account undermines the distinctiveness of Dasein even though it hopes to affirm it. Heidegger would succeed where Kant had failed. The difference (*Unterschied*) between history and nature, as Heidegger hopes to develop it, is so great that it is, he asserts, far greater than the traditional ontological difference drawn between God and man, between creator and creation.[27] His distinction is so radical that it would obviously disallow the Husserlian understanding of ourselves as natural beings.

Inasmuch as this distinction between two regions of beings is developed and prepared in fundamental ontology, that is, in the treatment of the meaning of being, we could say that with this ontological distinction Heidegger is attempting to drive the Kantian distinction of person and nature (implicit even in Descartes's *res cogitans – res extensa* distinction) back into the very treatment of being as such. But if the difference between the two is so great, then working out a unitary concept of being will become exceedingly difficult. And Heidegger explicitly set himself the task of working out a unitary concept of being, though he never succeeded in developing it. The "higher-level" problem of the relation of Dasein and nature in terms of temporality is at the same time a "deep" problem in the basic

account of the meaning of being as such. We should recall that the
immediate context for establishing this unitary concept of being is
the account of temporality that Heidegger begins in the *Basic Problems* lectures. Let us look a little more closely at this distinction,
which is so important to Heidegger's project.

First of all, we should note that Heidegger abandons, for the most
part, the term "nature," presumably because both in ordinary and in
philosophical usage the term has received interpretations that cover
over the distinction Heidegger wants to make. Thus, the distinction
that Heidegger draws in the temporal region "within time" is that
between Dasein (which we have used here as a technical term and
have not translated) and *Vorhandensein* (translated as "presence-at-
hand" in *Being and Time* and "being-extant" in *Basic Problems*).
According to Heidegger's sketchy account of the distinction in *Basic
Problems* (for which we can find the ground laid in *Being and Time*),
Dasein is a "who," not a "what." The formal structures laid out in
the phenomenological account of it are "existentialia" (a term coined
by Heidegger), and not "categories." Presence-at-hand (or extantness)
is appropriately considered a "what," and the appropriate philosophical treatment of it is by way of categories. That is, the philosophy of
nature was treated appropriately in modern philosophy (and particularly in Kant) by way of categories.[28] Methodologically the accounts
of the two regions are parallel (who/what; existentiale/category), but
we might ask about their intersection. That is, how is it that Dasein
knows or uses the extant? In more traditional terms, we might wonder how it is that we, as persons, find ourselves in a world not only
of persons (and history) but of nature as well.

It would be helpful here to look back at the treatment of extantness
in Section 15 of *Being and Time* (and again later in §69 b), where Heidegger treats our encounter with things in the world as exemplified
by work in a workshop. In the first place, according to the account
given there, we experience things practically as equipment (*Zeug*).
The equipment of the workplace is either "handy" (*zuhanden*, translated as "ready-to-hand" in *Being and Time*) or "not handy." Only
when the tool breaks down or cannot be found do we "theoretically"
attend to it as being present in a certain way, that is, as having certain
properties, or as not being present at all. Heidegger insists here that
"handiness is the way in which entities as they are 'in themselves'
are defined ontologico-categorially" (BT 101). With this assertion he

also rejects the suggestion that handiness be understood merely as "a way of taking them, ... a subjective coloring." Nonetheless, he also says that "yet only by reason of something present-at-hand [or "extant"] 'is there' anything handy" (BT 101). He then asks a question he does not answer: "Does it follow ... that handiness is ontologically founded upon presence-at-hand?" At stake in this question is the question as to which is ontologically prior – our practical approach to things or our theoretical approach.

It is telling that the opening scene of *Being and Time* is that of the craftsman at his workbench surrounded by his tools, and not a scene in a more "natural" setting. Tools, like the hammer or turn signals of an automobile (Heidegger's examples), are human constructs and are defined, as Heidegger points out, by a network of (human) involvements. But when Heidegger turns to another example and another scene, the scene of a farmer in Swabia (where Heidegger was born and grew up) surveying the sky for signs of rain, it seems to be an example of a different kind, since we should ask whether the wind can be understood as equipment in the same way that the hammer can. If it cannot be, it is hard to accept the claim that Heidegger makes here: "Only by the circumspection with which one takes account of things in farming is the south wind discovered in its Being," that is, as the herald of rain and good crops (BT 112).

The workshop and the fields are part of Dasein's world. Dasein is ontologically defined as worldly, as we have already seen; it is being-in-the-world. On the other hand, nature, or extantness, Heidegger tells us, does not belong ontologically to the world. Worldliness (*Weltlichkeit*) is not an ontological property of nature. Yet Dasein encounters nature only in the world. Accordingly, Heidegger calls nature (or the extant) as encountered in the world "intraworldly" (*innerweltlich*, translated as "innerworldly" in *Being and Time*). Yet to cite Heidegger once again: "Intraworldliness does not belong to nature's Being" (BP 169). We are left to ask, If nature is encountered only as intraworldly, yet intraworldliness does not belong to nature's being, do we encounter nature as it is in itself? This question is promoted by Heidegger himself when he insists with the example of the south wind in Swabia that only through farming do we discover it "in its Being." With the difference between Dasein and nature as great as it is, how can nature be what it is "in its Being" in Dasein's world?

This great difference between Dasein and nature is most starkly asserted in terms of time in the concluding paragraph of *History of the Concept of Time* lectures, where Heidegger simply states that "they [the movements of nature] are as such completely *time-free.*" He also says here, consistent with what we have already noted, that nature is "encountered 'in' the time which we ourselves are" (HCT 320). But we must recall the assignment of nature as a subdivision to the region "within time" in *Basic Problems.* Nature is "within time" only *as encountered* in Dasein's world. As encountered, it becomes a part of history and culture. Accordingly, *in Being and Time* we can find Heidegger saying that "even nature is historical." He quickly adds, however, that "it is *not* historical, to be sure, in so far as we speak of 'natural history'" (BT 440). The examples of nature as historical are cultural: the battlefield and the site of a cult. It is in the sense referred to as "natural history" that Heidegger later says in *Basic Problems* that "culture *is* not the way that nature is" (BP 169). We are left to wonder how Heidegger can say in *Basic Problems* that nature (or the extant), if it is indeed "time-free" and so different from Dasein, can together with Dasein constitute the region of being that is within time.

Their difference is emphasized in still another way in the *History of the Concept of Time,* where Heidegger utilizes Wilhelm Dilthey's distinction between understanding and explanation in saying that nature is explainable (*erklärbar*) but not understandable (not *verständlich*). Nature is "the incomprehensible [*Unverständliche*] pure and simple" (HCT 217). Yet to say that nature is not to be understood runs against the claim that the Swabian farmer knows the south wind "in its Being." We might wonder about the less practical, and more theoretical, knowledge of weather of the natural sciences. Presumably meteorology is derived from the more primordial experience of living with the weather. Clearly for Heidegger both the natural sciences and farming are aspects of culture, they have their place in the world and are historical. But nature is not "worldly," as we have just seen. This is made clear when Heidegger asserts that, though there is no world without Dasein, there would be nature without Dasein: "Nature can also be when no Dasein exists" (BP 170). Nature, then, is not merely a projection of the natural sciences or of our practical involvements with it. But it seems that our understanding of it, such as it is, comes from our practical involvements.

This raises the question as to whether nature for Heidegger can be encountered only instrumentally. It also suggests a parallel with the Kantian view that we cannot know things as they are in themselves, but only insofar as they appear to us.

On this reading of Heidegger's claims, it is tempting to sever the question of being (ontology) from the question of knowledge (epistemology). Yet the central motive of phenomenology for both Husserl and Heidegger was to overcome this break and to make the claim that in some important sense we can know things in themselves. Heidegger thinks that Husserl's transcendental idealism does not succeed, and that Husserl falls back into a version of Kant's idealism. As a result, Heidegger set out to develop a phenomenology that would not give precedence to the subject in the way that Kant and Husserl (in his egological approach) did. Yet he finds himself in a position with important parallels to Husserl and Kant. In one sense, Heidegger's problem is greater than Husserl's insofar as the difference between Dasein and nature is so much greater. Whereas Husserl thinks we are natural beings, this does not seem to be the case according to Heidegger.

CONCLUSION

Our discussion may seem to have taken us away from the theme of time. Yet we should recall that Heidegger (like Husserl before him) draws the distinction between extantness (or nature) and Dasein within the context of a treatment of the temporality of being. The boundaries of the regions of being are, in the first place, temporal boundaries, and the problems this creates parallel what I have called Husserl's "higher-level" problem of time. Both Dasein and extantness are "within time," yet we have just seen some of the problems that Heidegger faces in this regard.

Perhaps the clearest indication of Heidegger's initial orientation and its problems is his statement in the conclusion of the *History of the Concept of Time* lectures that "Dasein...temporalizes" (HCT 319). This is like Husserl's according time to the function of transcendental subjectivity. Dasein (in the case of Heidegger) or the transcendental ego (in the case of Husserl) originates time. Yet in *Being and Time* Heidegger writes that "temporality (*Zeitlichkeit*) temporalizes" (BT 377). And, further, he summarizes his position in *Being and Time* with the statement, "Time is primordial as the temporalizing of temporality, and as such it makes possible the Constitution of the structure of care" (BT 380). We can note again here the Husserlian language of "constitution" and "structure." But, more important, we see that it is time that makes care and Dasein possible. Time is somehow prior to Dasein. We are reminded of the priority of time over subjectivity in Husserl's late manuscripts. In *Basic Problems* Heidegger talks similarly about the temporalization of temporality (BP 319).

We might want to consider a later remark that seems to demand a basic reappraisal of Heidegger's approach, though we cannot fully address it here. In the late lecture "Time and Being" (1962), Heidegger tells us that "the attempt in *Being and Time*, section 70, to derive human spatiality from temporality is untenable" (TB 23). What Heidegger means by this largely unexplained comment is not entirely clear. But insofar as it challenges the Kantian precedent followed by both Husserl and the early Heidegger of giving both methodological and ontological priority to the temporality of inner sense, this comment challenges substantively the phenomenology of both Husserl and the early Heidegger. Husserl had considered the consciousness of temporality as the fundament of all experience of ourselves and the world. The early Heidegger rejects the language of consciousness, yet he follows Husserl in considering time to be primordial. If spatiality were, to use the Heideggerian term, equiprimordial, the phenomenological project would require substantial revision. The early Heidegger clearly does accord priority to time and does, in the words of the later Heidegger cited earlier, attempt "to derive human spatiality from temporality." It is hard to envision what shape an ontology based as much on spatiality as temporality would take. Perhaps the later Heidegger is attempting this in some way or other. Notions like "region" (*Gegend*, not *Region*) and "nearness" are clearly prominent, and the concept of *Zeit-Spiel-Raum* accords equal prominence to space and time.

Thus, we can say of Heidegger's early phenomenological attempt that his way of starting with Dasein and not transcendental subjectivity does not resolve adequately the problems that Husserl faced concerning temporality, but instead leads him to correlative ones. Methodologically, his account of being seems to require an indifference that is unjustifiable on his own account of Dasein.

Thematically, his attempt at a unitary concept of being is made hopelessly difficult by the great difference between Dasein and extantness. This difficulty is related to the first insofar as the methodological priority of Dasein makes it difficult to make sense of the extant as independent of Dasein, though such independence is ontologically, if not epistemologically, required. It is perhaps these difficulties that led Heidegger later to write that "the ecstatic-horizonal temporality delineated in *Being and Time* is not by any means already the most proper attribute of time that must be sought in answer to the Being-question."[29]

As a consequence, the planned shift or reversal from Dasein's temporality (*Zeitlichkeit*) to the temporality of being (*Temporalität*) cannot be satisfactorily carried out. Another turn is needed – one that leaves behind the project of a phenomenology that is transcendental, ontological, and hermeneutic. In his later writings Heidegger abandons the planned defense of the necessary apriorism of "scientific" philosophy. He abandons "philosophy" for "thought."

Yet it is precisely the central role given to time by Husserl and Heidegger that has brought about our current insight into the historicity and finitude of all human experience and all philosophical inquiry. Whether one sees this as ground for further philosophizing, or, with the later Heidegger, as leading us to a postphilosophical project of "thinking," or as a warrant for a new stance of postmodern "playfulness" and "decentering," it is clear that the phenomenology of time, with all its problems, has redefined our understanding of what philosophy can be.

NOTES

1. Gadamer tells us that one of his goals in *Truth and Method* (New York: Seabury Press, 1975) was to measure up to the "conscientiousness of phenomenological description which Husserl has made a duty for us all" (p. xv). He also says that "it is true that my book is phenomenological in its method" (p. xxiv). Ricoeur explicitly asserts that hermeneutics presupposes phenomenology in his essay "Phenomenology and Hermeneutics" in *Hermeneutics and the Human Sciences*, ed. and trans. John B. Thompson (Cambridge: Cambridge University Press, 1981), pp. 101–28. Moreover, time is a theme central to both Ricoeur and Gadamer. Note Ricoeur's recent three-volume work *Time and Narrative* (Chicago: University of Chicago Press, 1988). I have shown the significance of an

understanding of temporality for Gadamer's hermeneutics in my essay "Philosophical Discourse and the Ethics of Hermeneutics," in *Festivals of Interpretation*, ed. Kathleen Wright (Albany: State University of New York Press, 1990), pp. 63–88.

2. See *Speech and Phenomena*, trans. David Allison (Evanston, IL: Northwestern University Press, 1973).

3. Edmund Husserl, *Formal and Transcendental Logic*, trans. Dorion Cairns (The Hague: Nijhoff, 1969), p. 120. For the discussion of formal ontology in Husserl's earlier work of 1913, *Ideas I*, see §10, "Region and Category." This is available in English translation as Vol. 2 of *Edmund Husserl: Collected Works*, trans. F. Kersten (The Hague: Nijhoff, 1982).

4. Immanuel Kant, *The Critique of Pure Reason*, trans. Norman Kemp Smith (New York: St. Martin's Press, 1965), p. 59 (B 25 according to the standard pagination of the second edition of the *Critique*).

5. *Ideas II* and *Ideas III* are available in English translation in *Edmund Husserl: Collected Works*, respectively, as Vol. 3 (trans. Richard Rojcewicz and André Schuwer) and Vol. 1 (trans. Ted Klein and William Pohl). These two volumes were never published by Husserl and were first published in German in 1952 and 1971 (*Husserliana*, Vols. IV and V [The Hague: Nijhoff]). In a footnote in *Being and Time* Heidegger gratefully acknowledges his familiarity with these then-unpublished manuscripts (BT 489).

6. See the end of the chapter on the schematism in the *Critique of Pure Reason*, pp. 184–7.

7. For Husserl's treatment of space and spatiality, see his lectures from 1907, *Ding and Raum*, Vol. 16, of his collected works, *Husserliana* (The Hague: Nijhoff, 1973) – not available in English translation.

8. See Schrag's Introduction to *The Phenomenology of Internal Time Consciousness*, trans. James S. Churchill (Bloomington: Indiana University Press, 1964), p. 12.

9. Edmund Husserl, *Husserliana*, Vol. 10: *Zur Phänomenologie des inneren Zeitbewusstseins (1893–1917)*, ed. Rudolf Boehm (The Hague: Nijhoff, 1966). This has recently been translated by John Brough (with a complete retranslation of the 1905 lectures) as Vol. 4 of *Edmund Husserl: Collected Works – On the Phenomenology of the Consciousness of Internal Time (1893–1917)* (The Hague: Nijhoff, 1991). See Brough's helpful introduction concerning the history of the edition.

10. See Karl Schumann, *Husserl Chronik* (The Hague: Nijhoff, 1977), p. 325.

11. See his "Is the Present Ever Present?" *Research in Phenomenology*, 12 (1982):85–112, p. 87.

12. *Ideas I*, p. 192; translation revised.

13. Husserl, *Formal and Transcendental Logic*, p. 273.

14. Ibid., p. 274.
15. See §13 of Husserl's *Cartesian Meditations* (1931), trans. Dorion Cairns (The Hague: Nijhoff, 1960): "We are envisaging a science that is absolutely subjective.... It begins in pure egology." It should also be noted here, however, that the Cartesian approach is not the only way into phenomenology. The "way in" attempted in the *Crisis of the European Sciences* (1936) is through everyday experience, what Husserl calls the "life-world." Even when adopting the Cartesian mode, Husserl is substantially critical of Descartes.
16. There are many examples of this in the unpublished C manuscripts. For example, in No. 71, p. 5 of the typed transcription, Husserl writes that "the ego in its most original originality is not in time." And in No. 7 II, pp. 11–12, he discusses the absolute ego as the source or spring (*Quelle*) of all phenomena. Husserl wrote almost daily in shorthand, returning always to the theme of time. These manuscripts from the late twenties and early thirties are repetitive and sometimes contradictory, since Husserl is carrying out thought experiments trying to find out where different approaches might lead him. For example, Husserl sometimes comes close to identifying this "standing now" with God – Leibniz's God – as a way to consider the higher-level subjectivity that is not temporal but constitutes the temporality of subjectivity. In other contexts, he considers the possibility of an ultimate unconscious behind consciousness – e.g., *On the Phenomenology of the Consciousness of Internal Time*, p. 394.
17. C Manuscript No. 10, p. 25.
18. "*Die Zeitlichkeit ... zeitigt sich*" (SZ 328). It is important to note that what is the subject and agent here is temporality, not the ego (as it is sometimes for Husserl) or Dasein (as it is for Heidegger in the earlier lectures, *History of the Concept of Time*). In the same context as this quote concerning *Zeitlichkeit*, Heidegger asserts that "primordial temporality" is prior to Dasein (BT 380–2).
19. *Being and Time* first appeared in Vol. 8 (1927) of this yearbook, together with Oskar Becker's phenomenological account of mathematics. Becker was another of Husserl's assistants.
20. In the twenties Husserl often made the comment to Heidegger: "You and I are phenomenology." See Dorion Cairns, *Conversations with Husserl and Fink* (The Hague: Nijhoff, 1976), p. 9.
21. Note the comment about the possibility of working up a philosophical anthropology on the basis of *Being and Time* (BT 169–70). Philosophical anthropology is to be understood as a regional ontology. See the discussion of this in *Kant and the Problem of Metaphysics* §37. In *History of the Concept of Time*, lectures from 1925 that are an earlier version

of *Being and Time,* Heidegger begins and ends with a discussion of the distinction of nature and history. The subtitle of the published edition and the announced title of the lecture series is "Prolegomena to a Phenomenology of History and Nature."

22. In *The Metaphysical Foundations of Logic* (lectures of 1928) Heidegger acknowledges the importance of Husserl's account for his own view of time and temporality: "With regard to all previous interpretations, it was Husserl's service to have seen these phenomena [the unity of time and its various aspects] for the first time" (MFL 204).

23. The attentive reader is rightly puzzled about the modes of Dasein in *Being and Time.* Usually Heidegger writes as though there are two modes of Dasein, authentic and inauthentic, but sometimes he suggests that there are three. The third is neither authentic nor inauthentic but indifferent. I discuss this puzzle in "The Problem of *Indifferenz* in *Sein und Zeit,*" *Philosophy and Phenomenological Research,* 43 (September 1982): 43–58. I show how Heidegger's ambivalence between two or three modes is related to the methodological problems of the phenomenological method that are discussed briefly later.

24. A footnote to the first sentence of the lectures reads simply, "A new elaboration (*Ausarbeitung;* more literally, "working out") of division 3 of part 1 of *Being and Time.*"

25. The outline of the projected lectures in the introduction has three parts, each with four chapters: Part 1, a historical introduction; Part 2, the direct discussion of being; and Part 3, a treatment of phenomenology and its method. The lectures go only as far as the first chapter of Part 2, which discusses the ontological difference. The next (and undelivered and unpublished) chapter was entitled "The Problem of the Basic Articulation of Being." And the successive two chapters were to treat the unity of being and the truth of being.

26. See the discussion of thematization and objectification in science in *Being and Time* (BT 412–15). In *Being and Time* Heidegger never discusses the "scientific" and objective status of fundamental ontology, but he does discuss it briefly in *Basic Problems* (BP 281–2, 320–4). See also my "Problem of *Indifferenz.*"

27. "Existence [*Existenz*] and extantness [*Vorhandensein*] are more disparate than, say, the determinations of the God's being and man's being in traditional ontology" (BP 176).

28. See the treatment of categories and existentialia in *Being and Time,* §9.

29. See the letter to William Richardson of 1962 published as the preface to Richardson's book, *Heidegger: Through Phenomenology to Thought* (The Hague: Nijhoff, 1963), p. xiii.

5 Laying the ground for metaphysics: Heidegger's appropriation of Kant

A philosophy comes to have true validity, when its own power is released and the possibility is provided for it to deliver a shock and to make a difference.

(PIK 3)[1]

HEIDEGGER AND KANT'S "COPERNICAN REVOLUTION"

In Section 4 of *Being and Time*, Heidegger proposes that in order to answer the question what being means, we must first investigate the nature of our own existence. But why should this be so? At first blush, it is highly counterintuitive. After all, being is, in the words of *Being and Time*, "what determines entities as entities" (SZ 6).[2] Being is whatever is characteristic of anything simply in so far as it *is*. Ontology is a general account of being. To do ontology, one might therefore naturally think, we must survey the full range of entities and generalize to an account of what all entities have in common. In other words, ontology could be an intellectual discipline parallel with biology and philology: a direct study of some domain of objects. Whereas biology studies objects in so far as they are alive, ontology would study them in so far as they quite simply *are*. Now, we do not have to do a preliminary investigation into our own existence in order to do biology; so, why should such a procedure be called for in the case of ontology?

In order to understand Heidegger's motivations here, we must explore his encounter during the 1920s with the thought of Immanuel Kant. It was Kant, after all, who first advocated a "Copernican revolution" in philosophy: "We must therefore make trial whether we may not have more success in the tasks of metaphysics, if we suppose that objects must conform to our knowledge."[3] In short, if we presuppose that objects must conform to our knowledge, then we can develop a general account of objects, an ontology, by exploring the nature of our knowledge of them. Indeed, Heidegger characterizes the intention of Kant's *Critique of Pure Reason* as the attempt to "lay a ground for metaphysics": "The following investigation is devoted to the task of interpreting Kant's *Critique of Pure Reason* as laying the ground for metaphysics and thus as placing the problem of metaphysics before us as a fundamental ontology" (KPM2 1). Thus, we can see that Heidegger's announced ontological strategy in §4 of BT is fundamentally Kantian: to explore the meaning of being by developing an account of our understanding of being.

Such an account of our understanding of being can be offered, roughly, either *a priori* or empirically. Consider first a broadly empirical and/or sociological version of a "Copernican" ontology. We can ask ourselves, for example, what understanding of being is implicit in modern physics. Ontology might seek to give expression to this understanding of being embedded in scientific practice and theory, to put it into words hermeneutically. Proceeding this way, moreover, we realize that there is undoubtedly a *history* to the understanding of being implicit in physics, that physicists have held differing and incompatible visions of what it is to be a physical thing over the centuries. What is more, one might argue plausibly that our commonsense understanding of being lies closer to the sort of ontology presented by Aristotle, according to which the world is made up of substances with powers and properties, rather than the obscure posits of contemporary physics. By reflecting carefully upon all these differing and in some ways rival understandings of being, we can produce a catalog of understandings of being. The job of the philosopher might well then be to organize and edit this catalog, introducing whatever coherence she can find in it.

Throughout the enterprise, note, the empirical or sociological ontologist is beholden to the understanding of being implicit in the theories and practices that she studies. The philosopher cannot weigh into debate herself and introduce her own ontology. She cannot claim to have discovered the meaning of being from out of her own resources. She cannot proceed, in short, *a priori*. To be able to do so would require that she be in a position to argue that her own ontology somehow defeats or trumps the understandings of being implicit in science, common sense, theology, historiography, and so on. The philosopher would have to claim that her own contribution to ontology is somehow immune to empirical refutation.

Now, Heidegger seems to claim precisely this *a priori* authority for his ontological reflections.

The basic concepts of philology cannot be clarified with the help of philological methods; and the basic concepts of history cannot be determined by researching the sources, let alone be grasped by such research.... Latent in every science of a realm of entities there always lies a regional ontology which belongs to this science, but which can never in principle be developed by this science.   (PIK 25)

Heidegger adds in *Being and Time* that,

Such laying the ground for the sciences is fundamentally unlike the "logic" that limps along afterwards, which investigates the contingent condition of a science with respect to its "method." It [namely, Heidegger's ontological reflection] is productive logic in the sense that it leaps ahead into a determinate region of being, discloses it for the first time in its ontological constitution, and makes the structures that are disclosed in it available to the sciences as transparent directives for inquiry. So, e.g., what is philosophically primary is not a theory of historical concept formation, nor a theory of historical knowledge, nor even a theory of history as the object of the discipline of history, but rather the interpretation of authentically historical entities in terms of their historicality. Thus, the positive results of Kant's *Critique of Pure Reason* rest upon an approach to working out what belongs to a nature in general, and not upon a "theory" of knowledge. His transcendental logic is an *a priori* material logic of the region of being of nature.   (SZ 10–11)

Note that in the second of these two passages, Heidegger does not just say that giving hermeneutic expression to an understanding of being implicit in a science requires a special methodology. He insists more strongly that ontology is not beholden to the "contingent condition" of a science, that the results of ontological investigation are normative for or controlling of the ontologies implicit in current scientific practice. The ontological foundations of empirical science are not scientific, but rather *a priori* and philosophical. What could possibly justify such an immodest assumption?

If we turn to Heidegger's interpretation of Kant in order to answer this question, as Heidegger himself suggests in the passage just quoted from *Being and Time*, we meet an immediate obstacle: the premier expression of Heidegger's Kant-interpretation, *Kant and the Problem of Metaphysics* (1929), is an immensely obscure book. It has, moreover, given many fair-minded readers the impression of being not so much an interpretation, as an abuse of Kant. Kant is made to assert many doctrines that Heidegger himself held, but which it is far from clear Kant embraced. Further complicating matters, Heidegger was frying more than one fish with his work on Kant. He was, indeed, exploring Kantian possibilities for grounding the enterprise of ontology, but he was also waging a war with neo-Kantianism.[4] Fortunately, since 1977 we have had access to Heidegger's Winter semester 1927–28 lectures, *Phenomenological Interpretation of Kant's "Critique of Pure Reason."* These lectures are far more lucid and direct than *Kant and the Problem of Metaphysics*, and by looking at them closely, we may hope to reconstruct Heidegger's answer to our question.

TIME AND BEING

We have seen that Kant's "Copernican" strategy served as a guiding clue for Heidegger, as he set out to develop and ground his own approach to ontology. Heidegger did not, moreover, limit his appropriation of Kant to Copernican methodology; he also took over a fundamental aspect of Kant's ontological doctrines: that being is to be articulated in terms of time. The result of Kant's "analytic of the understanding" is that the world consists of causally interacting substances in time.[5] Temporality is an essential characteristic of anything that can be an object of our knowledge. We see here already a necessary connection between ontology and time. For Kant, however, the connection runs deeper: not only must any object of human understanding exist in time, but what it is for such an object *to be* an object is articulated *in terms of time*.

To be is, roughly, to be a causally interacting substance, according to Kant.[6] But what is it to be a substance? To be a substance, Kant argues, is to be an item that necessarily persists through change. Contents of experience that change are properties of underlying substances that do not change. For example, the color of a penny changes from copper to green. The color is a property of the penny, because while the color changes, the penny persists. Or at least, so says our commonsense ontology. Kant embraces the basic analysis here, but argues that the only item that persists through all changes is Newtonian matter. Thus, the things that populate our commonsense ontology, such as pennies, chairs, tables, human bodies, and the like, are not in the end viable candidates for substantiality. The only thing that survives scrutiny, that passes the test of persistence, in order to qualify as a genuine substance, is Newtonian matter, which is conserved in all material changes according to the science of Kant's day. Standing back from the details, we can see that substantiality is defined in terms of time for Kant: a substance is something that *persists through change.*

To offer such a time-oriented ontology, it should be clear, we must have some reason for being confident that everything that is exists in time. If to be is to be a substance, and if to be a substance is to *persist through change,* then in order to be, an item must exist in time. To be is in part to be in time. In the language of *Being and Time,* "time is the horizon for the understanding of being" (SZ 15–19). This draws our attention to the doctrinal aspect of Heidegger's appropriation of Kant. Like Kant, Heidegger believes that time is the horizon for the understanding of being. Thus, Heidegger must also have Kant's confidence that everything that is somehow exists in time.[7]

Why should we be so confident about this, however? Put a little differently, how can we know *a priori* that everything that is exists in time? Kant's way of framing the assertion is this: "time is an *a priori* representation." Put a little more colloquially, we can say, "we know *a priori* that all objects are temporal." How do we know this?

TIME, INTUITION, AND APRIORITY IN KANT

In order to explore Kant's argument for the apriority of the representation of time, we must first ask ourselves, What is it for a representation to be *a priori* anyhow? According to a common and traditional understanding of the matter, knowledge (or a claim to knowledge) is *a priori,* just in case it does not depend upon the data of experience for its justification. The data of experience do not provide us our *reasons to believe* what we know *a priori.* Let us call this *epistemological apriority*. Mathematics is usually thought to be epistemologically *a priori*, because for example, counting pennies neither confirms nor possibly refutes arithmetic truths, such as that $4 + 4 = 8$. We know that $4 + 4 = 8$, but not on the basis of the data of experience. We shall see that this epistemological apriority is *not* the key to understanding the representation of time. Nevertheless, we must stay with epistemological apriority a little longer in order to sort out how we should understand the apriority of the representation of time.

Epistemological apriority characterizes a piece of knowledge in virtue of the nature of its justification. Hence, to be epistemologically *a priori*, a piece of knowledge must have a justification (or must somehow be self-justifying). Justification is a relation among beliefs in which one belief or set of beliefs, the justifier(s), provides *reason* to believe another belief, the one justified. The justifier must imply the belief justified or in some other way make it more likely that the justified belief is true. For example, my belief that I read in the paper this morning that Barry Bonds hit yet another home run last night makes it more likely that it is true that he did. The beliefs that stand in relations of justification must all be capable of being either *true* or *false*, or else they could not imply one another or make one another more likely to be true. In Kant's jargon, this is to say that the representations that stand in justificatory relations are *judgments*, or are *objectively valid* (CPR B140, §19).[8] It follows that in order for a representation to be a candidate for epistemological apriority, it must be a judgment.[9]

In order to understand what Kant means by the term "judgment," we might consider a linguistic analogy (derived from Kant himself: A69/B94). The most basic form of linguistic expression that can be true or false is a complete sentence. Although we sometimes regard sentence fragments as true or false, that is only because we interpret them as elliptical for complete sentences. We may think of complete sentences as linguistic analogs of Kantian judgments. Every complete (basic) sentence, moreover, has a predicate, whether that be a simple property ascription (e.g., "... is green"), a sortal (e.g., "... is a cat"), or a more complex relation (e.g., "... is five feet to the left of ... "). Concepts are predicates, and the understanding uses these predicates when it applies them to or predicates them of some object. Such acts of predication are judgments, and like the complete sentences on which they are modeled, they may be true or false.[10]

Thus far we have seen that knowledge that is epistemologically *a priori* consists of judgments justified independently of the data of experience. So, for the representation of time to be epistemologically *a priori* would then be for it to be a judgment that can be justified independently of the data of experience. Here, however, we run into trouble, for Kant *denies* that the representation of time is a judgment, and this would appear, given the account so far, to disqualify it from being *a priori*. Let us, therefore, explore the nature of the representation of time in order to determine whether and in what way it can be *a priori*.

In one sense it is clear that Kant denies that the representation of time is a judgment. He officially classifies both it and the representation of space as "*a priori* intuitions," and intuitions are not judgments. In an intuition an object is "given" or presented to us. For this reason, Kant characterizes our general capacity to have intuitions as "receptivity," a form of cognitive passivity. A judgment, by way of contrast, is a reflective representation that predicates a concept of an object. The capacity to judge belongs to the understanding or spontaneity, not to receptivity.

The matter, however, is not so simple, for Kant also insists that intuitions are *implicit* judgments: "The same function which gives unity to the various representations *in a judgment* also gives unity to the mere synthesis of various representations in *an intuition*" (CPR A79/B104–105).[11] Our experience of objects is conceptually mediated. I do not experience a raw "this," but rather a "this-such." I experience, for example, a white cat before me. In this experience I take this thing before me *as* a cat, which is to say that I implicitly predicate " . . . is a cat" of it, implicitly judge of it that it is a cat. It is for this reason that we may speak of our visual experiences (our intuitions) as deceptive or false: the judgments they imply may be wrong; the thing I see before me may not be a cat. In short, intuitions are neither concepts nor judgments, but they do use concepts and are implicitly judgmental. If this is so, furthermore, then intuitions might be epistemologically *a priori* in an indirect sense: the judgments they imply might require no data of experience in order to be justified.

It is possible to defend an interpretation of Kant's account of the representation of time along just these lines. Kant does classify intuitions as a species of "cognition" (*Erkenntnis*), which for him means that they are objectively valid, that is, about objects. They are, thus, at least implicitly judgments (CPR A319–320/B376). What is more, he does say that "different times are but parts of one and the same time; and the representation which can be given only through a single object is intuition" (CPR A31–32/B47). This is to say the representation of time presents a single object to us, namely, time as a whole, and for this reason, it is an intuition. Since the presentation of time to us in our experience cannot be understood literally to be a judgment, Kant would have to mean that it is an implicit judgment, just as the presentation to me of my cat is an implicit judgment.

It is also possible, however, to press an interpretation according to which the representation of time is not even implicitly a judgment, and this is what Heidegger in fact does. Kant does sometimes characterize the representation of time as an intuition, but in other places he classifies it as a "form of intuition." Of the forms of intuition he writes, "These are indeed something, as forms of intuition, but are not themselves objects which are intuited" (CPR A291/B347). The forms of intuition do *not* present objects; they are, therefore, not themselves intuitions. This implies in turn that the representation of time is not epistemologically *a priori*. Recall, to be epistemologically *a priori*, a representation must be (either explicitly or implicitly) a judgment. Yet Kant does say that the representation of time is *a priori*. How can this be? Clearly, to avoid contradiction here, we must find a non-epistemological sense of apriority at work in the *Critique*.

What is the non-epistemological sense of the *a priori* in Kant, according to Heidegger? The representations of space and time function in experience in a special way: they *enable* experience. "Philosophically fruitful is that meaning of *a priori* according to which *a priori* means 'enabling'" (PIK 73). The forms of intuition (space and time) enable intuition by "determining" it. He writes, " . . . the term *form* designates *what determines (determining)*" (PIK 86). In what sense do the representations of space and time determine experience? By serving as their "ground." So, when Kant describes the representations of space and time as "necessary" representations that "underlie all intuitions" (CPR A24/B38, A31/B46), Heidegger glosses his point thus:

Positively, this means that space and time underlie what is present-at-hand as its "ground." . . . This is a distinctive term for Kant and means functioning as ground, i.e., making possible that things as such show themselves and appear as present-at-hand *here, there, now*, and *then*.   (PIK 79, translation altered)

In what way do the representations of space or time determine or ground empirical experience? Speaking of space, Heidegger writes,

In the empirical intuition of certain things that are ordered and present-at-hand in spatial relations, there is necessarily an advance viewing of pure spatial relations of space as such which is free of objectification. This advance viewing of the non-objectively disclosed space makes possible the empirical intuition of what is spatially present-at-hand. This means that it is this "having a view of" which *guides* empirical intuition in advance, *leads it, and in this sense determines it*. This "having a view of space," which occurs in advance and is non-objective, is a basic structure of that encounter which allows what is spatially present-at-hand to be encountered. As such, this "having a view" *determines* the empirical intuiting and for this reason can be called "form."   (PIK 89)

And again:

Only with an advance view of spatial relations *as such* – e.g., the three dimensions – is something disclosed to us in advance *wherein*, or *in terms of which*, what is encountered can be encountered as ordered by this *definite* next-to, before or in front of, and behind.   (PIK 88)

To explain this line of thought, Heidegger uses the following example:

Granting a manifold of balls of different color, weight, size, and material, and as regards each property there are respectively several specimens – all lying around pell-mell, chaotically and disordered. We can now order these balls with respect to their color, weight, material structure, or size. In order to be able to order these balls at all, we must look in advance at the intimate connection according to which these balls must be brought together. We must view the unity with regard to which the chaos is to be separated and brought together.   (PIK 88)

A natural, but as we shall see, misleading, way to explain the example offered would be this: in order to bring the manifold of balls into order, we must have a preconception of the ordering principle according to which the balls are to be ordered. Thus, if we are going to order them by color, we need an ordering principle something like this: "by color in order of the rainbow." Now, such a principle is essentially articulated in concepts: it involves at least the concepts of color and the rainbow. So, the example suggests that in order to bring a manifold into order, we need a conceptually articulated principle by which to order the manifold.

ARE SPACE AND TIME FORMAL OBJECTS?

If this were the way to understand Heidegger's example, his interpretation would be in serious trouble. Consider what the preceding paragraph implies. Space and time are forms of intuition that determine experience by serving as ordering principles for experience. As we have seen, ordering principles such as "by color in order of the rainbow" are conceptually articulated: they are rules or guidelines for ordering a manifold of data according to a certain *conception* of how the data is to be organized. Although a principle such as "by color in order of the rainbow" is not itself a concept, it *is* a directive to organize data *so that* a concept or conceptual construction applies to it. Now, in what way would the representations of space and time be *a priori*, if this model of their determining function were sound? Presumably, to say that such principles hold *a priori* is to say that we can know independently of experience that the data of experience can be ordered according to space and time, or more colloquially, ordered *in* space and time, ordered spatially and temporally.

This approach suggests, then, that space and time are special sorts of object after all, roughly, formal objects. Consider by way of analogy the concept of a baseball team. Right before the start of a baseball game, we can take the ten starting players on the Baltimore Orioles and order them in several different ways. We can have them line up by height, by age, by weight, and so on. We can also have them line up by position. The relations among the positions are a formal structure that can be occupied in principle by any ten people (on an American League team!). When we think about a baseball team, that is, *any arbitrary* baseball team, we are thinking about this formal structure. Similarly, perhaps space and time are formal structures in this way. They are systems of relations among positions, now positions in space and time, that can be occupied, in principle, by any given objects.

Heidegger rejects this analysis of the representations of space and time. Understanding how and why he does so is crucial to seeing what he thinks he has learned from Kant. To pursue this point, we have to introduce one more distinction. Some formal objects are entirely conceptual in nature: they are logical constructions out of concepts. Consider as an example the generic concept of chess. As has been pointed out repeatedly in the contemporary literature, the generic concept of chess is one that can be realized in a great variety of concrete objects. The standard conception of chess, as a game played on a middle-sized checkerboard with pieces of the typical shapes is *just* the standard conception. Generically, chess may be played without a board (e.g., electronically), in which case the pieces and positions are something along the lines of electronic or brain data. In short, the generic concept of a chess game does not imply anything in particular about the way in which the game presents itself to our senses, or even that it does so at all. Space and time are not purely conceptual, abstract structures in this way. A number line may well have the same formal properties as time, and this may allow us to infer facts about the structure of time from an analysis of the real numbers. But *time* is a concrete structure, a concrete ordering of items "intuitively" or concretely present to the mind. For this reason, Kant has to introduce a special sort of representation to capture our grasp of such a concrete, yet formal structure: formal intuition. The representations of space and time, conceived as formal objects, are formal intuitions, because they are at once concretely present to the mind, yet also defined by their formal structures.

In order to deny that the representations of space and time that determine experience are formal intuitions in this way, Heidegger places great weight on a passage in which Kant precisely distinguishes formal intuitions from forms of intuition (CPR B160n). Formal intuitions are concrete structures that are conceptually organized by formal principles. Forms of intuition are supposed to be somehow more basic than such formal structures. They are *not* supposed to be explained by formal principles. Before we explore what precisely this means, let us recall what hangs on this suggestion. If Heidegger is right that the spatial and temporal forms of intuition are not formal intuitions, then they are not directives to organize the data of experience so that it will conform to a concept or conceptual construction. And this implies that the way in which we explained the colored balls example above was incorrect.

HEIDEGGER, NEO-KANTIANISM, AND THE ROLE
OF LOGIC IN METAPHYSICS

This is a good place to pause and reflect upon a further implication of Heidegger's negative claim, that the *a priori* representations of space and time are not principles for organizing formal structures. What of more comprehensive philosophical import would follow from the conclusion that the *a priori* representations of space and time are not formal intuitions? Why are we so concerned with the *a priori* representations of space and time anyhow? Recall that according to Heidegger, "time is the horizon for the understanding of being." In other words, being makes sense in terms of time, time is the meaning of being. Now, if time were a formal object in the way in which we have considered, then the primary tools for analyzing or explaining time would be logic and physics.

If we reflect upon the representation of time as a formal intuition, we can distinguish two sources of content within it. There is, on the one hand, the formal structure exhibited by time. On the other hand, there is the content that gets organized by that formal structure. It is quite hard to know what to say about the latter, just as it is hard to know what to say about the basic elements of our experience of color. Our experience of color is organized by the formal structure of the color spectrum, or perhaps by various proposed color wheels, but the raw data that gets organized by the structures is fundamentally inarticulate. The same may be said about space and time: we can analyze at great length the formal structures of space and time, but when it comes to saying something about the raw data that gets organized by the formal structures, we run out of words. What is more, we have seen that the chief suggestion we have on board for how the representation of time plays a role in ontology is this: we spell out what it means for something to be in terms of the entity's temporal *structure*. For example, to be in the sense of substantiality is to persist through change, and persistence is just such a formal structure as we have considered. To analyze such a formal structure, therefore, we need those tools that are best designed for spelling out conceptual relations, namely, logical tools. Furthermore, since time is a concrete experiential structure, we must also rely upon those tools that are best designed for exploring the structure of the concrete phenomenon of time, namely, modern physics.

If this line of thought were fundamentally sound, then we would be driven to the conclusion that the primary means for developing and justifying a temporalized ontology of the sort Heidegger envisions are logic and physics. It is just this conclusion, however, that Heidegger rejects, and it forms the focal point of his disagreement with the neo-Kantians who dominated Kant studies in Heidegger's day. Hermann Cohen, Paul Natorp, and Ernst Cassirer were the leading lights of neo-Kantianism. They were all agreed that logic and physics were the proper tools of ontology. As Michael Friedman has shown, this aligns the neo-Kantians quite broadly with Carnap and the logical empiricist tradition of philosophy and helps to explain the chasm that opened up between Heidegger and those sympathetic with him, on the one hand, and the largely Anglophone, empiricist tradition on the other.[12]

In order to create space for an alternative to the logical orientation shared by Carnap, the neo-Kantians, and the logical empiricist tradition dominant in the English-speaking world, Heidegger must explain how the *a priori* representation of time is not a formal intuition.

FORMS OF INTUITION

We have seen that if the forms of intuition are not formal intuitions, that must be because they are not fundamentally formal principles for organizing the data of experience. Formal principles are directives to order data so that it conforms to a concept or conceptual construction. If the forms of intuition, the *a priori* representations of space and time, are not conceptually articulated, then they cannot be such formal principles. Put a little differently, if the forms of intuition are preconceptual, if they make sense prior to the application of concepts, then they are not formal principles. But why does Heidegger think that the *a priori* representations of space and time are preconceptual? To answer this question, it is helpful first to explore a dead end.

There are strong suggestions in PIK that Heidegger's line of thought may well run as follows: the forms of intuition are preconceptual, because we do not have to have articulated the concepts of space and time to ourselves in order to be guided by the forms of intuition. The emphasis here is on whether we have *articulated* or *made explicit* the principles by which we order the data of experience. To the extent to which we have already made the principles of order explicit, those principles are conceptually articulated. To the extent to which we have not already made the principles of order explicit, that is, to the extent to which they remain implicit, they are not conceptually articulated. To develop this line of thought in more detail, it is necessary to explore Heidegger's account of *concept formation*.

How does Heidegger understand concept formation in PIK? He appears to adopt an intuitive or commonsense account of concept formation as abstraction. To illustrate and motivate this account, he draws on Kant's presentation of abstraction.[13] Consider Kant's account of forming the concept of a tree by abstraction. I first have experiences of a pine tree, a willow tree, and a lime tree. I then compare these experiences and abstract away or remove the differences in order to abstract out or isolate the common element. Note that the ability to do this presupposes that I am already able to grasp what the trees have in common. Only if I have this prior grasp of or mastery over what is common, can I remove the differences to isolate the common element. Thus, Heidegger argues,

Noticing the differences [among diverse trees] already presupposes the leading regard, in whose range and in view of which we can take a look at many objects in advance and grasp the definite unity wherein the objects agree. Only by keeping in view this [unifying] one can we disregard everything in the objects which in terms of this unifying one, e.g., the trunk, is different in a certain way.   (PIK 158)

Only by being able already to experience the objects in terms of what they have in common am I able to disregard what differentiates them. Disregarding what differentiates them is the crucial step by which I give my cognition the *form* of a concept. The unity grasped or represented by that concept, however, is already, as it were, under my control, but not in the *mode* of a concept.

According to this abstractionist account of concept formation, a concept is *not* the capacity to recognize the unity or commonness in a sample of objects in the first place. It is not what Heidegger describes as "the leading regard" by means of which we "grasp the definite unity wherein the objects agree." Rather, a concept is an explicit representation of that unity formed by reflectively disregarding everything not common to the sample of objects. When concepts "spring up explicitly," we "bring to concept" forms of unity already implicit in experience (PIK 272). A concept is, thus, an explicit representation that articulates a hitherto inarticulate capacity we already possess.

With this abstractionist theory of concept formation in mind, we can reconstruct an interpretation of Heidegger's colored balls example in §8 of PIK, an interpretation that will, however, prove unsatisfactory. As we organize a sample of balls by color in order of the rainbow, we rely on a principle of order that is not, according to the theory we are currently considering, conceptually articulated. At least, it need not be. One may well have encountered rainbow ordering by exposure to rainbows and prisms and have "absorbed" the principle they exhibit, without ever having explicitly articulated that principle to oneself. One may further be able to apply the principle unreflectively by ordering a set of colored balls, again without ever thinking explicitly about the principle at work. That is, one can grasp the rainbow principle implicitly, without having "brought it to concept," without having let it "spring up explicitly." Thus, Heidegger might be seen to argue, we rely on a preconceptual grasp of ordering relations to bring the sample of balls into order.

Heidegger's argument as just reconstructed, is, however, deeply flawed. First, it relies upon a superficial theory of concepts, for after all, the mind already "preconceptually" grasps the very same forms of unity that are later made explicit in concepts. The argument grants that prior to making the ordering principle explicit in an articulate concept, we have a grasp of it, a mastery of it, which for all the world appears to be an implicit, yet *conceptual*, grasp, an implicit use of the very same form of mastery on display in an explicit concept. Put a little differently, we have identified two forms of understanding, one explicit, one implicit. What is understood in both cases is the same, however: a commonness or unity that can be made articulate in a reflective representation. Nothing very much seems to hang on the distinction between what is implicit and what is explicit. In either case, the proper set of tools for analyzing the ordering principle will be logical and scientific.

Second, the argument as presented is of no use in the larger context in which it occurs, for it establishes too much.[14] The argument works just as well for ordering the balls by color as for ordering sensory information by spatio-temporal relations. Heidegger is trying to explain what he means in interpreting Kant as arguing that the forms of intuition are forms in the sense of representations that guide the ordering of intuitive data. But the argument as presented would imply that the principle, "by color in order of the rainbow," is likewise a form of intuition. Thus, this reconstruction of Heidegger's interpretation of Kant's argument for the apriority of the representation of time results in a rather unsatisfactory picture: a defective argument based on a superficial theory of concepts.

Is there an alternative way to reconstruct Heidegger's interpretation of the forms of intuition? Heidegger offers a more promising line of thought in §9 of PIK:

> ... but *having a view* of spatial relations as such is not an *objectification* of them. In advance viewing, these relations are not comprehended, but are given to us non-objectively. Insofar as we exist, we always already exist into space without turning space into an object or even a theme. Being oriented in space is still free from objectification of space. We need a special science, that of geometry, in order to discover the plenitude of what lies in space as such.... But now it was also shown to what extent what is intuited [in advance in the forms of intuition] is neither something *present-at-hand* nor any kind of *object* comprehended in its own right.   (PIK 89)

What does Heidegger mean by denying that the *a priori* representations of space and time are *objectifications*? An objectifying representation is one that represents an object (PIK, p. 19), or in the language we were using earlier, an objectifying representation is objectively valid. The forms of intuition, however, "... are indeed something, as forms of intuition, but are not themselves objects which are intuited" (CPR A291/B347, quoted earlier). The forms of intuition *enable* objective representation, but are not themselves objective. In other words, the forms of intuition enable us to represent the world by means of concepts, but are not themselves conceptual. Why?

APPERCEPTION AND THE *A PRIORI* REPRESENTATION OF TIME

Heidegger's argument for nonobjective character of the *a priori* representation of time[15] runs through one of his central, and most controversial, theses about Kant, namely, that Kant implicitly embraces a preconceptual form of imaginative unity, one that lies at the foundation of all cognition. "*Prior to* conceptual unification the manifold must be 'gone through, taken up, and connected'" (PIK 184). This process of synthesis is a function of the pure productive imagination. It is a central doctrine of Heidegger's Kant interpretation that the term "synthesis" in the first *Critique* is systematically ambiguous between (a) a conceptual synthesis that belongs to the understanding and accounts for how we abstract an explicit concept from our implicit mastery of commonness or unity, on the one hand, and (b) a preconceptual synthesis that belongs to the pure productive imagination, on the other. According to Heidegger, the pure productive imagination is a faculty or capacity of the human mind more basic than either our passive receptivity to sensory data or our reflective ability to recognize conceptually articulable unity in that data (PIK 95 and §21).

According to Heidegger, conceptualization and intuition both require an "antecedent zone," "a dimension within which I can move while" either intuiting or forming concepts:

This "grasping in *one*" cannot at all be identical with seeing pre-given representations together in terms of the "unity of the concept." This "grasping in one" is by no means the logical act of concept-forming reflection, but rather is the act of the same synthesis on the basis of which a many is pre-given as *a* many for a thinking seeing. I see a pine tree *and* a willow tree *and* a lime tree. I do not see them successively by losing sight of the one seen before. Rather this many must be given to me *in one* so that I have a dimension within which I can move while comparing. What encounters [me] must in a certain way belong *to me*, must lie before me in a surveyable *zone* [*Umkreis*]. The unity of this zone, which, so to speak, antecedently holds the manifold together in advance, is what is ultimately meant by "grasping in one."   (PIK 187)

Concept formation requires that representations of a sample of objects be able to come before the mind, so that their differences can be excluded in light of what they have in common. There is much to say about how such a process works – and neither Kant nor Heidegger says much that is very illuminating about it, since they both rely upon abstractionism – but this much, at least, Heidegger thinks is presupposed: the representations that are compared and processed must all, as Heidegger says, belong *to me* and be available *to me.* Thus, the "surveyable zone" to which Heidegger refers is the zone of my self-consciousness, what Kant calls "transcendental apperception."

Heidegger argues that this "zone" of availability is the pure form of time. In order to learn to see unity in a sample of experiential data, I must be able to hold the data together through time.[16] This requires the abilities to "apprehend" the data in sequence, to "reproduce" or retain the data through the flow of time, and to "recognize" or identify their unity. These abilities in turn require that the temporal flow of my experience itself possess unity. Unless the past remains available to me, not as an explicit object of recollection, but as a retained repository of information, I could not "reach back" to the data once present to me in order to identify the specific regularity or commonness I am learning to see. This unitary temporal flow of experience is a necessary condition of my capacity to learn concepts. In a nutshell: *however it is that we learn or come to identify conceptual patterns in experience,* such identification presupposes the temporal unity of the flow of experience, what Heidegger calls "temporality" (*die Zeitlichkeit*).

The unity of temporality, therefore, enables or makes possible the formation of concepts, for it is only in virtue of the unity of temporality that I can even *have* a sample of data at all in which I identify a pattern of unity. Since concept formation, however exactly it takes place, presupposes the prior, temporal unity of experience, all those capacities that are themselves built upon the possession of concepts likewise presuppose the unity of temporality, and that includes both ordinary intuitive or sensory experience (e.g., seeing a cat), formal-mathematical experience (e.g., constructing a Euclidean triangle), and abstract logical reasoning (e.g., analyzing an abstract formal structure). Notice that this argument does not depend upon the abstractionist theory of concept formation, nor upon the associated superficial understanding of concepts discussed above. We can see, thus, how the unity of the temporal form of intuition (here understood as the temporal unity of the "antecedent zone") is of a different kind than the unity provided by the principle, "by color in order of the rainbow." Precisely because the color principle is conceptually articulated, it depends upon the unity of temporality. All conceptuality depends upon that unity. But that unity does not return the favor; the unity of temporality is possible without the color principle.

Thus, the unity of temporality is more fundamental than *any* conceptually articulated principle.

ASSESSING THE EXEGETICAL ADEQUACY OF HEIDEGGER'S RECONSTRUCTION OF KANT

As an interpretation of the *Critique*, Heidegger's argument is highly problematic, for according to Kant transcendental apperception is the highest principle of the faculty of the *understanding* or *concepts*, not a form of time (CPR B139). The *a priori* representation of time belongs to the faculty of intuition, whereas apperception is a logical principle of the understanding. The understanding and intuition are the two "stems" of knowledge, the two distinct sources of content or meaning in human experience. Heidegger appears just to have run the two together, illegitimately to have fused time as a form of intuition with apperception as the most general form of the understanding. It is therefore highly unlikely that Kant could have meant to suggest this interpretation of the apriority of the representation of time.

Heidegger is, of course, aware of this difficulty, and he confronts it head-on. We can analyze his response at two levels. At an exegetical level, Heidegger seizes upon certain passages in the *Critique of Pure Reason* that suggest that beneath the two stems of knowledge (the understanding and intuition) there is a "common root" out of which they both grow (see KPM2 24, CPR A15/B29 and A835/B863). Further, Kant sometimes identifies the imagination, or more precisely, the "pure productive" imagination, as a third source or faculty of knowledge alongside the understanding and intuition. Heidegger, going beyond anything indicated by the text, identifies the third faculty, the imagination, with the unnamed common root. Finally, Kant at least once suggests that apperception is grounded in the imagination (CPR A118), and he once describes the forms of intuition as *entia imaginaria* or products of the imagination (see PIK 84, CPR A291/B347). Forcing all this together, Heidegger concludes that the pure productive imagination, in the form of the temporal unity of apperception, is the common root that lies at the foundation of both intuitive experience and conceptual reflection.

As an exegesis of Kant this is at least a stretch. Dieter Henrich has forcefully argued that Kant cannot have meant this, because it contradicts the limits that Kant places on the mind's ability to know the ultimate sources of its operations.[17] To postulate a "common root" for the two stems of knowledge is to attempt to know something about the mind as it is in itself, something not present to us in our experience of ourselves. For this reason, Kant only suggests that there *could* be a common root; he neither argues that there *is*, nor does he attempt any characterization of it. To try to do so would be seek knowledge of the realm of things in themselves, forever and in principle closed off to human cognition. Heidegger responds that Kant misunderstood his own implication that intuition and conceptualization have their "common root" in the pure imagination as a *psychological* thesis, that is, as a factual thesis about the constitution of an object of knowledge, namely, the mind. Thus, in rewriting the *Critique* for the second edition, Kant deleted a crucial reference to the pure imagination and substituted for it a critique of psychologism.[18] Heidegger argues, however, that Kant was groping toward a *phenomenological* approach to the problem (which for our purposes we need not identify with anything more than our analysis of apperception and the a priori representation of time), and had Kant found it, he would have been able to accept Heidegger's analysis. So, Heidegger grants, in effect, that Henrich's reading of Kant is more exegetically precise, but less philosophically penetrating.

Heidegger repeatedly states in PIK that Kant misunderstood himself.

Not only will we let Kant say what he wanted to say; but we shall even let him say more, even if this "more" rests only on philosophical interpretation. On the basis of the philosophical understanding we have achieved, it is then easy subsequently to take back the surplus. However, it is difficult if not impossible to aim directly at what Kant wanted to say, unless we would simply repeat Kant's sentences.   (PIK 64, translation altered)

Heidegger's derision of more straightforward exegesis, the sort practiced by Henrich, as merely "repeating Kant's sentences" is silly, of course. It is noteworthy, moreover, that the neo-Kantians against whom he is arguing did not just repeat Kant's sentences; they too argued that Kant's thought was heading in a certain direction, namely, the subordination of metaphysics to logic. The real dispute is not a battle between Kant's words and the direction of his thought, but rather between two visions of the *proper* direction of his thought.[19]

Heidegger's view, then, is that Kant raised issues that he could not fully master, and that he took inconsistent positions in his attempt to work the issues through. *We* readers of Kant must resolve those tensions and inconsistencies by taking a *philosophical* stand on the issues and looking back at the text from the more lucid vantage point thereby gained.

LAYING THE GROUND FOR METAPHYSICS

How does Heidegger's philosophical reconstruction of Kant help lay the ground for ontology? We can see how it would, if the fundamental unity of the antecedent zone of temporality gave rise to an understanding of being. Indeed, this is the approach Heidegger suggests in PIK:

> But if the synthesis of understanding, as synthesis of recognition in the concept, is related to time and if categories emerge from just this synthesis as activity of understanding, that is, if the three syntheses are interrelated on the basis of time, then the origin of the categories is time itself.
> (PIK 247)

The categories together make up "the concept of the object in general." Note that the "concept of the object in general" is not a single, simple concept. It is, rather, a complex construction assembled from the Kantian categories. Instead of "concept of the object in general," it is probably clearer to say "conception of objectivity in general." This conception of objectivity in general is the correlate in Kant of ontology in Heidegger. Kant's "analytic of principles" in the *Critique of Pure Reason* is an analysis of the temporal structure of any object simply in so far as it is an object, just as the promised (but never completed) third division of Part I of *Being and Time* was intended to be a temporal analysis of any entity just in so far as it is. So, when in interpreting Kant Heidegger writes (above) that "the origin of the categories is time itself," that is, the origin of the conception of objectivity is time itself, Heidegger implies that for him the origin of ontology is time itself.

How does Heidegger's interpretation of time as the true nature of transcendental apperception show that the origin of ontology is time? We have seen that the concepts that go to make up an ontology *require* the temporal unity of experience. But to establish that time is the *origin* or *source* of ontology, we need to say something stronger, namely, that the unity of temporality is rich enough to *generate* the understanding of being *on its own*. But how can the resources of the pure form of time be rich enough to generate such an understanding of being? The pure form of time is not rich enough, it would seem, to generate much of anything! After all, the pure form of time is the original flux of time held together as past-present-future.

To begin to chip away at this difficulty, first note that the "present-at-hand" is the region of entities whose temporal form is the continuous flow of indistinguishable moments of time. What lies in the future can or must become present; what is present can or must become past. The pure flux of time that underlies our understanding of the present-at-hand is "content-neutral." This is the conceptual heart of what Heidegger calls "the ordinary conception of time" in *Being and Time*:

The nows [of the ordinary conception of time] are, as it were, cut off from these relations [of datability and significance, which give nows their distinguishing content] and are arranged, as thus cut off, each after the other, in order to make up the sequence [of time].   (SZ 422)

In PIK Heidegger alludes to the same idea, when he writes,

But just as apprehension is necessarily open toward what has already been retainable, in the same way and inversely everything retainable as something which can be brought forth must be capable of being displayed in each actual phase of the now of apprehension.   (PIK 239)

The pure flux of time is content-neutral and makes up a pure succession of past-present-future. Moreover, this is all there is to the ontology of the present-at-hand. To be present-at-hand is to take place in ordinary time.

One might object that this comparatively thin conception of the ontology of the present-at-hand just is not thick enough to underwrite everything that Heidegger wants ontology to do. As we have seen, Heidegger aimed not just to lay the ground for this abstract, general ontology of the present-at-hand, but more specifically to provide an *a priori* foundation for the sciences. The regional ontologies underlying the sciences are accounts of the fundamental nature of the entities investigated by the respective sciences. How can such science-specific regional ontologies be extracted from something as abstract as the pure flux of time explored above? They cannot.

The pure flux of time is in fact too thin to generate these *a priori*, science-specific, regional ontologies. But this is a happy result, not an unhappy one. Cristina Lafont has argued[20] that Heidegger's insistence that science is grounded in *a priori* regional ontologies makes his account of science aggressively anti-empirical. Because the fundamental concepts of a science are disclosed *a priori* by philosophy, rather than lying simply at the center of an on-going, empirical research project, they cannot be discredited through research. If biology arrives at a new conception of life, it cannot be thanks to empirical research in the field of biology, but rather must be the product of essentially philosophical reflection. Although the fundamental concepts of empirical science do shift – so that they are, in Hamman's words, as exploited by Lafont, "*a priori* arbitrary and indifferent, but *a posteriori* necessary and indispensable"[21] – their development through the history of science is not rational and empirical, but rather the product of inexplicable alterations in "the truth of being."

If we give up on Heidegger's aggressively anti-empirical vision of the ontological foundations of the sciences, then we need no longer defend his similarly anti-empirical vision of fundamental, scientific research. Thus, Heidegger *should* say that anything that goes beyond the thin ontology of the present-at-hand, as what occurs in the pure flux of contentless nows, is not properly *a priori*. The understanding of what makes up life, for example, is not *a priori* and external to empirical, biological research. What is more, and more central to our concerns with Heidegger's Kant, this thinner ontological project is all that Heidegger's argument in PIK authorizes. Heidegger wants something thicker, both in *Being and Time* and even in the Kant lectures, but he has not earned it. Perhaps we need here to understand Heidegger better than he understood himself. Perhaps we should look forward toward a position implied by Heidegger's argumentation, but one that he did not himself clearly grasp.

From another angle, however, grounding our thin *a priori* ontology of objects in the pure flux of time may appear not too restrained, but rather too unrestrained. If the pure flux of time generates an ontology that specifically describes the present-at-hand, then we seem committed to the conclusion that all entities are present-at-hand. What then becomes of the other modes of being analyzed by Heidegger, such as the ready-to-hand and the existent (human beings)? If our *a priori* ontology is grounded in the pure flux of time, so that it is necessarily an ontology of the present-at-hand, does that not force us to conceive the ready-to-hand and the human as present-at-hand as well?

The solution to this worry is to recognize that the temporal unity of the antecedent zone of self-consciousness is merely the *a priori* form of *detached cognition*. Detached cognition is directed at the present-at-hand. We also interact with entities, however, through engaged manipulation and through self-engagement (through living our lives). According to the analysis of the final quarter of *Being and Time*, these other modes of interaction have their own pure forms of time ("the temporality of circumspection" and "originary" or "primordial temporality"). Those modes of time generate ontologies alternative to that of the present-at-hand.[22] Kant (*Heidegger's* Kant) argues that the pure flux of contentless nows makes up the temporal form of self-consciousness and thereby generates an ontology of objectivity. Heidegger accepts the claim that the various modes of human interaction or engagement with entities are structured by time. But unlike Kant, even Heidegger's Kant, he holds that our modes of interaction are not limited to detached cognition. Rather, the central thrust of the phenomenology of *Being and Time*, one that Heidegger does not ascribe to Kant, is that detached cognition is but one form of engagement, and a comparatively superficial one at that. Heidegger thus takes it as his project in *Being and Time* to describe and analyze these other modes of interaction, and then ultimately to reveal their temporal structure. Through it all the strategy remains constant: to locate the temporal form of our access to entities. This strategy he learned from Kant.

We began by asking what it would take for the philosopher to be in a position to offer his own distinctive contribution to ontology, rather than merely to catalog, clarify, and organize the regional ontologies implicit in current scientific practice. We have seen that Heidegger intends to appropriate Kant in order to lay a ground for metaphysics, to show how the philosopher can do precisely this. According to Heidegger and Heidegger's reconstruction of Kant, our encounter with or experience of entities is structured always by a temporal form, one that the philosopher brings into view phenomenologically. This phenomenological ontology is independent of, and immune to refutation by, the empirical sciences, because it explores the form of our experience of any and every entity. It imposes form upon the sciences. Viewed in terms of these far-reaching aspirations, Heidegger's appropriation of Kant is not entirely successful. The argument that emerges from Heidegger's reconstruction of transcendental apperception does not show how the specific fundamental concepts of the sciences, such as physics, biology, history, and theology, belong primarily to philosophical reflection and are therefore *a priori*. Heidegger develops no argument through his encounter with Kant to justify this aggressively anti-empirical stance toward science. The philosopher can generate *a priori* ontologies of several very general regions of being, perhaps even of being in general, out of his own phenomenological resources, but cannot do much more than this. He cannot claim to understand life or matter better than the biologist or physicist. Kant's Copernican revolution can show us how the philosopher has title to his own *a priori* domain of inquiry, but it cannot demonstrate any philosophical claim to exercise unchallenged authority over the fundamental concepts of the sciences.[23]

NOTES

1. I have systematically changed some of the terminological choices of the translations of PIK and *Kant and the Problem of Metaphysics*.

2. All translations of *Being and Time* are my own, although I have consulted the standard Macquarrie and Robinson.

3. Immanuel Kant, *Critique of Pure Reason*, translated by Norman Kemp Smith (New York: St. Martin's Press, 1966), p. Bxvi (hereafter, in this chapter, cited as CPR).

4. See Michael Friedman, *A Parting of the Ways: Carnap, Cassirer, and Heidegger* (Chicago: Open Court, 2000).

5. All objects of human knowledge exist in time, and some necessarily exist in space. Objects "outside our minds" (tables, chairs, Newtonian matter) exist in space, whereas objects "inside our minds" (our mental states) exist only in time. This is a complexity of Kant's account that we need not worry about here. We will pay attention to Kant's analysis of space in passing below.

6. The sense in which the thinking subject exists is clearly problematic. It is an "abiding and unchanging 'I'" (CPR A123). On this basis, Heidegger charges Kant with having misinterpreted subjectivity as quasi-substantial, modeled on natural things. See BP §§13–14.

7. One crucial difference in official doctrine between Kant and Heidegger is that Kant claims to be offering only an analysis of objectivity, that is, of the structure that anything that can be an object for human consciousness, and not an analysis of being in general. This is especially clear when Kant eschews "the proud name of an Ontology" in favor of "the modest title of a mere analytic of the pure understanding" (CPR A247/B303). Kant's restriction to objectivity depends crucially upon his doctrine of transcendental idealism, which Heidegger decisively rejects in PIK §6.

8. When Kant uses the term "objectively valid" in this way he does not use it as a synonym for "true" or even "justified." He means the representation is valid (*gültig*) of or applies to an object. He contrasts this objective validity with merely subjective validity, the paradigm of which is association. When I associate my cat with whiteness, I am not actually thinking *about* my cat. When I think *that my cat is white*, I am. Judgments are objectively valid, Humean associations are not. Note, however, that in other places Kant uses the term "objectively valid" in a slightly different way. For example, in the *Prolegomena to Any Future Metaphysics*, he writes, "Therefore, objective validity and necessary universal validity (for everybody) are equivalent concepts...." (Immanuel Kant, *Prolegomena to Any Future Metaphysics*, translated by Paul Carus and revised by James W. Ellington [Indianapolis, IN: Hackett, 1977], p. 42.)

9. What if a representation is *self*-justifying? Then it would not need to be justified by another representation, and in that case, it might seem, it would not need to stand in a relation of being made more likely to be true. The problem with this line of thought is that unless a self-justified representation can stand in justificatory relations, it will be *a priori* at the cost of being inert: it will not be able to imply anything further and, thus, will be useless to the development of the edifice of human knowledge. See Wilfrid Sellars, "Empiricism and Philosophy of Mind," in *Science, Perception and Reality* (Atascadero, CA: Ridgeview, 1991), pp. 127–196.

10. There are a whole raft of difficulties with Kant's analysis, it should be noted. The account of judgments given here ignores both logically compound sentences (e.g., "The cat is on the mat, and the mat is blue" and "if you go outside, you'll get wet") and quantified sentences (e.g., "There is a home-run king"). Further, judgments can be formed not only by predicating something of an object, but also by predicating something of another concept (e.g., "Red is a color"). Part of the business of spelling out Kant's account of judgment is to work out all these details.

11. For a fascinating discussion of this issue, see Wilfrid Sellars, *Science and Metaphysics: Variations on Kantian Themes* (Atlantic Highlands, NJ: Humanities Press, 1968), chap. 1.

12. Friedman, *Parting of the Ways*.

13. Immanuel Kant, *Logic*, translated by Robert S. Hartman and Wolfgang Schwarz (New York: Dover, 1974).

14. See D. P. Dryer, *Kant's Solution for Verification in Metaphysics* (Toronto: University of Toronto Press, 1966), p. 173, for a related observation.

15. At this point the representation of space just drops out of the picture. Is this a defect of Heidegger's interpretation of Kant? Not obviously, since it is a peculiarity of Kant's argument that space drops out of the picture along the way anyhow. Heidegger could argue that Kant should never have claimed that the representation of space is *a priori* in the relevant sense.

16. I here restate Heidegger's analysis of the "threefold synthesis" in the A-Deduction (CPR A98–104). See PIK §24. It is obviously modeled upon Husserl's analysis of time-consciousness, the published version of which Heidegger edited during the period in which he was mulling over Kant. See Edmund Husserl, *The Phenomenology of Internal Time-Consciousness*, translated by James S. Churchill (Bloomington: Indiana University Press, 1966).

17. Dieter Henrich, "On the Unity of Subjectivity," in *The Unity of Reason: Essays on Kant's Philosophy*, edited by Richard L. Velkley (Cambridge, MA: Harvard University Press, 1994), pp. 17–54.

18. Kant, *CPR* B127–9 substituted for A94–95. See (*PIK* 215–216).

19. Cohen makes this quite clear in his path-breaking book on Kant, where he writes, "In so far as the history of philosophy should not be seen as philological history of literature, but rather as the ideal form of knowledge, which helps to bring philosophy itself to completion, so with respect to Kant we stand historically upon a higher vantage point than that upon which he stood" (Hermann Cohen, *Kants Theorie der Erfahrung*. Edited by Geert Edel. In *Werke*, edited by Helmut Holzhey, Vol. 1 [Hildesheim: Georg Olms, 1987], p. 7, my translation; see also the preface to the first edition). Note, however, that Heidegger may well overstate the connection between his interpretation and authorial intention, when he tries to connect his reading with "Kant's own intentions." See Heidegger, PIK 49.

20. Cristina Lafont, *Heidegger, Language, and World-Disclosure*, translated by Graham Harman (Cambridge: Cambridge University Press, 2000).

21. Hamman, as quoted by Lafont, p. 3.

22. I have explored this in more detail in William D. Blattner, *Heidegger's Temporal Idealism* (Cambridge: Cambridge University Press, 1999).
23. I would like to thank especially Charles Guignon, whose detailed comments on an earlier and more technical draft of this chapter dramatically transformed it. I want also to thank Bert Dreyfus, Sean Kelly, Jay Reuscher, Mark Wrathall, the participants in the second annual meeting of the International Society for Phenomenological Studies at Asilomar, CA, July 2000, as well as the discussants at my presentation during the annual meeting of the Society for Phenomenology and Existential Philosophy at State College, PA, October 2000, for their helpful feedback on earlier versions of this paper.

6 Heidegger and the hermeneutic turn

The closing decades of this century have been marked by a wide-ranging, multidisciplinary exploration of the theory of interpretation and its practical implications. To speak of a revolution in the history of thought is perhaps too grand, but certainly there has been a general movement that can be called the "hermeneutic turn." This turn has taken various forms, including poststructuralist cultural studies, deconstructive literary studies, interpretive anthropology and social science, and critical legal studies. Of course, the specific turns taken in each of these fields are reactions to older ways of practicing each discipline. But in each case the emphasis on interpretation is used as an antidote, usually to objectivistic conceptions of the discipline's methods. However, none of these particular turns would have been imaginable without a dramatic change earlier in this century, the change brought about in philosophy by Martin Heidegger in 1927 in *Being and Time*. Heidegger's hermeneutic turn is taken most explicitly in Sections 31 and 32 of that book, where Heidegger makes interpretive understanding the central mode of human existence (or Dasein).

In 1927 Heidegger himself could not have foreseen the diverse effects of his theory on later thought, and in the final section of this essay I will describe his influence on the hermeneutic and deconstructive philosophies that emerged in the latter half of the century. But at the time Heidegger did see his account of understanding as a revolutionary break from the traditional philosophical emphasis on problems about knowledge and on the dichotomy between subjectivity and objectivity. To explain this break, I will begin by working through the details of Heidegger's account of understanding and interpretation in *Being and Time*, situating this material against the background of traditional hermeneutics as well as of Cartesian and Kantian philosophy.

THE METAHERMENEUTIC TURN IN PHILOSOPHY'S SELF-CONCEPTION

Hans-Georg Gadamer, who in *Truth and Method* (1960) was the first philosopher to develop Heidegger's account of interpretation into a general hermeneutics, defines hermeneutics as the philosophical enterprise for which the central question is, How is understanding possible?[1] This formulation is a reasonably straightforward way to characterize the hermeneutic philosophy that Gadamer himself has contributed to twentieth-century thought. However, before Heidegger, or to anyone who has not read Heidegger, the question would be misleading, since hermeneutics might thereby seem to be merely one branch of philosophy, the one that analyzes the phenomenon of understanding in contrast to other human activities such as knowledge or language. Hermeneutic philosophers before Heidegger did think of understanding in this way, and they therefore distinguished disciplines that could acquire knowledge in an objective way, as in the natural sciences, from those that could not give lawlike explanations but instead offered interpretations, as in the humanities (or *Geisteswissenschaften*).

So classified, since the humanistic disciplines like history, law, literary and cultural studies (and perhaps philosophy itself) rarely or never give explanations emulating the causal laws of natural science, they seem to be poor cousins in the family of knowledge. One defense of these *Geisteswissenschaften* is to claim a separate status for them and to take them as examples of a distinct cognitive operation called understanding. This move, which ran through traditional hermeneutics from Friedrich Schleiermacher (1768–1834) to Wilhelm Dilthey (1833–1911), has a weakness in that it seems to leave understanding as a derivative and deficient subspecies of knowledge.

A central part of Heidegger's legacy comes from his strikingly different conception of hermeneutics. Heidegger's analysis of Dasein as being-in-the-world changes our understanding of understanding from a derivative phenomenon to the central feature, the keystone, of human experience. As Gadamer remarks, "Heidegger's temporal analytics of Dasein has, I think, shown convincingly that understanding is not just one of the various possible behaviors of the subject but the mode of being of Dasein itself . . . and hence embraces the whole of its experience of the world."[2] When understanding becomes the central phenomenon for philosophy, hermeneutics is no longer conceived of as simply one minor branch of philosophy. Instead, philosophy itself becomes hermeneutic. Or at least one can now speak of a distinctively hermeneutic approach to philosophy in contrast to the traditional approach running from Descartes through Kant to Husserl. This traditional approach conceived of the human being as a "subject," a knower disengaged from the world and from practical activity in the world.

Heidegger's hermeneutic turn is more radical than earlier philosophy, then, in that it avoids the traditional model of the subject as the knower standing over against what is to be known, the objective world. His hermeneutic turn shows both that the mentalistic vocabulary of the subject – object model is not the only possible starting point for philosophy and that this vocabulary is derivative from the more basic starting point where Dasein and world are coterminous in understanding. Heidegger conceives of Dasein and world as forming a circle, and he thus extends the traditional hermeneutic circle between a text and its reading down to the most primordial level of human existence. Traditionally, the paradigm for the hermeneutic circle is the reading of a text, where the parts cannot be interpreted without an understanding of the whole, but the whole cannot be grasped without an understanding of the parts. As I shall explain, in Heidegger's deeper conception of the hermeneutic circle as a feature of human existence in general, the relation of knowledge and understanding is one neither of antagonism nor of indifference, but one in which the legitimate task of achieving knowledge is a *subspecies* of the more general phenomenon of human understanding.

Heidegger begins his radicalization of the hermeneutic turn in Section 31 of *Being and Time* by distinguishing his conception of understanding from a different conception of how a philosopher might be interested in analyzing understanding: "'Understanding' in the sense of *one* possible kind of cognizing among others (as distinguished, for instance, from 'explaining') must, like explaining, be Interpreted as an existential derivative of that primary understanding which is one of the constituents of the Being of the 'there' in general" (BT 182). Traditional, pre-Heideggerian hermeneutics distinguished humanistic understanding and interpretation from the lawlike explanations of the natural sciences, and it thus put itself in a weak position when the metaquestion was raised, What is the status of the knowledge claimed by hermeneutic philosophy itself? Is hermeneutic philosophy itself the one right explanation, or is it only one possible interpretation? Obviously, hermeneutics is not itself giving causal explanations, so it appears to be at best only one possible interpretation, not the definitive explanation, of human inquiry and existence. Traditional hermeneutics, and Dilthey especially, was thus plagued by the threat of relativism, particularly by the relativism of its own philosophical status.

Now Heidegger too will want to say that *Being and Time* is an interpretation. But because he has a deeper conception of what understanding is, he will have a different conception of interpretation, and a different account of how interpretation arises from understanding. What he means by understanding is not simply one form of cognition among others, but our most basic ability to live in and cope skillfully with our world. Of course, this ability must take into account that the ways in which features of the world show up are constantly changing, and this constant change requires us to form particular interpretations. As our projects and needs change, we will change our interpretations. For instance, sometimes we must interpret ourselves as students, sometimes as family members, sometimes as consumers, and perhaps sometimes as philosophers. Yet Heidegger suggests that all these interpretations presuppose a primary understanding of the world that runs through them. Our shift from one interpretation to another at the appropriate moment is a sign that we do understand the world. So a change in interpretation is not necessarily a sign of lack of understanding, since in these cases the change of interpretation shows that we can cope with the various demands the world places on us.

Heidegger is describing the "primary understanding" that runs through our various ways of existing in and interpreting the world. What is the status, then, of this philosophical activity of description? The philosophical description is itself an interpretation, but it is on a plane different from the interpretations that flow naturally from our everyday ways of coping with the world. Heidegger thus distinguishes between *Auslegung* and *Interpretierung*. *Auslegung*, the standard translation of which is "interpretation" with a lowercase "i," includes the everyday phenomena of ordinary skills like hammering, typing, or driving. *Interpretierung*, translated as "Interpretation" with an uppercase "I," includes thematized, discursive articulation and theorization. *Interpretierung* is itself said to be a derived form of *Auslegung*, but Heidegger obviously does not mean to denigrate *Interpretierung* since that is what *Being and Time* is. An *Interpretierung* is a reflective working through of phenomena, such as is done in philosophy and philology. So Heidegger claims the status of philosophical *Interpretierung* and not "knowledge" or "explanation" as a description for what he is doing.

Whereas the ordinary interpretations are more or less automatic, philosophical Interpretation of these ordinary interpretations is reflective in two senses. First, it is reflective in that it must explicitly articulate or thematize what goes on more immediately and less explicitly in everyday coping. Second, it is logically self-reflective in that it must itself be one possible manifestation among others of primary understanding; it will not be a representation of something that is of a different order from it, but it will be of the same kind as what it captures. Philosophical Interpretation can be "true to" the phenomenal activity of ordinary world interpretations because it is itself a form of the same phenomenon, although a more articulated or explicit form. So philosophical Interpretation is not simply arbitrary, and not threatened by the problem of relativism, because it is a case of the primary understanding that it is trying to capture. Philosophical Interpretation may be refined, or it may be supplanted by later redescriptions of what philosophy should be, but if it is agreed that there is a primary understanding of the world, then the philosophical articulation of that understanding will be binding to the degree that it is adequate to phenomenal manifestations of understanding, which include philosophy itself.

Is there any way to *test* Heidegger's philosophical Interpretation? Such an Interpretation will aim not merely to clarify ordinary usages of terms like "understanding," "explanation," and "knowledge," but will *reinterpret* or *reorder* them. This reordering is what goes on when Heidegger argues that something is *derived* from something else. If Heidegger can argue successfully that explanatory knowledge is a derived case of understanding, he will thus be in a stronger philosophical position than traditional hermeneutics, where understanding is simply an alternative mode of cognition. Heidegger's "derivations" are reminiscent of Kant's "transcendental deduction" in the *Critique of Pure Reason*, where Kant claims to demonstrate and justify our assumption that our experiences are not simply subjective but objective. Heidegger points to Section 31 as an attempt to go deeper than Kant did by explaining what Kant left unexplained (BT 184). One metaproblem with Kant's attempt to explain the possibility for our scientific knowledge of nature is the status of the synthetic a priori knowledge claimed by the *Critique* itself. That is, Kant is often accused of trying to give philosophical explanations of scientific explanation without reflecting sufficiently on whether the philosophical knowledge propounded in the first *Critique* had the same conditions as scientific knowledge.

Heidegger can avoid this problem by consistently claiming that *Being and Time* is an Interpretation. This Interpretation does not eliminate ratiocinative operations like explaining, deliberating, reflecting, and deciding, but situates them within a more general account of how they fit together in a primary understanding that also includes our everyday interactions in and with the world. Heidegger's account tells a story about how cognitive explanation always inheres in a context of intelligibility that is projected in understanding. Heidegger's account is thus properly construed not as a single, decisive transcendental argument, but as an Interpretation, that is, a reasonably complete and plausible reconstruction of the conditions that obtain if the things of the world make sense, and if beings like ourselves are also part of the world. Understanding is among these conditions and is the projection of an inclusive context or pattern of intelligibility as the background against which particular instances of sense making succeed.

In sum, contrary both to Kant and to traditional hermeneutics, Heidegger is trying to show us that we need not take "knowledge" as primary and see "understanding" and "interpretation" as derived, but that we can reverse this derivation. Even if the reversal is successful, however, a further problem arises if this result tells us simply that either direction of derivation is equally valid. The entire strategy of reordering or deriving would be undermined if that were the only conclusion, and relativism would again threaten. But Heidegger thinks that since traditional philosophy has come up against unsolvable antinomies and unbridgeable dichotomies, his reordering acquires greater plausibility to the degree that it avoids such difficulties.

Also, Heidegger can urge that by starting from the more primary phenomenon of understanding, he can make better sense than the tradition of how knowledge is really possible. Traditional philosophy from Descartes to Kant wanted to offer not only a definition of knowledge (for instance, as correct representation of the real world), but also an account of how the knower is connected to the known. Heidegger's strategy is different from the Cartesian strategy, which starts by assuming a basic ontological disconnection (e.g., between mental and physical substance) and then looks for instances of epistemological connection that cannot be doubted (e.g., the knowledge of the existence of a thinking subject). Heidegger's strategy is to see Dasein as already in the world, which suggests that what needs to be explained is not the connection, which is the basis, but the disconnection. Instances of disconnection happen obviously and frequently, as when humans make mistakes, not only cognitively but practically. The Cartesian strategy runs into difficulty when it fails to explain (e.g., to skeptics) connection. The Heideggerian strategy must show that it does not run into similar problems when it tries to explain how apparent disconnections could arise, as in the breakdown of a ready-to-hand tool and its transformation into a merely present-at-hand object or piece of junk. A crucial part of Heidegger's account of the connection of Dasein and world is the section on understanding as the projection of possibilities, and I will now focus on how the details of that section contribute to the hermeneutic turn.

UNDERSTANDING, PROJECTION, AND POSSIBILITY

One question that arises if philosophy is itself a mode of interpretation is, How can one such Interpretation be said to be better than others? Is it "true"? Are there other such Interpretations that could be "true" in the same sense? To clarify these questions, Heidegger distinguishes two senses of truth. One is the ordinary philosophical sense of truth, where an assertion uncovers or discovers some fact about the world. Heidegger usually describes truth in this sense as being about things that do not have the character of Dasein (BT 118), using the term *Entdecktheit* (discoveredness). The contrasting term, "disclosedness" (*Erschlossenheit*), suggests that the total context is opened up through understanding. Understanding thus does not consist only of making assertions about the world, but also of grasping the entire mode of being-in-the-world. Understanding grasps the world as such, without which the discovery of particular features of the world would not be possible. However, understanding grasps not only the world, but also Dasein's way of being in the world. So an understanding of the world is always also a self-understanding.

To speak of self-understanding can be misleading, however, if it suggests a Cartesian or Kantian ego, which stands at a remove from the objective world as if it occupied a different, subjective world. Heidegger says instead that disclosure involves both the world and Dasein at the same time. Dasein's understanding of its world is thus not distinct from its understanding of itself, but is at the same time an interpretation of itself. This self-interpretation thus does not discover facts about the properties of a mental substance or a noumenal self, but discloses how Dasein has dealt with and is dealing with the question or "issue" of its own existence. A student of physics, for instance, is not simply learning some facts about the physical world, but is learning how to do physics. The student is thus becoming a physicist, at least to some degree. Being a student is generally best described neither as finding innate abilities in oneself nor as acquiring a mass of facts about the world. Instead, being a student on Heidegger's account is learning how to go about in the world in a certain way, for instance, as a physicist or as a philosopher, where who one is and what one does are inseparable.

Understanding involves, therefore, more than the discovery of facts about particular features of the world. Understanding is more primordially the disclosure of what Heidegger calls possibilities. Heidegger suggests that the disclosure of possibilities could not be derived from the discovery of factual features. His philosophical Interpretation is trying to show that both discovery and disclosure are necessary to human activity. Focusing on the discovery of facts alone (e.g., as empiricist philosophers might) will obscure the dimension of disclosure. So Heidegger's Interpretation shows that if the dimension of disclosure is recognized, then both discovery and disclosure can be accounted for, since disclosure makes the phenomenon of discovery intelligible. The isolated, atomistic discovery of one fact after another would not generate an understanding of a world that was significant and intelligible, but only of a disconnected aggregate. An interpretation is precisely not a heap of facts but an account of how these facts are *possible*.

Possibility for Heidegger is not simply logical possibility, since understanding is of real relations and situations. Possibility also does not mean not-yet-actual, since Dasein is itself currently one possible way of existing and understanding. Dasein exists as "definite" or concrete possibilities (BT 183), which it does not choose arbitrarily. Dasein finds itself as already having these possibilities. We can begin to see what Heidegger means by returning to my example of what it is to be a student. Heidegger is not describing the process of explicitly planning to be, say, a physicist or a philosopher, and possibilities are not the abstract thoughts a student might have about what it would be like to be a physicist or a philosopher. Possibilities are recognized only in the concrete activity of doing physics or philosophy and are what limit the range of what it makes sense to do or to try to do in those activities. What it is sensible to do in a particular situation is already laid out in advance in a genuine understanding of the concrete possibilities. Dasein may not be explicitly aware of those possibilities it has let go by, or even of the ones that currently characterize it. Dasein can also be mistaken about its possibilities, for instance, by trying to fix them so rigidly that it takes them as necessities instead of as possibilities, thereby misunderstanding itself and becoming disconnected from a more primary understanding of itself (BT 183).

Dasein's understanding of itself as possibility, and its "knowledge" of those possibilities of which it is capable, is thus a matter of degree. This "knowledge" is often more implicit "know-how" than explicit "knowing-that," and it is more a grasp of the worldly situation than a reflective turn inward. Insofar as Dasein finds itself already thrown into a situation that is not of its own making, it has "in every case already gone astray and failed to recognize itself" (BT 184). Dasein thus does not "know" itself from the start, but if it is to recover or "find itself," it must come to understand what it can do given its own possibilities in its particular worldly situation.

Understanding thus involves possibilities, and these are not simply subjective or inner phenomena, but are always tied to worldly situations. Heidegger wishes to distance himself from the traditional idea that these possibilities should be thought of as spontaneously free choices, and he rejects the "liberty of indifference" (BT 183). So he avoids making "choosing" the starting point for his analysis of primary understanding, and instead starts from what he calls "projecting." Projection involves an understanding of what matters, and there will always be two sides to what matters. First, there must be a context of significance, of meanings that are really possible in the "current world." Second, nothing could matter or make a difference unless it mattered or made a difference to beings who cared, so Heidegger suggests that Dasein's own being is also projected as that "for-the-sake-of-which" whatever matters or makes a difference.

Projection is not simply reasoning from a list of all the particular possible choices that one has, as well as the pros and cons for each choice, to some decision. Listing all the "facts" about oneself and one's situation would be an interminable process, and the idea of specifying all that could be known about anything may even be unintelligible. Furthermore, "facts" about humans are always already meaning-laden and interpretive. Heidegger thus draws a distinction between "factuality" and "facticity." Factuality has to do with nonhuman things, discrete facts about which could be entered in a list. Trying to draw up such a list for any particular instance of Dasein would always fall short of characterizing that Dasein, and thus Dasein itself always is something "more" than it is (factually). But a central aim of Heidegger's account of understanding is to show Dasein's inherence in the world, which is to say that Dasein is not some free-floating spirit that transcends its material situation. As a projection (Entwurf, from the German stem "to throw"), Dasein finds itself "thrown" into a world, and it finds itself as already projected or "thrown" into a situation with concrete possibilities. Possibilities that are concrete (or definite, bestimmte) differ from purely logical possibilities in that they come with concrete limitations. So Heidegger speaks of these limitations as Dasein's "facticity," in contradistinction to the other kind of fact that he calls "factuality."

Now exactly why something matters or makes a difference may be difficult to say or explain, either to oneself or to others. Hence, Heidegger wants to distance his concept of projective understanding not only from spontaneous choice, but also from deliberate decisions, conscious planning, or the weighing of alternatives. He denies that projection consists of making explicit plans or of grasping its possibilities "thematically" as explicit contents of the mind. Does explicit planning or conscious weighing of alternatives and deciding never enter human action? In Being and Nothingness Jean-Paul Sartre takes the strong position that conscious reflection (or deliberation) has little to do with real choice, and that one is really just fooling oneself by such reflection to put off the inevitable need to act. As Sartre says, "a voluntary deliberation is always a deception," one that really postpones a choice that has already been made; so conscious decision always comes too late, and "les jeux sont faits" (the dice are cast).[3]

Heidegger need not make such a strong claim, precisely because he has a different Interpretation of what understanding is. Understanding involves a holistic projection of a context in which particular possibilities first become intelligible. Much of what we understand thus remains largely inexplicit. However, it does not follow that when Heidegger says that understanding does not grasp its possibilities "thematically" that he must be denying that understanding is ever thematic in any way. Unlike Sartre, he need not assert that thematizing (deliberating and deciding) is only ever a way of postponing the need to take action and is thus inefficacious. The point is instead that more reflective operations such as explaining, deliberating, or deciding would ever be possible only by supervening on a larger background of features that could never be explicitly thematized, but that nevertheless were part of the understanding and thus of the concrete possibilities.

In contrast to Sartre's claim that "les jeux sont faits" Heidegger's argument is focused on a different claim, "Become what you are" (BT 186). This slogan has an ancient tradition, going back to the Greeks, but it also features famously in Nietzsche. The imperative that one should become who one is seems paradoxical, for one would seem able to become only what one was not (yet), and a being that already was what it was could not even try to become that way. Heidegger's solution is to say that the paradox may indeed hold for beings that do not have the character of Dasein. But he asserts that not only can Dasein become what it is, it can also fail to become what it is. The facticity – factuality distinction thus clarifies how "Become what you are" expresses an imperative that is genuine. Dasein is not its factuality, so it is not what it is *factually*. However, because Dasein is understanding, and understanding involves projection into a concrete "current world," Dasein is what it is *factically*. But because the projection also involves concrete possibilities, Dasein can *become* what it is by becoming what it is already possible for it to be. There is a genuine alternative here, for Dasein can equally well fail to face these possibilities, and thus it can become disconnected from itself by failing to own up to all that it has been and can be.

INTERPRETATION

Becoming who we are requires interpretation for two reasons. First, we cannot become who we are unless we have an interpretation both of who we are and of how we can continue to be who we want to be. Second, what we are interpreting is already interpretive. How we get to be who we are is through interpretations, not only of ourselves but also of the possibilities inherent in the public world, which is already interpreted meaningfully for us. A question that has plagued hermeneutics, however, is, What makes some interpretations better than others? Are some interpretations true and others false?

Since interpretations involve possibilities and not simply facts, the true – false distinction may not be the most pertinent one to use when judging interpretations. If an interpretation of any sort can be said to be "true," one must be using truth in a different sense from that in which a statement is said to be true. Interpretations typically contain or imply many statements, so in speaking of the truth of the set of statements, the sense of truth is extended. One might say that an interpretation is true only if all its assertions are true, but this reductive claim seems to misconstrue what is meant by calling an interpretation true. An interpretation may consist of more than simply those assertions that are uttered, since a good interpretation frees up the possibility of uttering many other significant assertions. There is also no reason to think that the set of possible assertions generated by an interpretation is closed. Furthermore, two interpretations could conflict with each other on some central claims while each one contained many other claims that either interpretation would grant to be true. In sum, interpretive understandings may be better judged by labels other than true or false, and Heidegger invokes such contrasting normative terms as authentic or inauthentic, genuine or not genuine, and transparent or opaque.[4]

Already this traditional philosophical obsession with the truth of falsity of interpretive claims may be on the wrong track in trying to understand Heidegger's account. In Section 32 of *Being and Time* Heidegger is not primarily concerned with explicit, deliberate Interpretation (*Interpretierung*) but with the phenomenon of *Auslegung*, that is, with interpretation of a practical sort that may not always involve articulated judgments or thematizing. Contrary to present tendencies to think of the reading of texts as the paradigm case of interpretation, Heidegger's paradigm cases are everyday activities like opening a door or hammering. Even Heidegger's philosophical Interpretation is an interpretation not of a text, but of Dasein. But these cases are analogues of texts insofar as Heidegger's point is that even the most obvious ordinary objects taken by themselves do not have their characteristics inscribed in them. Instead, the characteristics of the tools come into being in the concrete interpretation manifested in the activity of using them.

Contrary to an empiricist epistemology that presupposes that we first "perceive" objects with their particular properties and only secondarily apply or use them, Heidegger's suggestion is that this type of perception is not primary. Seeing is not simply perceiving the properties of external objects with the bodily eyes (BT 187). Instead of construing seeing as seeing *that* an object has such and such a property, Heidegger construes seeing as already interpreting something *as* something (e.g., seeing something as a hammer, as a door, or as a table). Another example of such "seeing-as" (not Heidegger's own) is found in the hermeneutic phenomenon of reading. When we read a text, we do not first perceive black marks on a white page and then construe their meaning. Instead, the meaning of the text, and indeed the text itself, comes to be only in the reading. Hence, for later hermeneutic theory the text and the reading form the paradigm case of the hermeneutic circle. While the early Heidegger does not emphasize textuality to the same degree, his account does underwrite the shift of philosophical attention from the epistemological model of perception to the hermeneutic model of reading.

Since reading involves grasping the meaning of the text, it is appropriate that Heidegger features the notion of meaning (*Sinn*) centrally. He does so in a way that will be congruent with this hermeneutic model and that will block some traditional problems that arise from construing meanings as private, internal, mental states. Meaning for Heidegger is not something that one imposes on an object, and it is neither a distinctive object of perception nor an intermediary between the subject and the object. Strictly speaking, says Heidegger, what is understood is not the meaning but the entity. There is thus a sense in which Heidegger eliminates the traditional philosophical notion of meaning from his vocabulary. He thinks that we grasp entities as entities in their webs of relations with other entities, not as aggregates of perceptual qualities. Thus, we do not first see some colors or hear some noises and only secondarily infer that we are seeing or hearing a motorcycle. Instead, we first encounter a motorcycle, and only secondarily (if at all) do we abstract its properties (perhaps to hear its "noise").

"Meaning" for Heidegger thus involves the holistic way in which something can become intelligible *as* something in a web of relations (BT 193). Independent of the web of meanings, entities are not meaningful (in this special sense). Since this web of meaning requires Dasein, only Dasein can be said to be meaningful or meaningless, as Heidegger understands the notions. In other words, unless objects inhere in an interpretive context, they could not be understood. So they cannot be said to have meanings that are prior to and independent of their interpretive uses.

The context of meaningfulness is thus what makes it possible to interpret something *as* something. For the most part, this context is not explicit but makes up the background of understanding, or what Heidegger calls the "fore-structure" of understanding. For an explicit interpretation of something as something to occur (e.g., in picking up the hammer and hammering), there are three levels at which understanding must be running in the background. First, there must be a general grasp of the whole situation (e.g., of the workshop as a whole). Heidegger calls this the "fore-having" (*Vorhabe*), where, before making any particular object explicit, we *have* a background grasp of the totality of possible practices involved. But to have a grasp of the whole is not yet to make any particular feature explicit, so the second level required before anything can become explicit is "foresight" (*Vorsicht*), where we *see* in advance the appropriate way in which things can appear. But for something to become fully explicit in an act of interpretation there would have to be some particular concepts under which it would be appropriate even to begin interpreting it. So the third level required before an explicit interpretation can occur is the "fore-conception" (*Vorgriff*), where we grasp conceptually in advance the appropriate way to interpret something.

Each of these levels brings the interpretation closer to being explicit, but none of them is fully explicit. Should we infer from this insistence on the fore-structure of understanding that it is "prior to," whether genetically or logically, the explicit articulation of an interpretation? That Heidegger might be giving a priority to the pre-reflective and prelinguistic levels is perhaps reinforced by his examples, which come from everyday activities such as using hammers and opening doors, not from more explicitly cognitive activities like reading texts. Heidegger warns us, however, not to break interpretation up "into pieces" (BT 192), and we should not infer that the implicit levels of the fore-structure of the understanding would function independently of explicit interpretations. The fore-structure of understanding goes together with the as-structure of interpretation, and the levels of *Vorhabe, Vorsicht,* and *Vorgriff* are all in play at once in any given act of interpretation.

Furthermore, while Heidegger wants to show that interpretation takes place in areas of activity other than those where language is involved, he would not need to claim that understanding is more essentially prelinguistic than linguistic. While not all interpretation involves uttering sentences or making assertions, Heidegger's point is not to deny but to affirm that asserting is itself an interpretive practice. He will have a separate argument in later sections that although not all interpretation involves explicit linguistic thematization, the being who is Dasein and is able to interpret would also need to be a being who could thematize and assert. In this section, moreover, he does include textual interpretation as a case of interpretation. If he says that philological Interpretation is a derivative case, he is not making a derogatory claim about textual interpretation (BT 194). On the contrary, he objects to the philosophical tendency to contrast the "textual" disciplines like historiography and literary studies with the natural sciences and to conclude that the former are "less rigorous" than the latter. While he recognizes that natural science is a "legitimate task" (BT 194), as we have seen, he thinks that science is a subspecies of understanding. So instead of thinking that science is a separate domain of knowledge, and then puzzling about whether history and literature should count as knowledge, Heidegger is giving an account of human understanding that will accommodate these different disciplines as subspecies. Hence, he does not see them either as unrelated enterprises or as a family in which the humanities are poor cousins of the natural sciences.

To make this case he need not privilege the textual disciplines over the sciences. So he does not invert the hierarchy and privilege historiography over mathematics. Mathematics is "narrower," he says (BT 195), which is not to say that it is poorer, but simply that it has defined its limits in a different way than the humanities. Historiography on his model is not criticized because it is incapable of precise definitions and rigorous demonstrations. Instead, when properly practiced, it can highlight the possibilities, and not simply the factual consequences, of human action. Historiographic understanding is circular, but this circle is not the vicious one of an allegedly rigorous deduction that succeeded only in proving what it already presupposed. Instead, all understanding is circular, says Heidegger, in the sense that "any interpretation which is to contribute understanding must already have understood what is to be interpreted" (BT 194). This "hermeneutic circle" thus characterizes all understanding, for there must already be a context of intelligibility for any discovery to be made, or for any conclusion to be proved.

This insistence on the circularity of understanding raises the problem of whether one is always trapped within one's own assumptions, or whether there is some way to get out of the circle. The solution to this problem will depend on how "getting out" is construed. Heidegger, of course, believes that interpretations can make discoveries and that they can correct their own inadequacies. Heidegger grants that we do not simply prove things that we already know, or limit ourselves to "popular conceptions." *Genuine, primordial* understanding will see that these popular conceptions or standard assumptions are hindrances to better ways of interpreting (BT 195). However, Heidegger's way of explaining how fanciful interpretations and popular conceptions are to be avoided may confuse some readers. He says that the task is to check our prior understanding of the subject matter against "the things themselves" (BT 195). This phrase "the things themselves" might suggest that there is a domain outside the circle against which our beliefs can be tested. However, Heidegger's main point is to undermine this strong philosophical assertion of a radically independent "outside." His point is instead that beliefs can be checked only against other beliefs. Understanding is holistic and includes a dense pattern of interlocking beliefs and skillful know-how, so the idea of "getting out" of it is not really intelligible. Heidegger thus insists that interpretation is never a "presuppositionless apprehending" of some *given* (BT 191).

Even if one is willing to abandon the idea of an independent given "outside" the circle of understanding, one still might object to the holism in the thesis that all understanding is interpretive.[5] That is, one might think that understanding is *prior to* interpretation. This claim could mean that there is an understanding of something, and that this understanding then gets "interpreted," for instance, by applying that understanding to a particular situation (as when a judge interprets a statute by applying it to a case not explicitly covered by the abstract legal language). Or the claim might be that when we really understand something we do not describe ourselves as interpreting it, since to say that we were interpreting would suggest that there were features that we had not yet grasped correctly or adequately. Either way expresses the feeling that there must be something "beneath" interpretation, such that interpretation is not a circle but an "arch" that remains firmly grounded in its object.[6] Behind this insistence on the priority of understanding over interpretation would be an *epistemological* intuition, since the worry would be that understanding needs to be adequate to its object, which somehow anchors interpretation.[7]

Although many philosophers before Heidegger started from this epistemological worry, Heidegger's own project is to show that this problem can only arise *within* the circle of understanding. To start from the problem is already to disconnect the interpretation and that which is being interpreted to such a degree that it becomes impossible to reconnect them. Heidegger's insistence on the circle sees a particular misunderstanding arising only against a tacit background of shared understanding. While any interpretation may involve particular points of misunderstanding, it would be a mistake to infer that all readings are misreadings or that, as Jonathan Culler characterizes the literary theories of Paul de Man and Harold Bloom (but not Jacques Derrida), "understanding is a special case of misunderstanding."[8] Understanding must generally be a successful practice before particular aspects of the interpretive understanding could even emerge as mistakes or misunderstandings. Of course, in the process of interpretive understanding, the interpreter has the sense that there is something "out there" that is to be understood. Heidegger himself insists on this phenomenon and gives the following explanation of what is really happening: "If, when one is engaged in a particular concrete kind of interpretation, in the sense of exact textual Interpretation, one likes to appeal to what 'stands there,' then one finds that what 'stands there' in the first instance is nothing other than the obvious (*selbstverständliche*), undiscussed assumption (*Vormeinung*) of the interpreter, which necessarily lies in every interpretive approach as that which has already been 'taken for granted' in interpretation as such, that is, as that which is pre-given through the fore-having, fore-sight, and fore-conception" (BT 192; translation modified). So Heidegger does not deny that interpretations include some apparent givens, commitments, or purchase points. However, these points do not lie outside the circle of understanding, but are already at play within the circle as tacit aspects of our prior understanding of our world and ourselves. The world is itself in the circle, both in general as its horizon and also concretely as the commitments of any successful practice of understanding. Any particular assumption may become problematic and therefore move from being tacitly taken for granted to being explicitly called into question. Then the assumption may show itself to be merely a popular misconception or a fanciful, superficial glossing over of difficulties. But any challenge to any particular assumption can be made only by appeal to other commitments that the interpretation is not willing to give up. So the challenge is from within the circle and is not to some independent given "outside" or "beneath" the circle.

If there is no outside to the circle, understanding should not itself be taken as a mental operation that is distinct from interpretation. Understanding is itself always realized in interpretation and is not a separate, prior operation that then gets reprocessed in a secondary operation of interpretation. Understanding functions concretely only as interpretation: "In interpretation, understanding does not become something different, but instead it becomes itself" (BT 188). Interpretation is the concrete working through of the possibilities projected by the understanding. That is, the context of intelligibility that is tacitly understood provides the background against which specific interpretive actions make sense. The tacit background and the explicit interpretive action are integral functions of any instance of interpretive understanding.

AFTER HEIDEGGER

If the pieces of Heidegger's account of understanding and interpretation are now in place, some concluding reflections on the outcome of the hermeneutic turn later in the twentieth century are in order. Two thinkers in the second half of the twentieth century whose work would not have been possible without these sections of *Being and Time* are Hans-Georg Gadamer and Jacques Derrida. Yet the hermeneutic theory developed by Gadamer and the deconstructive movement fathered by Derrida take the Heideggerian account in different and apparently opposed directions. Gadamerian hermeneutics appear to deconstructionists to harbor the hidden assumption that the text has an internal unity of meaning, and that meaning is a single thing that interpretation must aim at *reconstructing.* The deconstructionists see this faith in the unity and the coherence of the text as a vestige of metaphysical faith, which they aim to *deconstruct.* In contrast to the hermeneutic move to recover and reconstruct *the* meaning of the text, deconstruction is the operation of questioning this faith in the meaning of the text by finding in the rhetoric and style of the language of the text moments where the assumption of the unity of meaning fails.

At least two problems, then, are raised by these two different ways of developing Heidegger's analysis of the circle of understanding. One problem is whether interpretation should be reconstructive or deconstructive in intent. The other is whether the interpretation's account of the meaning of the interpreted entails a metabelief that the interpretation is approximating the ideal of the one right interpretation. I will call the position that believes that this ideal is posited in all interpretation *monism,* and the denial of monism I will label *pluralism.*

The debate about deconstruction is too complex to be summarized here, and I will therefore limit myself to the issue of what follows directly from Sections 31 and 32 of *Being and Time* for this controversy. The issue has two sides, a methodological one and a political one. The methodological one turns on the question whether Heidegger's insistence on the circle of understanding does not simply imprison us in our own outlook, blocking us from recognizing the otherness or alterity of the text. The political issue arises from Heidegger's further insistence that the fore-structure of understanding forms our interpretations *in advance.* Thus, interpreters inherit from their tradition much of the background of their readings. From the deconstructive point of view the hermeneutic position that accepts Heidegger's analysis is too traditionalist and thus politically suspect because it seems unable to challenge the cultural and political status quo.

The countercharges against deconstruction are easy to imagine. Methodologically, deconstruction will appear to be fantasizing an escape from the circle of understanding by its dalliance with an impossible "outside" where meaning is undecidable and thus hopelessly multiple and fractured. Politically, its critique will seem pointless, since the fantasy of a complete break with tradition can lead nowhere. Deconstruction will seem to be neglecting Heidegger's insistence that we find ourselves already thrown into a social situation, which has specific concrete possibilities but also real limitations. Deconstruction's own faith that any construction can be deconstructed will lead to an undirected resistance that will be ineffectual because of its inability to generate a positive construction of its own.[9]

Unfortunately, these charges and countercharges may obscure the reach of Heidegger's original account of the hermeneutic circle. That account did not envision the specific controversy that I have sketched. Without minimizing this controversy, which is stimulating much current work in literary theory and social philosophy, I will outline some ways in which Heidegger's account can accommodate central features of both the reconstructive and the deconstructive enterprises.

Before this reconciliation can begin, however, the issue of monism versus pluralism must be clarified. Part of the deconstructive worry about the hermeneutic recovery of meaning may be caused by a suspicion that this recovery presupposes the monistic ideal of the one final, right interpretation. Much can be said for that ideal; yet, in the exposition that I have given of Heidegger's account, I have deliberately stressed the elements in it that I find pointing toward an antimonistic pluralism. Heidegger's account of "meaning" in his technical sense may seem monistic because it posits a whole, a totality of involvements, a single context in which interpretation may take place. My insistence on the holistic nature of meaning in this special sense suggests, however, that the context is always revisable, and that revision will come from within the context of belief itself. This holism implies, therefore, that while the task of understanding strives to be coherent and unified, it must always recognize that there are elements in it that have not been worked through explicitly and that may be inconsistent with other central commitments. So the context can always turn out to include inadequate elements.

The drive of understanding toward a single coherent position is thus compatible with its allowance for the inevitability of hidden error and bias, and the recognition that no interpretation is final.

Other aspects of Heidegger's account that support the metaposition of pluralism include his revision of the ordinary conception of truth and his description of the fore-structure of projective understanding. While interpretations contain true statements, one cannot adjudicate between two conflicting interpretations simply by counting the true statements that would be entailed by each one. Other criteria (such as richness, relevance to the present, genuineness, or authenticity) come into play, and these more normative considerations can lead us to prefer some interpretations to others. But the criteria are themselves interpretable and do not obviously support the monistic belief in a single exclusive interpretation. Furthermore, Heidegger's account of understanding as projection suggests that explicit interpretations always arise from implicit needs. The appearance of a new interpretation is likely to generate new needs, and these will in turn stimulate further interpretation. That the circle of understanding is never closed need not raise the specter of epistemological relativism. The nihilistic conclusion that our present interpretations are mostly false does not follow from the pluralistic thought that they will be altered by future generations, for whom the context and the background conditions will have changed.

Heidegger himself may not have fully accepted this pluralistic conclusion about his own theory of Dasein in *Being and Time*. I noted Heidegger's apparent desire to outdo Kant with Heidegger's own suggestion that Section 31 rivals Kant's transcendental deduction. But I also pointed out another reading of Heidegger's enterprise, one that takes seriously his claim that the account of Dasein has the metastatus of an interpretation, in the sense of an *Interpretierung*. Taking seriously this metaposition of interpretive pluralism allows us to imagine ways in which Heidegger's account of understanding could be expanded and modified. One way it can be modified is to take the hermeneutic turn more radically than Heidegger did in 1927, allowing language a more central role by modeling the account of understanding more explicitly on reading, as Gadamer did in 1960. Another way would be to recognize more explicitly and strategically how understanding can directly challenge meaning and how much more conscious the rhetorical play of language can become.

The latter way was the achievement of Derrida and the deconstructive movement from the late sixties to the present.

If these modifications are granted, it must also be recognized that they are prefigured in *Being and Time* itself. Whatever Heidegger's personal politics were, the text of *Being and Time* allows for the deconstructivist suspicion of simply recovering the tradition. Heidegger insists that the tradition may need to be criticized, and he reminds us that the "tradition" is not simply the "past." The past is finished, and there would be no point in criticizing it since the criticism could have no effect on the past. What we (and poststructuralists like Derrida and Michel Foucault) may need to criticize is the present, or more specifically, the present's interpretation of how it has come to be what it is, which is what "tradition" is. The criticism of the "traditional" in the present need not be presented as a complete break with tradition, but more reasonably as a break with a prevalent but mistaken understanding of the tradition's possibilities. So an effective criticism will see places where the present has misconstrued the possibilities inherited from the tradition, and it will also draw our attention to concrete possibilities in the tradition that have currently been lost from sight.[10]

If political, social, and historical criticism is to be genuinely possible on the Heideggerian account, however, there must be some resolution of the methodological question that I raised about whether we are not always imprisoned in our own cognitive and normative standpoint. This problem seems to follow from Heidegger's general claim that we can understand something only from within a context that we bring with us already. If the circle of understanding were static, this worry would be justified. But close attention to Heidegger's text shows that he thinks of the circle as a dynamic process of making aspects of the implicit background explicit and then testing standard assumptions to see if they really hold up, given the rest of what we believe and do. Hence, he speaks of testing assumptions against the "things themselves" to make "the scientific theme secure" (BT 195).

Gadamer's own theory in *Truth and Method* (see pp. 254–71) is built around an explication of these sections of *Being and Time*. Gadamer replies to the charge that, on the hermeneutic account, understanding is always imprisoned in its own standpoint by pointing out that in interpreting a text our own preconceptions often do not work out. The text may give us a shock by showing us a side of the subject matter that we had not anticipated. So the circle of understanding is a dynamic one where preconceptions will either work out or fail. Heidegger himself had spoken of genuine understanding as that which gets beyond "fancies" and "popular conceptions," and these are precisely what come to nothing when the interpreter tries explicitly to work them out.

Gadamer thus insists that it is false to conclude that the hermeneutic circle cannot recognize the alterity of the text. I would add that deconstruction could indeed be a crucial moment in the circle of interpretation, for its techniques could be used to ensure that the alterity of the text was taken seriously enough. The circle of understanding should not be purely reconstructive, if by that is meant either that the interpreter reads only what is already familiar back into the text or that in the effort to find a unity of meaning the interpreter should overlook tensions and contradictions that are also at play. But the circle could also not be purely deconstructive, since there must first be an assumed meaning that is deconstructed, and the discovery of tension and contradiction is itself a projection of an understanding of what is really going on in the text.

Heidegger's model of projective understanding can therefore recognize both reconstruction and deconstruction as necessary moments of interpretation. How these are balanced in particular cases is itself a matter of judgment and may be part of what makes interpretations interestingly different. What makes some interpretations more interesting or insightful than others is a question that I suggested at the beginning of this essay and is an appropriate one with which to conclude. While the question is a large one, there is at least the outline of an answer in these sections of *Being and Time*. At least one central aspect of what makes an interpretation better will be whether it understands not only its object and subject matter, but also itself. Interpretations that are methodologically more self-aware are therefore better if they bring to light unnoticed features not only of the object of interpretation, but also of the conditions and procedures of interpretation. A good interpretation, on Heidegger's model, will show something about the possibilities of interpretation as such. An interpretation presupposes a self-understanding, and bringing crucial features of this implicit self-understanding to light will make the interpretation insightful (in Heidegger's special sense of sight, which is not simply the perception of present-at-hand objects, but the disclosure of the total background or context).

As I have suggested, however, self-understanding is not to be taken in the traditional sense in which it might suggest grasping some inner, private self. In German, "self-understanding" (*Sichverstehen*) has to do with knowing one's way around. So for Heidegger, who construes Dasein as being-in-the-world, self-understanding thus has to do with knowing one's way around in the world or in some specific worldly subject matter. That Heidegger was himself interpreting Dasein and not simply a text does not signify a conflict with later hermeneutic theory. Instead, his *Interpretierung* of Dasein brings out a double-sided possibility of interpretation. On the one side, genuine interpretation will reflect the being who is interpreting. So there must be some dimension of the interpreter's context that is itself brought into focus. On the other side, who this being is will itself depend on its interpretations of the world, including its beliefs and its activities. So on the Heideggerian account any good interpretation should disclose something about both Dasein and the world. Interpretation is, after all, the way that both meaningful human existence and a significant world become what they are.

NOTES

1. Hans-Georg Gadamer, *Truth and Method*, 2d rev. ed., trans. Joel Weinsheimer and Donald G. Marshall (New York: Crossroad, 1989), p. xxx.
2. Ibid.
3. Jean-Paul Sartre, *Being and Nothingness*, trans. Hazel E. Barnes (New York: Washington Square Press, 1956), p. 581.
4. For a detailed account of these terms, see Hubert L. Dreyfus, *Being-in-the-World: A Commentary on Heidegger's "Being and Time,"* Division *I* (Cambridge, MA: MIT Press, 1991), Chap. 11.
5. Or at least, all understanding is interpretive in the sense of *Auslegung*, not necessarily in the sense of *Interpretierung*. Richard Shusterman raises the objection under discussion here in his article "Beneath Interpretation: Against Hermeneutic Holism," *Monist* 73, No. 2 (1990): 181–204.
6. Paul Ricoeur appeals to the metaphor of the arch in the account of interpretation in "Qu'est-ce qu'un Texte? Expliquer et comprendre," in *Hermeneutik und Dialektik: Aufsäatze II*, ed. Rüdiger Bubner, Konrad Cramer, and Reiner Wiehl (Tüubingen: Mohr, 1970), pp. 181–200.

7. For the Heideggerian critique of epistemological foundationalism, see Charles Guignon, *Heidegger and the Problem of knowledge* (Indianapolis, IN: Hackett, 1983), esp. pp. 150–82.

8. Jonathan Culler, *On Deconstruction: Theory and Criticism after Structuralism* (Ithaca, NY: Cornell University Press, 1982), p. 176. Jacques Derrida explicitly rejects this thesis in *Limited Inc* (Evanston, IL: Northwestern University Press, 1988), p. 157.

9. Jürgen Habermas advances this line of attack on deconstruction in Chapter 7 of *The Philosophical Discourse of Modernity: Twelve Lectures*, trans. Frederick Lawrence (Cambridge, MA: MIT Press, 1987). For a response, see my article, "Splitting the Difference: Habermas's Critique of Derrida," *Praxis International*, 8, No. 4 (1989): 447–64.

10. See Section 74 of *Being and Time*, especially BT 438, and my article, "History, Historicity, and Historiography in *Being and Time*," in *Heidegger and Modern Philosophy: Critical Essays*, ed. Michael Murray (New Haven, CT: Yale University Press, 1978), pp. 329–53.

7 Engaged agency and background in Heidegger

I

Heidegger's importance lies partly in the fact that he is perhaps the leading figure among that small list of twentieth-century philosophers who have helped us emerge, painfully and with difficulty, from the grip of modern rationalism. Others on the short list would include Wittgenstein and Merleau-Ponty. But one might claim some preeminence for Heidegger, in that he got there first. In the case of Merleau-Ponty, the breakthrough plainly built on Heidegger's work.

The emergence these philosophers helped us toward has, alas, been only partial and is still very contested; indeed, it is always menaced with being rolled back – hence the continuing relevance of their works, some of which appeared more than half a century ago.

In this essay, I shall discuss Heidegger, though with a side-glance at the others from time to time. I shall try to formulate the way in which his thinking takes us outside the traditional epistemology, using the notions of engaged agency and background.

My use of the term "rationalism" at the beginning of this essay could be contested, even by people basically sympathetic to the current of thought I am trying to articulate. There are a number of ways of formulating the outlook, more a set of semiarticulate assumptions, that Heidegger helped "deconstruct." It has a number of features, and we can argue which are most fundamental. In speaking of "rationalism," I am supposing that a certain conception of reason played a determining role. My view is, in short, that the dominant conception of the thinking agent that Heidegger had to overcome was shaped by a kind of ontologizing of rational procedure. That is, what were seen as the proper procedures of rational thought were read into the very constitution of the mind and made part of its very structure.

The result was a picture of the human thinking agent as disengaged, as occupying a sort of protovariant of the "view from nowhere," to use Nagel's suggestive phrase.[1] Heidegger had to struggle against this picture to recover an understanding of the agent as engaged, as embedded in a culture, a form of life, a "world" of involvements, ultimately to understand the agent as embodied.[2]

The issue of engaged agency merits some discussion because it is still difficult and controversial. What does "engagement" mean here? It is to say something like: the world of the agent is shaped by his or her form of life, or history, or bodily existence. But what does it mean to have one's "world shaped" by something? This is a relation subtly different from the ordinary causal link it is sometimes confused with.

Let us take a particular aspect of engagement, namely, being embodied; that is, let us focus on the way our world is shaped by our being bodily agents of the kind that we are. This is something different from the way some of our functions as agents are determined by physical causes. For instance, as a perceiving agent, I cannot now see the wall behind me. This can be explained by certain causal relations in physical terms: the light refracted off the surface of the wall behind me cannot reach my retina. The behavior of light and my physical constitution are so disposed as to make this impossible. In this sense, my embodiment undoubtedly shapes my perception, and hence in a sense my "world."

But this relation is rather different from the following example. As I sit here and take in the scene before me, this has a complex structure. It is oriented vertically, some things are "up," others are "down"; and in depth, some are "near," others "far." Some objects "lie to hand," others are "out of reach"; some constitute "unsurmountable obstacles" to movement, others are "easily displaced." My present position does not give me "good purchase" on the scene; for that I would have to shift farther to the left. And so on.

Here is a "world shaped" by embodiment in the sense that the way of experiencing or "living" the world is essentially that of an agent with this kind of body. It is an agent who acts to maintain equilibrium upright, who can deal with things close up immediately and has to move to get to things farther away, who can grasp certain kinds of things easily and others not, can remove certain obstacles and others not, can move to make a scene more perspicuous, and so on. To say that this world is essentially that of this agent is to say that the terms in which we describe this experience – for instance, those in quotes in the preceding paragraph – make sense only against the background of this kind of embodiment. To understand what it is to "lie to hand" one has to understand what it is to be an agent with the particular bodily capacities that humans have. Some creature from another planet might be unable to grasp this as a projectible term. Of course, the creature might work out some descriptions that were roughly extensionally equivalent. But to project this term the way we do, one has to understand what it is to be human.

Thus, there are two quite different kinds of relationship that might be expressed by saying that our experience is shaped by our bodily constitution. In the first – the case of the wall behind me – we note some consequences of this constitution for our experience, however characterized. In the second, we point out how the nature of this experience is formed by this constitution, and how the terms in which this experience is described are thus given their sense only in relation to this form of embodiment. The first kind of relation is asserted in an ordinary statement of contingent causality. The second concerns, by contrast, the conditions of intelligibility of certain terms. It is this second relation that I invoke in speaking of our "world being shaped" by body, culture, form of life. The ways in which our world is so shaped define the contours of what I am calling engaged agency – what Heidegger sometimes referred to as the "finitude" of the knowing agent.[3]

Now the other half of my claim is that the dominant rationalist view has screened out this engagement, has given us a model of ourselves as disengaged thinkers. In speaking of the "dominant" view I am thinking not only of the theories that have been preeminent in modern philosophy, but also of an outlook that has to some extent colonized the common sense of our civilization. This offers us the picture of an agent who in perceiving the world takes in "bits" of information from his or her surroundings and then "processes" them in some fashion, in order to emerge with the "picture" of the world he or she has, who then acts on the basis of this picture to fulfill his or her goals, through a "calculus" of means and ends.

The popularity of this view is part of what makes computer models of the mind so plausible to lay people in our day. These models fit neatly into already established categories. The "information-processing" construal builds on a long-supported earlier conception, whereby atomic "ideas" were combined in the mind and made the basis of a calculation underlying action. Classical Cartesian and empiricist epistemologies provided earlier variants of this conception, which combine an atomism of input with a computational picture of mental function. These two together dictate a third feature: "factual" information is distinguished from its "value," that is, its relevance for our purposes. This separation is dictated by atomism, since the merely "factual" features can be distinguished from their having some role to play in our goals. But it is also encouraged by another underlying motivation, to be discussed later. In any case, the composite traditional conception has this third feature, which we might call "neutrality," whereby the original input of information is shorn of its evaluative relevance, is merely the registering of "fact."

Now in some respects this view has roots in the common sense of (in any case) our civilization, going back before the modern era. But in other important respects, this conception was shaped and entrenched in modern times. And one of the factors it was shaped by was modern reason – or so I want to suggest in my perhaps tendentious term "rationalism."

There are two facets of modern reason relevant here. The first is that the modern conception, starting with Descartes, focuses on procedure. Reason is not that faculty in us that connects us to an order of things in the universe, which itself can be called rational. Rather, reason is that faculty whereby we think properly. In its theoretical employment, reason serves to build a picture of the world. Rationality requires that we scrutinize this building closely and not let our view of things just form itself distractedly, or self-indulgently, or following the prejudices of our day. Rationality involves a careful scrutiny by thinking of its own processes. This determines the reflexive turn of modern rationalism. Careful construction of our picture of things requires that we identify and follow a trustworthy procedure. Modern thinkers differ on what this is, and there is a crucial and hotly contested difference in the seventeenth century between, for instance, that defined by the clear and distinct perception of Descartes and that organized around the rules of believable evidence of Locke. But both views call for reflexive self-policing in the name of a canonical procedure.

More to the point, both procedures require that we break down our too hastily acquired beliefs into their components and scrutinize their composition to see if they are properly to be trusted. They both require that we treat candidate beliefs in this sense atomistically. Now a "method" of this sort is, in certain domains, an uncontestable advance over earlier ways of proceeding. The fateful step was not so much its formulation, but rather what I earlier called its ontologizing, that is, the reading of the ideal method into the very constitution of the mind. It was one thing to call on us to break down our beliefs into their possibly separable components, another to think that the primitive information that enters the mind must do so in atomic bits. The "simple ideas" of Locke are a classical example of such a reification of procedure, pouring it, as it were, in theoretical concrete and building it into the constitution of the mind itself.

But this reification has been immensely influential, conferring on the resulting model of the mind all the prestige and unchallengeable force that the procedures of reason have acquired in our civilization. The more we learn to treat things rationalistically, the more we are inclined to accept the corresponding view of how we "really" operate. The atomist-computational view owes part of its powerful hold on common sense to this.

"Simple ideas" result from reifying the procedure of challenging too hasty interpretations and inferences in order to get back to the basic data. But there was another important feature of correct, scientific thought as conceived in the seventeenth-century revolution that has also strongly influenced our ontology of the subject. This is the feature that Nagel calls "objectivity." Our thinking is objective when it escapes the distortions and parochial perspectives of our kind of subjectivity and grasps the world as it is. Seventeenth-century thinkers were impressed with the way our embodied experience and our ordinary way of being in the world (to use contemporary language) could mislead us. Descartes pointed out how the way we take our everyday experience leads us to attribute, say, the color to the object or to situate the pain in the tooth. These localizations were fine for Aristotelian theory, but the new mechanism showed that they were illusory. Only "primary" properties were really "in" the objects; "secondary" properties, like color, were effects produced in the mind by concatenations of primary properties in things. Seeing things as really colored was one of those distorting effects of our peculiar constitution as substantial union of soul and body. What comes to be called "objectivity" requires an escape from this.

Again, because of our situation in the world, we tend to "see" the sun "rising" and "setting," we "feel" directly that objects stop when they are no longer being pushed, and the like. One of the recurrent themes of seventeenth-century scientific discovery was the gap it showed between the real underlying constitution of things and the way things appeared to common sense. Sometimes the common appearance "regestalted" under the impact of the discovery: before Galileo, people "saw" that cannonballs shot straight forward and then dropped to the ground. Later, it was "obvious" that their trajectory was curved. But in very many cases, we still cannot help seeing things in the old way. The development of science since then has only entrenched this sense of strangeness, of the distance between underlying truth and our ordinary ways of seeing. An experience of everyday space that remains Euclidean coexists with our settled convictions about the curvature of space.

All this has nourished the aspiration to objectivity as Nagel defines it:

The attempt is made to view the world not from a place within it, or from the vantage point of a special kind of life or awareness, but from nowhere in particular and no form of life in particular at all. The object is to discount for the features of our pre-reflective outlook that make things appear as they do, and thereby to reach an understanding of things as they really are.[4]

There is nothing wrong with this aspiration as it stands – except perhaps the hyperbolic form in which it is stated here. If we stated it slightly more modestly, as the goal of disengaging from those features of our prereflective outlook that we come to discover are distortive of reality, then it is not only unexceptionable but an indispensable condition of pursuing, say, modern physics. The fateful move was, once again, the ontologizing of this disengaged perspective, reading it into the depth constitution of the mind itself, and relegating the distortions to the periphery, either as a result of error, inattention, mere lapse or as a feature only of the brute preprocessed input, not touching the procedures of processing themselves.

Thus, the authors of the *Port Royal Logic* describe it as a culpable weakness in us that we tend to attribute color, heat, and the like to the things we experience.[5] They and the other foundational thinkers of seventeenth-century epistemology could agree that the input to our minds was extremely limited and lacunary, but the constitution of the mind as a thinking agency was unaffected by these limitations, which offered no real excuse for, even if they helped to explain the prevalence of, the distortions we typically fall prey to. The disengaged perspective, which might better have been conceived as a rare and regional achievement of a knowing agent whose normal stance was engaged, was read into the very nature of mind. This was the major motivation I alluded to earlier underpinning the third major feature in the modern "commonsense" view of the mind, the "neutrality" of the original input.

This ontologizing of the disengaged perspective took two major forms. One was dualism, as with Descartes. Disengagement can be seen as getting free of the perspective of embodied experience. It is this perspective that is responsible for our attributing the color to the object; it is this that makes us give disproportionate importance to the senses and imagination in our account of knowing. That the thinking activity of the mind is really in its essential character free from these distorting media shows that the mind is essentially nonbodily – so argues Descartes in the celebrated passage about the piece of wax that closes the second *Meditation*.

But what looks like a totally antithetical ontology could do just as well, that of monistic mechanism: thinking is an event realized in a body, mechanistically understood. This idea is given its modern form in Hobbes and thus has just as long a pedigree as the Cartesian alternative. Mechanism can do as well as dualism to underpin the disengaged perspective, because the underlying belief was that we need to attain this perspective in order to do justice to a mechanistic universe. This assumption is common ground to Descartes and his empiricist or mechanist critics. But to the extent that we understand our thinking mechanistically, we have to understand it outside of any context of engagement. The very relationship to something that defines a "world shaping," and hence identifies a form of agency as engaged, cannot be stated in a mechanistic perspective. The other relationship, that of the causal dependency of experience on some physical conditions, can of course figure in such an account. It is indeed of the essence of this kind of explanation. But nothing can be said about the conditions of intelligibility. That is why mechanists constantly misunderstand descriptions of experience as engaged as statements of causal dependency and are puzzled when they are described as denying such engagement. But, in fact, their denial is of the most effective sort, that of leaving a rival thesis no ontological room for coherent formulation.

To the extent that we explain thinking mechanistically, as with the present wave of computer-based theories of mind, what it means to say that the agent finds the input intelligible can be described only in terms of the operations it can put this input through. The unintelligible is what cannot be processed. But these operations are themselves mechanistically explained. So any statement of something like "conditions of intelligibility" for some input would have to take the form of some statement about how the mechanism is hard-wired or contingently programmed, that is, about the causal relations of the input to the series of steps it can trigger off. The "world-shaping" relation as defined earlier cannot be stated.[6]

Both dualism and mechanism are thus ontologies of disengagement. With the decline over the centuries in the credibility of the former, the latter has gained ground. But what has helped underpin the credibility of both, or rather of the view that sees these as the only two viable alternatives, is the power of the disengaged model of the mind, which draws on the prestige of the procedures of disengagement, channeling its authority, as it were, into a picture of the mind and its constitution that has the three features already mentioned. What I have called the ontologizing move brings about this (dubiously legitimate) transfer. The disengaged picture of mind then adds strength to mechanism; and since mechanistic explanations themselves have great prestige because of their association with the spectacular successes of natural science, support can also flow the other way as well. A picture of mind and an underlying theory of its explanation are thus locked into a posture of mutual support, and this complex has sunk deep into the common sense of our age. When one runs into trouble, the other comes to its support. If the picture can be made to seem implausible on the phenomenological level (and this is not hard to do), one can be reassured by the reflection that it all has to be explained mechanistically on a more basic level anyway and at that level that picture *must* be right. Reciprocally, the force of otherwise powerful arguments against mechanism is neutralized by the thought that in some sense we "know" that thinking is all information processing anyway, so surely some computer-based explanation must hold in the last analysis.

When I say that this rationalist model has entered common sense, I mean partly that the first reaction of most people when asked to theorize about thinking takes the form of this model, but also that it benefits from the onus of argument. That is, it stands as the default position. Powerful philosophical arguments have to be marshaled to convince people to think differently about these matters, to shake them out of what seems obvious. But in the absence of such a challenge the model itself seems to need no defense.

II

My claim here is that Heidegger is one of the principal sources of such powerful arguments that have helped to pry us loose from rationalism. In part, this was accomplished by our being made to appreciate the role of the background in one sense of this widely used term.

The sense I am pointing to here is that which arises inevitably in connection with any view of engaged agency. Engaged agency, as I described it earlier, is that agency whose experience is made intelligible only by being placed in the context of the kind of agency it is. Thus, our embodiment makes our experience of space as oriented up-down understandable. In this relation, the first term – the form of agency (e.g., embodiment) – stands to the second – our experience – as a context conferring intelligibility. When we find a certain experience intelligible, what we are attending to, explicitly and expressly, is this experience. The context stands as the unexplicited horizon within which – or to vary the image, as the vantage point from out of which – this experience can be understood. To use Michael Polanyi's language, it is subsidiary to the focal object of awareness; it is what we are "attending from" as we attend to the experience.[7]

Now this is the sense in which I use the term "background." It is that of which I am not simply unaware (as I am unaware of what is now happening on the other side of the moon), because it makes intelligible what I am uncontestably aware of; but at the same time I cannot be said to be explicitly or focally aware of it, because that status is already occupied by what it is making intelligible. Another way of stating the first condition – that I am not simply unaware of it – is to say that the background is what I am capable of articulating, that is, what I can bring out of the condition of merely implicit, unsaid contextual facilitator, and can make articulate in other words. In this activity of articulating, I trade on my familiarity with this background. What I bring out to articulacy is what I "always knew," as we might say, or what I had a "sense" of, even if I didn't "know" it. We are at a loss exactly what to say here, where we are trying to do justice to our not having been simply unaware.

But if the background is brought to articulacy, does it not then lose the second feature, that of not being the focal, explicit object? But this seemingly plausible inference is based on a misunderstanding.

Earlier I mentioned how the relation of "world shaping," which holds between a kind of agency and a certain form of experience, is easily confused with a psychophysical causal relation. But here we see that it can also be confused with another kind of relation, one between sentences, propositions, or thoughts. Someone's argument, for instance, can be "made more intelligible" by providing additional premises if it has initially been stated too elliptically. My enthymeme may not be fully plausible to you, but becomes so when I spell out the premises. There is a relationship of rendering intelligible that holds between speech acts – I explain to you what I was "on about" when I spoke earlier – which is based ultimately on logical relations between the sentences they put in play.

Now the "world-shaping" relation is neither of these. It is not a psychophysical link holding between states of affairs or events; nor is it a relationship of making intelligible holding between sentences. One of the great obstacles to winning recognition for this relation in our philosophical world is just that these two familiar forms of connection are thought to exhaust the space of possibilities. More specifically, it is often just taken for granted that if a relationship involves conferring intelligibility, it must hold between sentences or at least *representations* of some sort. The reasons behind my muddled and lacunary thoughts in the earlier example are further *thoughts*.

But the way in which my form of embodiment makes, for example, "lying to hand" or "too unwieldy" intelligible descriptions of some object is utterly different. The first term is not a representation or made up of representations. It is a really existent agent in the world. But, one might object, this is surely not the whole story. If my being humanly embodied makes "lying to hand" intelligible to me, this is because I have some "sense" of this embodied agency. This was the word I quite naturally had recourse to a few paragraphs back. That is perfectly true. Being this kind of agent means one has an implicit understanding, what Heidegger at one point calls a "pre-understanding" of what it is to act, to get around in the world, the way we do.

But this is not a matter of representations. The rationalist epistemology induces us to jump to this conclusion because it construes all our understanding as made up of representational bits in the way I described earlier. But this is not at all what preunderstanding is like. "Knowing our way about" is not a capacity that can be analyzed into a set of images on one side and a reality portrayed on the other. An analysis of this kind is certainly foreign to our lived experience, as Merleau-Ponty has shown.[8] To know one's way about is to be really moving around, handling things, dealing with things, with understanding. What is described in the last two words is not an extra layer of representations mirroring the effective actions; it conveys rather the way we inhabit these actions, differentiating them from certain autonomic processes in the body – digestion, for instance – or from what we may do in certain moments of blind distraction. An artificial-intelligence theory of bodily action may reconstruct an explanation in which inner representational states and computations on them play a role in enabling us to get about, but this has nothing to do with the way we live this capacity.

This background sense of reality is nonrepresentational, because it is something we possess in – that is inseparable from – our actual dealings with things. This is the point that is sometimes made by saying that it is a kind of "knowing how" rather than a "knowing that." The latter kind of knowledge is understood as consisting in having correct representations. We cannot do justice to our ordinary ability to get around if we construe it on the model of mind over against a world that it mirrors.

And it is also something that permits of what I called "articulation." I can become focally aware of where I am placing my feet; or I can say that I was taking your word in one way rather than another. This is neither a matter of fixing or saying expressly what was already formulated, nor is it one of totally fresh discovery. I am drawing on my sense of things to make these formulations or to rise to this explicit awareness. Articulation is a quite different process, for it calls on rather different skills and disciplines, even on quite different qualities of character, than describing independent realities. Think of the difference between articulating how you feel about someone and describing a scene involving that person. Of course, one may contaminate the other, but that is considered a vice. The tasks are distinct.

Our sense of things can be more or less articulate. But now we can see why the supposition that it could be totally articulate is misconceived in its very nature. I said that an engaged form of agency is one whose world is shaped by its mode of being. This mode of being provides that context in which the experience of this agent is intelligible, that is, has the sense it makes to the agent, as well as being understandable to an observer. World shaping is a matter of sense making. But the form can only determine the "sense" things make for the agent, because the agent has some "sense" of this form. The word in quotes in this sentence figures in two, closely related uses. "Up" and "down" have meaning for me because of my sense of what it is to be a creature embodied as I am. Engaged agents are creatures with a background sense of things.

But why can't it all be articulated? Because it isn't a matter of representations, but of a real context conferring sense. As a real context conferring sense, our form of life is also the essential background to any articulation being meaningful. The short answer to why complete articulacy is a chimera is that any articulation itself needs the background to succeed. Each fresh articulation draws its intelligibility in turn from a background sense, abstracted from which it would fail of meaning. Each new articulation helps to redefine us, and hence can open up new avenues of potential further articulation. The process is by its very nature uncompletable, since there is no limit on the facets or aspects of our form of life that one can try to describe or of standpoints from which one might attempt to describe it.

The supposition of complete articulacy arises out of the Procrustean outlook of modern rationalism. Our understanding is supposedly made up of a finite number of not yet expressly foregrounded representations that are in some sense already there. Beyond this it is all hard wiring. What this completely misses is the irreducible content–context structure of engaged agency.

One of the crucial distortions of the traditional rationalist epistemology was just that it had no place for this content–context structure. Ideas, the reified contents of the mind, were taken as bits of information. The background understanding in which they made sense either had to be ignored altogether or had to be treated like other bits of information. This leads to almost comical consequences at times, as in Hume's complaint that he can find no idea corresponding to the self. The same disability affects the contemporary heirs of this outlook who propound computer models of thinking.

The paradoxical status of the background can then be appreciated. It can be explicited, because we aren't completely unaware of it. But the expliciting itself supposes a background. The very fashion in which we operate as engaged agents within such a background makes the prospect of total explicitation incoherent. The background cannot in this sense be thought of quantitatively at all.

One of the features that distinguishes a view of human agency as engaged from the disengaged picture is that the former has some place for this kind of background. On the disengaged view, and in particular the mechanist theory that often underpins it, there is not, of course, an explicit rejection of this notion, but the entire issue to which it provides some answer does not arise. Intelligibility is assumed from the start and does not need a context to provide it. It is understood that the bits of input information are taken as such from the beginning and that the operations that follow amount to processing of that information. In the case of computer-based theories of the mind, this reading of input and process is built in to the very definition of what occurs as the realization of a program. Its being describable as such is a sufficient condition of its counting as such.[9]

Thus, it is not surprising that all the philosophies that have challenged the disengaged picture have had some place for a notion of the background. I already referred to Heidegger's notion of preunderstanding, or a prethematized understanding of our world. Wittgenstein makes use of a similar notion – for example, when he shows what has to be supposed as already understood when we try to define something ostensively or name something.

III

But the background does not just figure in these philosophies as a doctrine. It also plays a crucial role in their argumentative strategy.

They overturn the disengaged picture through an articulation of the background that it too has to suppose. In doing this, they can be seen as answering a potential challenge that a defender of the disengaged view might throw back at his critic: if you're right, and we are always drawing on a background understanding that gives intelligibility to our experience, then even my account of the knowing agent in terms of the disengaged picture must draw on such a background to be intelligible to me. For according to you, what I am really describing is the disengaged stance, which you see as a special and regional achievement by an agent whose experience as a whole is made intelligible only by a background of the kind you invoke. As a special stance, one among the many possibilities of this agent, having a determinate place in his or her world, this must as well be made intelligible by some background understanding. So articulate for me the implicit understanding that I am allegedly drawing on, show me the preunderstanding I could not be doing without. Then I will have to believe you. Otherwise, stop prattling on about my being held captive by a picture, caught in a fly bottle, or suffering from *Seinsvergessenheit.*

The line of argument of the major "deconstructors" of the disengaged picture could serve as an answer to this challenge. It undermines the picture by bringing out the background we need for the operations described in the picture to make sense, whereby it becomes clear that this background cannot fit within the limits that the disengaged view prescribes. Once understood against its background, the account shows itself to be untenable.

The pioneer in this kind of argument, in whose steps all deconstructors find themselves treading, is Kant. Not that he intended to refute the disengaged view as such. But he did manage to upset one of its crucial features, at least in an earlier variant. The arguments of the transcendental deduction can be seen in a number of lights. But one way to take them is as a final laying to rest of a certain atomism of the input that had been espoused by empiricism. As this came to Kant through Hume, it seemed to be suggesting that the original level of knowledge of reality (whatever that turned out to be) came in particulate bits, individual "impressions." This level of information could be isolated from a later stage in which these bits were connected together – for example, in beliefs about cause–effect relations. We find ourselves forming such beliefs, but we can, by taking a stance of reflexive scrutiny (which, as we saw earlier, is fundamental to the modern epistemology), separate the basic level from our too hasty conclusions. This analysis allegedly reveals, for instance, that nothing in the phenomenal field corresponds to the necessary connection we too easily interpolate between "cause" and "effect."[10]

Kant undercuts this whole way of thinking by showing that it supposes, for each particulate impression, that it is being taken as a bit of potential information. It purports to be about something. The primitive distinction recognized by empiricists between impressions of sensation and those of reflection amount to an acknowledgment of this. The buzzing in my head is discriminated from the noise I hear from the neighboring woods, in that the first is a component in how I feel and the second seems to tell me something about what's happening out there. So even a particulate "sensation," really to be sensation (in the empiricist sense, i.e., as opposed to reflection), has to have this dimension of "aboutness." This will later be called "intentionality," but Kant speaks of the necessary relation to an object of knowledge. "Now we find that our thought of the relation of all knowledge to its object carries with it an element of necessity."[11]

With this point secured, Kant argues that this relationship to an object would be impossible if we really were to take the impression as an utterly isolated content, without any link to others. To see it as about something is to place it somewhere, at the minimum out in the world, as against in me, to give it a location in a world that, while it is in many respects indeterminate and unknown for me, cannot be wholly so. The unity of this world is presupposed by anything that could present itself as a particulate bit of *information,* and so whatever we mean by such a particulate bit, it could not be utterly without relation to all others. The background condition for this favorite supposition of empiricist philosophy, the simple impression, forbids us giving it the radical sense that Hume seemed to propose for it. To attempt to violate this background condition is to fall into incoherence. To succeed in breaking all links between individual impressions would be to lose all sense of awareness of anything. "These perceptions would not then belong to any experience, consequently would be without an object, merely a blind play of representations, less even than a dream."[12]

The transcendental deduction, and related arguments in the *Critique of Pure Reason*, can be seen as a turning point in modern philosophy. With hindsight, we can see them as the first attempt to articulate the background that the modern disengaged picture itself requires for the operations it describes to be intelligible and to use this articulation to undermine the picture. Once one goes through this transition, the whole philosophical landscape changes, because the issue of background understanding is out in the open. A crucial feature of the reified views that arise from ontologizing the canonical procedures of modern epistemology is that they make this issue invisible. The conditions of intelligibility are built into the elements and processes of the mind as internal properties. The isolated impression *is* intelligibly information on its own, just as the house is red or the table is square. It has all the particulate, separable existence of an external object. Locke treats simple ideas as analogous to the materials we use for building.[13] This outlook forgets that for something to be intelligibly X is for it to *count as* intelligibly X, and that there are always contextual conditions for anything to count as something.

In its original Kantian form, this revolution sweeps away the atomism of modern epistemology. In this respect, all those who have come after follow Kant closely. In a sense the very move that dereifies our account of the knowing agent has an inherently holistic bent. What was formerly built into the elements is now attributed to the background they all share.

Heidegger follows this pioneering Kantian form of argument. In *Being and Time*, he argues that things are disclosed first as part of a world, that is, as the correlates of concerned involvement, and within a totality of such involvements. This undercuts the first and third features of the disengaged picture, and hence makes the second feature inoperative. The first feature, the atomism of input, is denied by the notion of a totality of involvements. The third feature, neutrality, is undercut by the basic thesis that things are first disclosed in a world as ready-to-hand (*zuhanden*). To think of this character as something we project onto things that are first perceived neutrally is to make a fundamental mistake.[14]

Heidegger's discussion in *Being and Time* is sometimes taken by unsympathetic readers to be an interesting discussion of everyday existence that has no relevance to the philosophical issues of ontology he claims to be discussing. So we usually treat things as tools or obstacles in their relevance to our activities – what does this show about the priority of neutral information? Of course, we are not *aware* of things most of the time as neutral objects, but this does not show that the disengaged account is not right. Our ordinary everyday consciousness must itself be seen as a construct. We must not make the pre-Galilean mistake of thinking that things are as they appear, even in matters of the mind – so runs a common complaint by supporters of the disengaged view against "phenomenology."

But Heidegger's intention is plainly other than just reminding us of what it is like to live in the world at an everyday level. The purport of the argument is the same as Kant's and could be invoked like his as an answer to the challenge I voiced earlier. The aim is to show that grasping things as neutral objects is one of our possibilities only against the background of a way of being in the world in which things are disclosed as ready-to-hand. Grasping things neutrally requires modifying our stance to them that primitively has to be one of involvement. Heidegger, like Kant, is arguing that the comportment to things described in the disengaged view requires for its intelligibility to be situated within an enframing and continuing stance to the world that is antithetical to it, hence that this comportment could not be original and fundamental. The very condition of its possibility forbids us giving this neutralizing stance the paradigmatic and basic place in our lives that the disengaged picture supposes.

This argument about the conditions of possibility – the conditions of intelligibly realizing the stance – is carried in Heidegger's use of the term *ursprünglich* ("primordial"). This term does not just mean "prior in time," but something stronger. Our *ursprünglich* stance comes before, but also as a condition of, what follows and modifies it. The argument about conditions of possibility is also carried in his repeated use of the phrase *zunächst und zumeist* ("proximally and for the most part," according to the standard translation). Once again this sounds deceptively weak. But it is applied to a way of being that is not just there earlier and more frequently, but that also provides the background for what is not it.

In this essay, I have tried to show how Heidegger has helped to free us from the thrall of modern rationalist epistemology. I have formulated his line of thinking in terms of the notion of engaged agency. This in turn brings us to the notion of the background. But the idea of a background we can articulate figures not only as part of a new *picture* of the knowing agent. The series of philosophical arguments of Heidegger's existential analytic is itself such an articulation. The picture puts itself in motion. This pragmatic self-confirmation is what gives the existential analytic its peculiar force – a force that is very much needed to combat the hold of the disengaged understanding of agency in our culture.

NOTES

1. See T. Nagel, *The View from Nowhere* (New York: Oxford University Press, 1983).
2. Merleau-Ponty, whom I consider another of these great twentieth-century "deconstructors," focused more than anyone else on this issue of embodied agency. See especially *La phénoménologie de la perception* (Paris: Gallimard, 1945).
3. These two senses in which experience is shaped by embodiment help to explain the dialogue of the deaf between critics and exponents of artificial-intelligence-inspired theories of the mind. The former, e.g., Hubert Dreyfus and John Searle, have often insisted that the computer offers a model of "disembodied" consciousness. See Dreyfus's *What Computers Can't Do* (New York: Harper & Row, 1979); and Searle's "Minds, Brains and Programmes," in *Behavioural and Brain Sciences*, 3 (1980): 417–57. Proponents of the artificial intelligence model, insulted in the very heart of their materialist commitment, generally find this accusation unintelligible. But it is easy to see why the criticism is not understood. Proponents of strong artificial intelligence are thinking of the first kind of relation. The second kind has not yet swum into their conceptual ken, and hence they have great trouble understanding what they are being accused of.
4. Thomas Nagel, *Mortal Questions* (Cambridge: Cambridge University Press, 1979), p. 208.
5. The soul "ne s'est pas contentée de juger qu'il y avoit quelque chose hors d'elle qui étoit cause qu'elle avoit ses sentiments, en quoi elle ne se seroit pas trompée; mais elle a passé plus outre." "Et comme ces idées ne sont point naturelles, mais arbitraires, on y a agi avec une grande bizarrerie." A. Arnaud and P. Nicole, *La logique ou l'art de penser*, Pt. I, Chap. 9 (Paris: Flammarion, 1970), p. 103.

6. This is, of course, what underlies the misunderstanding mentioned in note 3 about the issue of "embodiment." Mechanists cannot formulate the issue without transcending their favorite explanatory language. It is odd that they have such trouble seeing that this language is so framed as to exclude engaged thinking, because with another part of their minds they are aware of this, and often say so. Thus, one of the original motivations for constructing computer realizations of reasoning was that realization on a program was thought to be a good criterion of formal rigor. A formally rigorous proof is one in which the transitions depend purely on the shape of the expressions, regardless of their semantic "meaning." But a proof can sometimes seem rigorous in this sense, and fail really to be so, because we can unawares be "supplying" some of the missing steps through the intuitive leaps we make as we check it. "Subjective" intelligibility is filling the gaps in formal argument. But if such a proof can be automated, that is, run on a machine, then we *know* that there can be no such surreptitious input from subjective intelligibility, and the proof must be valid. See John Haugeland's "automation principle: wherever the legal moves of a formal system are fully determined by algorithms, then that system can be automated" (in *Artificial Intelligence: The Very Idea* [Cambridge, MA: MIT Press, 1985], p. 83]. Also Marvin Minsky: "If the procedure can be carried out by some very simple machine, so that there can be no question of or need for 'innovation' or 'intelligence,' then we can be sure that the specification is complete, and that we have an 'effective procedure' " (in *Computation: Finite and Infinite Machines* [Englewood Cliffs, NJ: Prentice-Hall, 1967], p. 105].

7. See Michael Polanyi, *Personal Knowledge* (Chicago: University of Chicago Press, 1958), and *The Tacit Dimension* (Garden City, NY: Doubleday, 1966).

8. See Merleau-Ponty, *La phénoménologie de la perception.*

9. See Daniel Dennett, *The Intentional Stance* (Cambridge, MA: MIT Press, 1988), Chaps. 2 and 7.

10. David Hume, *An Enquiry Concerning Human Understanding* (Oxford: Oxford University Press, 1966), Chap. 7.

11. "Wir finden aber, dass unser Gedanke von der Beziehung aller Erkenntniss auf ihren Gegenstand etwas von Notwendigkeit bei sich führe." Immanuel Kant, *Critique of Pure Reason*, trans. N. K. Smith (London: Macmillan Press, 1963), A 104.

12. "Diese [sc. Wahrnehmungen] würden aber alsdann auch zu keiner Erfahrung gehören, folglich ohne Objekt und nichts als ein blindes Spiel der Vorstellungen, d.i. weniger als ein Traum sein." Ibid., A 112.

13. John Locke, *An Essay Concerning Human Understanding* (Oxford: Oxford University Press, 1975), 2.2.2.

14. "The kind of Being which belongs to these entities is readiness-to-hand. But this characteristic is not to be understood as merely a way of taking them, as if we were talking such 'aspects' into the 'entities' which we proximally encounter, or as if some world-stuff which is proximally present-at-hand were 'given subjective coloring' in this way" (BT 101). ("Die Seinsart dieses Seienden ist die Zuhandenheit. Sie darf jedoch nicht als blosser Auffassungscharakter verstanden werden, als würden dem zunächst begegnenden 'Seienden' solche 'Aspekte' aufgeredet, als würde ein zunächst an sich vorhandener Weltstoff in dieser Weise 'subjektiv gefärbt'" (SZ 71).

8 Death, time, history: Division II of *Being and Time*

> This certainty, that "I myself am in that I will die," is the *basic certainty of Dasein itself....* The MORIBUNDUS *first* gives the SUM its sense.
>
> (HCT 316–17)

> Only in dying can I to some extent say absolutely, "I am."
>
> (HCT 318)

Modern philosophy turns away from things in the world and zeroes in on the human self that grasps them in thought and transforms them in action. The self becomes the repository of both their truth and their ultimate purposes. By the same token, the human self is given the status of the self-grounding ground of reality. In this new and exalted status, the self ceases to be viewed as part and parcel of some independent order of things. Beginning with Descartes's *cogito*, the self withdraws from the world and falls back on its own experiences and thoughts. The subjectivity of the self supplies both the point of departure and the validating ground for various philosophical attempts at a reconstruction of our knowledge of the world.

One of Heidegger's aims in *Being and Time* was to question and to overcome this subjectivist tradition of modern philosophy. I hope to show, however, that in Division II of *Being and Time* Heidegger reveals himself as an heir to that tradition and to its model of the human self.

THE HUMAN SELF

In the very first section of Division II (BT 274–8), Heidegger makes two claims whose importance to the entire philosophical project he is pursuing in his opus magnum cannot be overestimated. In the first place, since the aim of this project is to investigate the meaning of being in general, and since the meaning of being in general is disclosed by Dasein, the ultimate clarification of the meaning of being demands an appropriately ultimate ("primordial") interpretation of Dasein. In other terms, we cannot be satisfied with this or that partial or approximate view of Dasein; we must achieve the grasp of Dasein *as a whole*. In the second place, and as we shall see more clearly later, from the present vantage point "one thing has become unmistakable: *our existential analysis of Dasein up till now cannot lay claim to primordiality.* Its fore-having never included more than the *inauthentic* Being of Dasein, and of Dasein as less than a *whole* [als unganzes]" (BT 276). The entire Division I, then, must now be considered profoundly incomplete, since it failed to give us the required insight into both the *totality* and the *authenticity* of Dasein (BT 276).

Even at this, still provisional and still quite general stage of Heidegger's analysis, the joint appearance of "totality" and "authenticity" can be given some justification. For the authentic life (in contrast to the inauthentic life) is one in which not just this or that aspect of Dasein, but Dasein *as a whole*, comes to expression. And if, as it will soon become clear, Dasein's authenticity requires the lucid acceptance of one's own death, it is precisely because Dasein's totality can be revealed only in its being-toward-death.

This last statement can first be taken in its obvious and least controversial sense. As long as a human individual is alive – as long as he continues to take a stand on what it means to be – his identity is not a settled matter, for it is open to constant revision and reinterpretation. At every stage of my life I can always take this rather than that option open to me – and, in so doing, not only do I determine what the course of my life will be from now on, but I also reshape and redefine the meaning of what my life was all about until now. This is so because the options that I take shed light on what was important to me all along, on the endurance and the strength of my commitments (or lack thereof), and so on. To shift back to Heidegger's terminology: as long as Dasein is, it can choose its possibilities; hence, as long as this "ahead-of-itself" item in the structure of Dasein is not extinguished, Dasein will be characterized by a "lack of totality" (BT 279). And since death does extinguish – ultimately and irrevocably – man's ability to choose his possibilities, death puts to rest the ongoing process of reshaping and redefining an individual's identity. What his life was all about becomes now a settled matter.

So far, however, this characterization of death has been offered from a third-person standpoint, and this cannot be satisfying to Heidegger. We must ask about "the ontological meaning of dying of the person who dies, as a possibility-of-Being which belongs to *his* Being" (BT 283). Elsewhere (HCT 308–9), Heidegger spells out in more detail both the thinking behind this requirement and the difficulty it immediately leads to. Since Dasein is defined as being in each instance *mine*, the emergence of death as totalizing my life must appear from within *my own* first-person standpoint. But this requirement seems impossible to satisfy, for as long as I envision things from my own standpoint, I have *not* yet reached my totality, and, conversely, when *I have* reached my totality, there is no standpoint of mine from which to gain the experience of that totality. To put it plainly, if my identity is in principle incomplete while I am alive, then I cannot see what it would even *mean* to say, "This is what my life was all about," unless I construe my death as an event witnessed and interpreted by other people. But by doing this I *eo ipso* abandon the first-person account of my own death.

But the dilemma we have just noted – *either* I am, and then any talk about the completion of my identity is meaningless from my own standpoint, *or* such talk is meaningful, but then it is not conducted from my own standpoint – is a false alternative. It results entirely from our conception of death as a present-at-hand item, that is, as an event within the world (BT 280). I have assumed that in order to gain the first-person sense of what it would mean to say (irrevocably), "This is what my life was all about," I would have to *wait* until that event of my death actually takes place; the insurmountable alternative we have seen to emerge is then a foregone conclusion. But this need not be so. To be sure, I cannot grasp just *what* my complete identity will be. But I nevertheless know, even from within my own standpoint, *how* to view my life as something I have the potential to realize.

In effect, I do not have to wait until my life runs its course to gain a sense of being exposed to, and defined by, the power of death. For the *cogito sum*, we remember from the epigraph, must be restated as *moribundus sum*: I *am* only in that I find myself, at every moment of my life, powerless to escape the possibility of dying at precisely that particular moment (and not only tomorrow, or the day after tomorrow, etc.). As will be shown later, *this* is the one truth that I cannot doubt, though I may try to conceal it and cover it up. And as we shall see shortly, my ability to doubt all truths is itself dependent on that unshakable truth about my being always totally vulnerable to the power of death.

At the same time – and due to the very same circumstance of my total vulnerability to death – the complete identity that I envision as attributable to me remains *my* identity. For my first-person sense of death establishes my life not only as a *totality*, but also as uniquely *mine* – that is, not as an intersection of social and natural roles and functions that I share, or may share, with others.

Heidegger's justification of this important connection – death gives my life its "totality" and its "mineness" (*Jemeinigkeit*) as well – is simple (BT 283–4). Being a member of the public world I can be easily replaced ("represented") by another person. Somebody else could have filled the position I occupy in society; somebody else could have been the husband of the woman I married, the father of her children, and so on. Now this possibility of being "represented" by another individual breaks down in one case and in one case only: in the case of my death. It is true, of course, that when we speak loosely we can easily point to a number of other cases in which, apparently, our personal presence is indispensable; no one, it seems, can replace me at that operating table when the surgeon is about to perform an operation on me, or in that imposing office of the dean, who expects from me an explanation of my repeated absences from the university functions, and so on. But it is also easy to see why such counterexamples can have no bearing whatsoever on Heidegger's point about death, for I can always avoid the experiences I have just described: I can decide to take my chances without the surgery, or I can fail to appear at the dean's office, and so on. My presence or absence on those occasions is a matter of my own choice: if I think that I have lived long enough anyway, or if I don't care much about keeping my job, I will not find it difficult, and certainly not impossible, to miss my appointments with both surgeon and the dean. But in no case can I avoid appearing before the tribunal of death. In all other cases where it seems that no one can replace me, changing my own goals will make me capable of avoiding those experiences. But there is no goal and no strategy that would allow me to maneuver myself out of my rendezvous with death.

We can understand now why Heidegger attributes to death the power of *both* totalizing and individualizing Dasein. Death totalizes me, for due to death my identity will become complete. Death individualizes me, for it imposes upon me the one and only experience that is inescapably mine. Thus, "if 'ending,' as dying, is constitutive for Dasein's *totality*, then the Being of this wholeness itself must be conceived as an existential phenomenon which is in each case *one's own*" (BT 284, my emphasis). But although these two functions of death – to *complete* my identity and to establish it as uniquely *mine* – are inseparable, they nevertheless remain distinct. Since somebody else could have filled in for me with each and every one of the experiences making up my life history, all of these experiences are uniquely mine only because that life history as a whole is individuated *independently* of them by its ultimate term: by death. Of the latter, it can only be said that it is "in every case mine insofar as it is at all" (BT 284). Thus, our first-person encounter with the menace of death, demands the *repudiation of the principle of the identity of indiscernibles*: I am *this* particular person not on account of the totality of determinations attributable to me, but due to the "mineness" of death, where the mineness at issue is an underived and primitive term distinguished only by its sheer "thisness," and not by any property or set of properties.

We can now see with more clarity Heidegger's reliance on the modern idea of subjectivity, indeed his profound kinship with Descartes. For both philosophers, the human individual is thrown back upon *his own* self by a sense of *total powerlessness and vulnerability* in the face of an ultimate threat (of, respectively, the evil demon and death). I shall return to this idea later.[1] But there is an immediate difficulty standing in the way of that parallel, just noted, between Descartes and Heidegger. If in Descartes the threat of the evil demon seems indeed inescapable (at least before the self's discovery of God), it is because the demon is said to deceive me constantly.[2] Thus, the demon gives me no respite and no escape; his power holds me in its grip without the slightest letup or slackening. And it seems equally obvious, at least to common sense, that death does *not* have this sort of power over me. I can be said to be under death's real threat when I wake up in a hospital bed, after a complicated and dangerous operation. But I seem to confront no such threat at all when, healthy, vigorous, and fresh from my yearly medical checkup, I find myself walking leisurely on a sandy beach. Death does not seem to threaten me "constantly." And so it follows that the "mineness" I was said to acquire through the exposure to death's menace cannot be one of the core characteristics of human selfhood. Yet such was precisely the status attributed to this characteristic at the very beginning of Heidegger's analytic of Dasein.[3]

The difficulty is genuine, but it stems from a misunderstanding of Heidegger's interpretation of death. The difficulty is raised from within the *commonsensical* view of death, while for Heidegger, the commonsensical view of death is a gross distortion of the actual state of affairs. When that actual state of affairs – that is, the true face of death – is brought out and articulated, the threat of death reveals itself as being indeed constant and all-pervasive.

Heidegger's analytic of death takes off with a reminder that "care is the basic state of Dasein" (BT 293). For if death is to have the constancy and the all-pervasiveness required by its function of individualizing the human self, that status of death must be made clear in terms of the very basic state of Dasein. This is indeed the route Heidegger now takes. He has already, at the earlier stages of his analytic of human finitude, defined care as composed of "existence," "facticity," and "falling." He will now show how all these three aspects of care reveal the constancy and the all-pervasiveness of man's exposure to the threat of death.

But the essential connection between care and death can be grasped on a more general level as well. Dasein is care, for Dasein is always concerned about its being. My life (both in its "that" and in its "what") is not something indifferent to me, something that leaves me cold, as it were; on the contrary, it is something that *matters* to me. Now my life matters to me – indeed *must* matter to me – only because I am aware that I don't have it "forever" and "once for all," life matters only because I am aware that it can be snatched away from me by the power of death. And so care is Dasein's basic state only because Dasein is, and understands itself as being, a mortal creature: "I am this 'I can die at any moment.' . . . *I myself am this constant and utmost possibility of myself*, namely, to be no more. Care, which is essentially care about the being of Dasein, at its innermost is nothing but this being-ahead-of-itself in the uttermost possibility of its own can-be" (HCT 313). Conversely, just as Dasein's (basic) state of care is dependent on Dasein's sense of being a mortal creature so, too, "*as regards its ontological possibility, dying is grounded in care*" (BT 296). In other terms, the mere conception of a mortal creature that would remain unaffected by, and indifferent to, its own perishability is not at all logically contradictory. If death moves us to show concern about our life, it is because man's "basic state" is indeed care – and not some sort of total obliviousness to his own finitude. To summarize, if we were not threatened by death, our basic state would not be care; but if our basic state were not care, our death would not be felt as threatening. Care and the sense of one's mortality are thus, to use one of Heidegger's favorite terms, "equiprimordial."

Now since care is the *basic* state of Dasein – that is, the state in which Dasein *always* is, the state that underlies *all* of Dasein's experiences – and since care implies one's exposure to the menace of death, this exposure must be just as constant and all-pervasive as care itself. For if I could remove the menace of death from a certain stretch of my life, then at least within *that* stretch I would not have to worry about my life being snatched away from me (I could say, "I will think about crossing that bridge when I get to it – when I get sick, old, and so on.") and thus care would cease to permeate *all* of my experiences. If, then, care is to remain the "basic state" of Dasein, the threat of death must be constant to Dasein.

Now the constancy of death's threat to Dasein reveals itself with a particular clarity in the first and most fundamental aspect of care: in Dasein's being-ahead-of-itself, projected toward a field of its possibilities. Death is constant insofar as it is the only *pure* possibility of Dasein, that is, the sort of possibility free of any admixture of actuality (and of necessity as well). Ordinarily, Heidegger argues (BT 305–7), we lack any understanding of such a pure possibility – including the possibility of our own dying – for our control-oriented stance toward the world is bent on reducing every possibility to a predictable and manageable event or process. Owing to this stance, possibility loses its character of possibility and it becomes possible only "relatively to" certain circumstances and conditions. A possibility whose occurrence is thus made dependent on the *actuality* of such and such conditions becomes something less than a possibility to the precise degree to which it becomes more connected with actuality. To appear in all the purity of its character *qua* possibility, a possibility must thus be equally possible under any conditions whatever.

But this does not mean that such a possibility becomes transformed into a *necessity*. There are two kinds of necessity to be considered, and rejected, in this connection. If we try to connect (or, worse still, to reduce) the possibility of dying to some *real* necessity produced by the operation of causal laws in our universe, then we are once again on our way to depriving possibility of its quality of possibility by making it dependent on something foreign and external to it. If it is necessary that I die at some point given certain facts and laws of human biology then, by the same token, I will not die unless and until all the required conditions have actually taken place. But then I can anticipate (at least to some degree) when and how I am likely to die and I can make my plans accordingly. So if death is viewed as occurring due to a real necessity, then death is not always equally possible – and then its character of pure possibility is, once again, glossed over. On the other hand – and this is the second sense of necessity to be considered here and rejected – the constancy and the all-pervasiveness of the threat of death to us is not a matter of *logical* necessity either. Given certain general facts about the human condition, the threat of death must indeed shadow every individual at every stage of his life. But it is not logically necessary that these general facts about the human condition be such as they are.

The all-pervasiveness and omnipresence of death's threat to an individual is captured by Heidegger with the term "indefiniteness" (*Unbestimmtheit*). The possibility of death is indefinite, for it is not confined to any particular moment or time span. The possibility of death can materialize at any moment. Furthermore, since Heidegger argues (in §70 of *Being and Time*) that space is encountered from within the temporal project of Dasein, the indefiniteness of death's "when" (BT 302) implies its lack of connection with any particular "here" or "there." This is why the threat disclosed in anxiety – the threat of death (BT 310) – is perceived as coming at us from *"nowhere"* (BT 231). Now, since due to its indefiniteness, the possibility of death is disclosed to us as a "constant threat" (BT 310), the parallel we have drawn between the threat of the evil demon in Descartes and the threat of death in Heidegger is vindicated. Both threats are indeed constant and all-pervasive; both threats reveal to the individual the powerlessness and the vulnerability of his condition.

But there is an even stronger kinship to be discovered between the *cogito sum* of Descartes and the existential *moribundus sum* of Heidegger. Insofar as I view myself in the light of the possibility of being misled by the evil demon, I suspend my reliance on the truths of everyday life; but at the same time, I discover the unshakable truth of my subjectivity: "There is some deceiver or other, very powerful and very cunning, who ever employs his ingenuity in deceiving me. Then without doubt I exist also if he deceives me, and let him deceive me as much as he will, he can never cause me to be nothing so long as I think I am something."[4] In a similar vein, my coming face to face with the (indefinite) possibility of death not only forces me to abandon the ordinary, everyday framework of intelligibility and truth, but at the same time leads me to discover the unshakable certainty and truth of my *sum*. Let us consider these two steps one by one.

In the first place, then, insofar as anxiety brings an individual face to face with the indefiniteness of death's threat to him, his public world is suddenly discovered as failing him. For the public world cannot protect an individual against death, and so this world *as a whole* proves to be unreliable. The tie between the individual and his public world is broken; the individual does not "find" himself in the latter; the meanings and the truths making up the fabric of the world become alien to the individual: "anxiety . . . takes away from Dasein the possibility of understanding itself, as it falls, in terms of the world and the way things have been publicly interpreted" (BT 232).

But – in the second place – insofar as the individual thus withdraws his assent to the intelligibility and truth of the public interpretation of reality, he discovers and falls back upon the unshakable evidence of the existential *moribundus sum*. Not only is this evidence subjectively "certain" (BT 309) but – just as in the case of the Cartesian *cogito* – it has "truth" as well (BT 309). To be sure, Heidegger warns us explicitly (BT 309) not to attribute to the certainty and truth of death the character of "apodictic evidence." But it is even more important to pay close attention to what he means by this warning, and how he justifies it. The passage is worth quoting in full:

Dasein must first have lost itself in the factual circumstances [*Sachverhalte*] (this can be one of care's own tasks and possibilities) if it is to obtain the pure objectivity – that is to say, the indifference – of apodictic evidence. If being certain in relation to death does not have this character, this does not mean that it is of a lower grade, but that *it does not belong at all to the graded order of the kinds of evidence we can have about the present-at-hand.*

Holding death for true (death *is* just one's own) shows another kind of certainty, and is more primordial than any certainty which relates to entities encountered within-the-world, or to formal objects; for it is certain of Being-in-the-world. As such, holding death for true does not demand just *one* definite kind of behavior in Dasein, but demands Dasein itself in the full authenticity of its existence.   (BT 309–10)

In this crucial passage, Heidegger clearly spells out several things. In the first place, whereas the certainty and the truth of death should not indeed be confused with the "apodictic evidence" that characterizes our mental grasp of "formal objects" – that is, of objects of pure mathematics or else of the pure essences of things – death's omnipresent threat to us does not have, for that reason, a "lower" kind of evidence and truth. Quite the contrary, as Heidegger leads us to understand in the last part of the passage, our "holding death for true" permeates *all* of our attitudes and stances, while the truth attributed to, say, the axioms and theorems of mathematics is attributed in a special "theoretical" attitude, which – Heidegger argues in *Being and Time* – is not even basic and primordial to Dasein. To put it plainly, under certain circumstances, Dasein *can* withdraw its endorsement of the intelligibility and truth of "formal objects," while under no circumstances whatever is it possible for Dasein to liberate itself from the gnawing sense of its mortality.[5] And, in effect, the very same anxiety that alienates Dasein from the meanings and the truths of the public world – and hence also from the meaning and truth of "formal objects" – brings Dasein face to face with its *moribundus sum*. The evidence and the truth of that proposition are unique in that all other forms of evidence and truth are objects of assent or doubt performed by a creature that, throughout all those acts of assent and doubt, continues to acknowledge (authentically or inauthentically) its own mortality.

Now insofar as the evidence of Descartes's *cogito* is interpreted as a case of "apodictic evidence" accompanying our mental grasp of a present-at-hand item – of our own ego – then indeed there can be no analogy between Descartes's *cogito sum* and Heidegger's *moribundus sum*. In addition, there can be no doubt that this is how Descartes's claims were often understood and developed; and it is also true that there is ample support for this sort of interpretation in Descartes's own writings. Not only is the "ego" of the *ego cogito* interpreted as a (mental) substance, but our cognitive mode of access to that substance often exhibits the character of an "apodictic evidence" enjoyed by mathematical entities.

But there is another, and more correct, way of analyzing Descartes's *cogito*, and this analysis brings him very close to Heidegger's thinking on the *sum*. Jaakko Hintikka argued that Descartes's fundamental and self-founding principle has in fact a *performatory character*.[6] The "I am" is neither deduced from the "I think" nor logically true all by itself. Rather, when I say, "I do not exist," this sentence (or thought) is "existentially inconsistent" with my uttering this sentence or entertaining that thought.[7] What implies my existence, then, is not the thought itself, but my performance of the act of thinking that particular thought (or any other thought denying my being). Similarly, if we are prepared to agree with Heidegger's dictum "The MORIBUNDUS *first gives* the SUM *its sense*," then every attitude and stance of mine – including my very attempts, in whatever form, to deny my mortality – testifies to my existence as a mortal self. The structure of the argument is the same in both Descartes and Heidegger.

TIME AND HISTORY

Our endorsement of that Heideggerian dictum "The MORIBUNDUS *first gives* the SUM *its sense*" allows us to see why the instantaneity of the Cartesian *cogito* must be replaced with the inherently temporal character of Dasein. Mine is a finite, limited existence – the sort of existence that, inevitably, must meet its ultimate end. And this is another way of saying that I am aware of having a certain definite destiny ahead of me. Furthermore, my sense of that future destiny is instrumental in bringing me face to face with my past. For when I say that my life is bound to come to its end, I imply that I am a *determinate* self, a self endowed with a particular life history, with such and such social and cultural background, and so on. All of these items refer to my past and all of them come alive for me as making up my identity when I confront the finite future. This is why my sense of my past is dependent on my sense of that finite future (BT 373,435).

Since death is revealed in anxiety and since my sense of death as my ultimate end imposes upon my experiences their temporal structure, it is only to be expected that the latter, too, will have its roots in anxiety. And, in effect, Heidegger speaks explicitly of the *temporality of anxiety*, which he carefully distinguishes from both the inauthentic and authentic forms of temporality:

> In contrast to this making-present which is not held on to [this is the inauthentic present, the present in which Dasein loses and disperses itself], the Present of anxiety is *held on to*...But even though the Present of anxiety is *held on to*, it does not as yet have the character of the moment of vision which temporalizes itself in a resolution.   (BT 394)

> This bringing-back has neither the character of an evasive forgetting nor that of a remembering. But just as little does anxiety imply that one has already taken over one's existence into one's resolution and done so by a repeating.   (BT 394)

In the first of these passages, Heidegger opposes both the inauthentic present (the "making-present") and the authentic present (the "moment of vision") to the present of anxiety. In the second passage, he draws a similar contrast between the inauthentic past (evasive forgetting, remembering) and the authentic past (repeating), on the one hand, and the past of anxiety, on the other hand.

The temporality of anxiety is the underlying ground of both authentic and inauthentic temporality. Whereas inauthentic temporality expresses Dasein's flight from its anxious anticipation of death, authentic temporality is built upon a stance in which one confronts what is revealed in the temporality of anxiety and expresses this in one's attitude toward one's entire life, from birth to death.

Let us try to get some grip on the basic concepts with the aid of which Heidegger attempts to articulate the structure of human temporalizing. Let us begin with inauthentic temporality, for this form of temporalizing represents the understanding of time characteristic of the ordinary, commonsensical Dasein. Since the entire commonsensical way of life expresses Dasein's attempt to turn away from the ever-present menace of death, the inauthentic future takes the form of a (hopeful, fearful, etc.) "awaiting" and "expecting" (BT 386 – 7). In the general strategy of an inauthentic Dasein, our sense of radical vulnerability and powerlessness becomes glossed over and made manageable by being projected onto the world. Whatever threats to our existence there may be, they are now viewed as threatening us from *within* the world. In conformity with this overall strategy, our entire future is seen as a pursuit of a secure acceptance by the world of the "they" (*das Man*). This understanding of the future entails a selective, highly utilitarian attitude toward one's past. Since successes and failures on the road of the inauthentic future are defined by the trends and pressures of the public world, an inauthentic Dasein's past will be disclosed through "forgetting." An individual will repress and relegate into oblivion such parts of his past as may prove detrimental to his search for success in the rapidly changing world of the "they" with all of this world's trends, fashions, and clichés. Conversely, whatever it is that this type of individual will remember will be remembered on the basis of forgetting (BT 389). Since an inauthentic individual retains from his past only what serves his pursuit of a secure acceptance by the public world, he remembers A only insofar as he forgets B, or C, or D. Finally, the overall attitude of "expecting" one's future and of "forgetting" one's past shapes one's inauthentic stance toward the present, the stance of "making-present." The inauthentic Dasein's search for security is reflected in a collection of entities – of persons, things, goods, and so on – with which this sort of Dasein surrounds itself (and thus "makes present" these entities) in order to gain a sense of having a place within the reassuring world of the "they."

In authentic temporality, the temporality of anxiety is incorporated into Dasein's self-interpretation. In the "anticipated" (authentic) future, an individual faces up to the ever-threatening menace of death as the meaning of what lies ahead. By thus confronting the limitedness and the finiteness of his existence, he finds himself brought back to his past. This authentic sense of acknowledging one's past is gained in "repetition." Finally, in the authentic present's "moment of vision" (*Augenblick*) an individual can open up to the present realities of his life, since his abandonment of the singleminded pursuit of social acceptance allows him to adopt a free, nonmanipulative attitude toward his present situation.

Viewed merely as items in the temporality of Dasein, the future, past, and present are disclosed in "ecstases" – in Dasein's ways of reaching out toward its death, its roots, and its surroundings. The *ordering* of these ecstases is prior to and independent of any temporal chronology (BT 375–6). The ecstatic future is not "later" than the ecstatic present, for at any moment of my life I am equally vulnerable to the power of death, and hence that vulnerability of mine is always an actual, live issue for me. My past, too, is not something that has simply elapsed and is now left behind, something existing "no longer now – but earlier" (BT 375). This is so because my past is nothing other than my "thrownness" – that is, my rootedness in a culture, my already established preferences, skills, habits, and so on – and it is precisely in terms of this thrownness that my present experiences get to be organized and endowed with a meaning. Nor does the ecstasis of the present derive its name from its position within a chronological order. In this ecstasis, in this "being-alongside (entities encountered within-the-world)," I am "present" to those entities and I thus allow them to "have presence" to me – in the sense of being available to me, of being at my disposal.

Just as the *ordering* of the ecstases is independent of any chronological relations, so too the *becoming* of the ecstases (thus, the present becomes the past, the future becomes the present, etc.) is not a chronologically determinable alteration either. Indeed, temporality's "essence is a *process* of temporalizing in the unity of the ecstases" (BT 377, my emphasis). And this dynamic, process-like character of temporality both precedes and conditions all our notions of temporal flow as chronologically understood.

But then how can Heidegger derive our ordinary, chronologically understood notion of time from the temporality of Dasein? We have already seen how the temporality of anxiety gets perverted into inauthentic temporality – into the temporality of a Dasein unwilling to confront its ontological powerlessness and vulnerability. This form of temporality is at the source of time as ordinarily understood: "'Time' as ordinarily understood...arises from inauthentic temporality" (BT 374). We must now try to understand this claim in more detail.

Human temporality in general is mapped onto the world through the *horizonal schemata* of the three temporal ecstases. We have already noted that the ecstases are Dasein's ways of being "outside itself." This last expression includes an implicit reference to the horizonal-schematic structure of the ecstases: "There belongs to each ecstasis a 'whither' to which one is carried away" (BT 416). Now this "whither" is nothing other than the worldly counterpart of each ecstasis. For example, the horizonal schema of the past is defined as "that *in the face of which*" Dasein has been thrown. This means that my relationship to my past presupposes a reference to a certain condition of the world: to the society and the institutions within which I was born and raised, to my family environment, to my childhood friends, and so on. My past is thus mirrored in the past of the world. Heidegger gives a similar account of the link between the ecstases of the present and the future, on the one hand, and their own worldly counterparts, on the other hand.

Because of its grounding in human temporality, the world gains a temporal structure of its own. However, we are still one step short of accounting for the emergence of the temporal chronology. For example, "that *in the face of which* Dasein has been thrown" (the horizonal schema of the past) does not yet mean "earlier" than the horizonal schema of the present. But this still outstanding gap is rendered irrelevant within the context of the existential analytic of Dasein. For Dasein's temporality is schematized onto the world due to Dasein's practical, everyday absorption within the world, and this practical, everyday stance of Dasein imposes on it the necessity of "reckoning" with time, of taking time into account in all of our daily plans and projects (BT 456–7). And in order to respond to that necessity of reckoning with time we must *date* actions and events that take place in it. This is why the horizons and the schemata of the ecstases must be assigned a chronological standing vis-à-vis one another. And this is also why the origin of the temporal chronology must be looked for in the commonsensical, inauthentic temporality of Dasein. "In the 'then' concern expresses itself as awaiting [i.e., as the inauthentic future], in the 'on that former occasion,' as retaining [as the inauthentic past]" (BT 458). Only now can the horizons and the schemata of temporality receive the chronological significance they have been lacking so far: "The horizon for the retaining which expresses itself in the 'on that former occasion' is the '*earlier*'; the horizon for the 'now' is the '*today*'" (BT 459). From this stage on, when I think of the circumstances and conditions in the face of which I was thrown (the horizonal schema of the past), I think of them as being "earlier" than such and such circumstances and conditions that I confront right now or am about to confront in the near future, and so on.

The substitution of the *moribundus sum* for Descartes's *cogito sum* had proved to be instrumental in replacing the instantaneity of the Cartesian *cogito* with the temporality of Dasein. A further implication of this substitution is the rediscovery of the *historical* dimension of the human self. The reason is still the same: when I anticipate and endure the menace of death I find myself to be a limited, determinate self, and this means also a self with certain definite historical roots, a self with a "heritage" and a "fate" (BT 435). But in thus imposing upon Dasein a historical dimension, death works jointly with several other items in the structure of Dasein. "Only if death, guilt, conscience, freedom and finitude reside together equiprimordially in the Being of an entity as they do in care, can that entity exist in the mode of fate, that is to say only then can it be historical in the very depths of its existence" (BT 437).

Let us first say something about the "call of conscience" (*Ruf des Gewissens*), which imposes on the plain, ordinary Dasein a "demand" (BT 311) to turn away from the conformisms of the "they" and to live up to its authenticity and wholeness. What does the ordinary, everyday Dasein *hear* in the message delivered in the call of conscience? The answer to this question represents the next stage in Heidegger's deepening hermeneutics of conscience. In the message delivered in the call, the ordinary Dasein is told about its own *guilt*.

But while Dasein, as the addressee and the bearer of this message of guilt, is indeed the ordinary Dasein, the guilt in question is not ordinary guilt. The latter is always specific and determinate: I am guilty of having crossed that intersection at the red light, guilty of not having lived up to my administrative duties at the university, and so on. But the guilt addressed to the ordinary Dasein in the call of conscience is general and unconditional. It does not concern this or that, and it is not conditional upon my having (or not having) done this or that. What, then, am I guilty of according to the accusation raised against me through the call of conscience?

This "primordial existential meaning" (BT 326) of my guilt can be gathered "from the fact that this 'Guilty' turns up as a predicate for the 'I am'" (BT 326). If the "guilty" is to be taken as the predicate of the mere "I am," it's because my mere existence is discovered as making me guilty. If it were otherwise, I would have to refer to myself (at least implicitly) through some additional and still other predicates; I would have to say, "I *as* the father of a child am guilty of not paying child support," or "I *as* a driver am guilty of violating traffic regulations," and so on. Under such circumstances the predicate "guilty" would not apply to me *qua* merely being, but *qua* being only this or that. But the call of conscience tells me I am guilty insofar as I (merely) am.

Now Dasein is guilty in its (mere) being, for, to begin with, "Dasein is not itself the basis of being" (BT 300). While I can achieve a measure of mastery and control over various items making up my environment, I can achieve no mastery and no control at all over the basis of my life. Thus, for Dasein to exist means "*never* to have power over one's ownmost Being from the ground up. This '*not*' belongs to the existential meaning of 'thrownness'" (BT 330); and therefore our thrownness is shot through with "nullity" [*Nichtigkeit*]. This connection of thrownness with nullity is also discovered through one's anxious anticipation of death: "The 'nothing' with which anxiety brings us face to face, unveils the nullity by which Dasein, in its very *basis*, is defined; and this basis itself is as thrownness into death" (BT 356).

In effect, in order to recognize myself as being thrown into death, I must come to see myself as a finite, limited, and hence a *determinate* self. What makes me such a determinate, concrete self is my social and historical background, my personal life history, my habits, and so on. Thrownness encompasses all of these established characteristics of mine, that is, my entire past (BT 373). And if my thrownness is the source of guilt, I must be guilty for having adopted the wrong attitude toward my entire past self. This does not mean that there is something *special* about my past that makes me guilty (if such were the case we would be back to the ordinary sense of guilt), but this does imply that I am guilty not as some empty form of a mortal self "in general," but as a determinate self.

But how *can* my thrownness represent a source of guilt for me? Where have I failed – where *can* I fail – in taking up an attitude toward my thrownness?

But I *can* fail and, as an ordinary Dasein, I *have* failed in my attitude toward my thrownness. "The Self, which as such has to lay the basis for itself, can *never* get that basis into its power; and yet, as existing, it must take over Being-a-basis" (BT 330). The accusation of guilt understood in that "primordial ontological meaning" is addressed to me insofar as I fail to respond to that task of shaping my life within a thrownness that I can never master and control.

The groundwork is now laid for man's acceptance of his historical roots. Once again, and quite predictably, the strategy of denial – the strategy of the inauthentic Dasein – will be brought to its end by Dasein's anxious encounter with the same menace of death:

As a way of Being for Dasein, history has its roots so essentially in the future that death, as that possibility of Dasein which we have already characterized, throws anticipatory existence back upon its *factical* thrownness, and so for the first time imparts to *having-been* its peculiarly privileged position in the historical. *Authentic being-towards-death – that is to say. the finitude of temporality – is the hidden basis of Dasein's historicality.*   (BT 438)

What is still required is man's active response – in anticipatory resoluteness – to the call of conscience, to his *guilt* vis-à-vis his thrownness. Through such an active response an individual situates himself within the historical background of his life. In addition, this historical background – the individual's "heritage" – now ceases to be viewed as open either to one's attempts at control or to ("detached" and "objective") justification. As of now, the individual is ready to accept his heritage in the latter's full contingency and groundlessness ("nullity"). This stance toward one's historical past is its "repetition."

Now to find himself free *for* such a repetition of his heritage, an individual must first free himself *from* the conformism and the pressures of the "they" world. In this respect, too, death plays the pivotal role. First, death "shatters all one's tenaciousness to whatever existence one has reached" (BT 308): insofar as I find myself exposed to the indefinite and constant threat of death, all of my ordinary ties and attachments cease to offer me any security and they thus lose their hold over me. Second, death gives me a "freedom which has been released from the illusions of the 'they'" (BT 311), for due to my anxious grasp of death I come to see the everyday world as a stage dominated by impersonal pressures and conformism.

Repetition allows Dasein to have a "fate" (*Schicksal*), a "destiny" (*Geschick*), as well as a "hero" (*Held*). In repeating my heritage I find myself endowed with a fate, for I acknowledge that my life can express itself only within a certain spectrum of values and traditions. I now realize that I cannot be "anything and everything," since my life is bound up with such and such (and not any other) historical roots. For the same reason, I have a destiny: my life is part and parcel of a broader current of life of the historical community to which I belong. And since both my fate and my destiny must be lived in a concrete possibility of existence, my historical past will provide me with a pool of role models ("heroes") to choose from. Whereas by having a fate, a destiny, and a hero, I can act with *loyalty* toward my historical past, the inauthentic Dasein – a Dasein bent on finding secure acceptance within the ever-shifting trends of the "they" world – will remain disloyal to its past and helpless to resist the tyranny of the "they."

But Dasein's linkup with a historical community does not remove from Dasein's structure its dimension of subjectivity. On the contrary, Dasein reveals itself as rooted in its historical community only by exploring the full depths of its own subjectivity – of its finitude, its freedom, its guilt, and so on. And these themes – the key themes of Division II of *Being and Time* – can be found not only in the classical writers of the subjectivist tradition (in Descartes, Kant, Fichte), but indeed, in its final and most radical version, in existentialism. One is thus perfectly legitimate in drawing parallels between Heidegger and such radically subjectivistic writers as Kierkegaard, Sartre, and Camus. In fact, one of the tasks of Heidegger scholarship remains the task of coming to terms with the tension between those individualistic and subjectivistic aspects of Heidegger's philosophy, on the one hand, and his simultaneous stress on the inevitably public character of intelligibility and significance, on the other.[8]

NOTES

1. For more detail, the reader may consult my book *Doubt, Time, Violence* (Chicago: University of Chicago Press, 1986).
2. R. Descartes, *Meditations on First Philosophy*, in *The Philosophical Works of Descartes*, 2 vols., ed. E. S. Haldane and G. R. T. Ross (Cambridge: Cambridge University Press, 1972), Vol. 1, p. 150.
3. "We are ourselves the entities to be analysed. The being of any such entity is *in each case mine*" (BT 67).
4. Descartes, *Meditations*, Vol. 1, p. 150.
5. For this reason alone, our certainty of death cannot be an *empirical* certainty either (BT 301–2).
6. J. Hintikka, "Cogito, Ergo Sum: Inference or Performance," *Philosophical Review*, 71 (January 1962): 3–32.
7. Ibid., p. 25.
8. Here I must refer the reader again to my *Doubt, Time, Violence*. See also Charles B. Guignon's paper "Heidegger's 'Authenticity' Revisited," *Review of Metaphysics*, 37 (December 1984): 321–39.

9   Truth and the essence of truth in Heidegger's thought[1]

A central issue in Heidegger's thought, both early and late, is the nature of truth and its basis in what Heidegger calls "the essence of truth" or "unconcealment." Unconcealment or *aletheia* (the Greek word for truth) is, Heidegger writes, "*the* matter of thought," that is, "what is first of all to be thought, [but] to be thought as released from the perspective of the metaphysical representation of 'truth' in the sense of correctness."[2]

As this passage intimates, Heidegger's thought on truth involves both a critique of traditional accounts of truth, and an inquiry into the unconcealment that is prior to truth as correctness. On the critical side, Heidegger argues that the tradition has misunderstood the nature of the relationship between intentional contents and the world. When a belief or an assertion is true, it is because the holder of the belief or the maker of the assertion has succeeded in directing her thoughts or words at the world in such a way that they capture the way things[3] really are. But what does it mean for a proposition to capture the way things really are, and how can assertions and beliefs accomplish such a feat? Heidegger's thought on propositional truth as uncovering offers an alternative to traditional ways of exploring such matters. In the first section of this chapter, I review his account of a nonrepresentational form of correspondence as the uncovering of a state of affairs.

As important as the philosophical issues concerning propositional truth might be, however, they are never Heidegger's primary concern. Instead, his interest in truth grows out of the recognition that the question of propositional truth, properly raised, opens out into some of the most fundamental issues addressed in contemporary philosophy – issues such as the nature of language, and the reality or mind-independence of the world. This is because the philosophical discussion of truth can be pursued only against the background of assumptions about the nature of mind (in particular, how mental states and their derivatives like linguistic meaning can be so constituted as to be capable of being true or false), and the nature of the world (in particular, how the world can be so constituted as to make mental states and their derivatives true). Heidegger's focus on unconcealment in his discussions of the essence of truth is intended to bring such background assumptions to the foreground. The claim that unconcealment is the essence of truth, then, is motivated by the recognition that we have to see truth in the context of a more general opening up of the world, that is, in the context of an openness to the world and comportment toward things in the world that is more fundamental than thinking and speaking about them. In the second part of this paper, I will explore Heidegger's thought on unconcealment as the foundation of truth as correctness.

Because the analysis of unconcealment is an analysis of the ground of propositional truth, it should be clear that unconcealment is not to be taken as a (re)definition of propositional truth.[4] Hence, it is essential to see that the analyses of the unconcealment of beings and the clearing of being are not being offered as definitions of propositional truth. And, just as importantly, propositional truth cannot account for the unconcealment of beings and the clearing of being: "The correspondence or agreement of the nexus [i.e., the proposition][5] *with* what is, and their consequent accord, do not *as such* primarily make beings accessible. Rather beings, as the concern of any predicative determination, must already be manifest *before* such predication and *for* it."[6] But if unconcealment, the "essence" of truth, is not propositional truth, Heidegger nevertheless believes that an understanding of unconcealment is essential to establishing an account of truth that can withstand anti-realism and anti-essentialism.

PART I: PROPOSITIONAL TRUTH AND LANGUAGE

Propositional truth is the correctness of things that have as their content a proposition – things like assertions and beliefs. When it comes to propositional truth, Heidegger grants in traditional fashion that "an assertion is true if what it means and says corresponds with the matter about which it asserts" (GA 9, 178). The truth of a

belief, in a similar way, "means today and has long meant the conformity of knowledge with the fact. . . . Propositional truth is always,
and always exclusively, this correctness" (PLT 176–77). This does not
mean that Heidegger accepts traditional *theories* of correspondence.
But he does accept correspondence as the right starting point for an
analysis of truth: "we are relying precisely on the customary conception," he notes in his 1937–38 lectures on truth, "so much so that
we are seeking a foundation for this reliance and consequently want
to confirm it all the more" (BQP 36). The "old definition of truth is
indeed basically right," but "it is merely an approach to the problem
of asking what grounds in general the possibility of conforming to
something" (FCM 342, translation modified).

Heidegger accepts, then, that (at least many) propositions are true
by corresponding to, or agreeing with the way things are. He does not
believe, however, that the correspondence view of truth has been adequately grounded. For one thing, he questions the assumption that
propositional truth is the core or paradigmatic instance of truth –
an assumption that typifies, for instance, analytic approaches to the
question of truth. Heidegger suggests that this assumption is partially responsible for the way that unconcealment has been overlooked as the ground of truth.[7] Because propositions are thought of as
ideal entities, mere representations, it has also led, Heidegger argues,
to a tendency to view correspondence as a relationship in which a
representation mirrors or pictures reality. The medievals, however,
from whom we have inherited the terminology of correspondence,
believed that things, too, are true by corresponding.[8] Attention to
this fact could have helped the tradition to avoid problems in explaining propositional truth – namely, explaining in what sense an ideal
entity (the content of a belief or assertion) can be said to correspond
with a real state of affairs (a fact in the world). If we saw propositional
truth as a species of a more general kind of truth, Heidegger suggests,
it would shed light on the nature of correspondence.

So, for example, Heidegger notes that we predicate truth not just
of assertions and beliefs, but also of things (as in a "true friend,"
the "true God," or "true gold").[9] He also notes that when we predicate truth of an assertion, we can mean either that what the assertion states is true, or that the assertion itself is a truth. Or, we
sometimes use "truth" to refer to "an aggregate of true propositions" (GA 21, 9). If we ask in what sense all these different uses

of the truth predicate name a kind of correspondence, we will see, Heidegger suggests, that the structure of correspondence is a *"so-as"* or *"just-as"* relationship.[10] We can say that a correspondence holds, in other words, whenever our orientation in the world lets the situation appear "just as" it is. An assertion is true, that is, when it so directs us to a state of affairs as that state of affairs in fact is. A thing is true if it so appears as it in fact is (GA 21, 9–10).

Let us look in more detail at Heidegger's account of the way correspondence works for propositional entities. Here the question is, in what does a correspondence of thoughts or words with the world consist? For Heidegger, the first step in making sense of a correspondence relationship is to jettison a representationalist view of the nature of propositional states. A phenomenological examination of the way assertions work, Heidegger argues, demonstrates that the representational theory is in fact unfounded. By reflecting on our experience in hearing an assertion, we recognize that we are never directed toward or by means of a representational content, but rather directly to the being indicated by the assertion. Assertions and beliefs do not *represent* beings in the world, they *present* them; they are a way of being oriented within the world so that a state of affairs can show up.

This view of assertions has implications for truth which we can trace out, Heidegger suggests, by looking at the context of demonstration, that is, the context in which we verify that a proposition is true. To avoid confusing Heidegger's view of truth with the verificationism popular among pragmatists and among some in the analytical tradition, it should be emphasized that the reference to the verification of assertions is by no means intended to define truth itself as verification.[11] Instead, Heidegger is perfectly clear that he turns to the question of the demonstration of the truth of an assertion because "in the phenomenal context of demonstration, the relationship of correspondence must become visible" (BT 260, translation modified). The phenomenological analysis is offered as an alternative to a conceptual analysis, because in the phenomenology of a case of successful correspondence, one can catch sight of the correspondence itself. In this analysis, we discover that an assertion's truth consists in its orienting us to the state of affairs just as it is in itself. This confirms that the correspondence relationship between assertion and world is not mediated by representations at all, and thus cannot consist in the representation picturing or mirroring the state of affairs.

Heidegger's analysis focuses on the sample assertion: "the picture on the wall is hanging askew" (ibid.). We confirm that this assertion corresponds to the way things are by "perceiv[ing] the picture hanging askew on the wall." The assertion works by directing us to a state of affairs in the world, and it does this not just when we set about to confirm the assertion, but even when we merely entertain the assertion in thought: "If he who makes the assertion judges without perceiving the picture, but 'merely represents' it to himself, to what is he related? To 'representations,' shall we say? Certainly not." (ibid.) That is, it is not phenomenologically correct to say that even when merely thinking about an assertion, we are relating ourselves to or through a representation. "The asserting which 'merely represents' is related rather, in that sense which is most its own, to the real picture on the wall. What one has in mind is the real picture, and nothing else. Any interpretation in which something else is here slipped in as what one supposedly has in mind in an assertion that merely represents, belies the phenomenal fact of the case as to that about which the assertion gets made." (ibid.) From this phenomenological consideration of the way language functions, it emerges that "asserting is a way of being towards the thing itself that is" (ibid.). It follows that, in demonstrating the truth of an assertion through a perception of the state of affairs to which the assertion corresponds, the demonstration consists in seeing that the assertion directs one toward things as they in fact are:

And what does one's perceiving of it demonstrate? Nothing else than that it is the being itself which is meant in one's assertion. What comes up for confirmation is that the assertative being toward what is asserted is a pointing out of the being, that it uncovers the being toward which it is. In carrying out such a demonstration, the knowing remains related solely to the entity itself. In this entity the confirmation, as it were, gets enacted.   (BT 260–61)

Because assertions work by indicating rather than representing, there is no need to worry about the representation's adequacy in corresponding to the state of affairs – one thing can indicate another without mirroring or otherwise representing the other. Of course, a correspondence between an assertion and what makes it true is not a bare indication of or referring to a thing. As Heidegger notes, "a sign points at what is indicated. Such indicating is not a correspondence of the sign with what is indicated" (BT 258, translation modified). In addition to directing us to a thing, then, a proposition will correspond only if it shows us the thing *in its condition*:

> The entity itself which one has in mind shows itself just as it is in itself; that is to say, it shows that it, in its self-sameness, is just as it gets pointed out in the assertion as being – just as it gets uncovered as being. Representations do not get compared, either among themselves or in relation to the real thing. What is to be demonstrated is not an agreement of knowing with its object, still less of the psychical with the physical; but neither is it an agreement between "contents of consciousness" among themselves. What is to be demonstrated is solely the Being-uncovered [Entdeckt-sein] of the entity itself – that entity in the "how" of its uncoveredness. This uncoveredness is confirmed when that which is put forward in the assertion (namely the entity itself) shows itself as that very same thing.   (BT 260–61, translation modified)

An assertion, in other words, orients us toward a state of affairs. Rather than a bare pointing toward a thing, it gives rise to an anticipation of the thing in such and such a determinate condition or state. What makes the indication a *correspondence* relation, then, is that it succeeds or fails, not merely in directing us to the thing indicated, but in directing us in such a way that the thing can (or can fail to) show itself as it is in some one (or more) of its aspects. An assertion corresponds simply by directing us to the state of affairs "so as to let it appear in the assertion as it is" (BQP 15). And so, it becomes clear that the correspondence relationship is not a relationship in which a representation is appropriately like the thing it represents, but rather a relationship of pointing out or uncovering a fact – a thing in a particular condition. "To say that an assertion 'is true'," Heidegger concludes, "signifies that it uncovers what is as it is in itself. It asserts, it points out, it 'lets' what is 'be seen' (*apophansis*) in its uncoveredness. The *Being-true* (*truth*) of the assertion must be understood as *Being-uncovering*" (BT 261, translation modified). Thus, on a nonrepresentational account of language, assertion is a way of orienting ourselves in an engagement with the world – an "assertative being toward what is asserted" – and correspondence amounts to uncovering.

A true assertion uncovers a state of affairs by elevating it into salience or prominence, thus allowing it to be seen: "the basic achievement of speech," Heidegger argues, "consist[s] in showing or revealing that about which one is speaking, that concerning which there is discussion. In such revealing, the thing that is addressed is made manifest. It becomes perceivable, and, in discussion, the thing perceived gets defined" (GA 21, 6).

What is more, Heidegger believes that it is only through the assertion that entities become manifest in this particular way, namely, as objects with determinate properties. The assertion, Heidegger explains, "relates 'itself' to the thing in that it presents it and says of what is presented how it is ordered according to the particular perspective that guides the assertion.... [To] present here means to let the thing stand opposed as object" (P 141). In order to uncover entities in this way, the assertion must occur against the background of a nonpredicative ability to deal with things: "for it to be possible, predication must be able to take up residence in a making-manifest that is *not predicative* in character" (P 103, emphasis in the original). In a propositional orientation to a thing, the "'subject' is *given a definite character* by the 'predicate'" (BT 196, emphasis in original). "Subject" and "predicate" are put in scare quotes to indicate the fact that, in our pre-predicative experience of the world, things are not understood in terms of objects with properties. Heidegger understands the way predication "gives a definite character" as a "narrowing of content" – that is, reduction of our pre-predicative understanding of things in terms of our practical modes of coping with them:

The advance availability of what we encounter and the advance appearance of those whom we encounter in a with-world are well-known (*hexis* [state of having, habit], *aletheia* [truth, uncoveredness]), and this not in the sense of having knowledge of and about them, but rather in the sense that they are the wherein in which *one*, corresponding to what and who is to be encountered, knows one's way around, one-self. Everydayness thoroughly dominates the definite relations in these contexts of reference. Each knows his way around for a while at the particular time, knows others well, just as these others know him well. This being-well-known in the with-world is one which is average, thriving in everydayness and developing into its contentments.   (OHF 77).

Such practically constituted things are implicated in a complex variety of involvements with other objects, practices, purposes, and goals.[12] In pre-predicative comportment, things are thus articulated along the lines of our practices for dealing with them. In such an articulation, things show up *as* what they are, but in the whole complexity of their involvements.[13] In predication, by contrast, our experience undergoes an "explicit restriction of our view," and we "dim down" the whole richly articulated situation in front of us to focus on some particular feature of the situation (BT 197). It is that dimming down that first gives something a conceptual character by discovering the kind of determinate content that allows one to form conceptual connections, draw inferences, and justify one occurrent intentional state on the basis of another.[14]

Heidegger offers his clearest explanation of this idea in a pair of lecture courses offered in 1925 and 1926.[15] In these courses, Heidegger developed an account of assertion in the context of a reflection on the structure of natural perception – our perception of things in the course of our everyday commerce with the world. He noted that when we make an assertion about what we perceive in our fluid coping with the world, the "assertion makes certain relations stand out from the matter, which is at first apprehended directly and simply in its unarticulated totality" (HCT 57). In natural perception, then, we ordinarily perceive a whole context that lacks the logical structure of linguistic categories. When we apprehend things in such a way as to be able to express them in an assertion, however, the act of perception now is brought under the categories of the understanding. The assertion, Heidegger writes, "draws out" or "accentuates" "a state of affairs," thus allowing the entity to "become expressly visible precisely in what it is" (HCT 63). In doing this, the assertion "discloses anew" what is present at first in a nonconceptually articulated fashion, so that these things "come to explicit apprehension precisely in what they are" (HCT 62). The assertion nevertheless manifests things differently than they are given to natural perception. In it, things are defined or determined "as such and so" – as having a particular property or characteristic.[16] It is not the case that those properties or characteristics were not present in the entity before, but through the assertion they are isolated and cut off from their context, thereby being highlighted or lifted into prominence. As a result, we see an object with a thematic clarity that is not present in our natural perception of it, but we are no longer able to deal with it naturally – for that, we need to see it in its immediacy (GA 21, 144–147).

Because propositional modes of comportment (believing, asserting, and so on) function by determining and highlighting certain elements of our pre-propositional experience of things, they are a derivative form of comporting ourselves toward things in the world. The pre-predicative understanding of the world, Heidegger explains, is prior to any predication, and "first makes the structure of predication possible" (GA 21, 145). Thus, we can understand Heidegger's claim that correspondence depends on a prior manifestness of the objects about which we think and assert: "beings, as the concern of any predicative determination, must already be manifest *before* such predication and *for* it.... Propositional truth is rooted in a *more originary* truth (unconcealment), in the pre-predicative manifestness *of what is*, which may be called *ontic truth*" (P 103, translation modified). This is not only because assertions function only against the background of a pre-predicative manifestness of things, but also because things can serve as a standard for judging the adequacy of the proposition only if they are present to us prior to, and independently of, the proposition.

We will explore this latter point in more detail in the next section. But before going on, we can summarize Heidegger's views in the following way. Our most fundamental forms of comportment are practically rather than conceptually articulated. On the basis of this practical articulation, things show up as making demands on us, and constraining how we can use them. Through language, however, we are able to orient ourselves to objects in a way that is conceptually rather than pragmatically articulated. When this orientation allows us to see a state of affairs just as it is – when it uncovers an object in its condition – we say that it corresponds to the facts or the state of affairs.

Given the near consensus among philosophers in the analytical tradition that, in Strawson's words, "the correspondence theory requires not purification but elimination,"[17] it is worth asking how Heidegger's critique of the correspondence view of truth stands with respect to this consensus.

Strawson's objection to the correspondence theory was an objection to the idea that a correspondence relationship holds between independent entities – statements on the one hand, and facts or states of affairs on the other. Since we can specify a fact only through a statement, statements and facts are not, he argues, independent of each other. Strawson thus concludes that "correspondence" does not name a genuine relationship, and consequently that it is unilluminating to note that facts "correspond to" statements.

Heidegger's gloss of correspondence as uncovering is in some sense very much in the spirit of Strawson's critique. Because there is no entity, no representation, which needs to be related to the fact or state of affairs which makes it true, "correspondence" does not name a genuine relationship. It names a kind of "orientation" to an entity – namely, one that lets it appear as what it is. As soon as it appears, there is no need to compare a representation with a state of affairs to see if they agree with one another. Instead, the state of affairs is made manifest in and through the assertion. So, in fact, Heidegger would agree with Strawson that there is no way to pick out a fact independently of a sentence, since the sentence is what first uncovers the fact. If correspondence meant "a thing-like approximation between dissimilar kinds of things" (P 114), then Heidegger would agree that it is in need of elimination. Properly understood, however, it is an illuminating notion insofar as it allows us to name what distinguishes successful from unsuccessful propositional acts and states. More importantly, for Heidegger's concerns, it points us to unconcealment as what is first of all to be thought.

PART 2: THE UNCONCEALMENT OF BEING
AND THE "ESSENCE" OF TRUTH

So far we have seen that Heidegger's critique of the traditional correspondence notion of truth is, in large part, aimed at vindicating a nonrepresentational account of correspondence, and exploring the conditions under which a correspondence of thoughts or words to the world is possible. This latter issue leads to a recognition that propositional modes of comportment are grounded in a pre-predicative familiarity with the world. Heidegger explores the nature of this pre-predicative familiarity under the heading of "unconcealment," which encompasses both the pointing out or uncovering of an entity, and the clearing of a space within which it is possible to point out an entity. In Part 1, we saw that Heidegger treats correspondence as a species of the former sort of uncovering. In this section, we will look more closely at what is involved in the latter sort.

We have already touched on the fact that the pre-predicative understanding of the world includes a pre-predicative openness of the world. Our ability to mentally and linguistically uncover the way things are requires that objects make themselves available to our thought and talk, and that our thought and talk holds itself open to and responsible to the objects in the world around us. The unconcealment of beings is what gives us objects toward which we can be directed, and about which we are responsible for getting it right. Heidegger explains: "if our representations and assertions . . . are supposed to conform to the object, then this being . . . must be accessible in advance in order to present itself as a standard and measure for the conformity with it" (BQP 18). The unconcealment of beings, in other words, grounds an objective notion of truth, because unconcealment creates the possibility for the things themselves to make our thoughts and assertions true: "the matter must show itself to be such if knowledge and the proposition that forms and expresses knowledge are to be able to conform to it; otherwise, the matter cannot become binding on the proposition. How can the matter show itself if it cannot itself stand forth out of concealment, if it does not itself stand in the unconcealed? A proposition is true by conforming to the unconcealed, to what is true."[18]

This might seem like a trivial point, but understanding how things can open themselves to us is anything but straightforward. It is not enough that we have an idea or a representation of the object for it to be opened to us. For it to be truly manifest in itself, and thus a standard for truth, there must be a way that the world really is, and also it must show itself to us as it really is. So, Heidegger concludes, our thoughts and assertions about things cannot be either true or false unless the things we are thinking and talking about have an essence, a way that they are – that is, that the objects themselves possess properties in virtue of which they do or do not belong to the extension of the terms of the proposition. Unless there are constraints on what is involved in a thing being a thing, our thoughts and assertions about it run the risk of losing touch with anything about which they could be an assertion or a thought. For example, if there are no essential features of a table, then my assertion "there is a table in the room" could be referring to anything, and thus is incapable of being either true or false. So it is a condition of propositional truth that beings come to stand before us as objects with determinable properties.

It must be the case, in addition, that the speaker is taking the way that things are arrayed in the world as the measure of her assertion. This point is simply the consequence of the first – namely, that what we say is true or false only if something specific in the world satisfies or fails to satisfy the belief or assertion: "In keeping with their nature, 'truths' – true assertions – assume a relation to something *on whose grounds* they are able to be in accord" (P 102). This means that we must have some grasp of the essence of things; otherwise, there is no sense in which we can take the world as the measure of the success or failure of our propositions. All our comportments toward objects – using them, thinking about them, referring to them – "whether they are interpreted as pre-predicative or as predicative, would be incapable of making beings accessible *in themselves* if their making manifest were not always illuminated and guided in advance by an understanding of the being (the ontological constitution: what-being and how-being) of beings. *Unveiledness of being first makes possible the manifestness of beings*" (P 103, some emphasis supplied). "Unveiledness of being" means, Heidegger explains, "the disclosure of beings through which an openness comes into its essence [*west*]" (P 146, translation modified). The unconcealment of being grounds truth by opening up a world of things with essential properties, a world about which it makes sense to say that we are speaking and thinking either correctly or incorrectly.

The problem is that, when it comes to determining the truth of essential definitions, we discover something of a paradox. Heidegger compares these two assertions:

(1) The lights in this lecture hall are on now
(2) Truth is the correctness of an assertion,

where assertion (2) is intended to specify the essence of truth (BQP 69 ff.). The truth of assertion (1) seems in a straightforward and undeniable fashion to consist in its relating to a particular fact or state of affairs – namely, the condition of the lights in the lecture hall right now. How about the truth of assertion (2)? Heidegger makes two important observations about such assertions. First, while it might well correspond with the facts (the relevant facts would include all particular truths), its correspondence with the facts is not what makes it true. Rather, its being true is what guarantees that it will correspond with the facts. We can see this if we think about what facts we could possibly adduce for (2) to correspond to. If the notion of a fact or a state of affairs is meaningful, it must be some actual (whether past, present, or future) condition of an object or a state of affairs. But essential claims go beyond any claim about past, present, or future conditions to include all possible conditions. This is because the essence of a thing is not picked out by a mere empirical regularity, but must also be maintained in the face of counterfactual situations. If I were to claim that the essence of a table is to be a wooden item of furniture, for instance, it would not establish this claim to merely show that all past, current, and future tables are wooden items of furniture (even if I could, in point of fact, be certain that there is not, never had been, and never would be, for example, a plastic table-shaped object). It would, in addition, have to be the case that a plastic object with exactly the same shape, resistance, function, and so on, would not be a table. This means that for essential definitions, correspondence to the facts is a necessary but not sufficient condition for their being true.

Second, facts come too late for essential definitions, since we need to assume that the definition is true in order definitively to identify the fact or facts to which it corresponds. To get a feel for this, compare two other essential definitions – this time for gold:

(3) Gold is the noblest of the metals
(4) Gold is an element with atomic number 79.

When it comes to definitively founding simple factual statements like (1), we begin by finding the fact to which it corresponds, and we can do this by first finding the object referred to in the subject phrase – the lights – and then checking their condition. How about (3)? It seems like we would start by locating the object referred to in the subject phrase – gold. In fact, if (3) is an essential definition, the only way we can determine that gold is the noblest of the metals is by first finding some gold, and we do this by looking for instances of the noblest metal. Thus we see that in order to establish the truth of the essential specification, we first have to assume that it is true. And that means that we are never in a position to prove empirically that it is right. Suppose, for example, we are trying to decide between (3) and (4). The advocates of (3) would round up all the noblest metals to test their definition. The advocates of (4) would round up all the elemental stuff with atomic number 79 to test theirs. Neither camp could ever persuade the other that their essential definition was correct, because, on the basis of their respective definitions, each would reject exactly those particular substances that the other took as decisive evidence in favor of his or her definition. As Heidegger summarizes the situation, "every time we attempt to prove an essential determination through single, or even all, actual and possible facts, there results the remarkable state of affairs that we have already presupposed the legitimacy of the essential determination, indeed must presuppose it, just in order to grasp and produce the facts that are supposed to serve as proof" (BQP 71).

But it seems that both definitions cannot be right. Even if it so happens that (3) and (4) agree in their extension, we could imagine cases or possible worlds in which the definitions apply to some substance differently. That means that we have reason to believe that at least one of them names, at best, an accidental property of gold.

If the world gives us no basis for deciding which of the competing essential definitions is right, then perhaps we have to conclude that there are no genuine essences in the world. Instead, what we find in the universe is what we (arbitrarily) project into it. And if we conclude that, then we also might be forced to conclude that there is no way that the universe is independently of the way we conceive of it, because it seems that we are free to carve it up in any way that we want. Such anti-essentialist and anti-realist views threaten the possibility of our thoughts and claims being about the world at all, and thus threaten the possibility of their being either true or false.

We can summarize the situation in the following way. It seems that our ability to have true beliefs and make true assertions about the world depends on things having an essence, and our grasping that essence. This is because we cannot succeed in linguistically referring to things in the world unless they have an essence. However, if an understanding of essences consists in a grasp of a propositional definition, then nothing in the world can make the essential definition true, because nothing in the world could establish one definition as opposed to any other. Thus, it seems to follow, nothing in the world can make our beliefs or assertions true.

Heidegger, in fact, rejects this argument, because he denies that our understanding of essences consists in a grasp of a propositional definition. The "knowledge of essence," he claims, "cannot be communicated in the sense of the passing on of a proposition, whose content is simply grasped without its foundation and its acquisition being accomplished again" (BQP 78). This is because the knowledge of essence he is interested in is a way of being attuned to the world; for that, we have to be introduced to the practices that will eventually teach us to have a particular sensibility and readiness for the world. Thus, "the knowledge of the essence must be accomplished anew by each one who is to share it" (BQP 78). It is this latter understanding of our knowledge of essences – seeing them as consisting in being attuned by the world to consider certain properties or features of things as definitive – that, Heidegger believes, allows us to see our way clear of anti-essentialism and anti-realism. The unconcealment of being, or *alêtheia*, is precisely the way a certain precognitive understanding of essences comes to prevail in an attunement. Through the unconcealment of being, Heidegger says, "human comportment is tuned throughout by the openedness of beings as a whole" (P 147).

Before explaining this view in more detail, however, I think it is illuminating to compare Heidegger's solution to the problem with Kripke's. Where Heidegger denies that our understanding of essences is a cognitive grasp of an essential definition, Kripke denies the assumption that our ability to refer to a thing depends on our knowing what that thing is. Instead, Kripke proposes that we can refer to something like, say, gold, even if we do not know exactly what it is, by a kind of "ostension" or pointing. The "original concept" of gold, then, does not have as its content any essential definition. Instead, the original concept is *"that kind of thing*, where the kind can be identified by paradigmatic instances. It is not something picked out by any qualitative... definition."[19] While it is in a sense quite contingent what we decide to refer to with our words, once the reference has been fixed it is no longer up to us to decide what the essence of the referent – the thing we refer to – will be. The referent of the word "gold" has been fixed by the (contingent) way that someone originally picked out gold. From that point on, however, it is no longer up to us, but up to the structure of the universe, to decide what properties are essential to gold. The essential properties will be just those properties that are necessary to account for the way in which we picked out gold in the first place.[20]

In the case of gold, for example, somewhere long ago, people began picking out a kind of thing that was malleable, yellow, metallic, did not tarnish, and so on. These properties, Kripke argues, do not determine the essence of the stuff; instead, they are perhaps contingent properties of the thing we picked out – say, a particular chunk of gold. The essence of the gold, by contrast, will be whatever it is about the gold that makes it that particular thing we have picked out. To help pump up our intuitions about this, Kripke proposes the following thought experiment about the yellowness of gold–yellowness being one of the properties by which we pick out the kind of thing that gold is. "Could we discover that gold was not in fact yellow?" Kripke asks. He explains his affirmative answer in the following way:

Suppose an optical illusion were prevalent, due to peculiar properties of the atmosphere in South Africa and Russia and certain other areas where gold mines are common. Suppose there were an optical illusion which made the substance appear to be yellow; but in fact, once the peculiar properties of the atmosphere were removed, we would see that it is actually blue. Maybe a demon even corrupted the vision of all those entering the gold mines (obviously their *souls* were already corrupt), and thus made them believe that this substance was yellow, though it was not. Would there on this basis be an announcement in the newspapers: "It has turned out that there is no gold. Gold does not exist. What we took to be gold is not in fact gold."? Just imagine the world financial crisis under these conditions! . . . It seems to me that there would be no such announcement. On the contrary, what would be announced would be that though it appeared that gold was yellow, in fact gold has turned out not to be yellow, but blue. The reason is, I think, that we use "gold" as a term for a certain *kind* of thing.[21]

I think Heidegger would accept Kripke's intuitions about this.[22] He would say that, while it is contingent on our practices, dispositions, and our interests what things we happen to pick out with our language and in our thoughts, the nature of the things we pick out is not in general up to us. Consequently, if it turns out that we are mistaken about lots of the things we believe about gold, it does not follow that there is nothing there in the world that we have been picking out. The gold is there, and it has a nature that cannot be changed just by our agreeing to use our words differently than we do.

I also think that Heidegger would accept Kripke's claim that our ability to refer does not depend on our knowing in advance what the essence of a thing is. In fact, a weaker version of this claim is a corollary of Heidegger's view that we often lack a cognitive understanding of the essence of thing. "Addressing something *as* something,"

Heidegger notes, "does not yet necessarily entail *comprehending in its essence* whatever is thus addressed. The *understanding* of being (*logos* in a quite broad sense) that guides and illuminates in advance all comportment toward beings is neither a grasping of being as such, *nor is it a conceptual comprehending of what is thus grasped.*"[23] So, in some respects, their positions are quite similar. As this passage makes clear, however, an important difference remains. In particular, Heidegger does not believe that we ordinarily refer without *any* understanding of essences, but rather that we can do so without a *conceptual* grasp of the essence. Thus, he would reject as ungrounded and untenable one element of Kripke's position.

Because Kripke believes that there is a way to refer that requires no advance understanding of essences, he believes that there is a way to decide conclusively between competing essential claims. If what we ostensively designate does not depend in any way on what we understand or know about the thing, then it seems that everyone who ostensively defines it will pick out the exact same thing. To return to the example discussed above, for instance, Kripke argues that (4) is the right definition. Gold is and has always been the element with atomic number 79. We know this now, because our science can show how all the (most important) surface properties of gold are produced by its atomic structure. Consequently, until modern science discovered the atomic structure of gold, no one who talked about gold knew what they were talking about.

Let us briefly review in order to clarify this point. Earlier, it seemed that, to the extent that an essential description determines what a thing is, we are never in a position to decide between competing essential descriptions. This is because we cannot pick the thing out in the first place without having some sense for what it is, and so we can never find evidence that will contradict the essential description that we have arbitrarily adopted. Kripke breaks the deadlock by proposing that, in fact, an essential description is not needed to pick a kind of thing out. Instead, we can do it by an ostension – by pointing to that thing *there*. We are then in a position to test an essential definition; we start by finding gold ("it is *that* kind of thing") and then check it to see what underlying property accounts for all the salient surface properties. In doing this, we can be essentialists and realists, because it is up to the world, not us, whether the stuff we ostensively pick out in fact does have the property. Kripke avoids anti-essentialism and anti-realism by denying that we need to grasp the essence of a thing in order to refer to it. The result is that we get a robust realism – so robust, in fact, that we might end up being almost completely mistaken in all the things we say or believe about the things to which we refer.

Rather than denying that we need to grasp the essence of a thing in order to refer to it, Heidegger denies that our grasp of the essence consists in an understanding of a *proposition*. "The essence of things," Heidegger notes, is ordinarily something "which we know and yet do not know" (BQP 73). It is "not first captured in a 'definition' and made available for knowledge" (BQP 101). This is because, as he explains, the knowledge of essences is originally manifest in the way "that all acting and creating, all thinking and speaking, all founding and proceeding were determined by and thoroughly in accord with the unconcealedness of beings as something ungrasped" (BQP 101).

From Heidegger's perspective, then, the problems of antiessentialism and anti-realism are generated by our belief that we must ground all our knowledge of things on a proposition which, to be true, would have to correspond to something in the world. Since essential definitions cannot correspond to anything in the world, all our knowledge of the world is left radically ungrounded. The solution, Heidegger believes, is to see that our knowledge of things is not grounded in a proposition, but in a way of being disposed for the world. A disposition is true, not by corresponding to the facts, but by giving us a good existential grip[24] on the world. And we only have a good existential grip on the world to the extent that the world itself has attuned us to the things we encounter in the world.

Once again, this position of Heidegger's is well-illuminated by comparing it to Kripke's view. Whether Kripke is right about essences depends on whether, in fact, every society refers the same way – for instance, whether everyone has always been picking out the same kind of thing we pick out when we refer to gold. I can easily imagine that, and I take Heidegger as arguing that, inhabitants of different world ages could look at the very same particular instance of gold, and nevertheless pick it out *as* a different kind of thing. They would then take different paradigms as their basis for uncovering the essence of gold (in the traditional sense of "essence").

From Heidegger's perspective, this fact should lead us to ask: what is it that grounds an ostensive definition? Even an ostensive definition, he would observe, requires that the object indicated in the definition be manifest prior to the ostension. What makes it manifest? Reflection on such questions shows that Kripke, too, relies on a pre-predicative or pre-linguistic mode of access to the world without clarifying the nature of the pre-linguistic mode of access itself. And so, before we impose on other cultures our way of allowing essences to show up, we ought to ask whether we in fact share their pre-linguistic mode of unconcealment of beings, to use the Heideggerian terminology. According to Heidegger, we in fact, do not. What distinguishes each historical age from another, Heidegger claims, is that each has a different style of "productive seeing," of perceiving things in advance in such a way that they are allowed to stand out as essentially structured.[25]

We can illustrate this by going back to what Kripke called the "original concept" of gold – a concept forever determined by one or a few paradigmatic examples of golden things. Notice first that those particular things – perhaps chunks of gold – that were discovered at a particular time and particular place could not have been picked out if they were completely devoid of discriminating characteristics. Whoever first picked them out *could* pick them out only because they were responding to them in a particular way, that is, because they were responding to some evident property or properties that they possess. Those chunks of gold were already showing up as meaningful in some sense.

In fact, we should observe that there are an indefinite if not infinite number of ways to characterize the properties of any particular thing. A piece of gold, for instance, has a color and a weight and a texture and a shape, but also all sorts of other properties like being good (or bad) for making jewelry, gleaming in a way that seems divine, being directly in front of my favorite chair, and so on. When we decide what kind or type of thing this particular object is, we will do it on the basis of just those particular properties we are responding to, and these properties will be some subset of an indefinite or infinite set of properties we could be responding to.

Given that this is the case, it seems that we need to revise the story we told above. Kripke is right: we do not need an essential definition to pick out a thing in the first place. But we do pick out things only against the background of a particular way of being in the world, of finding certain properties and relations salient and others irrelevant.

And consequently, while it is not up to us what the essential properties of a thing will be, which thing we are picking out *is* a result of our pre-linguistic modes of comportment. Or, more precisely, it is a result of a kind of disposition or readiness for the world that leads us to see certain features as more important than others.

Any essential definition, Heidegger reminds us, works by naming a property that holds for all particular instances of the type. However, because the definition needs to be counterfactually valid, the essence is not really the property, but that which makes the property hold for all instances.[26] This leads Heidegger to use the term "essence" in a way unfamiliar to the philosophical tradition; for Heidegger, the essence of a thing is always what it is that leads us to recognize an essential property as essential – what it is that "concerns and moves us," or "what matters to us in all things" (OWL 95). All essential definitions thus arise on the basis of a background disposition to the world. We disclose the essences that we do, according to Heidegger, because the way we are moved by or disposed to things allows a particular "character of being...to be ascendant" (BQP 112).

In the unconcealment of being, then, an understanding of being comes to prevail in such a way that we bring in advance a certain way of being disposed to objects: "human comportment is tuned and determined throughout by the openedness of beings as a whole" (P 147).

We can illustrate this idea through the gold example. We can imagine that, because of the way different cultures are disposed for the world, there might be different ways of ostensively picking out objects in the world. One way of being disposed might lead us to find the true being of a thing in the extent to which it approaches God by being like Him. Another way of being disposed might lead us to find the true being of a thing in its ability to be turned into a resource, flexibly and efficiently on call for use. When someone disposed to the world in the first way points to a lump of gold, and defines gold as "that *kind* of thing," she will take as essential its nearness to God. When someone disposed to the world in the second way ostensively defines it, she will see its essence as whatever it is about it that allows us to break it down into a resource, and flexibly switch it around and order it.

As a result, we can see that there is no longer any need to see (3) and (4) as incompatible. There might be a culture whose sensibilities for the world lead it to pick out an instance of gold as having just those essential properties specified in (4) – in fact, Heidegger would probably argue, those are just the essential properties we would find in a lump of gold if we were oriented to the world in a technological fashion. We do not need to see (4) as true *a priori*, because whether it is true is up to the world. Instead, we will use our technological disposition to pick out objects as instances of *that kind of resource;* from there it is an empirical matter which features of it make it that kind of a resource. In our age, it seems plausible to say that the essential features (in the traditional sense) are found in its atomic structure, because knowledge of the atomic structure gives us the best grasp on how to turn gold into a resource. In this way, we have secured the possibility of truth by providing that the world is opened up or unconcealed in some way or other, and thus can serve as a standard for our thoughts and words.

In summary, then, the claim that unconcealment is the essence of truth is the claim that the truth of beliefs and assertions depend on the world opening up for us in a particular way, prior to and independently of predicative language. The unconcealment of beings is the "anticipatory gathering," which lays out certain properties and relationships as salient (see BQP 121). This means that the properties of a thing that we consider to be most important to it – the properties that determine its "essence" – are a function of the historical age. Inhabitants of different historical worlds will consider different features of objects to be essential, because their dispositions for the world are shaped in different ways. As a result, what things are, how they actually show up, differs according to the historical world to which a person belongs.

This historical view of essences is certain to raise concerns. It might sound once again as if Heidegger is getting perilously close to saying that it is arbitrary and up to us how we are going to pick things out. But this is not the way we experience things. We today, for instance, find the story that the modern chemistry tells about gold particularly compelling, and few would be tempted to say that atomic number is an accidental property of gold's nobility. Moreover, it is not really the case that we could just decide, by consensus, to start picking something else out as the referent of our word "gold." How we pick things out is contingent, but not really up to us. Why is this the case? Why are we so inclined to agree that chemistry has it right about what we are talking about when we refer to gold?

The answer is that our disposition for essences is not entirely up to us, but is built into us, in large part, by the way our world and our practices for dealing with the world are organized. What concerns us, moves us, matters to us is, Heidegger quite rightly notes, historically determined. We technological westerners are moved by quite different considerations than, for instance, a medieval Christian or an ancient Greek. Heidegger even goes so far as to offer a general characterization of what moves our age – he claims that it is flexibility and efficiency that "matters to us in all things." In the technological age, Heidegger argues, everything shows up as something to be "unlocked" (i.e., removed from its natural conditions), "exposed" (i.e., reduced to something on call and readily available for use), and "switched about ever anew" (i.e., flexibly employable in an indefinite variety of activities).[27] If this is right, then the reason we find the modern scientific essence so compelling as an explanation of what things really are is that we have a background sensibility for the world which moves us to seek flexibility and efficiency, and the modern scientific account picks out that property of the thing which, when understood, allows us to unlock, expose, and switch about all natural entities.

The fact that our dispositions are historical in this sense does not mean, however, that essences are created by us. An essence, Heidegger argues, is "not manufactured, but it is also not simply encountered like a thing already present at hand" (BQP 77). On the Heideggerian view, then, we are entitled to an essentialism and a kind of realism. There is a way that the universe is independently of us, and it is not entirely up to us to decide what kind of things we will find in the universe. This is an historical essentialism, and one that denies that there is any final, correct vocabulary which every historical age needs to accept, because it sees that the way we pick out *kinds* of things depends on a background sensibility for the world that is subject to historical change. To the extent that we are thrown into a way of being in the world, we inherit a background sensibility for things. And this means, in turn, that we are not really at liberty to decide what type of thing any particular object will show up *as*. Consequently, the essential properties we hit on will be historically contingent in the sense that a different culture would have been moved by different aspects or properties of the object, and thus have understood the essence of the object quite differently. Given the particular background sensibility I inhabit, it is not at all arbitrary what I find compelling in a thing. Nevertheless, there is nothing outside of human practices to make us see the atomic structure of a thing as essential to it – as that without which it would not be the thing it is. Once the thing matters to me on the basis of my technological drive for flexibility and efficiency, the atomic structure of the thing is the most important property of it. Because understanding the atomic structure allows me to unlock it, expose it, and switch it about, I will see its atomic structure as that without which it would not be the thing that it is.

The way an understanding of being shapes our dispositions, then, determines the truth of the essence of things in the modern world. And that they have a true essence secures the possibility, and thus is the very essence, of all the propositional truths we possess.

NOTES

1. The reading of Heidegger that I offer in this chapter has been profoundly influenced by numerous conversations with Bert Dreyfus, as well as by papers he has written on related topics (for example, his "How Heidegger Defends the Possibility of a Correspondence Theory of Truth with Respect to the Entities of Natural Science," in *The Practice Turn in Contemporary Theory*, ed. Theodore R. Schatzki, Karin Knorr Cetina, and Eike von Savigny (London, Routledge, 2001), 151–162). I am indebted to him for all the help he has given me in thinking through these topics, as well as for specific comments he has made on this chapter. Charles Guignon has offered a number of helpful suggestions and thought-provoking comments regarding this chapter, for which I thank him. I am grateful also to good questions posed, and helpful comments made, when I presented earlier versions of this chapter to the BYU Philosophy Club, and at Södertörn University. Hans Ruin is deserving of special thanks in this regard. Finally, I would like to thank Thomas Sheehan for generously supplying me with an advance copy of the translation of GA 21.

2. Martin Heidegger, "Hegel and the Greeks," in P 335 (translation modified). Heidegger's reference to truth as "correctness" is always shorthand

for traditional accounts of propositional truth, in which truth is understood to consist in the correspondence or agreement of an assertion or
belief with a fact or state of affairs: "What makes everyone of these statements into a true one? This: in what it says, it corresponds with the matters and the states of affairs about which it says something. The being
true of an assertion thus signifies such corresponding. What therefore
is truth? Truth is correspondence. Such correspondence exists because
the assertion orients itself [sich richtet] according to that about which
it speaks. Truth is correctness [richtigkeit]. So truth is correspondence
of the assertion with the matter which is grounded on correctness." GA
34, 2. As the word-play on richtigkeit indicates, the correctness of an
assertion consists, for Heidegger, in its orienting itself to the state of
affairs.

3.   The term "thing" in Heidegger's writing and lectures on truth lacks the
specific sense it bears in later works on "things thinging." For this later
sense, see "Building Dwelling Thinking" and "The Thing." In the works
on truth, "thing" (Ding) is ontologically uncommitted, a way to refer to a
specific entity without making any assumptions about the being of that
entity. Heidegger typically (but not always) refers to an entity as it shows
up for propositional states as an "object" (Gegenstand). "Entities" or
"what is" (Seiende) is Heidegger's most general mass term for anything
that is, and the term he typically uses to refer to beings as they figure
in pre-reflective experience. My thanks to Charles Guignon for forcing
me to clarify this point.

4.   Heidegger was emphatic about this both "early" and "late"; compare,
e.g., comments from the 1931 lecture course on the essence of truth in
GA 34, 11 ("The meaning of the Greek word for truth, unconcealment,
to begin with has nothing to do with assertion and with the factual
context, set out in the customary definition of the essence of truth:
with correspondence and correctness"), with the 1964 essay "The End of
Philosophy and the Task of Thinking," in BW 389: "to raise the question
of aletheia, of unconcealment as such, is not the same as raising the
question of truth." See also the comments in BT 262 ("To translate
this word [alêtheia] as 'truth,' and, above all, to define this expression
conceptually in theoretical ways, is to cover up the meaning of what the
Greeks made 'self-evidently' basic for the terminological use of alêtheia
as a pre-philosophical way of understanding it"); and the 1960 essay
"Hegel and the Greeks," P 335 ("if the essence of truth that straightaway
comes to reign as correctness and certainty can subsist only within the
realm of unconcealment, then truth indeed has to do with Alêtheia, but
not Alêtheia with truth").

5.   A "nexus" is a connection of subject and predicate – i.e., a proposition.
See "On the Essence of Ground," in P 102, or GA 26, 30 & 40 ff.

6. "On the Essence of Ground," in P 103. See also BQP 23 (representation "does not first create the openness of the things and the openness of man for what he might encounter").

7. For one thing, the correspondence view – the idea that an assertion is true only if it corresponds to a fact (i.e., an object in a particular condition) – works poorly for negative assertions. To what object in what condition does the assertion "there are no Olympian gods" correspond? If negative assertions were taken as the paradigm case, Heidegger suggests, we would be forced to notice that every assertion is capable of truth or falsity only on the basis of a prior, non-propositional ability to comport with the whole practical situation. We would see that "in every individual assertion, no matter how trivial or complicated, we always already speak *out of beings that are manifest as a whole*, and this 'as a whole' itself... [is] not in turn the result of a pointing out by way of assertion" (FCM 345).

Likewise in focusing on assertions to the exclusion of the way we predicate truth of things, Heidegger argues that we become blinded to the way that truth is grounded in the unconcealment of beings. "What is originarily true, i.e., unconcealed, is precisely not the assertion about a being, but rather the being itself – a thing, a fact. A being is true, understood in the Greek manner, if it shows itself as that and in which it is: true gold. Fool's gold, on the other hand, shows itself as something that it is not. It covers over, conceals its what-being, it conceals itself as the being that it actually is. The true is thus primarily a character of the beings themselves" (GA 34, 118).

Both negative assertions and material truth, in other words, force us to face the primacy of unconcealment over propositional truth.

8. See Heidegger's discussion of the *adaequatio rei ad intellectum*, "On the Essence of Truth," in P 138.

9. See, e.g., GA 21, 9: GA 34, 3; P 138.

10. "Knowledge is supposed *so* to 'give' the thing *as* it is. 'Correspondence has the relational character: '*so-as*'," BT 259 (translation modified). See also GA 21, 10: "Truth has the formal structure of the *so-as*."

11. Cf. the interesting verificationist interpretations of Heidegger offered by Cristina Lafont, *Heidegger, Language, and World-Disclosure* (Cambridge: Cambridge University Press, 2000), and Mark Okrent, *Heidegger's Pragmatism* (Ithaca, NY: Cornell University Press, 1988).

12. I have discussed Heidegger's account of this structure in more detail in "The Conditions of Truth in Heidegger and Davidson," *Monist* 82 (1999): 304–323.

13. In BT, Heidegger draws the distinction between a pre-predicative and predicative experience of what is in terms of a "hermeneutical" *as* versus an "apophantical" *as*. See BT 201, 260.

14. Following Bert Dreyfus and John Haugeland, among others, I translate Heidegger's term *Vorhanden* as "occurrent." *Vorhanden* means literally "before the hand," and in the colloquial German of Heidegger's day, something is *vorhanden* when it *exists* or is *extant*, that is, when it is *to be found* or *encountered*. The Macquarrie and Robinson translation renders this as "present-at-hand," trying to capture the literal sense of something being on hand. But I find this translation rather unwieldy. It also invites confusion with Heidegger's discussions of presence and the present (a worry that Macquarrie and Robinson acknowledge at BT 48, n. 1). Stambaugh's translation of *Vorhanden* as "objectively present" only intensifies the danger of confusion by emphasizing the present-ness of what is *vorhanden* and offering an interpretation of the kind of presence *Vorhanden* has. Such translations at best short-circuit, or at least confuse, the conclusions Heidegger wishes to draw about occurrent entities. The English term "occurrent," as long as it is understood in a colloquial sense, captures just the connotations we want – something is occurrent when it is actual, encounterable, existing.

15. See GA 20 and GA 21.

16. See, e.g., GA 21 66, 133–134.

17. P. F. Strawson, "Truth," *Proceedings of the Aristotelean Society* (1950), suppl. 24: 129–156.

18. "The Origin of the Work of Art," in Martin Heidegger, *Basic Writings* (2nd ed.), David F. Krell, ed. (San Francisco: Harper, 1993), pp. 176–177.

19. Saul Kripke, *Naming and Necessity* (Cambridge: Harvard University Press, 1980), p. 122.

20. A clarificatory note is in order here. In the traditional sense, which Kripke adopts, the essence of a thing is that property of the thing which explains all the other properties that we consider to be important about the thing. For Heidegger, the essence of a thing is whatever disposes us to consider certain properties to be the important ones.

21. Kripke, *Naming and Necessity*, p. 118.

22. Hubert Dreyfus has shown that Heidegger, with his notion of "formal indication," anticipates the Kripkean idea of rigid designation. See "How Heidegger Defends the Possibility of a Correspondence Theory of Truth with Respect to the Entities of Natural Science," in *The Practice Turn in Contemporary Theory*, pp. 151–162. Dreyfus sees formal indication as a basis for Heidegger's anti-anti-essentialism – an argument I accept, but will not pursue in this chapter.

23. P 104 (some emphasis supplied). See also BQP 73: "We are acquainted with the 'essence' of the things surrounding us: house, tree, bird, road, vehicle, man, etc., and yet we have no knowledge of the essence. For we immediately land in the uncertain, shifting, controversial, and

groundless, when we attempt to determine more closely, and above all try to ground in its determinateness, what is certainly though still indeterminately 'known': namely, house-ness, tree-ness, bird-ness, humanness."

24. By "good existential grip," I mean simply an ability to comport successfully in the world in which we find ourselves.

25. See especially section 24 of BQP.

26. See BQP 55 ("what is essential in the essence . . . [is] that which admits, or demands, that the essence be valid for the many individuals").

27. See QCT, especially 14 ff.

10 Authenticity, moral values, and psychotherapy

PSYCHOTHERAPY AND THE QUESTION OF THE GOOD LIFE

Heidegger's influence on psychotherapy in the English-speaking world has followed a convoluted path. The Swiss physician and therapist Medard Boss tells us that Heidegger expressed the hope that "his thinking would escape the confines of the philosopher's study and become of benefit to wider circles, in particular to a large number of suffering human beings."[1] His participation in Boss's seminars for medical students and therapists from 1946 on was motivated by this concern.[2] Yet when his writings became more widely known among professionals in the field, it was less through this route than through the impact of existentialism in the fifties and sixties. As a result, though Heidegger's thought is often treated as the cornerstone of existential psychotherapy,[3] what one usually finds is a Heidegger refracted through the lens of the far more accessible writings of Sartre, de Beauvoir, and Camus. In the mouth of this "existential-ized" Heidegger, the ideal of authenticity is pictured as the stance of the rugged individualist who, upon experiencing anxiety in the face of the ultimate absurdity of life, lives intensely in the present and creates his or her own world through leaps of radical freedom.

As the enthusiasm for existentialism has waned over the past two decades, however, so has the initial motivation for thinking that Heidegger has something important to contribute to therapy. The decline of existentialism can be attributed, I believe, to the growing suspicion that its image of the human condition is too limited to capture the concrete realities of actual existence. The conception of "terrible freedom" found in the French existentialists, for

268

instance, seems to conceal the sense we have of being embedded in a world where not all things are possible. Idealizing this notion of freedom runs the risk of glorifying sheer capriciousness, the kind of "do-your-own-thing" willfulness that created such misery for the "me-generation." Moreover, when authenticity is equated with the existentialist vision of freely creating one's life as a work of art, it is quite natural to conclude that this idea is consistent with an amoral or even immoral way of life.[4] Existentialist psychology, allied in the sixties with "humanistic" movements, was supposed to provide a "third force" to serve as an alternative to Freudian and empirical approaches.[5] Opposing what it perceived to be the scientific mechanism and determinism of standard theories, this movement sought to protect the dignity of humans by insisting on human freedom. But, in the end, its overblown notion of freedom came to seem as unrealistic and pernicious as the view it sought to replace.

At the same time, however, many therapists and mental health professionals continue to feel that the mainstream "scientific" theories designed to explain and guide psychotherapy fail to capture much of what actually goes on in the practice of therapy. One way to describe this gap between theory and practice is to say that standard theories fail to make sense of the rich and complex forms of moral discourse that characterize therapeutic dialogue. We can see why moral discourse is essential to therapy if we reflect on the events that created the need for psychotherapy in the first place. Ira Progoff describes how the rise of modern technological civilization first *generated* contemporary psychological problems. In earlier, preindustrial societies, according to Progoff, "individuals experienced the meaning of their lives in terms of local religious orthodoxies and accustomed national or tribal ways of life" of their communities. These traditional practices and institutions "provided built-in psychic security for the individual." When faith in these commonalities broke down, however, the individual was left unprotected. With no recourse to a spiritual past shared with others, the individual "was isolated and cut adrift; and it is this situation of the lone individual no longer sustained by the cultural resources of his ancestors that is the main root of the psychological problems that have arisen in modern times."[6]

As a result of these changes, therapists are now asked to serve as moral authorities, filling the vacuum left by the loss of older sources of guidance. C. Marshall Lowe observes that since "the theological priesthood has lost much of its authority, ... the scientist practicing counseling and psychotherapy assumes a new moral authority. He is asked to make moral pronouncements in the name of science in the way the clergy was called upon for religious directives."[7] Because of this demand placed on therapists, a central part of what goes on in helping people in the modern world will consist in addressing questions about what constitutes the good life and how we can be at home in the world. And these are clearly *moral* questions in the broad sense, where "morality" includes not just questions about right actions, but "questions about how I am going to live my life" – questions "which touch on the issue of what kind of life is worth living, ... or of what constitutes a rich, meaningful life – as against one concerned with secondary matters or trivia."[8]

The need for moral guidance is all the more pressing given the kinds of problems therapists are asked to treat today. Morris Eagle points out that people currently seeking professional help suffer less often from the classical neuroses Freudian theory was designed to treat and more often from problems of self "experienced as feelings of meaninglessness, feelings of emptiness, pervasive depression, lack of sustaining interests, goals, ideals and values, and feelings of unrelatedness." Often quite successful in their careers, these individuals feel purposeless, adrift, and deeply dissatisfied with life. Although the immediate cause of such "self disorders" may be faulty parenting, Eagle suggests that they ultimately spring from such social factors as "the lack of stable ideologies and values... or an atmosphere of disillusionment and cynicism in the surrounding society." These disorders of the self reveal more than ever "the importance of goals and guiding values as both a reflection of and a maintainer of psychic health."[9]

Nevertheless, therapists may feel poorly equipped by their training to take on this task. For, to the extent that psychotherapy thinks of itself as an "applied behavioral science," it seems to embody assumptions that cloud any attempt to think of the therapist as a "moral authority." This is so because scientific endeavor from the outset has aimed at being value-free and objective, basing its findings solely on observation and causal explanation. The result is a deep distrust of authoritarian pronouncements and value judgments. Such distrust is evident, for example, in Freud's initial vision of psychoanalysis as a science concerned primarily with devising explanatory models for psychic conflict. For Freud, morality is treated as part of the workings of a harsh and punitive superego, more a source of conflict than its potential cure. Though newer approaches may take a less jaundiced view of morality, they still tend to treat moral concerns either as the personal business of the client or as reducible to whatever principles of procedural justice are currently accepted as "self-evident" in its own academic and professional community.

This situation points to the need for a way of understanding the human condition that can make sense of its irreducible moral dimension. In what follows, I will suggest that Heidegger's early concept of authenticity, properly understood, has a great deal to offer for this purpose. I will first sketch out some of the assumptions in the modern scientific outlook that make it difficult to grasp the moral dimension of psychotherapy. What is most interesting here is the way even the early approaches influenced by Heidegger, despite their hopes of escaping from "scientism," tended to slip back into the same assumptions and problems. By working out Heidegger's alternative view of human existence and authenticity, I hope to show that moral concerns are an inescapable part of any project of understanding humans, and that they quite naturally will be central to any meaningful therapeutic dialogue. In trying to display the evaluative dimension of psychotherapy, my aim is not to propose a new technique, but to provide an ontological basis for understanding what always goes on in therapy though it is never fully comprehended in standard theories.

UNDERLYING ASSUMPTIONS OF PSYCHOTHERAPY THEORIES

Much of contemporary psychotherapy theory draws its conception of humans from a view of reality shaped by the natural sciences, a view now commonly called "naturalism." Naturalism, the common ground for both Freudian and empirical approaches, holds that because humans are a part of nature, we understand them by applying the same canons of explanation used for other parts of nature. We might distinguish three assumptions drawn from naturalism that underlie the conception of humans found in most psychotherapy theories. The first concerns the nature of the self. Part of the achievement of the new science of the seventeenth century was to dispel the traditional image of reality as a value-laden, meaningful cosmos in favor of our modern naturalistic view of the "universe" as a vast aggregate of objects in causal interactions. Correlative with this objectifying view of the universe is a picture of the self as a *thing* or *object* of a particular sort. Humans are physical objects among others in the natural order, but they are distinctive insofar as they have a consciousness and so can freely act on the world. Despite the presence of the mind, however, humans are still conceived of as objects only contingently related to other items in the world. The self understood as a thing – as a "subject of inwardness" or a self-encapsulated center of action – has been central to most psychotherapy theories.

The second assumption has to do with the nature of agency and the proper conduct of life. With the tremendous success of instrumental reason in achieving technological control over the world, a conception of action as based on means-ends calculations became widely accepted. Through a formalizable procedure, it seems, we can work things over in order to achieve our goals. This capacity for strategic calculation and technical control was quite naturally expanded to include a psychotechnology for self-improvement. With the guidance of experts, we should be able to reengineer our own lives according to a rational blueprint. Thus, one finds, in self-help programs and popularized workshops, procedures of self-transformation described in a vocabulary of reworking the self to achieve particular ends – vocabularies of "strengthening the ego," "restructuring cognitive strategies," "instilling hardiness," "learning coping skills," or "managing stress."

What is most striking about this calculative-instrumentalist approach, of course, is its inability to reflect on the question of which *ends* are truly worth pursuing. Older views of life generally made a distinction between (1) "mere living," just functioning and satisfying needs, and (2) a "higher" or "better" form of existence that we could achieve if we realized our proper aim in life. In contrast, the modern naturalistic outlook tries to free itself from such a two-tiered view of life. The aims of living are now thought of either as the satisfaction of those basic needs dictated by our biosocial makeup or as matters of personal preference. Psychotherapy, seen as a technique designed to help people attain their ends, remains indifferent to the ends themselves so long as they are realistic and consistent.

The third assumption concerns the nature of human relations. Given what has been called the "ontological individualism" of modernity – the view that human reality is to be understood in terms of self-encapsulated individuals who are only contingently aggregated into social systems – a conflictual model of humans seems inevitable. When I see myself as a strategic calculator competing for limited resources, I tend to see others either as aids or as obstacles to my pursuits. Relationships are then experienced as temporary alliances entered into in order to secure our mutual benefit. The outcome is a kind of "therapeutic contractualism" that treats marriage, friendships, and love relations as means to individual self-enhancement, that is, as contractual arrangements to be maintained only so long as I "continue to grow" or "still feel good about myself" in the relationship.[10]

The humanistic and existentialist approaches of the fifties and sixties arose as a backlash against the objectification and instrumentalism they perceived in naturalistic theories. Turning away from science, they generally drew their understanding of the self from the "expressivist" ways of thinking that characterized nineteenth-century romanticism. According to this expressivist view, the self contains an inner seed of potential that is capable of self-fulfillment through artistic creativity, communion with nature, and intense relationships with others. The image of self-realization through the expression of one's innermost feelings and capacities seemed to offer an alternative to the "dehumanizing" effects of the naturalistic outlook. Nonetheless, to the extent that these approaches still bought into the assumptions of ontological individualism, they tended to perpetuate the very view of human reality they sought to overcome.

Some examples will show how this problem arises. Rollo May's writings display a refined moral sensibility and a commitment to making moral concerns central to the understanding of human existence. We can understand who we are, May writes, only through a "search for our values and purposes.... Without values there would be only barren despair." The two-tiered view of life, with its distinction of "mere life" and a "higher life," is indispensable to being fully human. Humans just are the beings who make certain values "more important than pleasure and even more important than survival itself."[11] It is because mainstream theorizing fails to account for the role of values in human life that psychotherapy risks becoming "part of the neurosis of our day rather than part of the cure."[12]

Yet May is less convincing when it comes to formulating his own positive account of moral values. The only ideal he seems to endorse is *commitment,* that is, a "decisive attitude toward existence," "the attitude of ... the self-aware being taking his own existence seriously."[13] Indeed, commitment to values is necessary if one "is to attain integration," for values are needed to serve "as a psychological center, a kind of core of integration which draws together [one's] powers as the core of a magnet draws the magnet's lines of force together." Values make possible freedom and maturity: "The mark of the mature man is that his living is integrated around self-chosen goals"; such a person "plans and works toward a creative love relationship or toward business achievement or what not."[14]

It goes without saying, however, that the question here is precisely this "what not." When values and goals are chosen solely in order to attain integration and maturity, they are being treated as mere means to ends. The result, then, is that values come to be regarded as adventitious, presumably dispensable in favor of other means (perhaps brutality or destructiveness) if those would do the job better. In this respect May's writings display a paradox common to a wide range of psychotherapy theories.[15] On the one hand, theorists recognize the deep-felt need in the modern world for authoritative values to provide guidance and a sense of purpose to life. On the other hand, the deep distrust of authority in our culture leads them to feel that values can be justified only if they are treated as means to achieving such nonmoral ends as personal satisfaction or fulfillment or "empowerment." When looked at in this way, however, moral discourse is reduced to the very calculative-instrumentalist thinking May rightly sees as so debilitating. Moreover, this conception of values as tools on hand for our use threatens to reinforce the objectifying view of the self May wants to eliminate. For when values are thought of as items on hand for our free choice, we will tend to think of ourselves as dimensionless points of raw will, not attached in advance to anything, who can freely pick and choose among the smorgasbord of values set before us.[16] Thus, though May is right to say that "the degree of an individual's inner strength and integrity will depend on how much he himself believes in the values he lives by,"[17] he seems unable to account for how the autonomous, disengaged chooser of values could ever come to regard any values as genuinely binding in the first place.

Medard Boss and Ludwig Binswanger, two theorists profoundly influenced by Heidegger, try to give us a richer grasp of our "being-in-the-world" as embracing a wide range of possibilities of self-understanding and self-appraisal. Boss, for example, rejects Freud's notion of "guilt *feelings*," claiming that it conceals the deeper phenomenon of "existential guilt." "Man's existential guilt consists in his failing to carry out the mandate to fulfill all his possibilities," a failure exacerbated by a tendency to follow "acquired moral concepts," the "foreign and crippling mentality which his educators forced upon him." To overcome this form of inauthenticity, Boss envisions the ideal of an "authentic" individual who, "accept[ing] all his life-possibilities," can "appropriate and assemble them to a free, authentic own self no longer caught in the narrowed-down mentality of an anonymous, inauthentic 'everybody.'"[18] And Binswanger, though less critical of the "everybody," agrees with Boss in regarding psychological problems as resulting from an overly constricted "world-design." Problems arise when the individual's *Eigenwelt* (own world) "is narrowed and constricted to such a degree [that] the self, too, is constricted and prevented from maturing." The aim of therapy, then, is to help people recover "the *freedom* of letting 'world' occur."[19]

Boss is confident that, once genuine freedom is achieved, "mankind's ethics becomes self-evident" and we will be able to "define man's basic morality."[20] Behind this confidence, I suspect, is the romantic faith that we have something deep within us, a "child within," who is truer, purer, and somehow "better" than the dreary, rigid, duty-bound self imposed on us by our socialization. The belief in this "authentic self" – an idea that has become common currency through the writings of such theorists as D. W. Winnicott, Alice Miller, and John Bradshaw – is tremendously appealing. But it is not at all obvious that "carrying out the mandate to fulfill all our possibilities" will help clarify our basic morality or make us better people. One thing Freud taught us is to be suspicious of such ideas as the "noble savage" and the "child within." Today we cannot avoid facing the fact that our "possibilities" include not just love and compassion, but also hostility, selfishness, and aggression. Does the "mandate to fulfill all our possibilities" include these as well? And, if not, what moral map guides us in distinguishing the possibilities we ought to fulfill from those we should not?[21]

Central to both Boss and Binswanger is their belief in what is the core value of modern individualism: freedom understood negatively as freedom *from* constraints. It may be the case, however, that this ideal of unbounded freedom is self-defeating. For where all things are equally possible, nothing is really binding, and so no choice is superior to any others. Freedom then becomes, in Rieff's classic line, the "absurdity of being freed to choose and then having no choice worth making."[22] What these criticisms show is that "third-force" approaches tend to slip back into the very naturalistic assumptions they set out to overcome. To get beyond these assumptions, I believe, we need a fresh way of thinking about human existence.

EVERYDAYNESS AND INAUTHENTICITY

Heidegger proposes that we bracket the presuppositions of modern naturalism and turn directly to a phenomenology of our pretheoretical sense of ourselves as we are in "average everydayness." In our ordinary agency, according to Heidegger's description, the self is not so much an object as an unfolding *event* or *happening* – the "movement" of a life course "stretched out between birth and death" (BT 427). From this standpoint, it is wrong to think of oneself as a mind or a center of consciousness with its own *Eigenwelt*: "Even one's own Dasein [is] something it can itself proximally 'come across' only when it *looks away* from 'experiences' and the 'center of its actions,' or does not yet 'see' them at all. Dasein finds 'itself' proximally in what it does" (BT 155). Because we are generally outside our "selves," caught up in equipmental contexts in a shared world, Heidegger can say that being a "self" is "'only'... *a way of being* of this entity" (BT 153, my emphasis).

In Heidegger's view, there is no pregiven "human nature" that determines what we are. Instead, we *are* what we make of ourselves in the course of living out our active lives. This is what it means to say that the "*'essence' of Dasein lies in its existence*" (BT 67). We can clarify this conception of humans as self-constituting beings by contrasting it with the kind of romantic expressivist view found in third-force psychotherapy theories. We saw that, for the expressivist, each person is endowed with deep, inner feelings, talents, and potentialities definitive of his or her "true self." A person's actions, then, are regarded as a more or less genuine outward display or expression of this inner germinal seed. Actions are physical movements to be explained in terms of inner beliefs, desires, and feelings. Here there is a sharp distinction between mind and body: the inner, mental realm is distinguished from the realm of mere physical movement.

When we look at our "average everydayness," however, we are led to what might be called a "manifestationist" view of human agency. For the manifestationist, there is no way to draw a clear distinction between an inner, core self and what is merely outward show. Instead, to say that we *are* what we *do* is to say that our very identity as agents – our *being* – is defined and realized only through our ways of becoming manifest in the world. We can clarify this conception of human agency by considering how we encounter a person who is particularly blunt and forthright. Her snappy responses, her no-nonsense style, her firmness in confusing situations – her ways of doing things – present themselves directly as her *being* the straight, unpretentious person she is. What she *is* is "written on the face" of things; for her, what you see is what you get. It is pointless here to think of such a person's actions as only outward representations of some hidden, inner mental acts, for what she does *presents* her being as the honest and direct person she is. Her agency is the "emerging-into-presence" or "coming-into-being" of her identity as a person of a particular sort, just as my wearing loafers and old sweatshirts *is* my being a casual or informal dresser. For the most part, the idea of an inner, mental source of actions has no role here. Suspicions about "what is really going on in her mind" make sense only when there are breaks in the otherwise smooth flow of her agency in familiar contexts.

From the manifestationist perspective, the mental remains inchoate and ephemeral until it is given shape in action. Even my *own* feelings and beliefs usually come to be defined for me only through the ways they show forth in the course of my actions. For this reason Heidegger locates human existence not in the mind, but in the unfolding "happening" or "event" of a life: as he says, "being-a-self *is* . . . only in its process of realization" (MFL 139, my emphasis). Understood as a "happening" that unfolds throughout a lifetime, a person's identity can be grasped only in terms of his or her life story as a whole. The temporal unfolding of life, as Ricoeur has pointed out, has the structure of a narrative.[23] We can understand who a person *is* only in terms of where that person is coming from and where he or she is going. From a narrativist perspective, actions in the present are fully intelligible only in terms of their place within the narrative unfolding of the person's life – in terms of what has happened up to this point and where things are headed in general.

Regarded as a temporal unfolding with both cumulativeness and purposiveness, Dasein's life course exhibits certain essential structures. First, Dasein is always "ahead of itself": it is a projection into the future insofar as its actions involve a commitment as to what sort of person it will be as a totality. What this means is that, in taking a stand on its own life, Dasein takes over some range of possibilities as definitive of its identity – some set of personality traits, lifestyles, roles, or attitudes – and exists as a "being-toward" the realization of a final configuration of possibilities for its life overall. Since we will *be* something once and for all only at the culmination of our lives, Heidegger calls this futurity the "bringing itself to fruition" (*sich zeitigen*) of Dasein. We are "being-toward-the-end" or "being-*toward*-death" not in the sense of facing our demise or fulfilling a potential, but in the sense that everything we do contributes to making us people of a particular sort. Thus, whether I realize it or not, my ways of relating to my children involve a commitment toward the future: through my actions, I am making myself a parent who is neglectful or supportive or unavailable. Although I may always change the identity I have formed up to now by a radical shift in my ways of acting, so long as I continue acting the way I do, I am making myself into this sort of parent.

Where "projection" grasps the future-directedness of a life happening, "thrownness" refers to our being already enmeshed in a particular context. As a parent, for example, I find myself stuck with obligations rooted in my past undertakings that I must take up in my current actions. At the same time I also find myself enmeshed in a particular historical culture that predefines the range of possibilities of action that will make sense in my situation. For the most part, Heidegger says, Dasein is the "they" or the "anyone." Our everyday actions make sense only because they instantiate or exemplify the taken-for-granted patterns and norms of the shared life-world. In this respect, the public context provides the medium of intelligibility we draw on in making something of our lives. Or, to restate this idea in the narrativist mode, it is in terms of the plot lines made accessible in the anecdotes, tales, and stories circulating in our public language that we come to see what is at stake in situations, what is worth shooting for, and what courses of action will be appropriate. This rootedness of our personal life stories in the wider drama of our community's history is expressed in the claim that Dasein's "historicity" is embedded in the "co-happening" of a "community, of a people" (BT 436). Our participation in a social context is therefore a fundamental dimension of our existence as humans. Because we can *be* human agents only against the backdrop of such a shared medium of intelligibility, Heidegger says that the "they" is *"a primordial phenomenon* [which] *belongs to Dasein's positive constitution"* (BT 167).

As is well known, however, the "they" as Heidegger describes it is Janus-faced. On the one hand, our participation in the "they" is an enabling condition that first opens us onto a world and gives us the resources we need for *being* human. From the outset, Dasein draws its possibilities for self-understanding and action from the way things are interpreted by the "they." On the other hand, this involvement in public forms of life can have a pernicious effect. It threatens to level all decisions to the lowest common denominator of what is acceptable and well adjusted; it restricts "the possible options of choice to what lies within the range of the familiar, the attainable, the respectable – that which is fitting and proper" (BT 239). There is an inveterate tendency, then, to go along with the flow, content with "satisfying the easily handled rules and public norms of the 'they,'" and thereby being disburdened of all "responsibility" for ourselves (BT 334). "Dasein, as a they-self, gets 'lived' by the commonsense ambiguity of that publicness in which nobody resolves upon anything but which has already made its decision" (BT 345). The result is a "dimming down of the possible as such" (BT 239). Inauthentic Dasein is dispersed into a multiplicity of humdrum routines, drifting with the latest fads, tranquilly assured that "everything is 'in the best of order' and all doors are open" (BT 222). This "leveling down" of all possibilities obliterates the kind of two-tiered sense of life that lets us distinguish higher from lower, crucial from trivial, central from peripheral. Taking the familiar demands of the public world as of consummate importance – as "the only game in town" – we can become highly effective strategic calculators, convinced that everything is possible, yet lacking any overarching sense of what makes life worth living.

Inauthenticity is characterized by "falling" and "forgetting." In the ordinary busy-ness of handling daily affairs, Dasein tends to become ensnared in its immediate concerns and to drift along with the taken-for-granted practices of average everydayness. We hide behind social roles, enacting parts in familiar dramas and following the rules of socially approved games. This tendency to fall into mundane activities catches us up in the "turbulence" of life and tears us away from the possibility of taking hold of our existence in a coherent, integrated way. Our falling absorption in the public world is coupled with "forgetfulness." Although some degree of forgetting is unavoidable if we are to be agents in the world – "The self must forget itself if, lost in the world of equipment, it is to be able 'actually' to go to work and manipulate something" (BT 405) – what is insidious is the way this first-order forgetting is compounded by a second-order forgetting in which one "not only forgets the forgotten but forgets the forgetting itself" (BP 290). In other words, we become so mired down in ordinary chores that we forget that we are called upon to take a coherent stand in a world where things are genuinely at stake. This self-forgetfulness, paradoxically, tends to aggravate our own self-preoccupation and self-absorption. Constantly concerned with checking its performance against public criteria, Dasein becomes "entangled in itself," sinking into "the most exaggerated 'self-dissection'" (BT 222), into an "extravagant grubbing about in one's own soul which can be in the highest degree counterfeit" (BP 160).

An inauthentic life comes to have the warped temporal structure Heidegger calls "making-present." Absorbed in the demands of the moment, we understand ourselves in terms of what "is determined by the success or failure, the feasibility or unfeasibility, of [our] commerce with things" (BP 289). Everyday existence is fragmented into a series of means-ends strategies governed by the latest public attitudes about what constitutes success. Inauthentic Dasein "dwells with things, gets entangled in its own self, and lets itself be drawn along by things," with the result that it "loses itself within itself, so that the past becomes a forgetting and the future a mere expecting of what is just coming on" (BP 287). Making-present retains only what is relevant to the current context, and it merely awaits expected outcomes. As a series of strategies for coping with practical concerns, our everyday lives are contracted into a succession of episodes – the "one damned thing after another" of mere functioning or "getting by." The ends of living are seen as fixed, not themselves in question. They are the well-deserved rewards we expect for having performed well: the martini at the end of the day or the weekend in front of the television. Life is experienced, in Aristotle's terminology, as *techne* rather than as *praxis:* it is a matter of "production," which has its end outside itself, rather than "activity," whose "end is doing well itself," and so is internal to the practice.[24] The outcome of this disjointed way of living is alienation from oneself, an inability to see anything as really mattering, and feelings of futility only partially alleviated by occasional intense "peak experiences" that are supposed to "make it all worthwhile." The inauthentic form of life, as Heidegger describes it, seems to be a perfect breeding ground for the kinds of demoralization and self disorders found among current candidates for psychotherapy.

AUTHENTICITY

Heidegger's concept of "authenticity" is supposed to point to a way of life that is higher than that of average everydayness. It is important to keep in mind that authenticity has nothing to do with such romantic ideals as getting in touch with a deep inner self or rising above the herd. Heidegger says that authenticity "does not detach Dasein from its world"; the world "does not become another one 'in its content,' nor does the circle of Others get exchanged for a new one" (BT 344). Indeed, since our own life stories are inseparable from the wider text of a shared we-world, authenticity can be nothing other than a fuller and richer form of participation in the public context. Thus, we find that authentic understanding "is so far from extricating itself from the way of interpreting Dasein which has come down to us [from the 'they'], that in each case it is in terms of this interpretation, against it, and yet again for it, that any possibility one has chosen is seized upon in one's resolution" (BT 435).

Yet as Heidegger describes it, the *path* to this deeper involvement in the public world passes through a radical breakdown of our complacent absorption in everydayness. In his well-known description of anxiety, Heidegger suggests that our ordinary preoccupations in the busy-ness of the world are actually a form of "evasion" or "fleeing." We throw ourselves into the turbulence of day-to-day chores and they-roles in order to avoid facing up to something we find threatening. What we are fleeing from in everydayness is our own "thrownness toward death": the fact that we are finite beings and that we are "delivered over to ourselves" in the sense of being responsible for the task of making something of our lives. In the experience of anxiety, we are forced to confront our own finitude. Heidegger says that anxiety brings Dasein "face to face with the 'nothingness' of the possible impossibility of existence" (BT 310). Confronted with our being-toward-death, the roles we have been playing suddenly seem anonymous, and we are faced with the demand to own up to our lives.

If we can take a stand on our being-toward-death, our lives will be transformed. Facing death, one is pulled back from the dispersal, distraction, and forgetfulness of everydayness. The result is the ability to live with a clear-sighted grasp of the temporal continuity and future-directedness of one's own life-happening. This lucidity leads to a way of living we might call "self-focusing." The authentic Dasein, recognizing that not everything is possible, is "snatched back from the endless multiplicity of possibilities which offer themselves as closest to one" and focuses itself into a range of possibilities "which are determined by the *end* and so are understood as *finite*" (BT 435, 308). Such directedness into a coherent range of possibilities brings about a change in the way we relate to our thrownness and our being as projections toward the future. We take over our situatedness with "resoluteness" – a decisive dedication to what we want to accomplish for our lives. And our stance toward the future is that of "anticipation" or "forward-directedness": a clear-sighted and unwavering commitment to those overriding aims taken as definitive of one's existence as a whole.

Authentic self-focusing, understood as a resolute reaching forward into a finite range of possibilities, gives coherence, cohesiveness, and integrity to a life course. Authenticity is characterized by a distinctive temporal structure. Where inauthentic existence is lost in the dispersal of making-present, an authentic life is lived as a unified flow characterized by cumulativeness and direction. It involves taking over the possibilities made accessible by the past and acting in the present in order to accomplish something for the future. Or to rephrase this in the narrativist mode, such a life is lived as a coherent story. It is a life that is given focus by its future-directedness – what Hans-Georg Gadamer calls an "anticipation of completion" or Frank Kermode calls a "sense of an ending." This directedness toward the culmination of our lives lets us appropriate what has already happened as resources or assets whose latent significance is brought to realization through action in the present. Achieving the narrative continuity of authentic existence is what first makes possible personal identity understood as the "constancy of the self" – its "steadiness" and "steadfastness" – stretched out across a life span (BT 369). According to Heidegger, it is by taking a stand on one's life as a whole that one satisfies Pindar's counsel to "become what you are" (BT 186; cf. IM 101).

Heidegger's notion of "authentic temporality" might become clearer if we contrast two different ways of understanding the relation of actions to the whole of life.[25] The first is found in the "instrumentalist" approach to living we saw in discussing Rollo May. This stance treats life as a matter of finding the means to achieving ends, where the ends are usually goods external to the activities themselves – such "positive reinforcements" as what "feels good" or satisfies a need. In this instrumentalist, means-ends living, actions are done *in order* to get something; for example, I run everyday in order to get healthy, or I help a friend in order to get him in my debt. In contrast to this means-ends approach, the second way of living might be called a "constituent-ends" way of living. Here actions are not just routes to achieving extrinsic ends, but instead are experienced as central to *constituting* a particular way of life, a way of life that is good *because* it consists of this and comparable sorts of activities. Action here is undertaken *for the sake of being* such and such: I run as a part of being a healthy person, or I help someone for the sake of being a good friend.

It should be obvious that although the actions performed are the same in both cases, the *quality of life* will be quite different. In the means-ends case, life tends to be experienced as an episodic sequence of calculative strategies lacking any cumulative significance or overriding purpose. The activities themselves might well seem to be tedious chores I would rather avoid if I could find other means to the same ends. For example, running can feel like a grim imposition, and the quid pro quo, contractual approach to friendship can begin to feel cynical and manipulative. In contrast, the constituent-ends case reflects an experience of life in which one's actions are an integral part of *being* a person of a certain sort. Where the means-ends attitude trivializes the present by keeping us preoccupied with the carrot at the end of the stick, the constituent-end approach, by making us realize that what we are doing at this moment just *is* realizing the goals of living, throws us intensely into the present moment as the arena in which our coming-to-fruition is fulfilled. Running and being a friend are not just impositions I could as well do without; they make me the person I am. What is important is building myself *as* this kind of person, not scoring points or getting rewards "down the road." When life is lived as an ongoing process of self-building or self-composing, it has the kind of cumulativeness and continuity that makes up authentic temporality.

THE SELF AS A MORAL AGENT: IMPLICATIONS FOR PSYCHOTHERAPY

According to Heidegger's description of human existence, to know what we *are* is at the same time to know what we *can and should be* if we are to achieve coherence and unity in our lives. The idea that there is an unbridgeable gap between facts and values, an idea tied to the naturalistic outlook, seems less obvious on this account of humans. It may very well be true, as Hume claimed, that there is no way to *deduce* an "ought" from an "is" – no way to derive motivations from statements of fact alone. Yet the connections Heidegger is pointing to are not so much matters of logical entailment as connections whose overwhelming plausibility is rooted in our deepest understanding of life itself. To the extent that intelligibility and a sense of direction are tied to unity, cohesiveness, and future-directedness, it is hard to see how anyone could want the former and nevertheless not care about the latter. In contrast to naturalistic theories, then, Heidegger's account of life gives us a way of seeing substantive moral questions as an unavoidable part of any attempt to understand human beings.

One might object, however, that Heidegger's approach does not really represent much of an advance over traditional theorizing, for one might claim that merely acknowledging the inevitable presence of moral concerns does not yet give us any clue to *how* these concerns are to be dealt with in the therapeutic setting. Insofar as our culture is devoted to respecting diversity and freedom, the objection goes, any attempt to advocate some particular set of moral values would be dogmatic and so intolerable. In the therapeutic context, as in an open society generally, an "anything-goes" relativism seems preferable to *any* form of moral suasion. And so once again it appears that morality is the client's personal business, off-limits to the therapist.

The first thing to note about this objection is that it is itself based on a set of unargued-for, and so by its own standards "dogmatic," moral assumptions about the value of pluralism, tolerance, and individual rights. What this shows is that psychotherapy, and the human sciences generally, have always operated with a set of value assumptions they kept concealed under the guise of "value-neutrality." What is more important to note, however, is that the specific set of value assumptions underlying this objection – the glorification of "do-your-own-thing" individualism with its rejection of all binding authority – is very often the *source* of those problems that therapy is, by general consent, supposed to cure. If this is so, however, then standard approaches are in a deep sense self-defeating: they exacerbate the conditions they set out to cure, and they conceal in advance any alternative approaches that might be able to do what they fail to do.

These observations suggest that it will be worthwhile to explore Heidegger's alternative account of life to see if it can make better sense of what actually goes on in therapy. In this, I will look at some of the ways Heidegger's image of human existence might enrich our understanding of the role of moral discourse within professional counseling. First, though Heidegger is not concerned with proving that any one moral outlook is superior to all others, his description of authenticity does point to certain character ideals – what we might call "metavalues" – which provide a basis for being able to take a meaningful stand on whatever first-order moral commitments we make. Authentic self-focusing is said to require such traits as resoluteness, steadiness, courage, and, above all, clear-sightedness about one's own life as a finite, thrown projection. It calls for integrity and a lucid openness about what is relevant to one's actions. The authentic stance toward life makes us face up to the fact that to the extent that we are building our own lives in all we do, we are "answerable" for the choices we make. Heidegger tries to capture this by saying that the authentic person "chooses to choose." At the same time, however, to be authentic is to recognize that circumstances may arise that force us to take back our basic decisions. Thus, authentic Dasein "resolves to keep repeating itself" (BT 355); that is, it keeps renewing its commitments knowing that it might have to change its course. Repetition imparts "constancy" to one's life, making it clear that, in the end, we *are* what we *do*. For an authentic person, self-deceptive hiding behind roles and blaming others are ruled out. Heidegger also speaks of the "sober joy" of an authentic existence: when one seizes hold of one's life with decisiveness and clarity, one lives with intensity, openness, and exuberance.

Second, Heidegger's account of human existence points to a way of understanding why substantive moral reflection must play a crucial role in our self-understanding. This role becomes evident only when we consider a dimension of Heidegger's thought that is generally overlooked in the older existentialist interpretations: his concept of "authentic historicity." The concept of historicity grows out of the description of the embeddedness of Dasein in a wider context. We saw earlier that Dasein's possibilities of self-interpretation and self-evaluation are drawn from the background of intelligibility of the public world into which it is "thrown." As we become initiated into the practices of our community, we soak up the tacit sense of what is important that circulates in our world. This "attunement" to shared commitments and ideals cannot be regarded simply as a matter of having certain "life-style options" on hand for our choice. For these understandings and normative commitments are definitive for the kinds of people we are. They provide us with the possibilities of assessment and aspiration that first give us an orientation toward our own lives and a window onto the world. Given that we have become the kind of people we are – people who, for example, care about children and believe in justice – there is now no way to drop these commitments without ceasing to be who we are.

Now Heidegger wants us to see that these core, defining possibilities of understanding embodied in our everyday practices are themselves products of history. We react in knee-jerk ways to hate crimes and to cruelty because certain concerns have become fundamental to us in our heritage. The commitments to natural rights and the dignity of persons so dear to the humanistic Enlightenment, for example, were opened up by earlier Greco-Roman and Judeo-Christian traditions that saw order in the cosmos or experienced all souls as equal before God. In this sense, our lives are, so to speak, commentaries on the wider "clearing" of stories and interpretations passed down in our historical community. Long before we can engage in detached critical reflection, we have absorbed a tacit sense of what life is all about by becoming attuned to the patterns of living in our surroundings. Thus, though we are all composing our own autobiographies throughout our lives, we are doing so by falling into step with the sense of reality built into our practices. Our moral understanding is shaped by these practices and by the familiar folktales, stories, anecdotes, and histories that articulate and sustain those practices. As agents, then, each of us appropriates, transmits, and transmutes a sense of what is important that we have inherited from our historical tradition.

What is distinctive about authentic existence is the way it takes over this historical embeddedness. Where inauthentic Dasein just drifts along with the latest trends, authentic Dasein "remembers" its rootedness in the wider unfolding of its culture, and it experiences its life as indebted to the larger drama of a shared history. As a result, authenticity involves encountering one's possibilities as drawn from the "wellsprings" of a "heritage" and living one's life as part of the "mission" or "destiny" definitive of one's historical community as a whole (BT 435–6). The temporality of an authentic existence is therefore a matter of "retrieving" the possibilities of the "Dasein who came before." This is why Heidegger says that authentic Dasein "chooses its hero" and is "free for the struggle of loyally following in the footsteps of that which can be repeated" (BT 437). To be authentic, then, is not to rise above the crowd by discovering one's own personal morality. Rather, it calls for "revering the sole authority which a free existing can have, . . . the repeatable possibilities of existence" (BT 443).

The idea of choosing a hero, together with the vocabulary of "loyalty," "reverence," and "authority," suggests that to be authentic is to find guidance for the conduct of one's own life in terms of the lives of models or exemplars drawn from history. Or putting this into the narrativist mode, we might say that authentic Dasein achieves self-focusing by articulating its existence in terms of the guidelines laid out by certain paradigmatic stories circulating in our cultural world – the stories of such heroes and heroines as Abraham Lincoln,

Martin Luther King, Mother Teresa, Helen Keller, and Malcolm X. The lives of these cultural exemplars sketch out plot lines or *mythoi* for composing one's own life story – for "following in the footsteps" of those who have come before. Such paradigmatic stories generally show how strengths and weaknesses, assets and liabilities can be integrated into a coherent, meaningful life that succeeds in contributing something to the world. Because these stories already prestructure our self-understanding, making explicit the tacit commitments we all have in common can play a central role in therapeutic dialogue.

The recognition of our embeddedness in and indebtedness to the wider context of our culture leads to a third observation about the moral significance of the ideal of authenticity. Authentic historicity brings about a strong sense of our solidarity with others. "Our fates have already been guided in advance in our being with one another in the same world," Heidegger says; "Dasein's fateful destiny in and with its 'generation' goes to make up the full authentic happening of Dasein" (BT 436). Authentic existence involves a clearsighted recognition that human reality at the deepest level consists not of self-encapsulated individuals in unavoidable conflict, but of a "we" or a "co-Dasein" already attuned in the shared quest for goods definitive of a community – such goods, for us, as fairness, honesty, dignity, benevolence, achievement, and so on. Because we first find ourselves and become the people we are in the space of aspiration and assessment opened up by our shared historical practices, the goods that define our community cannot be treated as luxury items to be carried on board or left behind at our discretion. On the contrary, our very ability to live coherent, meaningful lives presupposes that we operate within the range of possibilities opened up by this background of shared intelligibility.

It follows, then, that genuine freedom is to be found not in the absence of all constraints, but in clarity and depth about the constitutive stories that lay out the guidelines along which we already shape our lives. We are free to the extent that we find ourselves enmeshed in contexts of shared meaningfulness that make it possible for us to grasp what situations demand from us and which options make sense. Heidegger's language of "loyalty" and "authority" shows that his concept of authentic freedom, far from pointing to some existentialist conception of "terrible freedom," is designed to bring out the role of those bedrock loyalties and commitments that already *inhabit* our lives, though often in a form distorted by ontological individualism.

Finally, the account of authentic existence can clarify and expand the conception, found in certain recent theorists, of therapy as the renarrativizing of a person's life story.[26] If it is true, as we have seen, that action makes sense only in the context of an ongoing story, and if greater narrative continuity implies greater intelligibility, then much of what goes on in therapy can be thought of as the joint composition of a more coherent and clear-sighted narrative. Understood as narrativizing, however, therapy must involve moral reflection. For insofar as composing a story always draws on the background of communal stories of trials, struggles, conquests, and defeats, such storyizing has a moral dimension: the narratives constructed have a "moral" to the extent that their resolution implies the achievement of some goods taken as normative by our historical culture – the worth of sacrifice, for instance, or the nobility of great strivings. This is why Jerome Bruner says, "Stories must necessarily... relate to what is morally valued, morally appropriate, or morally uncertain.... To tell a story is inescapably to take a moral stance."[27] Imparting narrative structure to a life involves emplotting events along the guidelines of a moral map of aspiration and evaluation that is rooted in the tacit background understanding of our moral heritage. Because narrative has this inescapable moral dimension, it is different from the explanations found in naturalistic approaches. Stanley Hauerwas points to the difference between stories and explanations when he says that a narrative is "not told to explain as a theory explains, but to involve the agent in a way of life.... I cannot make the story true by how I use it, but the story must make me true to its own demands of how the world should be."[28] Thus, narratives always have a normative dimension: they spring from and feed back into an understanding of the world not only as it is, but as it can and should be.

We began by looking at how naturalistic and third-force psychotherapy theories tend to presuppose a picture of the self as an essentially isolated individual in a morally neutral, objectified universe. What is troubling about such theories is the possibility that their picture of the self might be a major *source* of the emotional and behavioral problems that many people bring to therapists today.

If this is so, then modern therapy risks perpetuating the problem in the cure. Heidegger's conception of authenticity, in contrast, can help us make sense of dimensions of therapeutic practice not fully accounted for in most forms of theorizing. Its value lies not in offering recipes for new types of technique, but in providing a basis for understanding our embeddedness in a wider context of meaning, the role of constraints in genuine freedom, and the fundamental role of moral commitments in our ability to be humans in any meaningful sense. In this way it provides a counterweight to conventional therapeutic ideals of effective behavior and self-actualization, and it can open up therapeutic practice to an understanding of life that is left unintelligible by prevailing theories.[29]

NOTES

1. Medard Boss, "Martin Heidegger's Zollikon Seminars," trans. Brian Kenny, in *Heidegger and Psychology*, special issue of *Review of Existential Psychology and Psychiatry*, ed. Keith Hoeller, 1988 reprint of Vol. 16, Nos. 1, 2, and 3 (1978–9): 7–20, p. 7.

2. A record of this collaboration is available as the *Zollikoner Seminare: Protokolle, Gespräche, Briefe*, ed. Medard Boss (Frankfurt: Vittorio Klostermann, 1987). For an excellent overview of the key ideas in this work, see Fred Dallmayr, *Between Freiburg and Frankfurt: Toward a Critical Ontology* (Amherst: University of Massachusetts Press, 1991), Chap. 8.

3. Irvin D. Yalom, in his *Existential Psychotherapy* (New York: Basic Books, 1980), describes *Being and Time* as the "single most important philosophical text in the field" (p. 16).

4. I discuss these criticisms of existentialism in my "Existentialist Ethics," in *New Directions in Ethics: The Challenge of Applied Ethics*, ed. J. P. DeMarco and R. M. Fox (New York: Routledge & Kegan Paul, 1986), pp. 73–91.

5. The classic works of existentialist psychology in English are Rollo May, Ernest Angel, and Henri F. Ellenberger, eds., *Existence: A New Dimension in Psychiatry and Psychology* (New York: Basic Books, 1958); Ludwig Binswanger, *Being-in-the-World: Selected Papers of Ludwig Binswanger*, ed. Jacob Needleman (New York: Basic Books, 1963); and Medard Boss, *Psychoanalysis and Daseinsanalysis*, trans. L. B. Lefebre (New York: Basic Books, 1963). Newer works include Rollo May, *The Discovery of Being: Writings in Existential Psychology* (New York: Norton, 1983), and Yalom's *Existential Psychotherapy*. Additional

works are listed in Maurice Friedman, ed., *The Worlds of Existentialism: A Critical Reader* (Atlantic Highlands, N.J.: Humanities Press, 1991), Pt. 6 and p. xvii. Louis A. Sass provides a bibliography of recent works in humanistic psychology in "Humanism, Hermeneutics, and the Concept of the Subject," in *Hermeneutics and Psychological Theory: Interpretive Perspectives on Personality, Psychotherapy and Psychopathology*, ed. Stanley B. Messer, Louis A. Sass, and Robert L. Woolfolk (New Brunswick, N.J.: Rutgers University Press, 1988), pp. 222–71.

6. Ira Progoff, *The Death and Rebirth of Psychology* (New York: McGraw-Hill, 1956), p. 5.

7. C. Marshall Lowe, *Value Orientations in Counseling and Psychotherapy: The Meaning of Mental Health* (Cranston, R.I.: Carroll Press, 1969), pp. 16–17.

8. Charles Taylor, *Sources of the Self: The Making of the Modern Identity* (Cambridge, Mass.: Harvard University Press, 1989), p. 14.

9. Morris N. Eagle, *Recent Developments in Psychoanalysis: A Critical Evaluation* (New York: McGraw-Hill, 1984), pp. 72–3.

10. Robert N. Bellah, Richard Madsen, William M. Sullivan, Ann Swidler, and Steven M. Tipton, *Habits of the Heart: Individualism and Commitment in American Life* (New York: Harper & Row, 1985), pp. 128–30.

11. May, *The Discovery of Being*, pp. 10, 17.

12. Ibid., p. 87.

13. Ibid., pp. 166–7.

14. May, *Man's Search for Himself* (New York: Dell, 1953), pp. 175–6.

15. Frank C. Richardson, "Freedom and Commitment in Modern Psychotherapy," *Journal of Integrative and Eclectic Psychotherapy*, 8 (1989): 303–19.

16. This was part of Heidegger's criticism of the notion of "values" (a word first imported into German moral philosophy from economics in the nineteenth century). Because values are usually thought of as present-at-hand objects, Heidegger abjured the concept altogether.

17. May, *Man's Search for Himself*, p. 176.

18. Boss, *Psychoanalysis and Daseinsanalysis*, pp. 47, 271.

19. Binswanger, "The Existential Analysis School of Thought," in *Existence*, May et al., eds., pp. 194, 204, my emphasis.

20. Boss, *Psychoanalysis and Daseinsanalysis*, p. 271.

21. David Hiley and I have discussed these problems in connection with Richard Rorty's glorification of "self-enlargement" as the post-Freudian character ideal. See "Biting the Bullet: Rorty on Private and Public Morality," in *Reading Rorty: Critical Responses to "Philosophy and the Mirror of Nature" (and Beyond)*, ed. Alan R. Malachowski (Oxford: Blackwell, 1990), pp. 339–64.

22. Philip Rieff, *The Triumph of the Therapeutic: Uses of Faith after Freud* (New York: Harper, 1966), p. 93.
23. Paul Ricoeur, "Narrative Time," in *On Narrative*, ed. W. J. T. Mitchell, (Chicago: University of Chicago Press, 1980), pp. 169–90; idem, *Time and Narrative*, trans. K. McLaughlin and D. Pellaner (Chicago: University of Chicago Press, 1984–6).
24. *Nicomachean Ethics*, trans. Terence Irwin (Indianapolis, Ind.: Hackett, 1985), 1140b.
25. In making this distinction, I draw on David Wiggins, "Deliberation and Practical Reason," in *Essays on Aristotle's Ethics*, ed. Amélie O. Rorty (Berkeley and Los Angeles: University of California, 1980), pp. 221–40.
26. The key works are those of Roy Schafer: "Action and Narration in Psychoanalysis," *New Literary History*, 12 (1980): 61–85; "Narration in the Psychoanalytic Dialogue," in *On Narrative*, ed. Mitchell, pp. 29–53; and *Narrative Actions in Psychoanalysis* (Worcester, Mass.: Clark University Press, 1981). See also Donald Spence, *Narrative Truth and Historical Truth: Meaning and Interpretation in Psychoanalysis* (New York: Norton, 1984)
27. Jerome Bruner, *Acts of Meaning* (Cambridge, Mass.: Harvard University Press, 1990), pp. 50–1.
28. Stanley Hauerwas, *Truthfulness and Tragedy: Further Investigations in Christian Ethics* (Notre Dame, Ind.: University of Notre Dame Press, 1977), pp. 73, 80.
29. I am grateful to David Hoy, Frank Richardson, and Peter Tumulty for helpful comments on an earlier draft of this chapter.

11 Heidegger, Buddhism, and deep ecology

Many commentators have remarked on the affinities between Heidegger's thought and East Asian traditions such as Vedanta, Mahayana Buddhism, and Taoism.[1] In this essay, I shall examine critically some aspects of the apparent rapport between Heidegger's thought and Mahayana Buddhism.[2] One reason for recent interest in Heidegger's thought and in Buddhism is that both are critical of and claim to offer an alternative to the anthropocentrism and dualism that some critics say is responsible for today's environmental crisis.[3] According to such critics, Western humankind is particularly anthropocentric. Regarding humanity as the source of all meaning, purpose, and value, humans justify doing anything they want with the natural world. Western humanity also thinks in terms of dualisms and binary oppositions, such as mind versus body, reason versus feeling, humans versus nature, male versus female. Those possessing the "privileged" properties (mind, reason, human, male) allegedly have the right to dominate those possessing the "inferior" properties (body, feeling, nature, female). In an attempt to gain godlike security and power for humankind, modern Western ideologies call for transforming the earth into a titanic factory, thereby threatening to destroy the biosphere on which all life depends.

In my critical examination of the presumed similarities between Heidegger and Mahayana Buddhism, I shall focus particular attention on the claim advanced both by Heidegger and by Buddhism: that humans can learn to "let beings be" only by gaining insight into the nothingness that pervades all things. Such insight, we are told, spontaneously leads to the overcoming of anthropocentrism and dualism. In what follows, I first touch on the mystical origins of Heidegger's idea of nothingness; then I examine, in turn, his early and later accounts of the role of nothingness in authentic human existence. After some preliminary remarks about Heidegger's interest in Eastern thought, I examine the Buddhist conception of the relation between enlightenment and the revelation of nothingness. Then I compare what Heidegger and Mahayana Buddhism have to say about the relation between authenticity or enlightenment and insight into one's own nothingness. Finally, I explore briefly the extent to which these Heideggerean and Buddhist ideas are congruent with the claims advanced by deep ecology, a version of radical environmentalism.

EARLY HEIDEGGER ON NOTHINGNESS

The reader may be wondering how there can possibly be any philosophical importance to the idea of nothingness. For the most part, when we think of nothingness, we simply think of... nothing at all! Nothingness, to our minds, is merely the absence of anything: sheer lack, emptiness in a negative sense. Western thinkers who emphasized the importance of nothingness have been primarily mystics such as Meister Eckhart, the latter of whom greatly influenced Heidegger's writings. Eckhart insisted that "God" is far beyond our conceptual categories, which are appropriate only for understanding *creatures*. Instead of speaking of God in positive terms, it is better to speak of Divine Nothingness.[4] The Divine cannot be regarded as a super entity existing somewhere else, but instead constitutes the unconditioned openness or emptiness in which all things appear. Meister Eckhart argued that humans are at one with this openness. So lacking is any distinction between one's soul and the Divine, in fact, that one who is awakened to Divine Nothingness forgets all about God and lives a life of releasement (*Gelassenheit*), moved by compassion to free things from suffering.

Heidegger's interest in mystics such as Eckhart was reflected in his hopes of becoming a priest. After these hopes were dashed for health reasons, Heidegger became a professional philosopher. Although increasingly antagonistic toward Christianity, he nevertheless continued to draw upon the insights of Christian mystics in his philosophical writings. In particular, his notion that human existence is the openness, clearing, or nothingness in which things can manifest themselves is deeply indebted to mysticism. For mystics, the "self" is not an entity that stands opposed in a dualistic way to other entities. Instead, it is the clearing in which entities (including thoughts, feelings, perceptions, objects, others) appear. The idea that humans are not entities but the clearing in which entities appear eventually helped Heidegger overcome not only dualism, but also anthropocentrism, the attitude that humankind is the source of all value and that all things must serve human interests. By maintaining that humans are authentic only when they let a thing manifest itself in ways consistent with its own possibilities, not merely in accordance with its instrumental value, Heidegger countered the anthropocentrism of much of Western thought. In examining his conception of nothingness, let us turn first to his early writings, particularly *Being and Time* (1927). Later, we shall consider the role of nothingness in his later (post-1935) writings.

The mystical notion of nothingness is at work in *Being and Time*, despite the fact that it is disguised in the complex vocabulary of philosophers like Kant. Following Kant, Heidegger asked the following sort of question: How is it possible for humans to understand entities *as* entities? To answer this question, he distinguished between the human understanding of things and the understanding we ascribe to animals. Birds are clearly able to apprehend entities; otherwise, they could not build nests or feed their young. But, so Heidegger argued, birds and other animals are not able to notice explicitly *that* things *are*.[5] Presumably, birds don't step back from their work to say, "Now that is a fine nest I'm building!" Moreover, we assume that birds don't have identity crises; they don't ask, "Why am I here and what will become of me? Who am I?" We humans understand ourselves and other things *as* entities, that is, as things that *are*. Early Heidegger concentrated on the human capacity for understanding the *being* of entities, a capacity revealed in our ability to use the verb "to be" in so many different ways.

Normally, philosophers conceive of understanding as a faculty of the mind, the thinking thing that attempts to comprehend extramental things. Heidegger, however, sharply criticized the Cartesian epistemological tradition, which conceived of humans as self-conscious substances, or as worldless subjects standing over against objects. Drawing on his study of Eckhart and other mystics, as well as on Kant, Heidegger maintained instead that the human being is not a thing but rather a peculiar kind of nothingness: the temporal linguistic clearing, the opening, the absencing in which things can present themselves and thus "be." If humans are not things, then we have to define "knowing" in a different way than before. Knowing is not a relation between two things, mind and object. Rather, knowing occurs because the openness constituting human existence is configured in terms of the three temporal dimensions: past, present, future. These dimensions hold open the horizons on which entities may manifest themselves in determinate ways – for example, as instruments, objects, or persons. Heidegger's talk of the *a priori* character of the temporal horizons of human existence is analogous to Kant's talk of the *a priori* categories of the human understanding.

Human understanding, then, does not take place inside a mind locked in the skull. Instead, understanding occurs because human temporality is receptive to particular ways in which things can present or manifest themselves. Here it is important to emphasize that what we ordinarily take to be the ultimate constituents of "mind" – thoughts, beliefs, assertions, and so on – are for Heidegger phenomena that occur *within* the temporal clearing constitutive of human understanding. Hence, minds do not make thoughts possible; rather, *a priori* human understanding of being makes it possible for us to encounter and to conceive of ourselves as minds with thoughts separated from the external world. For Heidegger, thoughts are not radically other than allegedly external entities, such as trees, cars, and books. Thoughts and cars are both entities manifesting themselves within and thus being understood as entities within the temporal clearing of human existence.

Just as in the case of understanding, Heidegger defined "being" in a different way than most other philosophers. Traditionally, philosophers have defined the being of an entity as its ground or substance, that which provides the foundation for the thing. Plato called this foundation the eternal form of things; Aristotle their substance; medieval theologians, their Creator. Refusing to conceive of being as a kind of superior entity, an eternal foundation, ground, cause, or origin for things, Heidegger argued that for something "to be" means for it to disclose or to present itself. For this presencing (*Anwesen*) or self-manifesting to occur, there must be a clearing, an opening, an emptiness, a nothingness, an absencing (*Abwesen*). Human existence constitutes the openness necessary for the presencing (being) of entities to take place. When such presencing occurs through the openness that I am, I encounter an entity *as* an entity; that is, I *understand* what it *is*. Heidegger used the term "Dasein" to name this peculiar receptivity of human existence for the being (self-manifesting) of entities. In German, *da* means "here" or "there," while *sein* is the German verb "to be." Hence, Dasein means the place in which being occurs, the openness in which presencing transpires. For Heidegger, neither temporality (absencing, nothingness) nor being (presencing, self-manifesting) is an "entity." Rather, they are the conditions necessary for entities to appear as such. We never "see" time or "touch" the presencing of things; rather, we see and touch the *things* that manifest or present themselves.

In the light of these remarks, the significance of the title of Heidegger's major work, *Being and Time*, becomes comprehensible. His aim here was to study the internal relationship between being and time. Because being and time, presencing and absencing, manifestness and nothingness lack any phenomenal or empirical properties, they seem to be nothing in the merely negative sense of an "empty vapor" (Nietzsche). For Heidegger, however, presencing and absencing "are" that which is most worthy of thinking.

What evidence, we might ask, is there for the claim that humans are really this temporal nothingness through which entities can manifest themselves and thus be? To answer this question, Heidegger appealed in part to an argument taken from Kant: the best way of accounting for the possibility of our understanding of entities is to postulate that we humans simply *are* the temporal openness or nothingness in which entities can appear *as* entities. In addition to such an argument, however, Heidegger maintained that the mood of anxiety reveals the nothingness lying at the heart of human existence. While contending that anxiety is perhaps the most basic human mood, he also observed that it is such a disquieting mood that we spend most of our lives trying to keep it from overtaking us. Our unreflective absorption in the practices of everyday life – family relations, schooling, job activities, entertainment – keep us distracted enough that we manage to conceal from ourselves the weirdness of being human. Anxiety tears us out of everyday absorption in things; it reveals them to be useless in the face of the radical mortality, finitude, and nothingness at the heart of human existence.

Why is human existence weird? Because humans are not things, but the clearing in which things appear. Although we are not fixed things, we define ourselves as if we were simply a more complex version of the things we encounter in the world: rational animals. Ordinarily, we identify ourselves with our thoughts, beliefs, feelings, attitudes, memories, bodies, material possessions, and so on. Such identification gives us a sense of stability and permanence, which covers up the essential groundlessness and emptiness of human existence. There is no ultimate reason for our doing what we do. We have to postulate our own reasons for doing what we do; we invent our own identities, although those identities to a great extent are determined in advance by social practices and norms that have evolved historically. Moreover, as groundless nothingness, humans are essentially dependent and receptive, finite and mortal. The mood of anxiety is so disturbing because it reveals that at bottom we are nothingness, that our existence is ultimately groundless, and that we are essentially finite and mortal. In the face of such disclosures, little wonder that most people flee from the mood of anxiety.

Early Heidegger claimed, however, that if we submit resolutely to what the mood of anxiety wants to reveal to us, we become authentic (*eigentlich*) in the sense of owning our mortal existence. As authentic, we assume responsibility for being the mortal openness that we already are. Assuming such responsibility is essential to human freedom. Instead of existing in a constricted manner – as egos with firm identities – we allow the temporal openness that we are to expand. This expansion allows things and other humans to manifest themselves in more complex, complete, and novel ways, rather than as mere objects or instruments for our ends.[6] Conversely, by fleeing from anxiety into everyday practices and distractions, we conceal the truth about our own mortal nothingness and are thus incapable of allowing things to manifest themselves primordially.

What early Heidegger says about authenticity may be compared to the famous Zen story about the stages of enlightenment. Before enlightenment occurs, mountains are mountains; at the moment of enlightenment, mountains cease being mountains but then mountains become mountains once again. Zen enlightenment, *satori*, involves direct insight into one's radical groundlessness and nothingness. In the light of such a revelation, everyday practices (including working and eating) lose their meaning. Afterward, however, one reenters these practices, but in a way no longer burdened by ignorance about what it means to be human. Likewise for Heidegger, before becoming authentic one exists in accord with everyday practices; upon allowing anxiety to reveal one's utter groundlessness and nothingness, everyday practices slide away into meaninglessness; afterward, one takes up everyday-practices once again, but not in a merely conformist manner.[7]

Instead, being authentic means being free to invigorate and to transform practices in light of the realization of their utter groundlessness. As groundless, things could be otherwise than they are at present. It is important to note, however, that for Heidegger freedom did not mean boundless license for the ego, but instead the capacity for human Dasein to "let things be" in ways other than as mere instruments for the ego. As the Zen tradition puts it, being enlightened means chopping wood and carrying water – but in a manner attuned to the presencing of things as it occurs beyond the dualism of mind and body.

Heidegger's notion that humans are most free when they "let beings be" has been taken up as a slogan by some radical environmentalists, who object to treating nature merely as an instrument for human ends. Early Heidegger suggested that the instrumental disclosure of things played a primary role in human existence.[8] Later, however, he concluded that such instrumentalism was in fact a historical feature of Western history that began with the Greeks and culminated in the technological disclosure of things as nothing but raw material for human ends. Moreover, his early instrumentalism was intimately bound up with his twofold attempt to overcome the mind–body dualism that – especially in its scientific version – gave rise to the alienation at work in modern society.

One phase in this attempt involved conceiving of humans not as minds in skulls but rather as the temporal clearing or nothingness in which thoughts and trees, beliefs and cars can appear as entities. The other phase in overcoming dualism involved challenging those who privileged theoretical assertions and abstract knowledge over against pragmatic activity. Instead of conceiving of humans as worldless intellects making abstract assertions about external objects, Heidegger defined humans as being always already involved in myriad practices that utilize many different things. These things do not manifest themselves abstractly as objects, but instead as tools involved in a complex set of relationships that constitute the world of human existence. Human existence, temporally oriented toward the future, is always pressing forward into possibilities opened up within the world. The practical involvements and practices of everyday life precede and make possible the theoretical knowledge so prized by philosophers. Heidegger emphasized the practical dimension of human existence by defining the very being of Dasein as "care." To be human means to be concerned about things and to be solicitous toward other people.

While early Heidegger sometimes spoke as if the objectifying tendencies of modernity were a result of humanity's intrinsic tendency to conceal deeper truths, he later concluded that the objectifying scientific view did not result from any human decision or weakness, but was instead a proper part of the technological disclosure of entities, a disclosure that was itself a dimension of the "destiny of being." The famous "turn" in Heidegger's thinking occurred when he concluded that he could no longer conceive of being in terms of human understanding, but instead had to conceive of human understanding as an aspect of being itself.

LATER HEIDEGGER'S CONCEPTION OF NOTHINGNESS

Following Kant, early Heidegger sometimes spoke of Dasein's temporal openness as if it were a faculty or capacity of humankind. And he often spoke as if the being of entities was somehow a function of human Dasein's understanding. Moreover, he depicted anxiety primarily as a personal phenomenon that called individuals to a less constricted way of understanding things. Later Heidegger altered these views. Ceasing to speak of temporality or nothingness as a dimension of human existence, he made clear that human temporality arises within a more encompassing "openness" or "region" that cannot be reduced to anything merely human. Later Heidegger emphasized that human existence is appropriated as the site for the self-disclosure or being of entities. Instead of conceiving of being from the perspective of human Dasein, then, Heidegger began thinking being in its own terms. This move was central to his attempt to abandon any remaining anthropocentrism discernible in his earlier work. In this connection, he concluded that inauthenticity, that is, understanding things in a superficial and constricted way, was not a problem of individuals, but a widespread social phenomenon resulting from the self-concealment of being. The technological disclosure of entities, then, arose not because individuals were unable to endure anxiety, but instead because, since around Plato's time, being as such had increasingly withdrawn itself from human view. Correlatively, Western humanity was blinded to the fact that human existence is the clearing for the being of entities. Hence, Western humanity increasingly came to understand itself as a peculiar entity – the clever animal – driven to dominate all other entities for the sake of gaining power and security. Heidegger argued that the emergence of the technological age in the twentieth century was the inevitable result of the clever animals' craving for power.

From Heidegger's viewpoint in the thirties, Western humanity could be saved from technological nihilism only if Germany were granted another encounter with being and nothingness that was as powerful as the beginning granted to the ancient Greeks. Such an encounter, so he mistakenly believed, would be made possible by National Socialism, which revealed that the highest obligation and possibility of humanity were not to be the master of entities, but instead to be the historical clearing necessary for entities to manifest themselves in ways other than merely as flexible raw material.[9] Heidegger insisted that such a new beginning would require that humanity cease regarding itself as the lord and master, or the ground, of entities. A transformed humanity would acknowledge its radically receptive, dependent, mortal, and finite status, thereby allowing itself to be appropriated (ereignet) as the site required for the presencing or being of entities to occur. Only in this way could humanity learn to "let beings be," that is, to allow things to manifest themselves in accordance with their own limits instead of in accordance with the limits imposed on them by scientific constructs and technological projects. Heidegger eventually concluded that the historical reality of National Socialism betrayed its "inner truth and greatness" by promoting a particularly virulent version of the technological disclosure of things, instead of opening up a new phase of Western history. Heidegger's lifelong refusal to renounce unambiguously his own authentic version of National Socialism is a source of concern for students of his thought.

The fact that modern humanity came to regard itself as the ground or foundation for entities resulted not from human decision, Heidegger maintained, but instead from the self-concealment of being itself. Plato conceived of being not as the dynamic presencing of entities, but rather as the eternally present, unchanging blueprint, form (eidos), or model for things in the realm of becoming. By conceiving of being as the permanently present grounding for entities, Plato initiated the 2,500-year history of metaphysics. Heidegger sought to transform this history by revealing that there is no eternal or final "ground" for things, that in fact what we mean by "being" is always shaped by historical factors.

The Romans gave a crucial twist to the metaphysical tradition by depicting the metaphysical ground as that which causes things to come into being. Henceforth, metaphysics became concerned primarily with telling the story of where things came from, how they were produced or created. Appropriating the metaphysical tradition, medieval theologians argued that for something "to be" meant for it to be created (produced) and preserved by the supreme entity, the Creator of biblical faith. In early modern times, human reason arrogated to itself the divine role as the ground of entities. Beginning with Descartes, Western humanity began to encounter entities as objects for the self-certain rational subject. For something to be meant for it to be capable of being represented – measured, quantified, known – by the subject. Modern science forced entities to reveal themselves only in accordance with theoretical presuppositions consistent with Western humanity's ever-increasing drive to gain control of everything. While during the industrial age the achievement of such control could be described as a means for the end of improving the human estate, during the technological era – which may be said to have commenced with the horrors of World War I – humanity itself has become a means to an end without purpose: the quest for power for its own sake, which Heidegger described as the sheer Will to Will.

Later Heidegger differentiated his own meditations on being from theological and scientific accounts that search for the "causes" of things. He focused instead on the manifestness by virtue of which entities can first be encountered and only subsequently interpreted in terms of theoretical categories such as cause and effect, ground and consequent. He insisted that human reason cannot ground or explain the sheer presencing of things. Following the German mystic Angelius Silesius, he spoke of such acausal origination by saying, "The rose is without why; it blooms because it blooms" (SG 101–2). Moreover, later Heidegger also concluded that the "clearing" necessary for the self-manifesting of entities cannot be understood in terms of the Kantian model of temporal ecstases of human existence.

Rather, he argued that the clearing is constituted by a thing – whether natural or artifactual – that gathers mortals and gods, earth and sky into a kind of cosmic dance which frees up the inherent luminosity of things. The world constitutes itself by virtue of the spontaneous coordination or mutual appropriation of the appearances that arise – un-caused, from no-thing – moment by moment. Later Heidegger used the term *logos* to name this mutual coordination of appearances; hence, his claim that language (*logos*) lets things be. This account of the self-organization of uncaused appearances, which is close to Taoism, also provides the key to Heidegger's proximity to Mahayana Buddhism.

HEIDEGGER AND EASTERN THOUGHT: PRELIMINARY REMARKS

We know of Heidegger's debt to Meister Eckhart, whose writings reveal many congruences with Buddhism and other East Asian traditions.[10] And Heidegger himself was interested in Buddhism and Taoism. In one essay, for example, he noted the resonances between the Chinese term *tao* and his own notion of *Ereignis*, the "event of appropriation" that claims humanity as the site for the self-manifesting of entities. Such appropriation would change the course of Western history by freeing humanity from its compulsion to dominate things through technical means and by freeing humanity to adhering to the self-concealing "way" of things themselves (OWL 92; US 198). In fact, so intrigued was Heidegger by Taoism that he spent most of the summer in 1946 working with a Chinese student, Paul Shih-yi Hsiao, translating portions of the *Tao Te Ching*.[11] Otto Pöggeler, one of Heidegger's ablest commentators, reports that as early as 1930, to help settle a dispute on the nature of intersubjectivity, Heidegger cited a famous passage from Chuang-Tsu.[12] And William Barrett reports the possibly apocryphal story that upon reading one of D. T. Suzuki's books on Buddhism, Heidegger exclaimed that Suzuki voiced what Heidegger had been trying to say all along.[13] The fact that the Japanese have published seven translations of *Being and Time* gives credence to the idea that there is an important relation between Heidegger's thought and Buddhism.[14]

Those skeptical of the East Asian influence on Heidegger's thought point out his insistence that the new beginning that he envisioned for the West could arise only from the West itself, since it was in ancient Greece that there arose the first beginning, which culminated in the technological disclosure of all things – including humans – as flexible raw material. In 1966 Heidegger said that the transformation of the technological impulse "cannot happen because of any takeover by Zen Buddhism or any other Eastern experience of the world. . . . Thinking itself can only be transformed by a thinking which has the same origin and calling" (OGSU 28I; Sp 214–17).

In making such a distinction between East and West, Heidegger not only tended to downplay the impact of Eastern thinking on the German philosophical tradition (beginning with Leibniz and continuing through Nietzsche), but also seemed to be thinking metaphysically in accordance with a binary opposition between East and West, an opposition that seems to privilege the West as the origin of the technological disclosure of things that now pervades the planet.[15] Nevertheless, in calling for another beginning that would displace the Western metaphysical quest for the ultimate ground of things, Heidegger questioned the validity of the West's claim to cultural superiority. Belief in such superiority hinges on the conviction that Western rationality, especially as manifested in science and technology, constitutes the ground for things: to be means to be a representation for the rational subject. In deconstructing metaphysical foundationalism, however, Heidegger revealed the groundlessness not only of rationality, but also of the historical project of mastery based on such rationality.

Heidegger maintained that, despite pretensions to the contrary, Western humanity never had control over its own destiny, including the rise of planetary technology. If such technology arises from trends in Western history, one might well make the case that it can be thought in terms of Western discourse. While Heidegger himself believed that his own thinking could be enriched by his encounter with Eastern thinking, he also maintained that radically different kinds of languages forced Western and Eastern peoples to live in different "houses of being." His dialogue with the Japanese thinker and his incomplete translation of *Tao Te Ching* were efforts to bridge this linguistic gap. Before moving further into our examination of the Heidegger–Buddhism relation, we must pause to consider major features of Mahayana Buddhism, especially its idea of absolute nothingness.

THE BUDDHIST CONCEPTION OF NOTHINGNESS

Buddhism is a cosmological, psychological, and religious system which maintains that salvation arises from insight into the true nature of reality. A central teaching of Buddhism is *anatman*, the claim that the human being lacks a substantial self. As described in the *Abhidharma* literature, human experience is constituted by the interplay of five impersonal *skandhas* (heaps or collections): matter/form, sensation, perception, volitional elements, and mind. The *skandhas* are composed of basic units called *dharmas*, of which there are about eighty different kinds. Although *dharmas* arise and disappear rapidly in complex casual relationships, early Buddhists said that the *dharmas* are real "from their own side" (*svabhava*). Hence, *dharmas* are the primary reality out of which the secondary reality of the *skandhas* is constructed. The fourth *skandha*, composed of many kinds of volitional, motivational, and affective *dharmas*, involves karmic actions, that is, actions that affect the subsequent birth. Important examples of volitional *dharmas* are aversion and craving. If these are not extinguished in the present lifetime, they will profoundly influence the composition of the fourth *skandha* – and thus the whole psycho-physical organism – in the subsequent lifetime.

To describe the totally interrelated factors generating the cycle of birth and rebirth (*samsara*), Buddhists speak of a twelve-fold process of "conditioned coproduction" or "dependent co-origination," *pratitya samutpada*. Conditioned coproduction emphasizes the merely constructed and thus empty (*sunya*) nature of all secondary phenomena, that is, phenomena composed of *dharmas*. Despite appearing to be continuous and solid, then, the contents of human experience are "constructed" of *dharmas* that are constantly arising and falling. Flux, not permanence, and conditioning, not independence, characterize all phenomena. *Nirvana* names the one totally unconditioned state, the way to which involves eliminating – step by step – the processes involved in conditioned coproduction. Buddhism's major advance over Indian religions 2,500 years ago lay in explaining salvation not in terms of sacrifices made to irrational divinities, but instead in terms of understanding and altering basic causal processes. Expressed succinctly: If one does this, that follows; if one undoes that, this follows.

The great Buddhist philosopher Nagarjuna (ca. 150 C.E.), commenting on the *Prajnaparamita Sutras*, effected an important conceptual shift that is central to Mahayana Buddhism. He concluded that even the *dharmas* are characterized by emptiness (*sunyata*). Instead of being the primary reality forming the basis for phenomena constructed in the five *skandhas*, the *dharmas* themselves arise and fall along with everything else in conditioned coproduction. All phenomena whatsoever are empty, because they lack independent, substantial existence apart from the totality of mutually conditioned phenomena that arise and fall together. To be empty means to be empty of independent or self-caused reality. In everyday language, we may say that things exist in this way or that, but in language drawn from ultimate insight we say that no-thing exists at all. This distinction between everyday and ultimate ways of seeing phenomena is called the Two Truth doctrine. Seeking to overcome all dualisms, including *nirvana* versus *samsara*, Nagarjuna indicated that there is no perceiving subject and no perceived object.[16] Instead, so one could infer, experience is constituted of self-luminous phenomena that have no substance, origin, or destination.[17] This may amount to a phenomenalism that lacks a perceiver.

The most famous metaphorical expression of this insight, advanced by the Hua-yen school, is the jewel net of the god Indra. Into this infinite net, representing the universe, are set an infinite number of perfect gems, each of which reflects the light given off by all the other gems throughout the expanse of the net. The play of reflected light is codetermined simultaneously by all the gems, no one of which stands in a superior or causal relation to the others. Mahayana Buddhism holds that the phenomenal world is akin to such an interplay of reflected appearances, in which each thing is aware of its relation to all other things. These appearances have no ground; there is nothing behind what appears, no substantial ground or essence to cause them. All things arise together in an internally cosmic event of reflection, which is sentient though not usually self-conscious. Based on the insight that all appearances are ultimately empty, Mahayana Buddhists draw the conclusion that form *is* emptiness and emptiness *is* form, a paradoxical conclusion whose proof demands direct insight, which argument alone cannot provide.

Nagarjuna warned against turning emptiness, the lack of own-self, into a new metaphysical reality or absolute.[18] Nevertheless, some Buddhists moved in this direction, by suggesting that *sunyata* is somehow generative of the phenomenal display. This interpretation may be traced to the fact that the Sanskrit word *sunyata* is derived from a term meaning "to swell." Something that looks swollen is hollow or empty inside. One commentator has noted that "this relationship is made still clearer by the fact that the mathematical symbol for zero was originally none other than the symbol for *sunyata*."[19] Swelling also calls to mind pregnancy, a fact that suggests reading *sunyata* as a somehow the ultimate generative source that, because it transcends all conditions, cannot be said either to cause or *not* to cause anything. Commentators sometimes speak of absolute nothingness – which transcends the polarities of being and nonbeing, cause and effect, subject and object, time and eternity, finitude and infinity – as the groundless ground. This view of *sunyata* became important in Chinese Buddhism, influenced as it was by the notion of the Tao as the groundless ground.

The doctrine of the radical emptiness of all forms, derived from the doctrine of dependent coproduction, suggests that every form, every phenomenon, has equal worth. Since there are no essences, there is no hierarchy of phenomenal reality; hence, no one thing is subordinate to or lesser than any other. Each thing is uniquely itself, like a particular jewel reflecting the play of all other jewels in the cosmic phenomenal play. Insight into the interdependency of all things reveals the falsehood of anthropocentrism: humans are not radically different from or better than other beings, but instead are moments in the play of phenomena.

If all things are internally related, there is no internal substance or core of entities, including humans. Human suffering (*dukha*) arises because people posit and identify with a substantial, unchanging ego at the core of the flux of experience. By identifying with this supposedly permanent self, we enter into the state of ignorance known as subject–object dualism. Such dualism is characterized by craving, aversion, and delusion, which combine to produce suffering. From one perspective, of course, there do seem to be individual things (including the ego) that are apparently connected by causal relationships. Hence, we speak of the laws of cause and effect at work among entities. From another perspective, however, as David Loy points out, "every moment and experience is momentary, uncaused because an end in itself, complete and lacking nothing." Nothing here causes something else to happen there. Attempts to explain how anything – including the self or the cosmos – "originates" fails to comprehend the radicality of dependent coproduction. There is not even a process that causes one to enter into illusion and suffering, nor can one do anything to free oneself from illusion, for illusion already *is* enlightenment. There is no better "place" at which one should hope to arrive. Ultimately, there is no difference between *nirvana* and *samsara:* the nothingness of the phenomenal world of suffering is the same as the nothingness of *nirvana*. That is, form is emptiness, emptiness is form. Recognition of this fact is said to be the source of the extraordinary laughter that often accompanies *satori*, laughter that occurs when one apprehends that all attempts to transcend the phenomenal world in order to become enlightened are profoundly misguided. The longed-for *nirvana* is not other than the world of everyday life, although theoretical constructs prevent us from directly apprehending this liberating insight.

According to Buddhism, Gautama Buddha opposed the traditional doctrine of the Upanishads and Vedas, according to which eternal Atman, the unchanging Divine Self, permeates and sustains things by constituting their ultimate essence, their true "self." For the Vedantic tradition, suffering ends only when one overcomes dualism by ceasing to cling to the illusory ego and identifying instead with the Absolute Self; for Mahayana Buddhism, suffering ends only when one overcomes dualism by ceasing to cling to the illusory ego and recognizing that there is no Absolute Self either. The conception of Buddhism as a life-denying tradition may be attributed to those adherents of Hinayana Buddhism who conceived of *nirvana*, the cessation of suffering, as being possible only for those few individuals who followed the arduous process of deconstructing the ego, encountering its emptiness, and thereby transcending the illusions of the world of appearance. Mahayana Buddhism affirms the possibility of and the need for saving *all* beings, since all "beings" are internally related – hence, the increasingly active role played by Mahayana Buddhists in the movement to protect nature from human abuse.[20]

THE RELATION BETWEEN HEIDEGGER'S THOUGHT AND MAHAYANA BUDDHISM

Heidegger's thought is close to that of Mahayana Buddhism, particularly Zen, in several respects. First, both maintain that inauthenticity or suffering arises from conceiving of oneself in a constricted manner: as an isolated ego craving security, avoiding pain, and seeking distraction. Both maintain that the self is not a thing, but rather the openness or nothingness in which the incessant play of phenomena can occur. Both criticize the dualistic view of the self as a cogitating ego standing apart from the "external" world. Both emphasize that the un-self-conscious nature of everyday practices reveals that people are not separate from things, but are rather directly involved with them. Human hands, diapers, the baby being cleaned up, the mixed feelings of aversion and affection – all these are moments of the same phenomenal event. No particular moment is privileged.

Second, Heidegger's thought is in some ways consistent with the *Heart Sutra*'s teaching that form is emptiness and emptiness is form. The proximity of this statement to Heidegger's notion that being and nothingness "are" virtually the same, helps to explain why Buddhist-influenced Japanese thinkers have been so attracted to Heidegger's thought. Central to such comparisons, however, is the similarity between *sunyata* (emptiness) and *das Nichts* (nothingness). According to Nagarjuna, as we have seen, emptiness refers to the fact that all phenomena are empty of self (*atman*) or substance. Later Buddhists, however, suggested that absolute emptiness had generative ontological significance beyond the *anatman* doctrine. Such views of *sunyata* as the generative "clear light" bear resemblance to Heidegger's idea that nothingness refers to the temporal clearing as which appearing (being) takes place. Neither being nor clearing are entities, but instead constitute the conditions necessary for the possibility for things to manifest *themselves*. Despite differences between later Heidegger and Mahayana Buddhism, both suggest that things are in an important sense self-luminous. They arise and disappear not merely within, but *as* the absolutely clear light of no-thingness. Form or being is not other than emptiness or nothingness; the known is not other than the knower. Absolute non-duality constitutes ultimate realization.

Third, both Heidegger and the Zen tradition maintain that once one is released from the constricted self-understanding associated with dualistic egocentrism, other people and things in the world no longer appear as radically separate and threatening, but instead as profoundly interrelated phenomena. Surrendering one's constricted ego-identity, and thus moving beyond dualism, enables one to become the compassion (Buddhism) or care (Heidegger) that one always already is. "Authenticity" (Heidegger) and "enlightenment" (Buddhism), then, result from the insight into nondualism, the fact that there are "not two," neither an ego-mind here nor objects there.

There is a difference between Heidegger's early and later idea of authenticity. Early Heidegger maintained that the moment of authenticity required resoluteness, a decision to allow human temporality to transform itself into a more radical openness for the self-manifesting of things. Later Heidegger, however, played down the voluntaristic dimension discernible in resoluteness and conceived of authenticity in terms of *Gelassenheit*, releasement from will. Interestingly, similarities between these two ways of conceiving of authenticity – as resoluteness and as releasement – are detectable in the Rinzai and the Soto Zen traditions, respectively.[21] Rinzai Zen emphasizes resoluteness in the face of the ego's resistance to transformation, while Soto Zen maintains that enlightenment can never be willed but can be cultivated only by learning to "let things be" in everyday life. The differences between the voluntarism of early Heidegger and Rinzai Zen, on the one hand, and the "letting be" of later Heidegger and Soto Zen, on the other, should not obscure their shared belief that enlightenment involves becoming the nothingness that we already are, such that we are open for and responsive to the phenomena that show up moment by moment in everyday life.

While maintaining that one can never *resolve* to become authentic or enlightened, however, both later Heidegger and the Soto Zen master suggest that spiritual practices may help put one in the position of a paradoxical willingness not to will, thereby preparing one for the releasement that brings one into the world appropriately for the first time.[22] While we may be familiar with the Zen emphasis on sitting meditation, proper breathing, and working with paradoxical koans, we may be somewhat less familiar with later Heidegger's claim that releasement may be cultivated by meditative practices, by proper breathing, and by contemplating paradoxical questions (Heideggerean "koans"). All of these practices are designed to bring one to the utter silence and stillness needed to become attuned to the openness or nothingness pervading all things.[23]

Fourth, Heidegger and Buddhism emphasize the importance of human existence, without thereby promoting a narrow anthropocentrism. For early Heidegger, because only human Dasein constitutes the clearing through which things can manifest themselves, only human Dasein can be authentic (*eigentlich*). Later on, however, he indicated that the clearing cannot be understood as a strictly human capacity. Instead, Dasein exists authentically insofar as it is appropriated (*vereignet*) as a partner in the world-opening dance of the fourfold that grants to all things their appropriate place. Early Buddhism asserts that enlightened is possible only if one has been born a human being. Mahayana Buddhism emphasizes, however, that the wisdom accompanying enlightenment simultaneously gives rise to compassion for all beings. Moreover, according to the Mahayana doctrine of Buddha nature (*tathagatagarbha*) *all* sentient beings are endowed with the possibility of attaining supreme enlightenment as Buddhas.

Fifth, both Heidegger and the Zen master suggest that, when authentic or enlightened, the individual exists beyond dualistic constraints, including those imposed by the distinction between good and evil. In many different traditions, mystics have said – in effect – "Love God, and do what you will." The danger here, of course, is that a person may transgress moral boundaries when under the illusion that he or she has become enlightened or authentic. Heidegger seems to have been gripped by such an illusion during support for National Socialism, as did many leading Japanese Zen masters during their support of Japanese nationalism and militarism leading up to World War II.[24] Zeal for the mystical ideal of anarchy,[25] which allegedly brings forth boundless compassion, must be tempered by insight into humanity's enormous capacity for self-delusion.

Despite similarities, there are also important differences between Heidegger's thought and Mahayana Buddhism. Members of Japan's famous Kyoto school, such as Keiji Nishitani[26] and Masao Abe,[27] have offered the most extensive Buddhist discussions of the limits of Heidegger's thought. Nishitani and Abe are interested in Heidegger partly because his rigorous meditation upon nothingness may help to galvanize a Zen tradition that has become intellectually flabby. If Zen practitioners are willing to learn from Heidegger, however, Nishitana and Abe also suggest that Western proponents of his thought learn from Zen experience regarding the futility of metaphysical speculation.

Masao Abe argues that Heidegger, despite his interest in nothingness, never arrived at absolute nothingness because even his meditative thinking was still too connected with the metaphysical tradition.[28] Presumably, in the Zen Buddhist tradition someone truly enlightened would no longer think, even in Heidegger's meditative manner, but would instead live a life without goal or purpose, although a life of profound compassion as well. Heidegger's continued insistence on the importance of thinking also differentiates him from Meister Eckhart. As Reiner Schürmann points out, "For Meister Eckhart *gelâzenheit* as an attitude of man refers to thought only secondarily. Primarily it is a matter of a way of life – a life without representation of ends and purposes."[29]

According to Masao Abe, what follows the direct experience of absolute nothingness may be called Non-thinking to distinguish it from the usual opposition between thinking and nonthinking. Despite his critique of Heidegger's adherence to thinking, Masao Abe warns that

because of its standpoint of Non-thinking, Zen has in fact not fully realized the positive and creative aspects of thinking and their significance which have been especially developed in the West. Logic and scientific cognition based on substantive objective thinking, and moral principles and ethical realization based on Subjective practical thinking, have been very conspicuous in the West. In contrast to this, some of these things have been vague or lacking in the world of Zen. [Hence, Zen's] position in Not-thinking always harbours the danger of degenerating into mere not-thinking.[30]

Masao Abe charges that in spite of Heidegger's talk of nothingness, his emphasis on human existence "does not necessarily lead him to the completely dehomocentric, cosmological dimension alone in which the impermanence of all beings in the universe is fully realized."[31] Heidegger's own student, Karl Löwith, also argued that his mentor remained trapped within an anthropocentrism that blinded him to the cosmocentrism of ancient Greek thinkers such as Heraclitus.[32] Nevertheless, later Heidegger's notion of the "event of appropriation" (*Ereignis*), which gathers mortals together into the luminous cosmic dance with gods, earth, and sky, bears important similarities to Buddhism's dependent coproduction and Lao Tsu's *tao*, both of which are nonanthropocentric. *Ereignis, sun-yata, tao*: these may be different names for the acausal, spontaneous arising and mutually appropriating play of phenomena. In suggesting that *Ereignis* "gives" time and being, however, Heidegger opens himself to the criticism that he is inventing a metaphysics of nothingness. Nevertheless, Dogen (1200–53 A.D.), founder of Zen's Soto sect, analyzed the temporality of nothingness in a way that has significant affinities both with early Heidegger's notion of temporality as the "clearing" for presencing and with later Heidegger's notion of the mutually appropriative play of appearances.[33]

Another apparent difference between *Ereignis* and *sunyata*: the former supposedly "sends" the different modes of presencing that have shaped Western history in its Greek, Roman, medieval, modern, and technological eras.[34] Some Mahayana Buddhists think that *Ereignis*, understood in this manner, becomes a metaphysical category inconsistent with Heidegger's non-dualism. One could reply in a number of ways. First, instead of interpreting *sunyata* to mean simply that all things are empty of own-being or self, some Mahayanists themselves – despite Nagarjuna's warning – have turned *sunyata* into a metaphysical category, for example, the generative matrix for all phenomena. Other Buddhists, however, largely avoided such metaphysical tendencies and succeeded in interpreting *sunyata* as absolute non-duality. Second, precisely because Mahayana lacks the conceptual resources needed to confront planetary technology, Nishitani and other members of the Kyoto school looked to Heidegger's thought for insight into an alternative to the technological understanding of the being of beings.[35] As we shall see later on, however, far from constituting a proto-Green alternative to the technological disclosure of beings, Heidegger's thought may affirm the inevitability of humanity's domination of nature.

HEIDEGGER, BUDDHISM, AND DEEP ECOLOGY

Heidegger's notion of "letting things be" has made his thinking attractive for radical environmentalists interested in transforming humanity's currently destructive attitude toward nature. Both Heidegger's thought and Mahayana Buddhism have influenced contemporary environmental philosophy, as well as a radical form of environmentalism called "deep ecology."[36] Unlike reform environmentalism, which fights pollution but remains anthropocentric, deep ecology argues that only a transformation of Western anthropocentrism and humanity–nature dualism can save the biosphere from destruction. Following Heidegger and Mahayana Buddhists, as well as other nonanthropocentric traditions, deep ecologists call on people to "let beings be."

The most important deep ecology theorist, Arne Naess, emphasizes that the heart of the deep ecology movement is an eight-point
platform, which may be derived from a wide variety of philosophical and religious views. In what follows, I compare Naess's *particular* philosophical approach to deep ecology with the foregoing discussion of Heidegger and Mahayana Buddhism. Naess admonishes
that his own "ecosophy" (ecological philosophy) is *not* definitive
for the deep ecology movement! Hence, in what follows when I
refer to "Naess's deep ecology," I have in mind his *particular* philosophical justification for adhering to the eight-point deep ecology
platform.

Heidegger, Buddhism, and deep ecology each promotes its own
version of ontological phenomenalism, the doctrine that "to be"
means to appear or to be manifest. Phenomenalism does not have
to be subjectivistic; in other words, the event of appearing does not
have to be restricted to or dependent on human awareness. In cosmic
phenomenalism, human awareness is regarded as one mode through
which appearing can occur. Mahayana Buddhism, with its claim that
all things are empty of self or substance, but nevertheless intrinsically luminous and totally interrelated with the play of appearance,
is an instance of such cosmic phenomenalism. Heidegger's thought
is a more ambiguous case of such phenomenalism. A critic of Pla-
tonic essentialism, he was an equally strong opponent of subjective
idealism. Yet if one combines his antiessentialism with his claims
(1) that the ontological event of *appearing* is acausal and, hence,
incapable of being explained by any narrative (mythical, religious,
metaphysical, scientific) regarding how things may have been *produced*, (2) that being and appearing are in effect the same, and (3)
that things manifest themselves in a mutually appropriative dance,
then one discovers a position that is in many ways close to a kind of
phenomenalism.

Naess argues that our everyday experience of what it means for
things to be is shaped by gestalts that organize the concrete contents or phenomena. There are no primary qualities, substances, or
essences of thing; indeed, there are no things at all, if by "things" we
mean solid, unchanging, isolated material objects. Gestalts provide
some stability to constantly changing and internally related phenomena, thereby providing a basis for the names conventionally assigned
to things. Naess says that "there is a similarity between this view and

those expressed by the Buddhist formula *sarvam dharmam nihsv-abhavam*, "every element is without 'self-existence'."[37]

According to Naess, insofar as all things, including persons, lack self-being or substance, there is no ultimate ontological divide between self and other, between me and fungus, fox, or forest. As Naess puts it, there is not an environment, nor are there people placed "in" it.[38] People and the environment are *abstractions* resulting from intellectual activity, which projects interpretive schemata upon concrete contents, that is, upon the play of phenomena. Growing awareness of one's own insubstantiality brings with it, spontaneously, a growing *identification* with all phenomena. Conceiving nature as nothing more than a totality of matter–energy events has some validity, so long as one makes no absolute ontological claims about it. Such a conception, however, lacks the element of compassion. According to Naess, Heidegger, and Mahayana Buddhists, each in their own way, the scientific conception of nature results from projecting abstract categories – space and time, matter and energy – onto phenomena that ultimately cannot be accounted for in terms of such categories.

Reasoning vainly attempts to give ground to what is groundless: the inexhaustible and intertwining flux of phenomena arising together moment by moment. Insight into the interdependent origination of all phenomena eliminates clinging to the idea of an independent self "in here" that seeks either to defend itself against or to aggrandize itself at the expense of things "out there." Such insight reveals the ego and its objects to be gestalts whose contents are constituted by an infinite number of self-arising phenomenal events. Awakening involves non-dual awareness of (1) those concrete contents, (2) the organizing gestalt, and (3) the inherent luminosity of the contents.

It may be objected that this kind of phenomenalism includes what seems to be two different notions of "appearing": (1) the event of a thing's appearing, its presencing, its self-manifesting; and (2) the emergence of a thing into presence by virtue of its own capacity for self-generation, as in the case of an animal being born or a plant sprouting. The first kind of appearing seems to require a site, human existence; the second kind of appearing does not.[39] For Heidegger, Buddhism, and perhaps Naess, however, such a distinction continues to presuppose that there are entities in a way that is distinguishable from what is meant above by the appearing of entities. Phenomenalist ontology holds that human existence is a specific modality of the luminosity characterizing all phenomena.[40] Human awareness brings this cosmic luminosity to self-awareness. Buddhism, Heidegger, and Naess all assign to human existence the special role of apprehending the groundless, empty play of phenomena. Humans exist most appropriately when their luminous openness is unconstricted by dualistic ego-consciousness. Freed from such dualism, people can enter into a new, nondomineering relationship with all things. Humans can encounter birds and trees, lakes and sky, humans and mountains not as independent, substantial, self-enclosed entities, but rather as temporary constellations of appearances: self-giving phenomena arising simultaneously.

To support their own view that nondualism discloses the truth about reality, some deep ecologists often appeal to contemporary scientific trends that lead beyond atomism, mechanism, humanity–nature dualism, and reductionistic materialism and open the way for understanding natural processes as internally related, holistic events. Naess implies, however, that deep ecologists must keep in mind that what scientists mean by the "internal relatedness" of events is not necessarily the same as what Buddhism means by empty, self-arising phenomena.[41] Moreover, scientific findings regarding the interrelatedness of things cannot in and of themselves lead to the compassion (Buddhism, Naess) or care (Heidegger) required for letting things be. Required for such compassion or care is direct insight into the interrelatedness of things, insight that transforms the very structure of the one gifted with the insight.

In attempting to find common ground among Heidegger, Buddhism, and Naess's ecosophy, I have argued that each adheres to non-dual phenomenalism, according to which there is no perceiving subject and perceived object, but instead self-manifesting phenomena arise and fall interdependently. Some differences among these three kinds of phenomenalism may be noted when I show how Buddhism, Naess, and Heidegger might answer the following question: Do the three versions of non-dual phenomenalism provide a basis for criticizing and resisting the technological transformation of natural beings?

Buddhists would answer by saying that even though all beings are merely temporary phenomena lacking in own-being, they are nevertheless sentient. It is wrong to inflict pain on sentient beings, especially in connection with the desperate quest to make the ego permanent, all-powerful, and secure. Some beings are apparently more sentient than others, so Buddhists emphasize alleviating the suffering of humans, animals, and denizens of other realms. Inflicting some pain on others is unavoidable for embodied beings. By increasing their wisdom and compassion, however, people can minimize the greed, aversion, and delusion that give rise to practices that provoke suffering among humans and non-humans alike. Contemporary Buddhists, attempting to inform and expand these Buddhist, ideas maintain that protecting habitat and curbing pollution are crucial for alleviating suffering.

In addressing the question posed above, Naess would maintain that – despite my argument to the contrary – his ecosophy is in fact not a phenomenalism. He is concerned that such a designation would lead environmentalists not trained as philosophers to conclude that he regards nature as a mere appearance that lacks substantial reality of its own. Naess claims instead to adhere to "ontological realism in the sense that we have direct access to the contents of reality in our spontaneous experiences. These are not mere appearances or phenomena."[42] It may be that Naess adheres to some version of Nagarjuna's Two Truth doctrine. In terms of everyday experience, it is true to say that we encounter living beings that we can and ought to protect from unjustifiable damage. In terms of ultimate wisdom, however, we realize that there are no independently existing beings. According to Mahayana Buddhism, the *bodhisattva* vows to save all beings, even though (understood in terms of ultimate wisdom) there are no such beings to be saved.

Naess also criticizes me for ascribing to him the view that "Things are useful constructs for dealing with constantly changing, internally related phenomena, which constitute 'experience'."[43] Naess replies that "'Constructs' reminds me too much of postmodernism and suggests an activity on the part of us humans that is too pretentious. We do not construct things. We construct concepts of things – that is enough for me."[44] Naess's distinction, I believe, is primarily directed at those postmodern theorists who maintain that nature is a social construct.[45] According to this idea, there is no wild nature, defined as nature untouched by humans. One of the deep ecology movement's major missions, however, is to protect wild nature or wilderness from human exploitation! If there is no wilderness, deep ecology seems pointless. Naess appreciates that Buddhist phenomenalism is linked with the ideal of compassion for all beings; he suspects, however, that postmodern constructivism lacks such an ideal. Hence, he emphasizes the relative reality of natural beings, so as to resist those who say that because nature is a human construct to begin with, we may reconstruct it in whatever ways serve human ends. Some philosophers, however, such as Steven Vogel, argue that social constructivism imposes on humankind greater responsibility for the environment.[46]

In later Heidegger's version of phenomenalism, the fourfold of earth and sky, gods and mortals gives rise to the self-manifesting of beings. This fourfold differs in various ways from Buddhist *dharmas* and *skandhas*, as well as from Naess's gestalts. Although at times appearing to assign equal weight to these four elements, Heidegger emphasizes the importance of mortal existence. Authentic mortals care for beings, both in the sense of letting them manifest themselves and in the sense of protecting them from harm. Heidegger frequently criticizes technological modernity for disclosing all beings as flexible raw material. He justifies limiting technological control over natural beings in the following way. First, like Aristotle, he maintains that a living being develops and sustains itself according to its own internal possibilities, though he would not refer to these as the being's essence. Second, he argues that humans have a responsibility to respect those internal possibilities whenever possible. If Kant's doctrine of respect for persons is based on insight into the human mode of being, as Heidegger suggested, then respect for animals, plants, and even ecosystems may be based on insight into their own modes of being. Human Dasein has no license to treat living beings arbitrarily. Endowed with great disclosive power, Dasein is also burdened with unparalleled responsibility to care for being.

Heidegger always indicated that the most profound caring follows from authenticity, the auto-disclosure of the temporalizing nothingness constituting human existence.[47] Despite generating wonder and awe, however, such disclosure offers no necessarily valid insights about the internal structure of beings, nor any necessarily valid insights about political and ethical matters. Given that Heidegger used his thought to support National Socialism, efforts to use his thought as a basis for deep ecology gives ammunition to those who portray the latter as incipient ecofascism.[48] Deep ecology, however, may be theorized in ways consistent with a progressive view of human evolution.[49] Deep ecology theorists can criticize the ecologically destructive tendencies of modernity, without denying its noble achievements. Arguably, compassion or care for all beings can emerge only after people have attained postconventional levels of morality. The great majority of people, as contemporary world events demonstrate, remain at conventional levels, which are consistent with religious tribalism and militant nationalism. Global transformation lies centuries in the future, if it is to be achieved at all.[50] In the meantime, deep ecologists must work to minimize environmental damage while maximizing constructive forms of human development.

In addition being radically anti-modernist, Heidegger's thought exhibits at least two other factors that stand in the way of interpreting as compatible with deep ecology. First, Heidegger sharply criticized naturalism and thus distinguished dramatically between humans and animals, thereby challenging the Darwinian evolutionary theory taken for granted by most deep ecologists and other environmentalists.[51] Second, according to Thomas J. Sheehan, Heidegger's most basic philosophical concepts may be compatible with the inevitability of the technological domination of nature.

Sheehan contends that Heidegger's conservative, anti-urban, proto-Green politics explains his longing for a "new beginning" to supplant technological modernity, but such a longing cannot be reconciled with Heidegger's major idea, that there is no alternative to the historical development of the allegedly nihilistic technological disclosure of being. If Sheehan is right, Heidegger's utterance that "only a god can save us now" is best regarded ironically.[52] If human Dasein is openness for beings, those beings themselves are *inclined* to make themselves accessible to humans. Far from offering a constricted disclosure of beings, as Heidegger sometimes says, scientific analysis and technological manipulation enable the most complete possible disclosure of beings. Hence,

[W]e would be doing being itself no favors if we just let entities 'be' in the sense of leaving them pristine and untouched, perhaps even unknown. To let entities *be* means to let them *be present*, that is, to take them as endlessly engageable. And we do that by endlessly engaging them [...], and yes, by letting them be submitted to the domination of the worker in the inevitable humanization of nature and the naturalization of man.[53]

According to Sheehan, then, Heidegger's thought is consistent with the progressive – Marxist and liberal alike – views that humankind can and ought to become a godlike being, capable of transforming nature in infinite ways. This conclusion is palatable neither to those Heideggerians, nor to those environmentalists, who regard progressive ideology as a justification for exploiting nature. Criticizing Heidegger for developing his own version of Christian eschatology, according to which being will return some day to save us from technological nihilism, Sheehan argues instead that humankind must instead come to terms with the power, insecurity, and responsibility imposed by the capacity for disclosing and transforming beings. A few philosophers and seers might catch sight of the nothingness constituting human existence, but science and other modes of inquiry must disclose the structures of things, while individuals and moral communities must work out issues involving how to treat beings, human and non-humans.

There are good reasons to portray Heidegger's thought as friendly with Mahayana Buddhism's ideal of compassion for all beings, and with Naess's call to let all beings actualize their own potential. There are also good reasons, however, to be cautious about the limitations of such portrayals. If we attempt to apply Heidegger's thought to contemporary movements, we should keep in mind its problems as well as its powers.[54]

NOTES

1.   The best collection on Heidegger's relation to Eastern thinking is *Heidegger and Asian Thought*, ed. Graham Parkes (Honolulu: University of Hawaii Press, 1987). The following is a partial bibliography of works on Heidegger and Eastern thought: Chang Chung-yuan, *Tao: A New Way of Thinking* (Heideggerian translation of *Tao Te Ching*) (New York: Harper & Row, 1975); Charles Wei-Hsun Fu, "Heidegger and Zen on Being and Nothingness: A Critical Essay in Transmetaphysical Dialectics," in *Buddhist and Western Philosophy: A Critical Study*, ed. Nathan Katz (New Delhi: Sterling, 1981); Peter Kreeft, "Zen in Heidegger's *Gelassenheit*." *International Philosophical Quarterly*, 11 (December 1971): 521–45; Michael Heim, "A Philosophy of Comparison: Heidegger and Lao Tsu," *Journal of Chinese Philosophy*, 11 (1984): 307–35; Carl Olson, "The Leap of Thinking: A Comparison of Heidegger and the Zen Master Dogen," *Philosophy Today*, 25 (Spring

1981): 55–61; *Philosophy East and West*, 20 (July 1970), entire issue; John Steffney, "Transmetaphysical Thinking in Heidegger and Zen," *Philosophy East and West*, 27 (July 1977): 323–35; idem, "Man and Being in Heidegger and Zen Buddhism," *Philosophy Today*, 25 (Spring 1981: 46–54; idem, "Mind and Metaphysics in Heidegger and Zen Buddhism," *Eastern Buddhist*, new ser., 14 (Spring 1981): 61–74; Rolf von Eckartsberg and Ronald S. Valle, "Heideggerian Thinking and the Eastern Mind," in *The Metaphors of Consciousness*, ed. R. Valle and R. von Eckartsberg (New York: Plenum Press, 1981): 287–31; Reinhard May, *Heidegger's Hidden Sources: East Asian Influences on His Work*, trans. Graham Parkes (New York: Routledge, 1996). See also J. L. Mehta's essay, "Heidegger and Vedanta: Reflections on a Questionable Theme," *International Philosophical Quarterly*, 51 (June 1978): 121–44, and Medard Boss, *A Psychiatrist Discovers India*, trans. H. Frey (London: Oswald Wolf, 1965).

2. Although a separate essay would be required to explore affinities between Heidegger's thought and Taoism, I shall on occasion mention such affinities because of Taoism's influence on both Chinese and Japanese Zen.

3. Concerning the deep ecological critique of anthropocentrism, see my essays "Toward a Heideggerean *Ethos* for Radical Environmentalism," *Environmental Ethics*, 5 (Summer 1983): 99–131; "Anthropocentric Humanism and the Arms Race," in *Nuclear War: Philosophical Perspectives*, ed. Michael Fox and Leo Groarke (New York: Lang, 1985), pp. 135–49; "The Crisis of Natural Rights and the Search for a Non-Anthropocentric Basis for Moral Behavior," *Journal of Value Inquiry*, 19 (1985): 43–53; "Implications of Heidegger's Thought for Deep Ecology," *Modern Schoolman*, 64 (November 1986): 19–43.

4. On Eckhart and his importance for Heidegger, see John D. Caputo, *The Mystical Element in Heidegger's Thought* (Athens: Ohio University Press, 1977), and Reiner Schürmann, *Meister Eckhart: Mystic and Philosopher* (Bloomington: Indiana University Press, 1978). Both Caputo and Schürmann include comparisons of Heidegger and Zen as well. On St. Thomas Aquinas's mystical side, see Caputo, *Heidegger and Aquinas* (New York: Fordham University Press, 1982).

5. Heidegger discusses the question of animal understanding in great detail in *Die Grundbegriffe der Metaphysik: Welt-Endlichkeit-Einsamkeit*, *Gesamtausgabe* 29/30 (winter semester, 1929–30), ed. Friedrich-Wilhelm von Hermann (Frankfurt am Main: Vittorio Klostermann, 1983).

6. On the topic of authenticity, see Michael E. Zimmerman, *Eclipse of the Self: The Development of Heidegger's Concept of Authenticity*,

2nd ed. (Athens: Ohio University Press, 1986). The final chapter includes a comparison of Heidegger and Buddhism.

7. On this topic, see Hubert L. Dreyfus and Jane Rubin, "You Can't Get Something for Nothing: Kierkegaard and Heidegger on How Not to Overcome Nihilism," *Inquiry*, 30 (1987): 33–76.

8. See Hubert L. Dreyfus, "Between *Techne* and Technology: The Ambiguous Place of Technology in *Being and Time*," in *The Thought of Martin Heidegger*, ed. Michael E. Zimmerman, Tulane Studies in Philosophy, 32 (New Orleans, LA: Tulane University Press, 1984), pp. 23–35. See also idem, *Heidegger's Confrontation with Modernity* (Bloomington: Indiana University Press, 1990), Chaps. 10 and 11.

9. See my essays "The Thorn in Heidegger's Side: The Question of National Socialism," *Philosophical Forum*, 20 (Summer 1989): 326–65; and "Philosophy and Politics: The Case of Heidegger," *Philosophy Today*, 33 (Summer 1989): 3–19. Concerning Heidegger's misguided view that National Socialism promised to offer an alternative to industrial nihilism, see my *Heidegger's Confrontation with Modernity*.

10. See, e.g., Rudolf Otto, *Mysticism East and West*, trans. Bertha L. Cracey and Richenda C. Payne (New York: Meridian Books, 1959); S. Radhakrishnan, *Eastern Religious and Western Thought* (Oxford: Oxford University Press, 1974); Daisetz T. Suzuki, *Zen and Japanese Culture* (Princeton, NJ: Princeton University Press, 1970).

11. Paul Shih-yi Hsiao, "Heidegger and Our Translation of the *Tao Te Ching*," in *Heidegger and Asian Thought*, ed. Parkes, pp. 93–103.

12. Otto Pöggeler, "West-East Dialogue: Heidegger and Lao-Tzu," trans. Graham Parkes, in *Heidegger and Asian Thought*, p. 53.

13. William Barrett, Introduction to D. T. Suzuki, *Zen Buddhism* (Garden City, NY: Doubleday, 1956), p. xi.

14. In an unpublished essay, "Die Übersetzbarkeit Heideggers' ins Japanische," Noriko Idada (Tokyo Metropolitan University) has commented on the difficulty of translating Heidegger into Japanese.

15. On this issue, see Evan Thompson, "Planetary Thinking/Planetary Building: An Essay on Martin Heidegger and Nishitani Keiji," *Philosophy East and West*, 36, No. 3 (1986): 235–52.

16. See David Loy's excellent book, *Nonduality: A Study in Comparative Philosophy* (New Haven, CT: Yale University Press, 1988).

17. For this point, I am indebted to David Loy.

18. David Loy, personal communication.

19. Hans Waldenfels, *Absolute Nothingness: Foundations for a Buddhist-Christian Dialogue*, trans. J. W. Heisig (New York: Paulist Press, 1980), 19.

20. See Allan Hunt Badiner, ed., *Dharma Gaia* (Berkeley, CA: Parallax Press, 1990), and Mary Evelyn Tucker and Duncan Ryuken Williams, eds., *Buddhism and Ecology* (Cambridge, MA: Harvard University Press, 1996).

21. See Zimmerman, *Eclipse of the Self*, Chap. 8.

22. Western philosophers, including Nietzsche, have frequently interpreted Buddhism as preferring "nihilation" or "extinction" (*nirvana*) to life itself. In *Beiträge zur Philosophie* (GA 65 170–1), Heidegger spoke in a way which suggests that he shared Nietzsche's view, one that is inconsistent with Mahayana Buddhism. Heidegger's remark is somewhat cryptic: "The more un-entity [is] man, the less he anchors himself in the entity as which he finds himself, ever so nearer does he come to being. (No Buddhism! the opposite)."

23. On these issues, see my essay "Heidegger and Heraclitus on Spiritual Practice," *Philosophy Today*, 27, No. 2 (1983): 87–103.

24. See James W. Heisig and John C. Maraldo, eds., *Rude Awakenings: Zen, the Kyoto School, and the Question of Nationalism* (Honolulu: University of Hawai'i, 1995), and Brian A. Victoria, *Zen at War* (New York and Tokyo: Weatherhill, 1997).

25. In his book *Heidegger on Being and Acting: From Principles to Anarchy*, trans. Christine-Marie Gros (Bloomington: Indiana University Press, 1987), Schürmann draws from Heidegger's writings the possibility of an anarchistic life, a life led "without why."

26. Keiji Nishitani, *Religion and Nothingness*, trans. Jan Van Bragt (Berkeley and Los Angeles: University of California Press, 1982).

27. Masao Abe, *Zen and Western Thought*, ed. William R. LaFleur (Honolulu: University of Hawaii Press, 1985).

28. Ibid., p. 119.

29. Schürmann, *Meister Eckhart*, p. 204.

30. Masao Abe, *Zen and Western Thought*, pp. 119–20.

31. Ibid., p. 67.

32. See, e.g., Karl Löwith, "Zu Heideggers Seinsfrage: Die Natur des Menschen und die Welt der Natur," *Aufsätze und Vorträge, 1930–1970* (Stuttgart: W. Kohlhammer, 1971), pp. 189–203.

33. On this topic, see Steven Heine, *Existential and Ontological Dimensions of Time in Heidegger and Dogen* (Albany: State University of New York Press, 1985). While his book is informative, Heine sometimes promotes Dogen's views at the expense of Heidegger's.

34. See Charles Wei-hsun Fu, "The Trans-onto-theo-logical Foundations of Language in Heidegger and Taoism," *Journal of Chinese Philosophy*, 1 (1975): 130–61.

35. See, e.g., Nishitani, *Religion and Nothingness*, Chap. 6.

36. See especially Bruce V. Foltz, *Inhabiting the Earth: Heidegger. Environmental Ethics, and the Metaphysics of Nature* (Atlantic Highlands, NJ: Humanities Press, 1995). Also see George S. Cave, "Animals, Heidegger, and the Right to Life," *Environmental Ethics*, Vol. 4, No. (1982), 249–254; Bruce V. Foltz, "On Heidegger and the Interpretation of Environmental Crisis," *Environmental Ethics*, Vol. 6, No. 4 (Winter, 1984), 323–338; Laura Westra, "Let It Be: Heidegger and Future Generations," *Environmental Ethics*, Vol. 7, No. 4 (Winter, 1985), 341–350; Leslie Paul Thiele, "Nature and Freedom: A Heideggerian Critique of Biocentric and Sociocentric Environmentalism," *Environmental Ethics*, Vol. 17, No. 2 (Summer, 1995), 171–190; Frank Schalow, "Who Speaks for the Animals? Heidegger and the Question of Animal Welfare," *Environmental Ethics*, Vol. 22, No. 3 (Fall, 2000), 259–272. On the Heidegger–deep ecology relation, see Dolores LaChapelle, *Earth Wisdom* (Los Angeles: Guild of Tutors Press, 1978), 80–86; Zimmerman, "Toward a Heideggerian *Ethos* for Radical Environmentalism," *op cit.*; Zimmerman, "Implications of Heidegger's Thought for Deep Ecology," *op cit.*; Zimmerman, *Contesting Earth's Future: Radical Ecology and Postmodernity.* (Berkeley and Los Angeles: University of California Press, 1994); Zimmerman, "Rethinking the Heidegger–Deep Ecology Relationship," *Environmental Ethics*, Vol. 15, No. 3 (Fall, 1993), 195–224.

37. Arne Naess, "The World of Concrete Contents," *Inquiry*, 28 (December 1985): 417–28, p. 419. For a fuller exposition of Naess's views, see his *Ecology. Community and Lifestyle: Outline of an Ecosophy*, trans. and revised by David Rothenberg (Cambridge: Cambridge University Press, 1989).

38. Ibid., p. 424.

39. See my essay "On Vallicella's Critique of Heidegger," *International Philosophical Quarterly*, 30 (March 1990): 75–100.

40. Note that in order to be true to the insight that being and nothingness, form and emptiness, are "the same," I should speak of the nothingness *as which* things come into presence, but such an expression defies good English.

41. For an exploration of whether modern science may contribute to the development of nondualistic awareness, see Ken Wilber, ed., *The Holographic Paradigm and Other Paradoxes* (Boulder: Shambhala, 1982).

42. Arne Naess, "Heidegger, Postmodern Theory and Deep Ecology," *The Trumpeter*, Vol. 14. No. 4 (Fall, 1997), 181–183; citation is from 181.

43. Zimmerman, *Contesting Earth's Future*, 123.

44. Naess, "Heidegger, Postmodern Theory and Deep Ecology," 181.

45. See William Cronon, *Uncommon Ground: Rethinking the Human Place in Nature* (New York: W. W. Norton University & Co., 1996).

46. Steven Vogel, *Against Nature: The Concept of Nature in Critical Theory* (Albany: SUNY Press, 1996).

47. Rüdiger Safranski, *Heidegger: Between Good and Evil*, trans. Ewald Osers (Cambridge: Harvard University Press, 1998), pp. 163–170, 194–201.

48. See Zimmerman, "Ecofascism: A Threat to American Environmentalism?" in *The Ecological Community*, ed. Roger S. Gottlieb (New York: Routledge, 1997), 229–254.

49. Zimmerman, *Contesting Earth's Future*, Chapters 2 and 3.

50. See Ken Wilber, *Sex. Ecology. Spirituality: The Spirit of Evolution* (Boston: Shambhala Press, 1995).

51. Zimmerman, "Rethinking the Heidegger–Deep Ecology Relationship."

52. Martin Heidegger, "Only a God Can Save Us: *Der Spiegel*'s Interview with Martin Heidegger," trans. Maria P. Alter and John D. Caputo, *Philosophy Today*, Vol. 20, No. 4 (Winter, 1976), 267–284; quotation is from 277.

53. Thomas J. Sheehan, "Nihilism: Heidegger/Jünger/Aristotle," in *Phenomenology: Japanese and American Perspectives*, ed. Bert C. Hopkins (Dordrecht: Kluwer Academic Publishers, 1998), 273–316; quotation is from 297.

54. My thanks to Charles Guignon and David Loy for their helpful critical comments on an earlier version of this essay.

12 Heidegger and theology

Heidegger's thought was from the start deeply interwoven with religious and theological concerns. We have recently learned from the searching historical investigations of Hugo Ott the details of Heidegger's early upbringing and education in the Catholic church. Heidegger was born in the conservative, Catholic farmlands of southern, central Germany, and his father was a sexton in St. Martin's Church, which stood across a quaint little courtyard not fifty yards from the Heidegger house. The Heidegger family was steadfastly loyal to the church in the controversy that followed the First Vatican Council when "liberal" Catholics rejected the proclamation of papal infallibility. The youthful Heidegger, brilliant and pious, was marked from the start for the Catholic priesthood. Through a series of scholarships funded by the church, one of which was intended for students seeking to do doctoral work on Thomas Aquinas, the poor but gifted young man was lifted out of these rural farmlands into the eminence of a German university career. Hugo Ott has discovered that Heidegger's earliest publications appeared in 1910–12 in *Der Akademiker*, an ultraconservative Catholic journal that toed the line of Pope Pius X. There in a series of book reviews the youthful Heidegger, still in his early twenties, spoke out against the danger of "Modernism" to the ageless wisdom of the Catholic tradition. Heidegger cites with approval the saying of "the great [Josef von] Görres": "Dig deeper and you will find yourself standing on Catholic ground."

Forced to break off his studies for the Catholic priesthood in 1911 for health reasons, Heidegger turned first to mathematics and the natural sciences and then to philosophy, where he was openly identified with the Catholic confession. His first teaching position was as a temporary substitute in the Chair of Catholic Philosophy at Freiburg, and his first serious professional disappointment was his failure to secure permanent appointment to that chair in 1916.[1]

Heidegger's earliest philosophical and theological interests in those days centered on a new and promising appropriation of medieval scholastic philosophy in the light of his research into the foundations of modern logic and Husserl's refutation of psychologism. As a philosopher Heidegger rejected psychologism – the attempt to found logic and mathematics on the psychological makeup of the human mind – as a form of empiricism and relativism, even as he was opposed theologically to modernism as a form of historical relativism that threatened to undermine ageless theological truth. Heidegger saw a continuity between Husserl's "logical investigations," which put logic and mathematics on the foundation of pure phenomenology, and the Scotistic tradition of "speculative grammar" in the late Middle Ages. According to this tradition, which was profoundly antirelativist and antipsychologistic, the forms of grammar and of language (*modus significandi*) are a function of and reflect pure, universal forms of thought (*modus intelligendi*), which are themselves reflections of being itself (*modus essendi*).

But Heidegger also saw another side to the medieval tradition, let us say its "living" side as opposed to its logical and logocentric side, which is to be found in the religious life that animated what he called, following Dilthey, the medieval "experience of life" (*Lebenserfahrung*). We must understand, Heidegger insisted in the postscript to his habilitation dissertation, that the abstract and difficult theories of medieval philosophers and theologians proceed from a concrete experience of life, that such theories give conceptual expression to the "soul's relationship to God" as that is experienced in medieval life. To gain access to that dimension of medieval tradition Heidegger says that we must attend to medieval moral theology and medieval mysticism, in particular that of Meister Eckhart (GA 1 404, 410). For it is the mystical notion that the soul belongs wholly to God, that it is constituted by a kind of transcendence toward God, which we see writ large in the corresponding metaphysico-conceptual notion that the intellect has an inner harmony with and belongingness (*convenientia*) to being. This notion that thinking "belongs" (*gehört*) to being is one that Heidegger would always in some way or another maintain as a part of his own later views.[2]

By invoking the living significance of medieval mysticism Heidegger makes his first attempt at a "destruction" of the tradition – which does not mean to level or raze but rather to break through the conceptual surface of traditional metaphysics in order to "retrieve" or recover (*wieder-holen*; BT 437) its living roots and life-giving experiences. This is a gesture that Heidegger would repeat again and again throughout his life, so that the famous "de(con)struction" of metaphysics or of the "history of ontology" in *Being and Time* is always to be understood as a fundamentally "positive" operation, not a negative one (BT 44).

THE EARLY WRITINGS

In 1919, at the age of thirty, and on the occasion of the baptism of his first child, Heidegger broke with the Catholic faith. Writing to Engelbert Krebs, the young priest who had married Martin and Elfride in 1917 and who would have performed the baptism, Heidegger said:

Epistemological insights, extending as far as the theory of historical knowledge, have made the *system* of Catholicism problematic and unacceptable to me – but not Christianity and metaphysics (the latter, to be sure, in a new sense).[3]

This is the first "turn" in Heidegger's thought, and its importance cannot be emphasized enough. For with the turn from Catholicism to Protestantism, the philosophical interests of the young thinker shifted from the questions of logic to those of history, from pure (Husserlian) phenomenology to what he called the "hermeneutics of facticity" (i.e., concrete life), and from dogmatic theology to the theology of the New Testament. He took his lead not from scholastic theologians like Aquinas, Scotus, and Suarez but from Pascal, Luther, and Kierkegaard, who in turn led him back to Augustine and Paul. Between 1919 and 1922 Heidegger – who identified himself in 1921 to Karl Löwith as a Christian theologian[4] – undertook an intensive study of the "factical experience of life" of the New Testament communities (in particular of their experience of time) in an effort to recover authentic Christian experience. Heidegger's model in this project was Luther's critique of Aristotle and medieval Aristotelian scholasticism. Luther, as has been pointed out by a recent historian of these affairs, even used the word "destruction" to describe his project of recovering an authentic scriptural Christianity beneath the conceptual scaffolding of medieval theology.[5] It is no exaggeration to say that Heidegger's attempt to formulate a "hermeneutics of facticity," or what came to be called in *Being and Time* an "existential analytic" (see BT 490, n. 1), which would mark out the distinctive traits of "factical life" – of Dasein – was inspired by Luther's critique of medieval metaphysical theology and Kierkegaard's critique of Hegelian speculative Christianity. The record of those investigations is now open as more and more of the early Freiburg lectures become available in the *Gesamtausgabe*. One of the most interesting of these lecture courses, the publication of which has been promised in the near future (GA 59/60), is Heidegger's lectures on St. Augustine, in which Heidegger attempts to retrieve the Christian experience of time that is concealed beneath the superstructure of Neoplatonic metaphysics in Augustine's writings.

The nearest prototype of the "destruction of the history of ontology" in *Being and Time*, and of what was later called "overcoming metaphysics," was this essentially theological project of 1919 in which Heidegger set out to recover the original categories of factical Christian life. At the same time, Heidegger was also undertaking a parallel project with regard to Aristotle. Unlike Luther, the young philosopher was not prepared to admit that God had sent Aristotle into the world "as a plague upon us on account of our sins."[6] On the contrary, Heidegger sought to break through Aristotle's system of metaphysical concepts, which was the side of Aristotle that medieval theology had seized upon, in order to discover its sources in "factical life." Aristotle had the greatest phenomenological sensitivities in the ancient world, Heidegger thought (BP 232; GA 24 328–9), and the task of the interpretation of Aristotle on which he had set out was to recover the living experiences – the factical structures of Greek and Aristotelian existence – that had taken conceptual form in Aristotelian philosophy. Heidegger's interpretations of Aristotle at this time were so rich and innovative that they inspired a generation of Aristotelian scholarship and were directly responsible for the appointment that Heidegger received from Marburg, where he began teaching in 1923 in close collaboration with the great Protestant New Testament theologian Rudolph Bultmann.

The work that eventually issued in the appearance of *Being and Time* – work thoroughly interwoven with theological questions – consisted of a twofold retrieval, of Aristotle on the one hand and of

New Testament life on the other. It appears to me that Heidegger thought that these two tasks were one, that the deconstructive retrieval of the categories of factical life would achieve the same results whether this was a matter of retrieving Greek or early Christian life, whether one were reading Aristotle's *Nicomachean Ethics* or the New Testament. For the categories of factical life – the categories of care and existence, of concern and instrumentality, of temporality and historicity – are what they are, wherever they are found. There is a peculiar kind of ahistoricism in Heidegger at this point, very likely one that was inspired by his attachment to phenomenology as a universal science and to the Husserlian ideal of the universal structures of the life-world that would be the same no matter where they would be realized. The goal of *Being and Time* – a very Husserlian and neo-Kantian goal indeed – was to "formalize" these factical structures, to give them a formal-ontological conceptualization that would be ontologically neutral to their concrete instantiation. That is what lay behind the famous distinction between the "existential" and the "existentiell," or the "ontological" and the "ontic," which is so central to the existential analytic. Heidegger's aim was to set forth universal *a priori* structures of existential life, of existing Dasein, without regard to whether such structures were in actual fact – that is, as an existentiell matter – Greek or Christian.

The goal of *Being and Time* was to keep the existential analytic free of any "existentiell ideal," any concrete, factical way to be – like Christian or Greek life: There is no suggestion at this point in Heidegger's writings that Greek existence was any more or less "primordial" than Christian existence. On the contrary they both represented "existentiell ideals" from which the existential analytic prescinded, of which the existential analytic represented the ontological formalization (BT 311; SZ 266).

Now it was precisely because *Being and Time* was in part the issue of an attempt to formalize the structures of factical Christian life that it was greeted with such enthusiasm by Protestant theologians like Bultmann (with whom it had in part been worked out). When Christian theologians looked into the pages of *Being and Time* they found themselves staring at their own image – formalized, ontologized, or as Bultmann said "demythologized." What *Being and Time* had discovered, Bultmann said, was the very structure of religious and Christian existence but without the ontico-mythical worldview that was an idiosyncratic feature of first-century cosmologies. The task of demythologizing Christianity for Bultmann came down to isolating the universal-existential structure of religious existence in general. Demythologizing sorts out existential structures like care, decision, temporality, and authenticity in the face of death from cosmological myths about heaven "above," hell "below," and the earth in between, myths about heavenly messengers who shuttle back and forth among these regions. Of the "historical" Jesus himself and what he actually taught we know nothing. Of the historical communities that were formed shortly after his death and that gave mythological formulation to their collective memories of Jesus we know a great deal, and they contain the essence of the Christian message, the saving truth. The task of theology, armed now with the Heideggerian analytic of existence, is to deconstruct and demythologize the canonical Gospels in order to retrieve their *kerygma*, the living-existential Christian message, one of existential conversion (*metanoia*), of becoming authentic in the face of our finitude and guilt, a task that faces every human being.[7]

When Bultmann "applied" *Being and Time* to Christian theology he was "de-formalizing" the existential analytic and articulating it in terms of a historically specific, existentiell ideal, namely, historical Christianity. The reason this deformalization worked so well was that the existential analytic was in the first place and in no small part itself the issue of a formalization of Christian factical life. Bultmann was largely reversing the process that had brought *Being and Time* about in the first place. I believe that much the same thing can be said of Paul Tillich – also a Marburg colleague of Heidegger – whose early existential theology draws on motifs in *Being and Time* that are themselves originally drawn from an analysis of the New Testament.[8]

Heidegger set forth his views on the relationship between universal phenomenological science and theology in one of his last lectures at Marburg, "Phenomenology and Theology."[9] Philosophy, as the science of being itself, differs "absolutely" from theology, which is an "ontic" science of a particular region of beings, not of universal being. Theology is a "positive" science because it deals with a positive, posited entity (a *positum*), which makes it more like chemistry than philosophy (PT 6–7; GA 9 48–9). The positum of Christian theology is "Christianness" (*Christlichkeit*), by which Heidegger means the factual mode of existing as a believing Christian, of existing in the history that is set into motion by the Cross, by the Crucified, by Christ on the cross (PT 10; GA 9 53–4). (These formulations reflect Heidegger's interest in the early twenties in Luther's theology of the cross.)[10] Theology is the work of bringing the existential rebirth that comes by faith to conceptual form. Theology is a science of faith, of existing faithfully, of existing historically as a Christian. It does not make faith easier, but harder, because it does not give faith a rational grounding but shows rather that that is exactly what theology cannot do.

Theology is founded on faith and faith does not need philosophy; but theology, as a positive science, does (PT 17; GA 961). The "cross" and "sin" can be lived only in faith, but they can be conceptualized only with the help of philosophy. For faith is rebirth from sin, but sin is an onticoexistentiell determination of the ontological structure of guilt that is worked out in *Being and Time*. The Christian concept of sin depends on an adequate elucidation of the "pre-Christian" (universal ontological) concept of guilt. This dependence is not a matter of "deducing" it from guilt, but rather of receiving conceptual help and direction – or rather "codirection" and "correction" – from ontology. The theological concept of sin arises from the experience of faith, but it reaches conceptual *form* only with the help of philosophy. None of this denies, Heidegger thinks, the Pauline view of the mortal opposition between faith and philosophy. Indeed, it is this strife, this very foolishness that philosophy and faith seem to be to each other, which keeps each strong (PT 20–1; GA 9 66–7). Faith is philosophy's existentiell enemy, but it must consort with the enemy if it wants to assume conceptual theological form.

THE WAR YEARS

"Phenomenology and Theology" was Heidegger's farewell to Christian theology as a matter of explicit and personal concern. After he returned to Freiburg as Husserl's successor in 1928, his thought underwent another fundamental shift, a shift that once again was keyed to a changed theological attitude. This is the beginning of the darkest days of Heidegger's life and work. It culminated in his hellish endorsement of National Socialism and his ardent efforts to Nazify the German university. He became an enthusiastic reader of

Nietzsche, while Kierkegaard, Luther, and Aristotle faded into the background. Deeply influenced by the bizarre work of Ernst Jünger, his thought became excessively voluntaristic and heroic, far in excess of anything to be found in *Being and Time* itself. He told the tale of an encroaching nihilism, by which he meant the unwelcome effects of modernity and of modern liberal democratic institutions, all of which he saw as a bourgeois softness and love of comfort and which he simply identified with "value theory." In opposition to this "moribund semblance of a culture"[11] Heidegger argued for the love of danger, the need to expose oneself to the abyss of being, to venture to the outer limits of the groundlessness of being. That alone would give greatness and strength to the "German spirit" – the whole notion of "Dasein" and of universal *a priori* structures having now been contracted to a specifically German mode of being.[12] Such hardness of spirit would in turn keep the West safe from "the boundless et cetera" of American consumerism, on the one hand, and of Russian communism, on the other hand (IM 46; GA 40 49). All of this reached a philosophical crest, first in the famous "Rectoral Address" of 1933 and then in the 1935 lecture course *An Introduction to Metaphysics*.

This ominous development in Heidegger's thought is intimately related to a changing theological attitude. If he had begun as an ultraconservative Catholic, and if he had after 1917 become deeply involved in a dialogue with liberal Protestant historical theology, he was after 1928 deeply antagonistic to Christianity in general and to the Catholicism of Freiburg in particular, and he gives indications of having become personally atheistic. He became in his personal conduct at Freiburg a hostile opponent of Christianity. He would not accept the young Jesuits who came to Freiburg as his doctoral students, and he treated other Catholic students like Max Müller exceedingly badly. When their dissertations were submitted – under the direction of Martin Honecker, who held the Chair of Catholic Philosophy – Heidegger treated them with distance and even disdain. (After 1945 he claimed them as his students.) When Honecker died unexpectedly in 1941, Heidegger succeeded in having this chair abolished, the very one to which he himself had aspired a quarter of a century earlier.[13]

His philosophical work, always "methodologically" atheist, lost its ontological neutrality and became hostile to Christianity. If he thought, up to 1928, that both Greek and Christian existence, taken in their historical concreteness, exemplified the universal structures of factical existence, his position during the thirties was that Christianity was a decadent falling away from the primordiality of Greek experience. By "Greek" he meant the early Greeks, and he took Plato and Aristotle to represent the beginning of the metaphysical oblivion of being. The hostility that had invaded Heidegger's portrait of the relationship between philosophical questioning and Christian faith, between his methodological atheism and a more aggressive atheism, can be seen quite clearly in the following contrast. In 1922 he wrote:

Questionability is not religious, but rather it may really lead into a situation of religious decision. I do not behave religiously in philosophizing, even if I as a philosopher can be a religious man. "But here is the art:" to philosophize and thereby to be genuinely religious, i.e., to take up factically its worldly, historical task in philosophizing, in action and a world of action, not in religious ideology and fantasy. Philosophy, in its radical self-positing questionability, must be in principle *a-theistic*.   (GA 61 197)

The trick is to maintain oneself in radical "questionability," that is, the ability to raise radical questions, while responding to the claim of faith. Philosophical questioning is not and cannot become faith, without ceasing to be questioning, but the believer can hold his faith open and keep it free from dogmatic ideology only by sustaining the life of questioning. But in *An Introduction to Metaphysics* we read:

Anyone for whom the Bible is divine revelation and truth has the answer to the question "Why are there beings rather than nothing" even before it is asked.... One who holds to such faith can in a way participate in the asking of our question but he cannot really question without ceasing to be a believer and taking all the consequence of such a step. He will only be able to act "as if."   (IM 6–7; GA 40 5)

Later on in the text, Heidegger assails a work entitled *What Is Man?* by the Christian theologian Theodore Haecker, whose recent lecture at Freiburg had been angrily protested by the Nazi students:[14]

If a man believes the propositions of Catholic dogma, that is his individual concern; we shall not discuss it here. But how can we be expected to take a man seriously who writes "What is Man?" on the cover of his book although he does *not* inquire, because he is *un*willing and *un*able to inquire? ...

Why do I speak of such irrelevancies in connection with the exegesis of Parmenides's dictum? In itself this sort of scribbling is unimportant and insignificant. What is not unimportant is the paralysis of all passion for questioning that has long been with us.   (IM 142–3; GA 40 151)

Heidegger now clearly holds that there is an existential (if not a logical) contradiction between real philosophical questioning and religious faith. The believer does not have the passion – or the honesty – to enter the abyss of the questionability of being. In the view that he held at the time, that also makes the Christian faith a counter-revolutionary force from the standpoint of the National Socialist "renewal." The façade of questioning the believer puts up will always have a kind of fraudulent "as if" quality. The dishonest labors of Christian writers should not be mentioned in the same breath as the greatness of Greek thinkers like Parmenides.

Ironically, and in testimony to the power of Heidegger's thought as opposed to the smallness and perversity of the man, Heidegger was to exert enormous influence on Catholic theology precisely during this time. A series of Catholic luminaries heard these lectures during the thirties, including, in addition to Müller, Gustav Siewerth, Johannes Lotz, and above all Karl Rahner, all of whom were German Jesuits. Rahner unfolded the problematic of questioning in the direction of a "transcendental Thomism" first marked off by the Belgian Jesuit Maréchal. He held that questioning, as the radical opening of thinking to being, represented the dynamism or momentum of the mind toward God. He treated the fore-having of being by the understanding as a preunderstanding of God inasmuch as God is the being that is sought in all of our thought and action. In his second major work, *Hearers of the Word*, Rahner appropriated the thematics of speaking and hearing, claiming and being claimed, that Heidegger had begun to enunciate for the first time in the thirties in connection with his readings of the early Greeks. Rahner put Heidegger's reflections to a theological use, which argued that the believer is ontologically disposed to revelation, that there is a kind of ontological structure in Dasein in virtue of which its very being is to be addressed by being itself. That ontological structure, worked out in Heidegger's philosophical writings, articulates the condition of possibility of being claimed by the Word itself that the Father speaks to humankind. (Rahner also made significant use of Heidegger's conception of being-unto-death in a short treatise entitled *The Theology of Death*.)[15]

Once again, the question can be asked whether these young Catholic theologians found Heidegger's thought so amenable to theological application only because that thought had in the first place been significantly inspired by theological resources. Heidegger was giving a reading of the early Greeks that it is impossible to believe was not the result of a transference of the categories of Christianity to early Greek texts. He called in quasi-prophetic terms for an "other beginning" that resembled a kind of *metanoia* (conversion) and the coming of the kingdom, or even of the Second Coming. He viewed the relationship between being and thinking in Parmenides and Heraclitus in kerygmatic terms, arguing that these early Greeks took being to be "addressed" to man, that it laid claim to man, and that the Greeks conceived the being of man in terms of responsiveness and answerability to this claim. Heidegger went on to say that his deeply historical conception of being, which included even an "eschatological" conception of the "history of Being," was fundamentally Greek in inspiration. But it is clear to everyone but Heidegger's most fanatic disciples that he is clearly Hellenizing and secularizing a fundamentally bibilical conception of the history of salvation. He was in the most literal sense building a rival *Heilsgeschichte* to the biblical one that he had discovered in his New Testament studies.

One might object to this interpretation that Heidegger was simply demythologizing the history of salvation and giving it an ontological sense, which is no different from what he was doing in *Being and Time*. The difference, on my view, is that the later "history of Being" is every bit as mythological and just as much in need of demythologizing as the history of salvation it would purport to demythologize.[16]

As Kierkegaard had said a century earlier, the discovery of time and history was a Judeo-Christian one[17] – as was, we may add, the whole thematics of speaking and answering, claiming and being claimed. Heidegger had baldly appropriated the *kairological* – the *kairos*, the appointed time, the "moment" (*Augenblick*) of truth and decision in *Being and Time* (§67a) – and *kerygmatic* conceptions of human existence that he had learned from Christianity in the first place and that were quite alien to the Greeks. It was these elements in his thought that the young Catholic theologians found so congenial to their own theological work. That is hardly surprising. Like Bultmann and the Protestant existential theologians before them, when they looked into Heidegger's texts, they beheld their own image.

THE LATER WRITINGS

After the war Heidegger largely succeeded in covering up his past involvement with National Socialism. A steady stream of new publications forged the image of the "later" Heidegger, previously known only to the small number of those who were able to follow his lectures during the war years. A whole new wave of Heideggerian thinking swept over Continental philosophy, encouraged especially by the enthusiastic reception Heidegger received from the French, which began with the French existentialist "misunderstanding" and continues today with French postmodernists. The 1947 "letter" to the French (to Jean Beaufret and to the philosophical world) set forth the "humanistic" limits of existentialism and the real demands of the "thought of Being" (BW 206–9). It was clear to everyone that Heidegger's thought had taken still another turn, one that we know today can be dated back to the 1936–8 manuscript entitled *Contributions to Philosophy*, which has only recently been published (GA 65).[18]

This later thinking had become radically antivoluntaristic, anti-Nietzschean. It construed classical Western "metaphysics" from Plato to the present age as the "oblivion" and "withdrawal" of being itself (and not a human error). It construed the metaphysics of the "will to power," whose most extreme expression is the contemporary technologizing of world and man, as the culmination of this history of oblivion. The task of "thinking" was now identified precisely as not willing, first by willing *not* to will and then by not willing at all (DT 59–60; GA 13 38–9). Here "willing" was taken in a general sense to mean not only choosing and willing in the determinate sense, but all conceptual or "representational" thinking, which goes to the very essence of the Western philosophical and scientific tradition. The heroic accents of the mighty "strife" between being and humanity – Heraclitus's *polemos*, which Heidegger liked to translate during the mid-thirties as *Kampf* (IM 61–2; GA 40 66) – disappeared. Instead of willing, Heidegger spoke of "letting be," using at this point the word *Gelassenheit*, one of the oldest and most revered parts of the vocabulary of the Rhineland mystics, in particular Meister Eckhart. Being is not something that human thinking can conceive or "grasp" (*be-greifen, con-capere*) but something that thinking can only be "granted." Thoughts come to us; we do not think them up (PLT 6; GA 13 78). Thinking is a gift or a grace, an event that overtakes us, an address visited upon us. The role of human beings is not, however, one of utter passivity but one of cooperation with and remaining "open" to being's advent. The work that man can do is not to will but to not-will, to prepare a clearing and opening in which being may come. This is not quietism but asceticism, the hard work of a kind of poverty of spirit. A debate began that continues to now about the place of "action" and ethics in Heidegger's thought, a debate that replays disputes in the classical literature on mysticism and ethical action, which itself goes all the way back to the biblical story of Mary and Martha and the medieval disputes about the relative merits of the *vita activa* and the *vita contemplativa*.[19]

Once again a fundamental shift in Heidegger's thinking took place and again with overt religious overtones. The strident antagonist of Christianity during the war years – himself a sometime Protestant and a sometime very ardent Catholic – had taken on a mystical air. With this latest turn Heidegger was, as he himself said, returning to his theological beginning (OWL 10; US 96). He was, we recall, quite interested in medieval mysticism as a youth and had intended to write a book on Meister Eckhart. He also had announced a lecture course on medieval mysticism for 1919, but the preparations for the course were apparently interrupted by the First World War and the course was never given.[20]

Heidegger's postwar relations with both Catholic and Protestant theologians were dramatically reversed. In the denazification trials held immediately after the war, a besieged Heidegger (he eventually had a minor breakdown) turned first for help from his old friend and counselor, the Archbishop of Freiburg Conrad Gröber, who had gained wide respect for holding his ground against the Nazis during the war (something of which Heidegger hardly approved in those years).

This is by no means to say that Heidegger's later thinking had returned to the faith of his youth. The mystical dimension of the later thinking is strictly a structural affair, a matter of a certain proportionality: the relationship of "thinking" to "being" is structurally like the relationship of the soul to God in religious mysticism. Thinking is directed toward being, not God. Being is not God but the event of manifestness, the happening of the truth of being, the coming to pass of the history of the epochal manifestations of being – from the early Greeks to the will to power. Being means very much what we might otherwise call history, but with two important differences: (1) history is understood as a history of truth or manifestness, of the various looks that being takes on over the ages (as *eidos* in Plato, as spirit in Hegel, as will to power in late modernity), as opposed to a political, military, social, or economic history;[21] (2) history is not human history but being's own, unfolding under the "initiative" of being's giving to and withdrawing from thought.

The status of God in Heidegger's later and more religiously, mystically keyed thinking is much debated. Heidegger does talk about God (and the gods) but it is a God who, from a Judeo-Christian point of view, has lost his sovereign lordship over history and become a function of being's history.[22] Thus, the epochal sending of the gods, the age of the Holy, has passed away and we now await a new god, a new and unpredictable sending of the Holy's graciousness, which appears to be a function of being's sending, not of God's will (BW 210). Heidegger at one point identified the lost age of the Holy as the time of the religion of the Greeks, of the Old Testament, and of the preaching of Jesus, indicating a kind of historicism about the various ways that the Holy can manifest itself or take on various historical forms, none of which is absolute (PLT 184; VA 183). Yet Heidegger shows a decided preference in these writings for the world of the early Greeks, for the Greek experience of being as *physis* and *aletheia*, and for an experience of the "gods" as a part of the "Fourfold." The Fourfold – earth and sky, mortals and gods – is a deeply Hölderlinian conception that Heidegger derived from his reading of Hölderlin's poetizing of the Greek world. So the god that emerges in Heidegger's late writing is a profoundly poetic god, a poetic experience of the world as something sacred and deserving of reverence. This god is a much more pagan-poetic god and much less Judeo-Christian, ethicoreligious God. It has virtually nothing to do with the God whom Jesus called *abba* or with the religion of the cross that Heidegger found in Luther. In fact, Heidegger's later writings are more suggestive of a kind of Buddhism, a kind of meditative, silent world reverencing, than of Judaism or Christianity.[23]

Understandably, Christian theologians have shown a remarkable interest in and been much nourished by Heidegger's later writings. These writings are marked by Heidegger's deeply – albeit generically – religious discourse of giving and receiving, grace and graciousness, saving and danger, address and response, poverty and openness, end time and new beginning, mystery and withdrawal and by a new thematics of the truly divine God. A new wave of post-Bultmannian Protestant theologians emerged that moved beyond Bultmann's "existential theology" and adopted a position that reflected Heidegger's own turn beyond the existential analytic. These theologians had a sharpened appreciation of the historicality and linguisticality of Heidegger's "thought of Being" and that is what they brought to bear on their theological work.

The key figure in this post-Bultmannian movement is Heinrich Ott. In his 1959 work entitled *Denken und Sein* (Thinking and Being) Ott, a student of Karl Barth, who also has studied extensively with Bultmann, showed in effect that the later Heidegger's rejection of humanism opened up new possibilities for theology. It confirmed Karl Barth's long-standing objections to Bultmann (and to the Heidegger of *Being and Time*) and shows that Barth's theology of the primacy of God is in fact accommodated by the later Heidegger's turn toward being. Theology for Ott arises out of the experience of faith and is not a matter of scientific theological objectification, even as for Heidegger thinking speaks "out of the experience of thought" (PLT 1–14), out of thought's experience of being. Ott went on to construe the history of salvation as a history of disclosure comparable to Heidegger's history of the disclosure of being, and he put Heidegger's conception of language as "call" to use in interpreting biblical language. The sentences of the New Testament about the resurrection, for example, are not to be taken as propositional assertions of matters of fact but as a call to a new mode of being. Ott's work, and the whole impact of the later Heidegger on theological reflection, reached the United States in a volume entitled *The Later Heidegger and Theology*.[24]

In 1959, at a meeting with the old Marburgers, Heidegger led a day-long discussion on the relationship between his later "thinking" and Christian faith, in which he held that if his thought ruled out the God of metaphysics, it was by no means inconsistent with a nonmetaphysical relationship to God (PT 22–31; GA 9 68–79). The upshot of "thinking" for theology is to cease to think of God as *causa sui*, as the causal energy that creates and sustains the cosmos, and to turn instead to the God before whom one can dance or bend one's knee. This he calls the truly "divine God" (ID 72), and it reminds us of Pascal's injuncture to lay aside the God of the philosophers in favor of the God of Abraham and Isaac. This was a very open ended formulation of thinking in relation to religious faith, and it was precisely the path that Ott was pursuing.

This suggestion was also taken up in a forceful and interesting way on the Catholic side by the Freiburg theologian Bernard Welte. Welte argues that Heidegger's conception of the history of being tells the story of a technological darkening of the earth in which the illusion of human mastery overshadows the appearance of God. The "other beginning" of which Heidegger speaks signals a new age of the Holy, an epoch in which God can indeed be God. Welte also wrote sensitively about Meister Eckhart and the notion of *Gelassenheit*, and he produced an excellent essay comparing the later Heidegger, Meister Eckhart, and Thomas Aquinas (whose Dominican Chair at Paris Meister Eckhart had later occupied).[25]

Martin Heidegger died in 1976, in his eighty-sixth year. He was buried in the Catholic churchyard in Messkirch between his mother and his father. At Heidegger's request a Catholic mass was celebrated by Bernard Welte in the church of St. Martin's where Heidegger's father had been sexton, in whose shop in the basement of the church the young Martin had often played as a youngster. Welte, who was also a fellow townsman of Heidegger, delivered the eulogy. Welte said, quite rightly, that Heidegger's thought had shaken this century, that it was a thought that was always seeking, always under way. He related this being "on the way" to the Gospels' notion that he who seeks shall find:

"He who seeks" – that could well be the title for all of Heidegger's life and thought. "He who finds" – that could be the secret message of his death.[26]

Had Heidegger come full circle, confirming what he said in *On the Way to Language* that his future lay in his theological beginning (OWL 10; US 96)? Was this Catholic end the repetition of his Catholic beginning? Was this the final turn on the path of thought?

NOTES

1. Hugo Ott, *Martin Heidegger: Unterwegs zu seiner Biographie* (Frankfurt: Campus, 1988), pp. 44–104; the Görres citation, p. 64; the grant to study Thomism, 79; passed over for chair, 91–2. For more on Heidegger's early Catholicism, see my *Heidegger and Aquinas: An Essay on Overcoming Metaphysics* (New York: Fordham University Press, 1982), Chap. 1.

2. The habilitation dissertation is found in GA 1. It has not been translated. I have discussed it in some detail in "Phenomenology, Mysticism, and the *Grammatica Speculativa*," *Journal of the British Society for Phenomenology*, 5 (1974): 101–17. See also Roderick Stewart, "Signification and Radical Subjectivity in Heidegger's 'Habilitationsschrift,'" *Man and World*, 12 (1979): 360–86.

3. This letter can be found in *Heidegger and Aquinas*, p. 60; cf. 56.

4. Karl Löwith, "The Political Implications of Heidegger's Existentialism," *New German Critique*, 45 (1988): 117–34, at 121–2. For a commentary see Theodore Kisiel, "War der frühe Heidegger tatsächlich ein 'christlicher Theologe'?" *Philosophie und Poesie: Otto Pöggeler zum 60. Geburtstag*, ed. Annemarie. Gethmann-Siefert (Berlin: Frommann-Holzboog, 1988), pp. 59–75. The letter itself can be found in D. Paperfuss and O. Pöggeler, eds., *Zur philosophischen Aktualität Heideggers*, vol. 2: *Im Gespräch der Zeit* (Frankfurt: Klostermann, 1990).

5. Edward John Van Buren, "The Young Heidegger," Ph.D. dissertation, McMaster University (1988), a revised version of which is forthcoming from Indiana University Press. See Van Buren's "The Young Heidegger: Rumor of a Hidden King (1919–1926)," *Philosophy Today*, 33 (Summer 1989): 99–108. See also Löwith, "Political Implications," as well as Otto Pöggeler, *Heidegger's Path of Thought*, trans. D. Magurshak and S. Barber (New York: Humanities Press, 1988), pp. 24–32, and idem, "Being as Appropriation," *Philosophy Today*, 19 (1975): 152–78; at 156–8.

6. *Selected Writings of Martin Luther* (1517–1520), ed. T. G. Tappert (Philadelphia: Fortress Press, 1967), p. 337.

7. See Rudolph Bultmann, *Kerygma and Myth* (New York: Harper & Row, 1961). On Heidegger and Bultmann, see John Macquarrie, *An Existentialist Theology: A Comparison of Heidegger and Bultmann* (New York: Harper Torchbooks, 1965); Hans-Georg Gadamer, "Martin Heidegger and Marburg Theology," in *Philosophical Hermeneutics*, trans. D. Linge (Berkeley and Los Angeles: University of California Press, 1976), pp. 198–212.

8. See, e.g., Paul Tillich, *The Courage to Be* (New Haven, CT: Yale University Press, 1952).

9. "Phenomenology and Theology," in Martin Heidegger, *The Piety of Thinking*, trans. J. Hart and J. Maraldo (Bloomington: Indiana University Press, 1976), pp. 3–22.

10. See Alister E. McGrath, *Luther's Theology of the Cross: Martin Luther's Theological Breakthrough* (Oxford: Blackwell Publisher, 1985). See the work of Van Buren cited in note 5.

11. Martin Heidegger, "The Self-Assertion of the German University," trans. K. Harries, *Review of Metaphysics*, 38 (1985): 467–502, p. 480.

12. Jacques Derrida has discussed the nationalism of Heidegger's use of the word "spirit" in *Of Spirit: Heidegger and the Question*, trans. G. Bennington and R. Bowlby (Chicago: University of Chicago Press, 1989), Chap. 5.

13. Ott, *Martin Heidegger*, 259–67.

14. Ibid., pp. 255–9.

15. Rahner said that he had many good professors (*Schulmeister*) but only one teacher (*Lehrer*); see *Martin Heidegger in Gespräch*, ed. R. Wisser (Freiburg: Alber, 1970); pp. 48–9. See Rahner's *Spirit in the World*, trans. William Dych (New York: Herder & Herder, 1968); idem, *Hearers of the Word* (New York: Seabury Press, 1969); idem, *On the Theology of Death* (New York: Seabury Press, 1971). He also discussed *Being and Time in* "The Concept of Existential Philosophy in Heidegger," trans. A. Tallon, *Philosophy Today*, 13 (1969): 126–37. On Heidegger and Rahner, see Thomas Sheehan, *Rahner: The Philosophical Foundations* (Athens: Ohio University Press, 1985). For a discussion of Heidegger and Lotz, Siewerth, and Müller, see my *Heidegger and Aquinas*, Chap. 7.

16. See my "Demythologizing Heidegger: *Aletheia* and the History of Being," *Review of Metaphysics*, 41 (March 1988): 519–46.

17. Søren Kierkegaard, *The Concept of Anxiety*, trans. Reidar Thomte (Princeton, NJ: Princeton University Press, 1980), pp. 89–90.

18. The only commentator who had access to *Contributions* was Otto Pöggeler. There are then three such turns: 1917–19, from Catholicism to Protestantism; ca. 1928, toward the extreme heroic, Nietzschean voluntarism; 1936–8: beyond voluntarism toward the "thought of Being."

19. John D. Caputo, *The Mystical Element in Heidegger's Thought* (Athens: Ohio University Press, 1978; rpt. New York: Fordham University Press, 1986), pp. 137–9.

20. Käte Oltmanns, a Heidegger student since 1925, published a book on Eckhart in 1935, which had been a dissertation done under Heidegger's direction; see Käte Oltmanns, *Meister Eckhart*, 2d ed. (Frankfurt: Klostermann, 1957). For a full account of these matters, see my *Mystical Element*.

21. It is for just this reason that Charles Taylor in an unpublished essay, quite rightly criticizes Heidegger for a "monomanic" conception of the history of the West.

22. John D. Caputo, "Heidegger's God and the Lord of History," *New Scholasticism*, 57 (1983): 439–64. For a famous exchange on this point, see Hans Jonas, "Heidegger and Theology," *The Phenomenon of Life* (New York: Harper & Row, 1966), pp. 244–9; and William Richardson, "Heidegger and God – and Professor Jonas," *Thought*, 40 (1965): 13–40.

23. There is a vast literature on Heidegger and Eastern religion. The best single volume is *Heidegger and Asian Thought*, ed. Graham Parkes (Honolulu: University of Hawaii Press, 1987). See also my *Mystical Element*, pp. 203–17.

24. Heinrich Ott, *Denken und Sein: Der Weg Martin Heideggers und der Weg der Theologie* (Zollikon: Evangelischer Verlag, 1959); idem, "The Hermeneutic and Personal Structure of Language," in *On Heidegger and Language*, ed. Joseph Kocklemans (Evanston, IL: Northwestern University Press, 1972), pp. 169–93; idem, *Theology and Preaching*, trans. Harold Knight (Philadelphia: Westminster, 1965). See also J. Robinson and J. Cobb, eds., *The Later Heidegger and Theology* (New York: Harper & Row, 1963).

25. Bernard Welte, "The Question of God in the Thought of Heidegger," *Philosophy Today*, 26 (1982): 85–100; idem, "La Métaphysique de Saint Thomas d'Aquin et la pensée de l'histoire de l'être de Heidegger," *Revue des Sciences Philosophiques et Théologiques*, 50 (1966): 601–14. A good account of the later Heidegger and Catholic theology can be found in Richard Schaeffler, *Frömmigkeit des Denkens: Martin Heidegger und die Katholische Theologie* (Darmstadt: Wissenschaftliche Buchgesellschaft, 1978). See also *Heidegger et la question de dieu*, ed. R. Kearney and Joseph O'Leary (Paris: Grasset, 1980). The best recent work by a Catholic theologian with a distinctly Heideggerian inspiration is Joseph O'Leary, *Questioning Back: The Overcoming of Metaphysics in Christian Tradition* (Minneapolis, MN: Winston Press, 1985).

26. "Seeking and Finding: The Speech at Heidegger's Burial," in *Heidegger: The Man and the Thinker*, ed. Thomas Sheehan (Chicago: Precedent, 1981), pp. 73–5. See also Sheehan's useful biographical piece on Heidegger's early years (Chapter 2, this volume).

13 Heidegger on the connection between nihilism, art, technology, and politics

Martin Heidegger's major work, *Being and Time*, is usually considered the culminating work in a tradition called existential philosophy. The first person to call himself an existential thinker was Søren Kierkegaard, and his influence is clearly evident in Heidegger's thought. Existential thinking rejects the traditional philosophical view, which goes back to Plato at least, that philosophy must be done from a detached, disinterested point of view. Kierkegaard argues that our primary access to reality is through our involved action. The way things show up for a detached thinker is a partial and distorted version of the way things show up to a committed individual.

Kierkegaard defines the self as a relation that relates itself to itself. That means that who I am depends on the stand I take on being a self. Moreover, how I interpret myself is not a question of what I think but of what I do. I have to take up what is the given or factical part of my self and, by acting on it, define who I am. I understand myself as being a student, a teacher, the lover of a specific person, or the follower of a specific cause. Thus, the self defines itself by taking up its past by means of present actions that make sense in terms of its future. For Kierkegaard, then, the self can be understood as a temporal structure.

Given his emphasis on involvement, Kierkegaard was convinced that philosophical reflection has undermined commitment in the West. In his book *The Present Age*,[1] written in 1846, he gave a prophetic description of how all authority was disappearing, all concrete differences were being leveled, everything was becoming indifferent, giving rise to alternate fits of lethargy and excitement. Such was the victory of critical detachment over involved commitment. His whole work was devoted to the question: How can we get

345

meaning and commitment back into our lives once we have gotten into the passionless, reflective attitude we are now in?

Heidegger calls the basic structure of human being – that each human being's way of being is an issue for it – *Dasein*. In his "existentialist" phase, during the twenties, Heidegger was interested in the ahistorical, cross-cultural structures of everyday involved experience. He worked out an interpretation of three basic ways of being (availableness, or "readiness-to-hand"; occurrence, or "presence-at-hand"; as well as Dasein) and their general structure (temporality) grounded in Dasein's ability to take a stand on its own being. These existential structures, Heidegger demonstrated, provided the conditions of the possibility of all modes of intelligibility. He also investigated the way the conformity to norms necessary for intelligibility opens up the possibility of flight into conformism, which levels down all meaningful distinctions.

But whereas Kierkegaard thought that leveling and lack of commitment had been accentuated to nihilistic proportions by the media, Heidegger in *Being and Time* writes as if leveling has been with humankind as long as tools have, and he sees nothing special in the present age. Around 1930, however, Heidegger began to investigate the understanding of being peculiar to modern Western culture. As he put it, in *Being and Time* "'phenomenology' and all hermeneutical-transcendental questions had not yet been thought in terms of the history of being" (EP 15). His early interest in the existential structure of the self had shifted to another Kierkegaardian concern – the lack of meaning and seriousness in the present age.

NIHILISM

In his lectures on Nietzsche in 1936, Heidegger quotes with approval Nietzsche's Kierkegaardian condemnation of the present age:

Around the year 1882 (Nietzsche) says regarding his times, "Our age is an agitated one, and precisely for that reason, not an age of passion; it heats itself up continuously, because it feels that it is not warm – basically it is freezing... In our time it is merely by means of an echo that events acquire their 'greatness' – the echo of the newspaper." (N I 47)

Heidegger agrees with Nietzsche that "there is no longer any goal in and through which all the forces of the historical existence of peoples can cohere and in the direction of which they can develop" (N I 157).

Nihilism is Nietzsche's name for this loss of meaning or direction. Both Kierkegaard and Nietzsche agree that if nihilism were complete, there would be no significant private or public issues. Nothing would have authority for us, would make a claim on us, would demand a commitment from us. In a non-nihilistic age there is something at stake; there are questions that all can agree are important, even if they violently disagree as to what the answers to these questions are. But in our age, everything is in the process of becoming equal. There is less and less difference among political parties, among religious communities, among social causes, among cultural practices – everything is on a par, all meaningful differences are being leveled.

Kierkegaard thought that the answer to nihilism was to make one's own individual absolute commitment. If you can commit yourself unconditionally – in love, for instance – then that becomes a focus for your whole sense of reality. Things stand out or recede into insignificance on the basis of that ultimate concern. You do not discover a significance that is already there. There is no basis for this commitment in the cosmos. Indeed, such a commitment is exactly the opposite of belief in an objective truth. You are called by some concrete concern – either a person or a cause – and when you define yourself by your dedication to that concern, your world acquires seriousness and significance.

The only way to have a meaningful life in the present age, then, is to let your involvement become definitive of reality for you, and what is definitive of reality for you is not something that is in any way provisional – although it certainly is vulnerable. That is why, once a society like ours becomes rational and reflective, such total commitments begin to look like a kind of dangerous dependency. The committed individual is identified as a workaholic or a woman who loves too much. This suggests that to be recognized and appreciated, individual commitment requires a shared understanding of what is worth pursuing. But as our culture comes more and more to celebrate critical detachment, self-sufficiency, and rational choice, there are fewer and fewer shared commitments. So commitment itself begins to look like craziness.

Heidegger comes to see the recent undermining of commitment as due not so much to a failure of the individual as to a lack of anything in the modern world that could solicit commitment from us and sustain us in it. The things that once evoked commitment – gods, heroes, the God-man, the acts of great statesmen, the words of great thinkers – have lost their authority. As a result, individuals feel isolated and alienated. They feel that their lives have no meaning because the public world contains no guidelines.

When everything that is material and social has become completely flat and drab, people retreat into their private experiences as the only remaining place to find significance. Heidegger sees this move to private experience as characteristic of the modern age. Art, religion, sex, education – all become varieties of experience. When all our concerns have been reduced to the common denominator of "experience," we will have reached the last stage of nihilism. One then sees "the plunge into frenzy and the disintegration into sheer feeling as redemptive. The 'lived experience' as such becomes decisive" (N I 86). That is, when there are no shared examples of greatness that focus public concerns and elicit social commitment, people become spectators of fads and public lives, just for the excitement. When there are no religious practices that call forth sacrifice, terror, and awe, people consume everything from drugs to meditation practices to give themselves some kind of peak experience. The peak experience takes the place of what was once a relation to something outside the self that defined the real and was therefore holy. As Heidegger puts it, "The loss of the gods is so far from excluding religiosity, that rather only through that loss is the relation to the gods changed into mere 'religious experience'" (QCT 117; GA 5 76). Of course, private experience seems attractive only once the shared public world has lost its meaning and reality. Then one thinks (as if somehow it had always been the case and one had just discovered it) that, after all, it is the experience that matters. But sooner or later one finds that although private experience may have "energy" or "spontaneity" or "zing," it provides nothing in terms of which one can give consistency, meaning, and seriousness to one's life.[2] In Nietzsche's words "God is dead, and we have killed him."

Nietzsche, however, unlike Heidegger, finds the death of God liberating. He foresees a new stage of our culture that he calls "positive nihilism," in which each "free spirit" will posit, that is, create, his or her own values. Heidegger is not so sanguine. He sets out to investigate the history of the understanding of being in the West in order to understand how we did the terrible deed of killing God. One way he tells the story of the loss of meaning is by tracing the history of the very idea of values taken over uncritically by Nietzsche. Heidegger argues that to think of nihilism as a state in which we have forgotten or betrayed our values is part of the problem. Thinking that we once had values but that we do not have values now, and that we should regain our values or choose new ones, is just another symptom of the trouble. Heidegger claims that thinking about our deepest concerns as values *is* nihilism.

The essence of a value is that it is something that is completely independent of us. It is perceived, and then chosen or rejected. Values have an interesting history. Plato starts with the claim that they are what shows us what is good for us independent of our interests and desires. The idea of the good shines on us and draws us to it. Only with the Enlightenment do we arrive at the notion that values are objective – passive objects standing over against us – and we must *choose* our values. These values have no claim on us until we *decide* which ones we want to adopt. Once we get the idea that there is a plurality of values and that we choose which ones will have a claim on us, we are ripe for the modern idea, first found in the works of Nietzsche, especially in *Thus Spoke Zarathustra*, that we *posit* our values – that is, that valuing is something we do and value is the result of doing it. But once we see that we posit values, we also see that we can equally "unposit" them. They thus lose all authority for us. So, far from giving meaning to our lives, thinking of what is important to us in terms of values shows us that our lives have no intrinsic meaning. As long as we think in terms of value positing rather than being gripped by shared concerns, we will not find anything that elicits our commitment. As Heidegger says, "No one dies for mere values" (QCT 142; GA 5 102).

Once we see how thinking of the problem of nihilism in terms of lacking values perpetuates rather than combats the problem, we are ready to diagnose and seek a cure for our condition. According to Heidegger our trouble begins with Socrates' and Plato's claim that true moral knowledge, like scientific knowledge, must be explicit and disinterested. Heidegger questions both the possibility and the desirability of making our everyday understanding totally explicit. He introduces the idea that the shared everyday skills, concerns, and practices into which we are socialized provide the conditions necessary for people to make sense of the world and of their lives. All intelligibility presupposes something that cannot be fully articulated – a kind of knowing-how rather than a knowing-that. At the deepest level such knowing is embodied in our social skills rather than in our concepts, beliefs, and values. Heidegger argues that our cultural practices can direct our activities and make our lives meaningful only insofar as they are and stay unarticulated, that is, as long as they stay the soil out of which we live. If there is to be seriousness, it must draw on these unarticulated background practices. As Heidegger puts it in "The Origin of the Work of Art," "Every decision ... bases itself on something not mastered, something concealed, confusing; else it would never be a decision" (PLT 55; GA 5 43). Critical reflection is necessary in some situations where our ordinary way of coping is insufficient, but such reflection cannot and should not play the central role it has played in the philosophical tradition. What is most important and meaningful in our lives is not and should not be accessible to critical reflection.

The cultural know-how that embodies our concerns is certainly not conscious, but neither does it appear to be unconscious. To get a sense of what this know-how is like, let us take a very simple case. People in various cultures stand different distances from an intimate, a friend, a stranger. Furthermore, the distances vary when these people are chatting, doing business, or engaging in courtship. Each culture, including our own, embodies an incredibly subtle shared pattern of social distancing. Yet no one explicitly taught this pattern to each of us. Our parents could not possibly have consciously instructed us in it since they do not know the pattern any more than we do. We do not even know we have such know-how until we go to another culture and find, for example, that in North Africa strangers seem to be oppressively close while in Scandinavia friends seem to stand too far away. This makes us uneasy, and we cannot help backing away or moving closer. It is through such responses that we got this know-how in the first place. As small children, when we began to interact with other people, we sometimes got the distances wrong. This made our parents and friends uneasy, and they either backed away or moved closer so that we gradually picked up the whole pattern. It was never made explicit. As a skill or *savoir faire* it is not something like a set of rules that could be made explicit.[3] Yet it embodies rudiments of an understanding of what it is to be a human being – hints of how important body contact is, and the relative importance of intimacy and independence.

Now practices like how far to stand from people are not all that are passed on by training and imitation. Our everyday know-how involves an understanding of what it is to be a person, a thing, a natural object, a plant, an animal, and so on. Our understanding of animals these days, for example, is in part embodied in our skill in buying pieces of them, taking off their plastic wrapping, and cooking them in microwave ovens. In general, we deal with things as resources to be used and then disposed of when no longer needed. A Styrofoam cup is a perfect example. When we want a hot or cold drink it does its job, and when we are through with it we throw it away. This understanding of an object is very different from what we can suppose to be the Japanese understanding of a delicate, painted teacup, which does not do as good a job of maintaining temperature and which has to be washed and protected, but which is preserved from generation to generation for its beauty and its social meaning. Or, to take another example, an old earthenware bowl, admired for its simplicity and its ability to evoke memories of ancient crafts, such as is used in a Japanese tea ceremony, embodies a unique understanding of things. It is hard to picture a tea ceremony around a Styrofoam cup.

Note that an aspect of the Japanese understanding of what it is to be human (passive, contented, gentle, social, etc.) fits with an understanding of what it is to be a thing (evocative of simpler times, pure, natural, simple, beautiful, traditional, etc.). It would make no sense for us, who are active, independent, and aggressive – constantly striving to cultivate and satisfy our desires – to relate to things the way the Japanese do; or for the Japanese (before their understanding of being was interfered with by ours) to invent and prefer Styrofoam teacups. In the same vein *we* tend to think of politics as the negotiation of individual desires, while the Japanese seek consensus. In sum, the practices containing an understanding of what it is to be a human being, those containing an interpretation of what it is to be a thing, and those defining society fit together. Social practices thus transmit not only an implicit understanding of what it is to be a human being, an animal, or an object, but, finally, an understanding of what it is for anything to be at all.

The shared practices into which we are socialized, moreover, provide a background understanding of what matters and what it makes sense to do, on the basis of which we can direct our actions. This understanding of being creates what Heidegger calls a *clearing* in which things and people can show up as mattering and meaningful for us. We do not produce the clearing. It produces us as the kind of human beings we are. Heidegger describes the clearing as follows:

Beyond what is, not away from it but before it, there is still something else that happens. In the midst of beings as a whole an open place occurs. There is a clearing, a lighting... This open center is... not surrounded by what is; rather, the lighting center itself encircles all that is.... Only this clearing grants and guarantees to human beings a passage to those entities that we ourselves are not, and access to the being that we ourselves are.   (PLT 5 3; GA 5 39–40)

As we have noted, our cultural practices and the understanding of being they embody allow us to direct our activities and make sense of our lives only insofar as they are and stay unarticulated, that is, stay the atmosphere in which we live. These background practices are the concealed and unmastered that Heidegger tells us give seriousness to our decisions. Mattering lies not in what we choose, but in "that on the basis of which" we choose. The more our know-how is formulated and objectified as knowing-that, the more it is called up for critical questioning, the more it loses its grip on us. This is part of what Kierkegaard saw in his attack on modern critical reflection, and Heidegger in his attack on value thinking.

But this cannot be the whole story about nihilism. For there must always be a clearing – background practices containing an understanding of being – in order for things and people to be intelligible at all. And these will never be fully accessible to reflection. So there must be a deeper problem that Heidegger is pointing to. There must be something wrong with our current background practices that leads us to ignore them, causing us to seek meaning by choosing objective values and finally by positing personal values for ourselves. So Heidegger raises new questions: What is it to have a nihilistic clearing, how did we come to have one, and what can we do about it? Only when we have answered these, he holds, can we ask: Are there still left in our practices some remnants of shared meaningful concerns? If so, where are such remnants to be found? The strongest argument that some meaningful practices must have survived is that without some remnant of them we would not be distressed by nihilism. But before we can answer these questions, we must ask a prior one: How do practices give shared meaning to the lives of those who practice them?

THE WORK OF ART (WORLD AND EARTH)

For everyday practices to give meaning to our lives and to unite us in a community, they must be focused and held up to the practitioners. Clifford Geertz and Charles Taylor have discussed this important phenomenon. Geertz, for example, describes the role of the cock fight in Balinese society:

It provides a metasocial commentary upon the whole matter of assorting human beings into fixed hierarchical ranks and then organizing the major part of collective existence around that assortment. Its function, if you want to call it that, is interpretive: it is a Balinese reading of Balinese experience, a story they tell themselves about themselves.[4]

Heidegger calls that interpretive function "truth setting itself to work," and anything that performs this function he calls a work of art. As his illustration of an artwork, Heidegger takes the Greek temple. The temple held up to the Greeks what was important, and so let there be meaningful differences such as victory and disgrace, disaster and blessing:

It is the templework that first fits together and at the same time gathers around itself the unity of those paths and relations in which birth and death, disaster and blessing, victory and disgrace, endurance and decline acquire the shape of destiny for human beings. The all-governing expanse of this open relational context is the world of this historical people. (PLT 42; GA 5 29)

The Greeks whose practices were manifested and focused by the temple lived in a moral space of gods, heroes, and slaves, a moral space that gave direction and meaning to their lives. In the same way, the medieval cathedral made it possible to be a sinner or a saint and showed Christians the dimensions of salvation and damnation.[5] In either case, one knew where one stood and what one had to do. Heidegger would say that the understanding of what it is to be changes each time a culture gets a new artwork. Then different sorts of human beings and things show up. For the Greeks, what showed up were heroes and slaves and marvelous things; for the Christians, saints and sinners, rewards and temptations. There could not have been saints in ancient Greece. At best there could only have been weak people who let everybody walk all over them. Likewise, there could not have been Greek-style heroes in the Middle Ages. Such people would have been regarded as pagans – prideful sinners who disrupted society by denying their dependence on God.

Generalizing the idea of a work of art, Heidegger holds that "there must always be some being in the open (the clearing), something that is, in which the openness takes its stand and attains its constancy" (PLT 61; GA 5 48). Let us call such special things cultural paradigms. Talking of a paradigm focusing the practices seems almost inevitable. Compare Geertz: "It is this kind of bringing of assorted experiences of everyday life to focus that the cockfight... accomplishes, and so creates what, better than typical or universal, could be called a paradigmatic human event."[6]

A cultural paradigm collects the scattered practices of a group, unifies them into coherent possibilities for action, and holds them up to the people who can then act and relate to each other in terms of that exemplar. Works of art, when performing this function, are not merely representations or symbols, but actually produce a shared understanding. As Geertz put it: "Quartets, still lifes, and cockfights are not merely reflections of a pre-existing sensibility analogically represented; they are positive agents in the creation and maintenance of... sensibility."[7]

Charles Taylor makes the same point when he distinguishes *shared meanings*, which he calls intersubjective meanings, from *common meanings* "whose being shared is a collective act":

It is part of the meaning of a common aspiration, belief, celebration, etc. that it be not just shared but part of the common reference world. Or to put it another way, its being shared is a collective act....

Common meanings are the basis of community. Inter-subjective meanings give a people a common language to talk about social reality and a common understanding of certain norms, but only with common meaning does this common reference world contain significant common actions, celebrations, and feelings. These are objects in the world that everybody shares. This is what makes community.[8]

In *The Structure of Scientific Revolutions*, Thomas Kuhn shows that scientists engaged in what he calls normal science operate in terms of such an exemplar or paradigm – an outstanding example of a good piece of work. The paradigm for modern science was Newton's *Principia*. All agreed that Newton had seen exemplary problems, given exemplary solutions, and produced exemplary justifications for his claims. Thus, for more than two centuries natural scientists knew that, insofar as their work resembled Newton's, they were doing good science.

The Newtonian paradigm was later replaced by the Einsteinian paradigm. Such a paradigm shift constitutes a scientific revolution. After such a revolution scientists see and do things differently. As Kuhn puts it, they work in a different world. They also believe and value different things, but this is less important. Kuhn is quite Heideggerian in holding that it is the paradigm that guides the scientists' practices and that the paradigm cannot be explained as a set of beliefs or values and so cannot be stated as a criterion or rule. As Kuhn notes: "That scientists do not usually ask or debate what makes a particular problem or solution legitimate tempts us to suppose that, at least intuitively, they know the answer. But it may only indicate that neither the question nor the answer is felt to be relevant to their research. Paradigms may be prior to, more binding, and more complete than any set of rules for research that could be unequivocally abstracted from them."[9] Kuhn further points out that "the concrete scientific achievement, as a locus of professional commitment, [is] prior to the various concepts, laws, theories, and points of view that may be abstracted from it." He adds that the paradigm cannot be rationalized: "The shared paradigm [is] a fundamental unit for the student of scientific development, a unit that cannot be fully reduced to logically atomic components which might function in its stead."[10] That the paradigm cannot be rationalized but only imitated is crucial to the paradigm's authority. It requires that the paradigm work by way of the background practices, in terms of which the scientists have a world. It also makes it possible for the scientists to agree without having to spell out their agreement.

At the time of a scientific revolution, however, Kuhn tells us that the paradigm itself becomes the focus of conflicting interpretations, each interpretation trying to rationalize and justify itself. Similarly, Heidegger holds that a working artwork is so important to a community that people must try to make the work clear and coherent and to make everyone follow it in all aspects of their lives. But the artwork, like the scientific paradigm, exhibits a resistance to such rationalization. Any paradigm could be paraphrased and rationalized only if the concrete thing that serves as an exemplar symbolized or represented an underlying system of beliefs or values abstractable from the particular exemplar. But the whole point of needing an exemplar is that there is no such system, there are only shared practices. Heidegger calls the way the artwork solicits the culture to make the artwork explicit, coherent, and encompassing the *world* aspect of the work. He calls the way the artwork and its associated practices resist such totalization the *earth*.

Heidegger points out that world and earth are both necessary for an artwork to work. The temple must clarify and unify the practices – it must be "all-governing" – but being a concrete thing it resists rationalization. Such resistance is manifest in the very materiality of the artwork. Such materiality is not accidental. The temple requires the stone out of which it is made in order to do its job of showing man's place in the natural world, so that a temple made out of steel would not work. Likewise a tragedy requires the sound of poetry to create a shared mood and thus open up a shared world. Since it is made out of rock or sounds, the artwork shows that what is at stake cannot be captured in a system of beliefs and values. All those aspects of a cultural paradigm and the practices it organizes that resist being rationalized and totalized are included in Heidegger's notion of the earth. Earth is not passive matter, but comes into being precisely as what resists the attempt to abstract and generalize the point of the paradigm. And since no interpretation can ever completely capture what the work means, the work of art sets up a struggle between earth and world. This struggle is a necessary aspect of the way meaning inheres in human practices. It is a fruitful struggle in that the conflict of interpretations it sets up generates a culture's history.

Next Heidegger generalizes the notion of a cultural paradigm from a work of art to any being in the clearing that can refocus and so renew cultural practices:

One essential way in which truth establishes itself in the beings it has opened up is truth setting itself into work. Another way in which truth occurs is the act that founds a political state. Still another way in which truth comes to shine forth is the nearness of that which is not simply a being, but the being that is most of all. Still another way in which truth grounds itself is the essential sacrifice. Still another way in which truth becomes is the thinker's questioning, which, as the thinking of being, names being in its question-worthiness.   (PLT 61–2; GA 5 49)

One can recognize an allusion to the covenant of God with the Jews and the Crucifixion. There is also a reference to the political act that founds a state. For example, the U.S. Constitution, like a work of art, has necessarily become the focus of attempts to make it explicit and consistent and to make it apply to all situations, and, of course, it is fecund just insofar as it can never be interpreted once and for all. The founding of a state could also refer to the act of a charismatic leader such as Hitler. This possibility will concern us later in this essay.

TECHNOLOGY

Cultural paradigms do not, however, always establish meaning-ful differences. There can be nihilistic paradigms. Such paradigms, instead of showing forth the earth on the basis of which our actions can matter to us, conceal the struggle between earth and world and celebrate our ability to get everything clear and under control. Thus, the current paradigms that hold up to us what our culture is ded-icated to and is good at are examples of flexibility and efficiency, not for the sake of some further end, but just for the sake of flexi-bility and efficiency themselves. We admire the way computers are getting faster and faster and at the same time cheaper and cheaper, without knowing how we will use the incredibly flexible computing power they give us. Likewise, fast-food chains that give us cheap and instant service at any time of day or night stand out as technological triumphs of efficiency and adaptability. Heidegger's example is the power station of the Rhine:

The hydroelectic plant is set into the current of the Rhine. It sets the Rhine to supplying its hydraulic pressure, which then sets the turbines turning. This turning sets those machines in motion whose thrust sets going the electric current for which the long-distance power station and its network of cables are set up to dispatch electricity .... the energy concealed in nature is unlocked, what is unlocked is transformed, what is transformed is stored up, what is stored up is, in turn, distributed, and what is distributed is switched about ever anew. In the context of the interlocking processes pertaining to the orderly disposition of electrical energy, even the Rhine itself appears as something at our command. (QCT 16; VA 23)

All such paradigms deny that an understanding of being necessar-ily involves receptivity and mystery, and so they deny Heideggerian seriousness.

Again, a comparison with Kuhn can help us see Heidegger's point. According to Kuhn, a science becomes normal when the practitioners in a certain area all agree that a particular piece of work identifies the important problems in a field and demonstrates how certain of these problems can be successfully solved. Thus, a modern scientific paradigm sets up normal science as an activity of puzzle solving. It is the job of normal science to eliminate anomalies by showing how they fit into the total theory the paradigm sketches out in advance. In a similar way, the technological paradigm embodies and furthers our technological understanding of being according to which what does not fit in with our current paradigm – that is, that which is not yet at our disposal to use efficiently (e.g., the wilderness, friendship, and stars) – will finally be brought under our control, and turned into a resource. The contrast with the Greek temple is obvious. The temple is not a totalizing paradigm that makes everything clear and promises to bring it under control. The temple not only shows people what they stand for, but shows them that there is an earthy aspect of things that withdraws and that can never be articulated and dominated.

In the face of the totalizing tendency of the technological artwork, the earth's resistance to total ordering shows up as a source of what Kuhn calls anomalies. What cannot be ordered is treated as recalcitrant human beings who are deviant and must be reformed or as natural forces that have yet to be understood and mastered. All cultures inculcate norms of human behavior and find some order in nature, but ours is the only culture that tries to make the social and natural order total by transforming or destroying all exceptions. Kierkegaard already saw that the individual or exceptional was menaced by leveling. Heidegger sees that all our marginal practices are in danger of being taken over and normalized. It looks to us, of course, as if this is for our own good.

Heidegger, however, sees in these marginal practices the only possibility of resistance to technology. Greek practices such as friendship and the cultivation of the erotic are not efficient. When friendship becomes efficient networking, it is no longer the mutual trust and respect the Greeks admired. Likewise, the mystical merging power of the erotic is lost when we turn to private sexual experience. Similarly, Greek respect for the irrational in the form of music and Dionysian frenzy do not fit into an efficiently ordered technological world. Indeed, such "pagan" practices did not even fit into the Christian understanding of being and were marginalized in the name of disinterested agape love and peace. These Christian practices in turn were seen as trivial or dangerous given the Enlightenment's emphasis on individual maturity, self-control, and autonomy.

In order to combat modern nihilism Heidegger attempts to point out to us the peculiar and dangerous aspects of our technological understanding of being. But Heidegger does not oppose technology. In "The Question Concerning Technology" he hopes to reveal the essence of technology in a way that "in no way confines us to a stultified compulsion to push on blindly with technology or, what comes to the same thing, to rebel helplessly against it." Indeed, he promises that "when we once open ourselves expressly to the *essence* of technology, we find ourselves unexpectedly taken into a freeing claim" (QCT 25–6; VA 33).

We will need to explain opening, essence, and freeing before we can understand Heidegger here. But already Heidegger's project should alert us to the fact that he is not announcing one more reactionary rebellion against technology, although many take him to be doing just that. Nor is he doing what progressive thinkers would like to do: proposing a way to get technology under control so that it can serve our rationally chosen ends. The difficulty in locating just where Heidegger stands on technology is no accident. Heidegger has not always been clear about what distinguishes his approach from a romantic reaction to the domination of nature, and when he does finally arrive at a clear formulation of his own original view, it is so strange that in order to understand it we are tempted to translate it into conventional platitudes. Thus, Heidegger's ontological concerns are mistakenly assimilated to ecologically minded worries about the devastation of nature.

Those who want to make Heidegger intelligible in terms of current antitechnological banalities can find support in his texts. During the war he attacked consumerism: "The circularity of consumption for the sake of consumption is the sole procedure which distinctively characterizes the history of a world which has become an unworld" (EP 107; VA 96). And as late as 1955, in an address to the Schwarzwald peasants, he points out: "The world now appears as an object open to the attacks of calculative thought.... Nature becomes a gigantic gasoline station, an energy source for modern technology and industry" (DT 50; G 19–20). In this address he also laments the appearance of television antennas on the peasants' dwellings and gives his own version of an attack on the leveling power of the media:

> Hourly and daily they are chained to radio and television.... All that with which modern techniques of communication stimulate, assail, and drive man – all that is already much closer to man today than his fields around his farmstead, closer than the sky over the earth, closer than the change from night to day, closer than the conventions and customs of his village, than the tradition of his native world.   (DT 50; G 17)

Such quotes make it seem Heidegger is a Luddite who would like to return from consumerism, the exploitation of the earth, and mass media to the world of the pre-Socratic Greeks or the good old Schwarzwald peasants.

Nevertheless, although Heidegger does not deny that technology presents us with serious problems, as his thinking develops he comes to the surprising and provocative conclusion that focusing on loss and destruction is still technological: "All attempts to reckon existing reality... in terms of decline and loss, in terms of fate, catastrophe, and destruction, are merely technological behavior" (QCT 48; TK 45–46). Seeing our situation as posing a problem that must be solved by appropriate action is technological too: "The instrumental conception of technology conditions every attempt to bring man into the right relation to technology.... The will to mastery becomes all the more urgent the more technology threatens to slip from human control" (QCT 5, VA 14–15). Heidegger is clear this approach will not work. "No single man, no group of men," he tells us, "no commission of prominent statesmen, scientists, and technicians, no conference of leaders of commerce and industry, can brake or direct the progress of history in the atomic age" (DT 52; G 22).

Heidegger's view is both darker and more hopeful. He thinks there is a more dangerous situation facing modem man than the technological destruction of nature and civilization, yet this is a situation about which something *can* be done – at least indirectly. Heidegger's concern is the human *distress* caused by the *technological understanding of being*, rather than the *destruction* caused by *specific technologies*. Consequently, he distinguishes the current problems caused by technology – ecological destruction, nuclear danger, consumerism,

and so on – from the devastation that would result should technology
solve all our problems:

> What threatens man in his very nature is…that man, by the peaceful
> release, transformation, storage, and channeling of the energies of physical
> nature, could render the human condition…tolerable for everybody and
> happy in all respects. (PLT 116; GA 5 294)

The "greatest danger" is that

> the approaching tide of technological revolution in the atomic age could
> so captivate, bewitch, dazzle, and beguile man that calculative think-
> ing may someday come to be accepted and practiced *as the only way* of
> thinking. (DT 56; G 27)

The danger, then, is not the destruction of nature or culture but
certain totalizing kinds of practices – a leveling of our understanding
of being. This threat is not a *problem* for which we must find a
solution, but an *ontological condition* that requires a *transformation
of our understanding of being*.

What, then, is the essence of technology – that is, the technological understanding of being, or the technological clearing – and
how does opening ourselves to it give us a free relation to technological devices? To begin with, when he asks about the essence of
technology we must understand that Heidegger is not seeking a definition. His question cannot be answered by defining our concept
of technology. Technology is as old as civilization. Heidegger notes
that it can be correctly defined as "a means and a human activity."
But if we ask about the *essence* of technology (the technological
understanding of being) we find that modern technology is "something completely different and…new" (QCT 5; VA 15). It even goes
beyond using Styrofoam cups to satisfy our desires. The essence of
modern technology, Heidegger tells us, is to seek to order everything
so as to achieve more and more flexibility and efficiency: "Expe-
diting is always itself directed from the beginning…towards driving on to the maximum yield at the minimum expense" (QCT 15,
VA 23). That is, our only goal is optimal ordering, *for its own sake*:
"Everywhere everything is ordered to stand by, to be immediately
at hand, indeed to stand there just so that it may be on call for a
further ordering. Whatever is ordered about in this way has its own
standing. We call it standing-reserve" (QCT 17; VA 24). No more

do we have subjects turning nature into an object of exploitation: "The subject–object relation thus reaches, for the first time, its pure 'relational,' i.e., ordering, character in which both the subject and the object are sucked up as standing-reserves" (QCT 173; VA 61). Heidegger concludes: "Whatever stands by in the sense of standing-reserve no longer stands over against us as object" (QCT 17; VA 24). He tells us that a modern airliner, understood in its technological essence, is not a tool we use; it is not an object at all, but rather a flexible and efficient cog in the transportation system. Likewise, we are not subjects who use the transportation system, but rather we are used by it to fill the planes.

In this technological perspective, ultimate goals like serving God, society, our fellows, or even ourselves no longer make sense to us. Human beings, on this view, become a resource to be used – but more important, to be enhanced – like any other: "Man, who no longer conceals his character of being the most important raw material, is also drawn into this process" (EP 104; VA 90). In the film *2001*, the robot HAL, when asked if he is happy on the mission, says: "I'm using all my capacities to the maximum. What more could a rational entity want?" This is a brilliant expression of what anyone would say who is in touch with our current understanding of being. We pursue the development of our potential simply for the sake of further growth. We have no specific goals. The human potential movement perfectly expresses this technological understanding of being, as does the attempt to better organize the future use of our natural resources. We thus become part of a system that no one directs but that moves toward the total mobilization and enhancement of all beings, even us. This is why Heidegger thinks the perfectly ordered society dedicated to the welfare of all is not the solution to our problems but the culmination of the technological understanding of being.

Heidegger, however, sees that "it would be foolish to attack technology blindly. It would be shortsighted to condemn it as the work of the devil. We depend on technical devices; they even challenge us to ever greater advances" (DT 53, G 24). Instead, Heidegger suggests that there is a way we can keep our technological devices and yet remain true to ourselves as receivers of clearings: "We can affirm the unavoidable use of technical devices, and also deny them the right to dominate us, and so to warp, confuse, and lay waste our nature" (DT 54; G 24–25). To understand how this might be possible, we need an illustration of Heidegger's important distinction between technology and the technological understanding of being. Again we can turn to Japan. In contemporary Japan traditional, nontechnological practices still exist alongside the most advanced high-tech production and consumption. The television set and the household gods share the same shelf – the Styrofoam cup coexists with the porcelain teacup. We thus see that the Japanese, at least, can enjoy technology without taking over the technological understanding of being.

For us to be able to make a similar dissociation, Heidegger holds, we must rethink the history of being in the West. Then we will see that although a technological understanding of being is our destiny, it is not our fate. That is, although our understanding of things and ourselves as resources to be ordered, enhanced, and used efficiently has been building up since Plato, we are not stuck with that understanding. Although the technological understanding of being governs the way things have to show up for us, we can be open to a transformation of our current cultural clearing.

Only those who think of Heidegger as opposing technology will be surprised at his next point. Once we see that technology is our latest understanding of being, we will be grateful for it. Our technological clearing is the cause of our distress, yet if it were not given to us to encounter things and ourselves as resources, nothing would show up *as* anything at all, and no possibilities for action would make sense. And once we realize – in our practices, of course, not just as a matter of reflection – that we *receive* our technological understanding of being, we have stepped out of the technological understanding of being, for we then see that what is most important in our lives is not subject to efficient enhancement – indeed, the drive to control everything is precisely what we do not control. This transformation in our sense of reality – this overcoming of thinking in terms of values and calculation – is precisely what Heideggerian thinking seeks to bring about. Heidegger seeks to make us see that our practices are needed as the place where an understanding of being can establish itself, so we can overcome our restricted modern clearing by acknowledging our essential receptivity to understandings of being:

Modern man must first and above all find his way back into the full breadth of the space proper to his essence. That essential space of man's essential being receives the dimension that unites it to something beyond itself... that is the way in which the safekeeping of being itself is given to belong to the essence of man as the one who is needed and used by being.

(QCT 39; TK 39)

This transformation in our understanding of being, unlike the slow process of cleaning up the environment, which is, of course, also necessary, would take place in a sudden gestalt switch: "The turning of the danger comes to pass suddenly. In this turning, the clearing belonging to the essence of being suddenly clears itself and lights up" (QCT 44; TK 43). The danger – namely that we have a leveled and concealed understanding of being – when grasped *as* the danger, becomes that which saves us. "The selfsame danger is, when it is *as* the danger, the saving power" (QCT 39; TK 39).

This remarkable claim gives rise to two opposed ways of understanding Heidegger's response to technology. Both interpretations agree that once one recognizes the technological understanding of being for what it is – a historical understanding – one gains a free relation to it. We neither push forward technological efficiency as our sole goal nor always resist it. If we are free of the technological imperative we can, in each case, discuss the pros and cons. As Heidegger puts it:

We let technical devices enter our daily life, and at the same time leave them outside, ... as things which are nothing absolute but remain dependent upon something higher. I would call this comportment toward technology which expresses "yes" and at the same time "no," by an old word, *releasement towards things.*[11]   (DT 54; G 25)

One natural way of understanding this proposal holds that once we get in the right relation to technology, namely, recognize it as a clearing, it is revealed as just as good as any other clearing.[12] Efficiency – getting the most out of ourselves and everything else, "being all you can be" – is fine, as long as we see that efficiency for its own sake is not the *only* end for man, dictated by reality itself, but is just our current understanding. Heidegger seems to support this acceptance of the technological understanding of being as a way of living with technological nihilism when he says:

That which shows itself and at the same time withdraws (i.e., our understanding of being) is the essential trait of what we call the mystery. I call the comportment which enables us to keep open to the meaning hidden in technology, *openness to the mystery.*

Releasement toward things and openness to the mystery belong together. They grant us the possibility of dwelling in the world in a totally different way. They promise us a new ground and foundation upon which we can stand and endure in the world of technology without being imperiled by it.

(DT 55; G 26)

Nevertheless, such acceptance of the mystery of the gift of an understanding of being cannot be Heidegger's whole story about how to overcome technological nihilism, for he immediately adds, "Releasement toward things and openness to the mystery give us a vision of a new rootedness which *someday* might even be fit to recapture the old and now rapidly disappearing rootedness in a changed form" (DT 55; G 26). When we then look back at the preceding remark, we realize releasement gives only a "possibility" and a "promise" of "dwelling in the world in a totally different way"; it does not enable us to do so. Mere openness to technology leaves out much that Heidegger finds essential to overcoming nihilism: embeddedness in nature, or localness, and new shared meaningful differences. Releasement, while giving us a free relation to technology and protecting our nature from being distorted and distressed, cannot by itself give us any of these.

For Heidegger, then, there are two issues. One is clear: "The issue is the saving of man's essential nature. Therefore, the issue is keeping meditative thinking alive" (DT 56; G 27). This is a matter of preserving our sense of ourselves as *receivers* of understandings of being. But that is not enough: "If releasement toward things and openness to the mystery awaken within us, then we should arrive at a path that will lead to a new ground and foundation" (DT 56; G 28). Releasement, it turns out, is only a stage, a kind of holding pattern we can enter into while we are awaiting a new understanding of being that would give a shared content to our openness – what Heidegger calls a new rootedness. That is why each time Heidegger talks of releasement and the saving power of understanding technology as a gift, he then goes on to talk of the divine: "Only when man, in the disclosing coming-to-pass of the insight by which he himself is beheld...renounces human self-will...may (he), as the mortal, look out toward the divine" (QCT 47; TK 45). This is reflected in Heidegger's famous remark in his last interview: "Only a god can save us now."[13] But what does this mean?

To begin with, Heidegger holds that we must learn to appreciate marginal practices – what Heidegger calls the saving power of insignificant things – practices such as friendship, backpacking in the wilderness, and drinking the local wine with friends. All these practices remain marginal precisely because they resist efficiency. These practices can, of course, also be engaged in for the sake of health and greater efficiency. Indeed, the greatest danger is that even the marginal practices will be mobilized as resources. That is why we must protect these endangered practices. But just protecting non-technical practices, even if we could succeed, would still not give us what we need, for these practices by themselves do not add up to a shared moral space of serious, meaningful options.

Of course, one cannot legislate a new understanding of being. But some of our practices could come together in a new cultural paradigm that held up to us a new way of doing things – a new paradigm that opened a world in which these practices and others were central, whereas efficient ordering was marginal. An object or event that would ground such a gestalt switch in our understanding of reality Heidegger calls a new god, and this is why he holds that only a god can save us.

What can we do to get what is still nontechnological in our practices in focus in a non-nihilistic paradigm? Once one sees the problem, one also sees that there is not much one can do about it. A new sense of reality is not something that can be made the goal of a crash program like the moon flight – another paradigm of modern technological power. A new paradigm would have to take up practices that are now on the margin of our culture and make them central, while deemphasizing practices now central to our cultural self-understanding. It would come as a surprise to the very people who participated in it, and if it worked it would become an exemplar of a new understanding of what matters and how to act. There would, of course, be powerful forces tending to take it over and mobilize it for our technological order, and if it failed it would necessarily be measured by our current understanding and so look ridiculous.

A hint of what such a new god might look like is offered by the music of the sixties. Bob Dylan, the Beatles, and other rock groups became for many the articulators of a new understanding of what really mattered. This new understanding almost coalesced into a cultural paradigm in the Woodstock music festival of 1969, where people actually lived for a few days in an understanding of being in which mainline contemporary concerns with order, sobriety, willful activity, and flexible, efficient control were made marginal and subservient to certain pagan practices, such as enjoyment of nature, dancing, and Dionysian ecstasy, along with neglected Christian concerns with peace, tolerance, and nonexclusive love of one's neighbor. Technology was not smashed or denigrated; rather, all the power of electronic communications was put at the service of the music, which focused the above concerns.

If enough people had recognized in Woodstock what they most cared about and recognized that many others shared this recognition, a new understanding of being might have been focused and stabilized. Of course, in retrospect it seems to us who are still in the grip of the technological understanding of being that the concerns of the Woodstock generation were not organized and total enough to sustain a culture. Still we are left with a hint of how a new cultural paradigm would work. This helps us understand that we must foster human receptivity and preserve the endangered species of pretechnological practices that remain in our culture, in the hope that one day they will be pulled together in a new paradigm, rich enough and resistant enough to give a new meaningful direction to our lives.

POLITICS

Heidegger's political engagement was predicated upon his interpretation of the situation in the West as technological nihilism, and of National Socialism as a new paradigm that could give our culture a new understanding of being. But the very same interpretation of the history of being that led Heidegger to support Hitler in 1933 provided the ground for his decisive break with National Socialism somewhere between 1935 and 1938. Between 1933 and 1935 Heidegger seems to have thought that following Hitler as a charismatic leader was the only way to save and focus local and traditional practices in the face of global technology as exemplified by the Soviet Union and the United States. In 1935 he says in a lecture course:

From a metaphysical point of view, Russia and America are the same; the same dreary technological frenzy.... Situated in the center, our nation incurs the severest pressure.... If the great decision regarding Europe is not to bring annihilation, that decision must be made in terms of new spiritual energies unfolding historically from out of the center.   (IM 31–2)

But by 1938, in "The Age of the World Picture," Heidegger sees technology as the problem of the *West*, and National Socialism, rather than the USSR and the United States, as the most dangerous form of what he calls, in Nazi terms, "total mobilization" (QCT 137; GA 5 97). Heidegger also criticized the belief in a *Führer* as the organizer of a total order as an example of faith in technological ordering.

> Beings have entered the way of erring in which the vacuum expands which requires a single order and guarantee of beings. Herein the necessity of "leadership," that is, the planning calculation . . . of the whole of beings, is required.   (EP 105; VA 93)

After 1938, then, Heidegger thought of National Socialism not as the answer to technology and nihilism, but as its most extreme expression.

This gets us to one final question: To what extent was Heidegger's support of National Socialism a personal mistake compounded of conservative prejudices, personal ambition, and political naïveté, and to what extent was his engagement dictated by his philosophy? We have seen that Heidegger, like Charles Taylor and Robert Bellah more recently, holds that we can get over nihilism only by finding some set of shared meaningful concerns that can give our culture a new focus. Moreover, Heidegger sees no hope of overcoming nihilism if one accepts the faith in rational autonomy central to the Enlightenment. In fact, he sees the pursuit of autonomy as the cause of our dangerous contemporary condition. He counters the Enlightenment vision with a nontheological version of the Christian message that man cannot be saved by autonomy, maturity, equality, and dignity alone. Heidegger holds that only some shared meaningful concerns that grip us can give our culture a focus and enable us to resist acquiescence to a state that has no higher goal than to provide material welfare for all. This conviction underlies his dangerous claim that only a god – a charismatic figure, or some other culturally renewing event – can save us from nihilism.

To many, however, the idea of *a* god that will give us a unified but open community – one set of concerns that everyone shares if only as a focus of disagreement – sounds either unrealistic or dangerous. Heidegger would probably agree that its open democratic version looks increasingly unobtainable and that we have certainly seen that its closed totalitarian form can be very dangerous. But Heidegger holds that given our historical essence – the kind of beings we became in fifth century B.C. Greece when our culture gained its identity – such a community is necessary to us or else we will remain in nihilism. It is, he thinks, our only hope or, as he puts it, our destiny.

It follows for Heidegger that our deepest needs will be satisfied and our distress overcome only when our culture gets a new center. Our current condition is defined by the absence of a god:

The era is defined by the god's failure to arrive, by the "default of god." But the default of god . . . does not deny that the Christian relationship with God lives on in individuals and in the churches; still less does it assess this relationship negatively. The default of god means that no god any longer gathers men and things unto himself, visibly and unequivocally, and by such gathering disposes of the world's history and man's sojourn in it.   (PLT 91; GA 5 269)

Heidegger's *personal* mistake comes from having thought that Hitler or National Socialism was such a god. Yet Heidegger had already, in "The Origin of the Work of Art," developed criteria that could serve to determine whether a charismatic leader or movement deserved our allegiance. He stresses there that a true work of art must set up a struggle between earth and world. That is, a true work of art does not make everything explicit and systematic. It generates and supports resistance to total mobilization. Yet Heidegger chose to support a totalitarian leader who denied the truth of all conflicting views and was dedicated to bringing everything under control. Heidegger no doubt interpreted Hitler as setting up some sort of appropriate struggle. Unfortunately, there is no interpretation-free criterion for testing a new god, and such mistakes are always possible. Heidegger's *philosophy*, then, is dangerous because it seeks to convince us that only a god – a charismatic figure or some other culturally renewing event – can save us from falling into contented nihilism. It exposes us to the risk of committing ourselves to some demonic event or movement that promises renewal.

What sort of claim is Heidegger making when he tells us that Enlightenment welfare and dignity are not enough and that only a god can save us? How can one justify or criticize Heidegger when he reads our current condition as the absence of a god and our current distress as a sign of the greatest danger? – for only such a reading of the present age justifies risking commitment to some new cultural paradigm.

The first answer we might try to give is that Heidegger is offering a genealogical interpretation. He will focus on and augment our distress and show that it can be accounted for by telling a story of the progressive narrowing, leveling, and totalizing of the West's understanding of being. Such an interpretation has to make sense of more details of our history and present situation than any rival interpretation, and ultimately it must convince us by the illumination it casts on our current condition, especially on our sense of ontological distress or emptiness, if we have one.

But how could we know that our distress was due to the absence of a god rather than personal and social problems? One answer might be that we will just have to wait for the perfected welfare state and then see how we feel. If defenders of the Enlightenment are right, distress will be eliminated, whereas Heidegger, one might suppose, would expect that, as technology succeeds, the suffering will grow. But Heidegger does not make this claim. Heidegger admits and fears the possibility that everyone might simply become healthy and happy, and forget completely that they are receivers of understandings of being. All Heidegger can say is that such a forgetting of our forgetting of being would be the darkest night of nihilism. In such an "unworld," Heidegger could no longer expect to be understood. Only now, and only as long as he can awaken our distress and our sense of our receptivity to a mysterious source of meaning that creates and sustains us, can he hope that we will be able to see the force of his interpretation.

Such thinking is far from the "infallible knowledge"[14] many think Heidegger claims. Indeed, Heidegger goes out of his way to point out that he can claim no infallibility for his interpretation. He writes to a student that "this thinking can never show credentials such as mathematical knowledge can. But it is just as little a matter of arbitrariness" (PLT 184; VA 183). He then goes on to repeat his reading of the West as having lost touch with the saving practices excluded by totalizing technology – practices that are nonetheless all around us:

The default of god and the divinities is absence. But absence is not nothing; rather it is precisely the presence, which must first be appropriated, of the hidden fullness and wealth of what has been and what, thus gathered, is presencing, of the divine in the world of the Greeks, in prophetic Judaism, in the preaching of Jesus.   (PLT 184; VA 183)

And he immediately adds that he can claim no special authority: "I can provide no credentials for what I have said... that would permit a convenient check in each case whether what I say agrees with 'reality'" (PLT 186; VA 184). This is an appropriate warning since Heidegger's own political mistake reminds us that any guidelines must always be interpreted, and that if one opts for the charismatic one cannot avoid the risk. Thus, Heidegger's letter to the student fittingly concludes: "Any path always risks going astray.... Stay on the path, in genuine need, and learn the craft of thinking, unswerving, yet erring" (PLT 186; VA 185).

NOTES

1. Søren Kierkegaard, *The Present Age*, trans. Alexander Dru (New York: Harper & Row, 1962).
2. For evidence that Heidegger is right on this point, see Robert N. Bellah, Richard Madsen, William M. Sullivan, Ann Swidler, and Steven M. Tipton, *Habits of the Heart* (Berkeley and Los Angeles: University of California Press, 1985).
3. See H. L. Dreyfus and Stuart Dreyfus, *Mind over Machine* (New York: Free Press 1982).
4. Clifford Geertz, *The Interpretation of Cultures* (New York: Harper Colophon Books, 1973), p. 448.
5. For a description of the dimensions and directions of moral space see Charles Taylor, *Sources of the Self* (Cambridge, MA: Harvard University Press, 1989).
6. Geertz, *Interpretation*, p. 450.
7. Ibid., p. 451.
8. Charles Taylor, "Interpretation and the Sciences of Man," *Philosophy and the Human Sciences* (Cambridge: Cambridge University Press, 1985), p. 39.
9. Thomas Kuhn, *The Structure of Scientific Revolutions*, 2d ed. (Chicago: University of Chicago Press, 1970), p. 46.
10. Ibid., p. 11.
11. Why Heidegger speaks of "things" here is a long and interesting story. In his essay "The Thing" in *Poetry, Language, Thought*, Heidegger spells out the way that certain things like a jug of wine can focus practices and collect people around them. Such things function like local, temporary works of art in giving meaning to human activities, but they do not focus a whole culture and so do not become the locus of a struggle between earth and world. Rather, they produce a moment of stillness and harmony. Albert Borgmann interprets and develops this idea in

his account of "focal practices" (see A. Borgmann, *Technology and the Character of Contemporary Life* [Chicago: University of Chicago Press, 1984]). For an illuminating discussion of the importance for Heidegger of the thing, see also Charles Taylor's "Heidegger, Language and Ecology," in *Heidegger: A Critical Reader*, ed. H. Dreyfus and H. Hall (Oxford: Blackwell Publisher, 1992), pp. 247–69.

12. See Richard Rorty, "Heidegger, Contingency and Pragmatism," in *Heidegger: A Critical Reader*, ed. Dreyfus and Hall, pp. 209–30.

13. "Only a God Can Save Us," *Der Spiegel*, May 31, 1976.

14. Jürgen Habermas, "Work and Weltanschauung: The Heidegger Controversy from a German Perspective," *Critical Inquiry*, 15 (Winter 1989): 431–56, p. 456, rpt. in *Heidegger: A Critical Reader*, ed. Dreyfus and Hall, pp. 186–208.

14 The fourfold

Among the many mysteries surrounding "the fourfold" is the almost total absence of any attempt by Heidegger scholars to explain what it is. Usually the topic doesn't even make it to the index, and even when it does, it does so only in virtue of statements like "this conception [of the fourfold] is developed in a way one can only call mythic, and its philosophical import is therefore far from clear,"[1] which is not really very helpful. Baffled by Heidegger's poetic brevity, commentators have consigned it to the silence of the too-hard basket.

Yet without understanding the fourfold – the fourfold of earth, sky, gods, and mortals – one can understand almost nothing of later Heidegger. Heidegger says that "dwelling," as he calls it, is the human "essence" (QCT 28, P 257, PLT 213 ff.). But to dwell is to "belong within the fourfold of sky and earth, mortals and divinities" (QCT 49; compare PLT 149). He also says that the fourfold is what "we call the world" (PLT 179). Without understanding the fourfold, therefore, one can understand neither later Heidegger's conception of the human being nor his conception of "world."

To dwell is to be "at home" (QCT 49). It is to be in the world as in a *Heimat*, to be in it as, not a foreign place, but as a homeland. To dwell is for one's place to show up as a *dwelling*-place.

Geviert (Heidegger's word translated as "fourfold") is an obscure word for "square" or "courtyard" – the courtyard of, for example, a farm surrounded on all four sides by farm buildings. As such it is an essentially spatial notion. The fourfold is Heidegger's account of what makes a place or space a dwelling-space. One's place is a dwelling place (a *Te Papa*, as the Maori put it) to, and only to, the extent it shows up as a *Geviert*. To understand how this happens and in what it consists, we must begin by trying to understand each of the elements that belong to it.

"Earth," says Heidegger, "is the building bearer, nourishing with its fruits, tending water and rock, plant and animal" (PLT 178). Dwellers dwell "on" the earth (PLT 149). "Sky," he continues, "is the sun's path, the course of the moon, the glitter of the stars, the year's seasons, the light and dusk of day, the gloom and glow of night, the clemency and inclemency of the weather, the drifting clouds and the blue depth of the aether" (PLT 178). Dwellers dwell "under" the sky (PLT 149).

Thought less pictorially, "earth" seems to embrace the totality of things, animal, vegetable and mineral, with which we share our world. And "sky" embraces, as well as the literal sky, that which is thought of as belonging to or coming from it – the predictable rhythms of the planetary motions, of the seasons, of day and night, as well as the unpredictable motions of the weather.

The element of the fourfold that is most difficult to understand is "the gods," *die Göttlichen*, literally "the godly ones." Heidegger says of Greek tragedy that it "brought the presence of the gods, [i.e.,] brought the dialogue of divine and human destinings to radiance" (QCT 34). In some sense, therefore, the gods *are* the "divine destinings." What are these?

The divine destinings, "laws" (HE 312) or "edicts" (I 116), are the fundamental *ethos* of a community. In a certain essential way "unspoken," they are what Sophocles' Antigone appeals to in resisting the unjust laws of Creon's state (*ibid.*). (Creon orders that, as a traitor, Polynices' body is to be left unburied. Antigone, appealing to a higher authority, buried the body of her brother and is condemned to death.) And it is the divine laws which create the possibility of a critique of "the voice of the people," contemporary public opinion (HE 312).

In his early magnum opus, *Being and Time*, Heidegger's word for the divine destinings is "heritage." And he speaks there of heritage as being embodied in "heroes" (BT 385, 391), more or less mythologized figures preserved in the collective memory of a culture, who embody, collectively, what it is to live properly as an Athenian, a German, a New Zealander, or whatever. Heroes are, in a word, "role" or – much better – "life" models.[2] The gods of later Heidegger are, I suggest, the reappearance of *Being and Time's* heroes, rethought in a deeper and richer way. This is why he calls them "the beckoning messengers of the godhead" (PLT 149, 179). By being who they are, they give voice to that which is most sacred to us. As members of a given community, and whether we heed their inspiring example or not, we live our lives in the light of our gods. As we live "on" earth and "under" the sky, we live "before" the divinities (PLT 149)

"Mortals," those "with" whom we live (*ibid.*), are of course human beings (PLT 150). Why does Heidegger say "mortal" rather than just "human being"?

Partly, I think, for pictorial and metaphorical reasons. As "earth" contrasts with "sky," so the "mortal" earth dwellers contrast with the "immortal" denizens of the *Himmel* – which means, in German, both "sky" and "heaven." Mainly, however, I think Heidegger wants to stress that to die, to be "capable of death as death" is a defining feature of human beings. While animals merely "perish," human beings are capable of approaching death with an understanding of what it truly is, namely, "the shrine of the Nothing," "the mystery of Being itself" (PLT 178). If they exercise this capacity then, Heidegger adds, they become capable of the "good death" (PLT 151). Showing up to oneself as a "mortal" is somehow a touchstone of having the right relationship to "Being." I shall try to elucidate these dark sayings shortly.

"Sky" and "Earth," evidently, add up, in some sense of the word, to nature. And individuals, mortals, gathered together by a common "heritage," by a shared pantheon of gods, are clearly culture or community: it is by, and only by, dwelling "in the sight of the gods," says Heidegger, that "man become[s] a people (*Volk*)" (GA 39 216). So the fourfold of earth, sky, gods, and mortals is really the twofold of nature and culture (or "history," as the Germans tend to call it.)

But if this is all it amounts to, then why the elevated, poetic language in Heidegger's own descriptions of it? Not, I think, out of casual literary hyperbole, but rather to *show* something. Heidegger uses poetic language to describe how the world is experienced when it shows up as a dwelling-place because he wants to show that – as one of his best loved lines from Hölderlin puts it – "poetically man dwells" (PLT 213 ff.).

What has poetry to do with dwelling? What *is* poetry?

"Intelligibility," the possibility of statements that are unambiguously either true or false, depends on what Heidegger calls "horizons of disclosure" (DT 63). For me to get the point when you say, pointing to the river, "You'll never bathe in that again," I need to understand that, for the moment, the horizon of discussion is a "stuff" rather than the usual "thing" horizon.[3]

In everyday life, the all-embracing horizon of experience is that of, in a broad sense of the word, "equipmentality" – a point emphasized (actually over-emphasized) in *Being and Time*. Because we are essentially practical agents, because we are given over to "toil" (PLT 220), we are, in a broad sense of the word, "workers" (we cannot but bring about intentional changes in the world), things show up for us in "work"-suitable ways. The object in front of me, for example, shows up not as a subtle symphony of delicately variegated whites reflecting off a semi-abstract, Henry Moore-like, hollowed-out, elongated sphere but as, and only as, a urinal. This reduction of things to the single dimension (horizon) of equipment is reflected in a characteristic of the language of everyday communication: such language is (or aspires to be), says Heidegger, *eindeutig* (GA 52 15): in normal usage "unambiguous," but here to be taken in its literal meaning of "one-meaning," one-dimensional.

There is nothing wrong with horizons of disclosure in general, or with the horizon of equipmentality in particular. We could not engage in successful communication without them, could not survive as practical agents without the horizon of equipmentality. (This is a point that seems to be missed in the universal paranoia directed toward "epistemes" or "regimes of meaning" displayed by Foucault and Derrida, the demand that they all be "deconstructed.")

What can easily happen, however, is that we lose sight of the fact that the horizon of equipmentality is just *a* horizon, *one* disclosure of Being (reality) among indefinitely many. Our everyday horizon ossifies itself into *the* way reality is so that we loose sight of the fact that horizons of disclosure always "conceal" other horizons, as, for example, the "thing" horizon conceals the "stuff" horizon. We lose sight of the fact that behind every disclosure is a "reservoir" of the "not-yet-disclosed" (PLT 60). Heidegger, perhaps not very helpfully, calls this reduction of many-aspected Being (PLT 124) to a single aspect, "metaphysics."

Whereas everyday prose, the language in which everyday experience happens, is *eindeutig*, the language of poetry is *vieldeutig* – normally "ambiguous," but here, says Heidegger, to be read literally as "of many meanings," possessed of a "multiplicity" or "richness of meaning." For to every "genuinely" poetic word belongs an "inexhaustible" range of "complex spaces of [semantic] resonance" (GA 52 15, compare OWL 192).

This is partly a repetition of Kant's account of the poetic word (or "aesthetic idea") as that which "induces much thought, yet without the possibility of any definite thought, that is *concept*, being completely adequate to it."[4] But whereas Kant, it seems to me, thinks of all these resonances of a poetic word as belonging within our ultimate – "transcendental" – horizon of disclosure, Heidegger, I believe, thinks of them as bringing to presence the sense of the word's designata as extending beyond the "transcendental" (DT 63) horizon constituted by the language we speak. If I name my love poetically, I think of her as a foundation, a blessing, a grace, a rose, a summer's day, a.... What is important here are the dots. Whereas, for Kant, they represent merely what we might call intra-worldly resonances, for Heidegger, they bring to experiential presence the fact that many-faced Being transcends, infinitely, anything of which our language is capable.

In poetic experience or in poetry-mediated experience, therefore, we "grasp" our lives as lived "in the face of the ungraspable" (I 136), come face to face with the "mystery" (QCT 25) of Being, with its "awesomeness" (PLT 68). This is why Heidegger says that the essence of poetry is that it "found[s] the holy" (GA 52 193, I 138, GA 4 148). In delivering us from the flatness of "metaphysics," it allows us to experience reality as that before which we must bow down in awe.

We are now in a position better to understand "poetically man dwells." What it means is that human beings dwell in, and only in, the holy. To become a dwelling-place, our world must show up – to deploy a metaphor Heidegger takes over from Hölderlin – as possessing the "dimension" of the holy, a dimension that can be "measured" only by the poet (PLT 220–225). In addition to the, as we might call them, "dimensions" of earth, sky, gods and mortals, the dwelling-place must possess the fifth dimension of the holy. Looked at in this way, we must say that the fourfold is really a five-dimensional place.

"Poetically man dwells" accords with our intuitions. Nothing moves the generally unlyrical to lyricism more than the homeland – particularly the homeland in danger, or the homeland viewed from afar (Auckland from a wet, winter's evening in London) – a fact which suggests one interpretation of Heidegger's remark that poetry is "politics in the highest and most authentic sense" (GA 39 214). But why, philosophically, should we believe that man dwells only in the poetic? What, indeed, *is* dwelling? What is it to be at home in the *Heimat*?

"The fundamental character of dwelling" says Heidegger, is "caring-for (*Schonen*)." But caring-for is double-aspected. On the one hand, the dweller is the *object* of caring-for, is "preserved from harm and danger . . . safeguarded . . . at peace" (PLT 149). The difference between the homely (in the sense of the German *heimisch*) and the foreign is that one feels secure in the former in a way one does not in the latter. On the other hand, the dweller is the *subject* of caring-for: she is the one who "spares and preserves" (*ibid.*) the things of the dwelling-place, becomes, as Heidegger puts it, its "shepherd" or "guardian" (P 252, PLT 184). To be at home in a place is to care for it. People do not litter their homes – if homes they have – in the way they litter motorways.

What is the connection between this double-aspected caring-for and the holy? Why should grasping the homeland in its mysterious and awesome "depth" (compare BT 152) make me feel "safe" and "at peace," and why, secondly, should it dispose me to *keep* the homeland safe, to become its caretaker?

The *ultimate* threat to our safety is, of course, death. Fear of death (as opposed to fear of judgment) is fear of nothingness, fear before "the nothing." But only to one who has succumbed to the illusion of "metaphysics" does his this-worldly manifestation represent the totality of his being. To one who has overcome metaphysics – who has intuitive insight into the real nature of Being and truth – "death and the realm of the dead" (Heidegger's discussion, here, take the form of a thinking-with Rilke) is simply "the side of life that is

averted from us" (PLT 124–5). In a sense, of course, death is entry
into the nothing, is, as already recorded, the "shrine of the nothing"
(PLT 178). But this is only the nothing of the "nothing comprehensible to us," the nothing that is "the mystery of Being itself" (ibid.),
is that which lies beyond our most ultimate horizon of intelligibility. Not the absolute, "privative-negative" (GA 15 363) nothing of
the abyss, it is rather something "positive" (PLT 124). To overcome
"metaphysics" is to become a "mortal," to be "capable of death as
death" rather than as mere "perishing." To overcome metaphysics is
to be initiated into the mysterious but unfrightening nature of death
and so to become capable of the "good death" (PLT 151).

Why, to turn to the second aspect of caring-for, should the disclosure
of my world as a holy place turn me into a "guardian of Being"?
Because, evidently, the showing of respect, of reverence, is what it is
to apprehend my place as a holy place. If I am not moved to respect
for the ground on which I stand, I do not know that it is sacred
ground.

Guardians, of course, cannot avoid making changes to the
dwelling-place. To the best of their ability, however, the changes
they bring about are harmonious with, rather than an "assault" upon
(QCT 16), the dwelling-place. Rather than assertively seeking to bull-
doze a new order of things, they seek to "bring forth" (QCT 10–11)
potentialities already implicit in the place itself. If, for example, they
are architects or gardeners they will, as the Sakutei-ki, the classic,
eleventh-century manual of Japanese gardening tells us, "Listen to
the request made by the land." As well as respecting the fundamental
order of things, they will allow the place to complete itself through
their actions. As well as "letting things be" in the sense of conserv-
ing them, they will "let them be" in the active sense of, as Heidegger
puts it, letting what is "coming" arrive (QCT 10–11).

So much for the exposition of Heidegger's basic idea. I want now
to pose some exploratory questions in the hope that the attempt to
answer them will provide a deeper understanding of the fourfold and
therefore of dwelling.

My first question, put with deliberate crudeness, is: how big is
the fourfold? How many are there? Is there more than one? As
observed, Heidegger identifies "fourfold" with "world" (PLT 179).

But since "world" is a notoriously elastic notion, this hardly provides an answer to the question.

The homeland is, says Heidegger, that which is "near" to us. But nearness implies farness; it fails to "appear" if "remoteness... remains absent" (PLT 166). If one has no conception of "the foreign," of what one is not and where one does not belong, then one can have no conception of what one is and where one belongs. (This, of course, is the danger of modern information technology, of TV and the Internet. It threatens to destroy the possibility of homeland by creating, as Heidegger puts it, a "uniform distancelessness" [ibid.], in which everything is equally near and equally remote. Marshall McLuhan's metaphor, it is worth reminding ourselves, is but a metaphor. The global village is not a village.)

So a dwelling-space is a *bounded* space. It is a space "cleared and free... within a boundary," a boundary being "not that at which something stops but... that from which it *begins its presencing*" (PLT 154). There are therefore *many* fourfolds. The fourfold in which one dwells, if one dwells, is a *local* fourfold. This means, to turn to what one might call the "ethics of dwelling," that there is, in Heidegger, a combination of universalism and localism. On the one hand, to stand in the right relationship to Being, to stand in a relationship based on "insight into that which is" (QCT 47) rather than the illusion of "metaphysics," is – universally – to care-for, to become a "guardian" of, the dwelling-place. On the other hand, since the dwelling-place is local rather than universal, the concrete implications of the ethics of dwelling will vary from place to place and person to person. The primary object of my guardianship is not the universe or the planet, but rather the particular fourfold to which I belong. (In the current context, of course, since the major threats to both my nature and my culture are global in character, I can only care-for my place by caring-for the globe. To think locally I must, as the saying goes, act globally.)

My second exploratory question concerns what Heidegger calls the "unity" or "simple oneness" of the fourfold. The fourfold is, he says, no mere collection of disconnected entities. Rather, "each of the four mirrors in its own way, the presence of the others." They "belong... to one another," have "essential being toward one another" (PLT pp. 178–80). What is Heidegger getting at here? Is he right?

The mutual "mirroring" between earth, sky, gods, and mortals, says Heidegger, "does not portray a likeness" (PLT 179). It is not iconic, not a matter of picturing. Rather, I think, it is more like a functional relationship. Given any one element of a fourfold, we can "read off" the other three (though, remembering that we are not doing mathematics, "read off," I think, must be understood in a relatively loose and approximate kind of way). "When we say earth [or sky, or gods, or mortals] we are already thinking of the other three along with it" (PLT 178, see also 149–50). Why so?

If we remember that "earth" embraces flora and fauna and "sky" embraces climate, the idea of a mutual "mirroring" between the two, the idea that from the "earth" of the dwelling-place you can "read off" its "sky," and conversely, is not difficult to make sense of. There is an obvious symbiosis between climate and species of animals and plants, even between climate and land formation. Under an arctic sky one finds only arctic wastes, over rain forests sky must be full of rain.

Similarly, the idea of a mutual mirroring between gods and mortals is not hard to understand – not hard, at least, if one is acquainted with early Heidegger, with *Being and Time.*

Being "authentic," according to *Being and Time,* is a matter of being true to the fundamental values that constitute the "heritage" of one's community.[5] Unlike Sartrean existentialism, which holds that my fundamental values are unavoidably *chosen* by me, Heidegger argues that my fundamental values – who I fundamentally am – are *given* to me as my "heritage." It follows that being authentic, being true to myself, is being true to heritage.[6] But "the gods," as we have seen, are the embodiments of heritage. So, from the gods of a community, one can read off the fundamental character of "mortals," both as a "people" and as individuals. And conversely.

Sky and earth are nature, gods and mortals – mortals living in community "before" their gods – are, we have said, culture. What we have seen so far is that the ideas of an intra-natural and of an intra-cultural "mirroring" are relatively easy to understand. What seems to me problematic and hard to understand, however, is the idea of a mirroring between nature and culture. Why should we believe that there is a mutual mirroring between the gods of a people on the one hand, and their sky and earth, on the other?

Nietzsche says that "once you have recognised the need and land and sky ... of a people you may also guess the law of their overcomings"[7] guess, that is to say, their virtues, or, in Heideggerian language, their "gods." Nietzsche's point is that particular virtues have a natural affinity with particular environments. Prudence, foresight, thrift, essential virtues in cold climates where food must be stored for winter, make no sense in a simple South Pacific community where food is almost effortlessly available throughout the year. "Gods" mirror nature, one might be tempted to conclude, because nature determines virtues.

There is an obvious objection to this claim, namely, that history provides many examples of two or more cultures with separate pantheons of "gods" inhabiting the same "sky" and "earth." For example, consider the Arab and French communities in twentieth-century Algeria, European and Maori in New Zealand.

The initial Heideggerian reply to this objection must consist, I think, in pointing out that inhabiting a geographical region is not the same as dwelling in a fourfold. *Bodenständigkeit*, rootedness of life in the soil, is a fundamental Heideggerian concept. Rejecting, in 1934, a second invitation to accept a chair in Berlin, he explained, in a radio broadcast entitled "Why do we stay in the Provinces?" that his

philosophical work does not take its course like the aloof studies of some eccentric. It belongs right here in the midst of the peasants' work. When the young farm boy drags his heavy sledge up the slope and guides it, piled high with beech logs, down the dangerous descent to his house, when the herdsman, lost in thought and slow of step, drives his cattle up the slope, when the farmer in his shed gets the countless shingles ready for his roof, *my work is of the same sort. It is intimately rooted in and related to the life of the peasants.* ... The inner relationship of my own work to the Black Forest and its people comes from a centuries-long and irreplaceable rootedness in the Alemanic-Swabian soil.[8]

The life of the philosopher is "rooted" in the life of the Black Forest peasant,[9] and the life of the peasant is rooted in the thin and impoverished character of the Black Forest "soil." As, too, are their virtues; the granite-like steadfastness with which Albert Schlageter faced the French rifles (he had been condemned to death in 1923 for acts of sabotage in protest at the French occupation of the Ruhr) is rooted in the "hardening of the will" of this "farmer's son" who grew up amidst the granite of the Black Forest, his "clarity of heart" developed by the "clear light" with which "the autumn sun of the Black Forest" bathes the mountain ranges."[10] Of course, Heidegger would say, one can *inhabit* a region without one's "gods" being the ones that are native to it. But if they are not, one lacks *Bodenständigkeit*, does not *dwell* there.

Heidegger surely has a point, here. The British in India, for example, as E. M. Forster shows, with only very few (despised) exceptions, did not *dwell* there. The incongruity between their "gods" and the Indian "earth" and "sky" – the *absurdity* of their heavy dress, rigid discipline and pompous manners – showed this. They did not, indeed, *want* to dwell there, found the idea of, as they called it, "going native" deeply threatening. They *prided* themselves on their out-of-placeness, treating Noel Coward's "Mad dogs and Englishmen go out in the mid-day sun," not as a satire, but as a *celebration* of themselves. They did not want to dwell there because, as Mrs. Moore realises on hearing the terrible Om echo in the Miribar caves, the price of dwelling in India is the destruction of one's European identity.

But this is not at all to say that colonial communities can never come to dwell in the colonized place. Albert Camus' intense and abiding homesickness for Algeria is evidence of that. What happens, however, when colonizers begin to dwell in the new homeland is that the immigrant culture begins to acquire *Bodenständigkeit*, and begins, therefore, to converge with the native culture. Camus takes note of this. In the sun of Algiers, on the beaches where people are not "nudists" – those boring "Protestants of the flesh" – but simply "comfortable in the sunlight," in a land where one says not "go for" but rather "indulge in" a swim, life, for the French as much as the Arabs, is no longer something to be "built up," as it is in Paris, but something rather to be "burnt up."[11] The same phenomenon is visible in New Zealand. In predominantly Maori areas, Pakeha (European) styles of living and speaking take on Maori inflections.

All this being said, however, one should resist the temptation, I think, to turn the idea that environment *influences* culture into the

idea that it *determines* it. Though European–Algerian culture perhaps *approaches* the Islamic culture of the Arabs, it never became
anywhere near *identical* with it. Though rural Pakeha culture
approaches that of the Maori, they remain separate. *Different cultures, different gods, may be "rooted in the soil" of the same nature*
(which is, of course, the source of many postcolonial tragedies). What
is true, I think, is that nature determines a range (or, perhaps better,
family) of gods as "at home" in a given place. But within that range
different communities may worship different pantheons.

I doubt that Heidegger ever thought about the parallel communities of colonialism – since Germany had no colonies to speak of, it
would have been somewhat surprising if he had. Implicitly, it seems
to me, he always thought within the unspoken presupposition of a
one-to-one correspondence between ethnic communities and natural places. The Black Forest is, for Heidegger, "Alemanic-Swabian
soil" since the dawn of history. When, in 1961, in one of his wilder
moments, he called all modern art worthless since it "arises no
longer from the shaping boundaries of an ethnic or national world,"[12]
it is clear, I think, that he views modernity's mingling of populations
as simply the destruction of dwelling, clear that the idea of different
communities of dwellers sharing the same "earth" and "sky" simply
does not cross his mind. The result, I think, is an exaggeration of the
strictness with which the "gods" of a community are determined by
its earth and sky.

"Things," says Heidegger, "gather" the fourfold (PLT 153). "Staying
with things is the only way in which the fourfold stay within the
fourfold is accomplished" (PLT 151). What does this mean? What, in
Heidegger's specially elevated use of the word, is a "thing"?

Heidegger observes that the Old High German *"thing"* – the origin
of the modern German *"Ding"* (thing) – referred to a gathering of the
people in order to discuss some matter of especial importance, a kind
of occasional parliament (PLT 175). This idea of a gathering of the
people points us, it seems to me, to the ancestor in Heidegger's earlier
thought of the later notion of the "thing."

In "The Origin of the Work of Art" of 1935–6, Heidegger had
argued that the "worlding of world," its emerging out of background obscurity into foreground clarity and radiance, could happen

through, and only through, the communal "artwork": the Greek temple, the Olympic games, or the medieval cathedral (PLT 41–3). Only through the community's ("people's") being gathered by the artwork into the charismatic presence of "the gods" could it *be*, and be preserved as, a community. Heidegger does not use the language of "dwelling" in "The Origin" (his Hölderlinian "education,"[13] still in the future, was necessary to his grasping the nature and importance of dwelling) but, in effect, what he argues is that since dwelling requires being-in-community, dwelling presupposes the communal artwork.

In his thinking of the 1950s, his thinking about dwelling, the fourfold and the "thing," Heidegger came, I believe, to grapple with the following problem. In this post-religious age, this age of the "flight of the gods," this age, that is, of the absence of a communal "artwork," how (if at all) is dwelling possible? How can I be in, and be "appropriated" by (PLT 179), a fourfold where there is no "artwork" to bring it to charismatic presence? Heidegger's answer is: through the "thing."

Dwelling doesn't just happen, in a general, unfocused kind of way. It needs a medium or focus through which it happens. To be such a focus is to be, in the elevated sense, a "thing." When the thing "things" (PLT 182), when it, as it were, rings or sings for me, my world comes to charismatic salience as the fourfold it is. When this happens, then in an occurrent sense, I dwell; as Heidegger puts it, I "experience and take over [my] . . . dwelling" (P 257). Without having, "from time to time" (PLT 182), such an occurrent experience of the "worlding of world" (PLT 179), I could not be a dweller. To dwell in my world I must, "from time to time," "experience and take over" my dwelling.

But what, to repeat, *is* a "thing'? Heidegger's paradigm is the simple peasant jug that is used to pour out wine for the gathering of friends around the *Stammtisch* (table reserved for regulars) in the village pub, somewhere in Southwest Germany. In the wine – the wine of the region, of course – are "gathered" the local earth and sky – the *terroir*, as French wine makers call it. And in the gathering of "mortals," deeply rooted in the richness of their tradition or "heritage," are gathered, too, the gods. Hence, "in the gift (*Schenk*, from *schenken*, which means both to give and to pour) of the outpouring dwells the simple singlefold of the four" (PLT 173).

Let me try to translate this into something closer to Anglo-Saxon experience: the Christmas dinner, focused around the turkey. Outside, the already dimming light of the Yorkshire afternoon is reflected off the snow through the low-set, mullioned windows and onto the faces and the walls. The family is gathered round the table. In the small silence that descends before the carving of the turkey begins, suddenly, in a way that is "inexplicable and unfathomable" (PLT 180), one experiences an epiphany, is visited by a profound sense of being in place, being in the right place, of belonging to a unique and indissoluble unity of earth, sky, divinities and mortals. One's world "worlds" which is the same as saying that the "thing things" (PLT pp. 180–1).

In *Heidegger's Philosophy of Art* (*op. cit.* Chapter 1), since the account of "the artwork" offered in "The Origin of the Work of Art" is heavily focused on Greece, I call that account "the Greek paradigm." Things which "thing" in the above manner one might call "mini-Greek-paradigm artworks." Though they do not gather an entire culture in the manner of the Greek temple or medieval cathedral (the manner the Bayreuth Festival and the Nuremberg rally attempted to revive) the context in which world rises out of background inconspicuousness into radiant salience is one of communal gathering.

At the end of "The Thing," however, Heidegger makes it clear that anything at all, no matter how "unpretentious" (PLT 182), can come to "thing" that any occasion, whether communal or solitary, can be an occasion of "thinging": "the jug and the bench, the footbridge and the plough[14] . . . tree and pond, brook and hill . . . heron and roe, deer, horse and bull, . . . clasp, book and picture, crown and cross," "each in its own way . . . thinging from time to time," are all "things" (PLT 182). In Greece and the Middle Ages, "things" gathered the fourfold to presence for an entire culture. In the modern ages they can still gather for an *us*, though for a smaller, more private "us" than in the past. But things can also gather just for me.

Heidegger's idea about the nature and importance of the "thing" is, I think, basically correct. To dwell is to be disposed to epiphanies of dwelling. One needs one's fourfold to come, "from time to time," to explicit presence, a presence which, because it is "radiant" (PLT 181), "appropriates" (PLT 179) one into one's fourfold, makes it the place where one belongs. But such appropriation can happen only through a focus of presencing. One person who understood this was the New Zealand writer Bruce Mason. "Consider, if you will," he invites the reader, "Te Parenga. A beach, three-quarters of a mile long, a hundred yards wide at low water.... This is Te Parenga: my heritage, my world."[15] Another was Camus. In the 1952 essay "Return to Tipasa" Camus returns from grey, post-War Paris to one of the "sites of his ... youth," the Roman ruins above the Bay of Tipasa in Algeria (now a "World Heritage" site). Though he knows it to be "sheer madness almost always punished" to "try to relive at forty what one had loved ... at twenty," he revisits the ruins "looking for a certain lift."[16] For when "one has once had the good luck to love intensely, life is spent in trying to recapture that ardour and illumination." Without it

A day comes when, thanks to rigidity, nothing causes wonder any more, everything is known.... These are the days of exile, of desiccated life, of dead souls. To come alive again one needs a special grace, self-forgetfulness, or a homeland. Certain mornings, on turning a corner, a delightful dew falls on the heart and then evaporates. But its coolness remains and this is what the heart requires always.[17]

"Inexplicably and unfathomably," in Heidegger's language, the return to Tipasa works. The thing things, Camus' fourfold shines forth:

under the glorious December light [Camus records], as happens but once or twice in lives which ever after can consider themselves favoured to the full, I found exactly what I had come seeking.... From the forum strewn with olives could be seen the village down below. No sound came from it; wisps of smoke rose in the limpid air. the sea likewise was silent as if smothered under the unbroken shower of dazzling, cold light. From the Chenoua a distant cock's crow alone celebrated the day's fragile glory. In the direction of the ruins, as far as the eye could see, there was nothing but pock-marked stones and wormwood, trees and perfect columns in the transparence of the crystalline air. It seemed as if the morning were stabilised, the sun stopped for an incalculable moment. In this light and this silence, years of wrath and night melted slowly away. I listened to an almost forgotten sound within myself as if my heart, long stopped, were calmly beginning to beat again.... I also listened to the happy torrents rising within me. It seemed to me that I had at last come to harbour, for a moment at least, and that henceforth that moment would be endless.[18]

A final question concerns the topic of, as I shall put it, dwelling and the city.

To dwell, we have seen, is to be in the fourfold. It is to be "on the earth" – "spreading out in rock and water, rising up in plant and animal" – and under the "sky" – "the year's seasons and their changes, the light and dusk of day, the gloom and glow of night, the clemency and inclemency of weather. . . . " But in the city there are no rocks or plants; covered shopping centers block out the "clemency and inclemency of the weather," while street- and flood-lighting obscure the "gloom and glow of night." They "turn night into day," while city life in general, it seems, turns "day into harassed unrest" (PLT 150). It would seem, then, that in the city no fourfold is to be found and that in it, therefore, there can be no dwelling.

In a (hostile) review of my *Heidegger, Philosophy, Nazism* (op. cit.) (*Times Literary Supplement* 15.18. 1997), George Steiner endorses this reading of later Heidegger as fundamentally anti-modernist, accusing him of an "anti-industrial, anti-urban, radical pastoralism." This familiar interpretation – often coupled with the accusation that Heidegger's notion of dwelling is really little more than nostalgic kitsch – is reinforced by Heidegger's biography: his taste for peasant costume, the hut in the Black Forest, the refusal of the chair in Berlin, and so on.

As a reason for at least pausing before embracing this anti-modernist reading, it may be pointed out that Heidegger actually lived, not in the hut, but in a suburb of Freiburg, and continued to do so even after his retirement from the university. And that the 1934 radio talk, referred to earlier, defended life in the "provinces," not life in the "countryside."

Still, there can be no doubt that Heidegger was a critic of a great deal of modern building and of the city in its characteristically modern form. The motorway (freeway) bridge (PLT 152) is Heidegger's paradigm of the building that fails to "thing," and is contrasted unfavorably with the "old bridge" in Heidelberg (PLT 152, 156) and with the Black Forest farmhouse (PLT 160). (Notice, however, that the "Old Bridge," as it is known locally, is actually a nineteenth-century, and the farmhouse an eighteenth-century construction; both, that is, works of, in the world-historical sense, "modernity.") And, explicitly discussing dwelling in a speech celebrating the seven hundredth anniversary of the founding of his home town of Messkirch in 1961, Heidegger says the following:

> Homeland is most possible and effective where the powers of nature around us ["earth" and "sky"] and the remnants of historical tradition ["heritage," "the gods"] remain together, where an origin and an ancient, nourished style of human existence holds sway. Today, for this decisive task, perhaps only the rural counties and small towns are competent – if they recognise anew their unusual qualities, if they know how to draw the boundaries between themselves and life in the large cities and the gigantic areas of modern industrial complexes.... [19]

Dwelling in the city is, therefore, for Heidegger, at the very least, problematic.

But this, it might be said, calls into question the connection between dwelling and "the fourfold." For there are surely many people who feel utterly "at home" in an environment where "earth" and "sky" show up hardly at all. Socrates is one example – to Phaedrus' accusation that he never steps outside the walls of Athens, he replies that he is "a lover of learning, and trees and open country won't teach me anything, whereas men in the town do" (*Phaedrus* 230 d). Another is Sartre, who said he never felt at home anywhere save in a fifth-floor Paris apartment. Is there a Heideggerian reply to this objection? Leaving aside Heidegger's personal tastes and prejudices, is there a way of using Heideggerian philosophy productively to think about dwelling in the city?

The first point to make is that Sartre's city, at least, is nothing like a "concrete jungle." There is, of course, a "sky," reflected, as Pissarro, Sisley, and Renoir saw, in the changing moods of the eighteenth-century terraces. And there is an "earth," the Seine, the Tuileries, Luxembourg, Champ de Mars and Palais gardens, the handsome avenue of trees along the Champs Elysées, and so on.

But let us put all this aside and suppose Sartre to have lived in a pure concrete jungle. Why, under this supposition, can he not dwell?

Dwelling, remember, is more than merely being on an earth, under a sky, before gods, and among mortals. It is for the place they constitute to show up as a radiant, "appropriating" presence, for it to show up as a holy place. In a post-Christian sense of the word, a dwelling-place is a place in which God reveals himself.

Bismarck (of all people) advises one never to trust a man who is immune to the wonders of nature. And Heidegger says that for "god-less" modern humanity, "traces of the fugitive gods" can appear, "if anywhere," only in the "site" of "earth and sky" (PLT 93). Both express the idea that to be immune to the wonders of nature is to be immune to the holy.

Why this special connection? Why, for most of us, is it Pan who speaks to us most readily? Why are we moved by mountain, forest and stream in a way we are not moved by streets and houses? Why are we moved by nature's "buildings" – Heidegger, it may be remembered, calls "earth" "the building bearer" (PLT 178) – in a way we are not moved by our own?

Just because, I think, they are *nature's* buildings. God, that is to say, is essentially the *other* of humanity, and, for most of us, if we experience it at all, otherness speaks to us only (or at least, principally) in nature. If, like Camus, we have the good fortune to come upon our own Tipasa (to have, what Heidegger calls an "*Ereignis* experience" [GA 65 70]), then we experience, with "gratitude" (GA 52 197), nature's (Being's) gift of our visible world, celebrate "the wonder that around us a world worlds, that there is something rather than nothing, that there are things, and we ourselves are in their midst" (GA 52 64). In the city, on the other hand, we can be proud only of our own cleverness. In the city we are alone, in nature we are not.

This, of course, is rhetorical oversimplification. The city may be built of materials which allow the local "earth" to speak to us in the midst of the city, as it does so eloquently in Oxford. It may be dominated, like Hobart, by the ever-changing but inescapable presence of a mountain. Or it may, like Constance, be enlivened at every turn by unavoidable views of the lake. It may, by good luck or good planning, be, like Wellington, a city infiltrated by "earth," a "garden city." It may (one day) be built by enlightened architects like Frank Lloyd Wright, who allow the city to be, in his words" "of" rather than "on" the earth.

Whatever Heidegger's personal prejudices, Heideggerian thinking is not anti-city, anti-modern. Productively used, it is a profoundly fruitful inspiration for thinking about how the city ought to be.[20]

Architects and town-planners – who have understood Heidegger very much better than philosophers – have known this for fifty years.

NOTES

1. Frederick A. Olafson, "The Unity of Heidegger's Thought," *Cambridge Companion to Heidegger* (1st ed.), ed. C. Guignon (Cambridge: Cambridge University Press, 1993): 97–121, p. 117.
2. What is important about Edmund Hilary and Peter Blake for New Zealanders, George Washington and Martin Luther King for Americans, is that, qua mythologized, they exemplify, *par excellence*, not just the virtues of being a good sailor or politician but rather the virtues of being a good human being.
3. A full discussion of Heidegger's account of truth is provided in my *Heidegger's Later Philosophy* (Cambridge: Cambridge University Press, 2002), Chapter 1.
4. *The Critique of Judgment*, trans. J. C. Meridith (Oxford: Oxford University Press, 1952), pp. 168–9.
5. For a full exposition and defence of this account of *Being and Time's* conception of authenticity, see my *Heidegger, Philosophy, Nazism* (Cambridge: Cambridge University Press, 1997), Chapter 2.
6. Notice that this is not the same as saying that being authentic is a matter of being true to the fundamental values of the society of one's birth – a point perhaps missed in *Being and Time*. One may, for example, emigrate and – slowly and always with difficulty – come to dwell in another fourfold. What shows up as holy and therefore authoritative for me may be not the birth-place, but the "second homeland." If this happens, however, I am, in a strong sense, no longer the person I was. Changing places – changing *dwelling*-places – I would maintain, is changing people.
7. F. Nietzsche, *Thus Spoke Zarathustra*, in *The Portable Nietzsche*, ed. and trans. W. Kaufmann (New York: Viking, 1954), I: 15.
8. Quoted in Michael Zimmerman *Heidegger's Confrontation with Modernity* (Bloomington: Indiana University Press, 1990), p. 71. This talk, given during the period of Heidegger's active involvement with Nazism, was delivered in a context of Nazi anti-intellectualism. But since Heidegger repeated similar sentiments all his life, there is no reason to doubt its sincerity.
9. On a visit to the Black Forest village of Todtnauberg (if I may be allowed a personal anecdote), I asked for directions to Heidegger's hut. "Did you know the Heideggers?" I asked the inhabitants of the farmer's house. "Of course, they collected their bread and milk from us." "What were they like?" "*Ganz einfache Leute* (very simple people)," was the reply.

10. *The Heidegger Controversy*, ed. Richard Wolin (Cambridge MA: MIT Press, 1993), p. 41. This is taken from a political speech delivered in May 1933 in praise of a former student of Freiburg University who had become a Nazi hero and martyr. Once again, however, there is no reason to doubt the sincerity of the sentiments expressed.

11. A. Camus, *The Myth of Sisyphus*, trans. J. O'Brien (London: Penguin, 1975), p. 33.

12. Quoted in my *Heidegger's Philosophy of Art* (Cambridge: Cambridge University Press, 2001), p. 120. Heidegger had an intense admiration for many modern artists and a considerable involvement in the "world" of modern art. In Chapter 4 of the above work, I discuss the apparent contradiction between his life, on the one hand, and his many condemnations of modern art as such, on the other.

13. See *Heidegger's Philosophy of Art* (*op. cit.*), Chapters 2 and 3.

14. For the thinging of ploughs, see the extraordinarily luminous series of late plough studies executed by Heidegger's friend, Georges Braque: *The Plough* of 1959–60, *The Belgian Plough* of 1962, and *The Weeding Machine* of 1961–3, Braque's last completed canvas.

15. *The End of the Golden Weather: A Voyage into a New Zealand Childhood* (Wellington: Victoria University Press, 1970), p. 31. Quoted in Jeff Malpas *Place and Experience* (Cambridge: Cambridge University Press, 1999), p. 183.

16. Camus, *Myth of Sisyphus*, pp. 175, 177.

17. Ibid, p. 178.

18. Ibid, pp. 179–80.

19. Quoted in Michael Zimmerman's *Heidegger's Confrontation with Modernity* (*op. cit.*) p. 71.

20. I try to demonstrate this claim in detail – with special reference to architecture – in Chapter 8 of *Heidegger's Later Philosophy* (*op. cit.*).

BIBLIOGRAPHY

A complete, up-to-date bibliography of works by and about Heidegger would be a vast undertaking. Hans-Martin Sass's 1975 bibliography, which covered the period from 1917 to 1972, included entire chapters called "Heidegger in Japan" and "Literature on Heidegger in the Soviet Union" and already contained more than 3,700 entries! Fortunately, some excellent bibliographies are available. The bibliography offered here is therefore quite selective, emphasizing recent books and collections in English most likely to be helpful to students and nonspecialists.

BIBLIOGRAPHIES

Franzen, Winfried. *Martin Heidegger*. Stuttgart: J. B. Metzler, 1976. (This volume provides a thorough overview of Heidegger's work in German, with carefully selected bibliographies arranged by topic.)

Groth, Miles. *Translating Heidegger*. Amherst, NY: Humanities, 2004. Professor Groth also provides an exhaustive bibliography on his Web page (http://www.wagner.edu/departments/psychology/grothpubs).

Nordquist, Joan, ed. *Martin Heidegger: A Bibliography*. Santa Cruz, CA: Reference and Research Service, 1990.

Sass, Hans-Martin. *Martin Heidegger: Bibliography and Glossary*. Bowling Green, OH: Bowling Green State University, Philosophy Documentation Center, 1982.

Sheehan, Thomas, ed. *Heidegger: The Man and the Thinker*. Chicago: Precedent, 1981. (This valuable collection contains, in addition to important works by Heidegger and by scholars writing about him, a bibliography matching original writings to translations and a detailed bibliography of writings about Heidegger.)

In addition, the annual journal, *Heidegger Studies*, provides an updated list of volumes published in the Collected Works and their translations into English. The most complete bibliography of secondary literature on Heidegger – found at http://www.ub.uni-freiburg.de/referate/02/heidegger/heidgg90.html – contains nearly 4,000 articles published between 1990 and 2005. Also see: http://www.webcom.com/~paf/ereignis.html, http://www.heidegger.org/bibliographie.htm, http://www.freewebs.com/m3smg2.

SELECTED WORKS IN GERMAN

In 1974 the German publisher Vittorio Klostermann (Frankfurt am Main) began preparations for the publication of Heidegger's collected works (*Martin Heidegger: Gesamtausgabe*). Around 100 volumes are planned. The series will consist of four divisions: (I) published writings, 1910–76; (II) lectures from Marburg and Freiburg, 1923–44; (III) unpublished papers; and (IV) notes and fragments (including notes on previously published works, letters, summaries, notes on seminars, etc.). Heidegger, who worked extensively with the editors of the *Collected Works* during the final years of his life, specified the form he wanted the volumes to have (e.g., no volume may contain an index). There is, however, some question whether these volumes will be the definitive edition for Heidegger scholarship. Those familiar with the project have suggested that Heidegger made revisions to the earlier manuscripts without this fact being explicitly noted in the texts. On this subject, see Thomas Sheehan, "Caveat Lector: The New Heidegger," *New York Review of Books*, December 4, 1980, pp. 39–41.

As of 2005 the publication schedule for the *Collected Works* was as follows (volumes already published have publication dates in brackets; an asterisk denotes the anticipated date of publication):

Division 1

1. *Frühe Schriften* (1912–16). Edited by Friedrich-Wilhelm von Herrmann [1978].
2. *Sein und Zeit* (1927). Edited by Friedrich-Wilhelm von Herrmann [1977].
3. *Kant und das Problem der Metaphysik* (1929). Edited by Friedrich-Wilhelm von Herrmann [1991].
4. *Erläuterungen zu Hölderlins Dichtung* (1936–38). Edited by Friedrich-Wilhelm von Herrmann [2nd ed., 1996].
5. *Holzwege* (1935–46). Edited by Friedrich-Wilhelm von Herrmann [2nd ed., 2003].

6. Vol. 1, *Nietzsche* I (1936–39) [1996]; Vol. 2, *Nietzsche* II (1939–46) [1997]. Edited by Brigitte Schillbach.
7. *Vorträge und Aufsätze* (1936–53). Edited by Friedrich-Wilhelm von Herrmann [2000].
8. *Was heisst Denken?* (1951–2). Edited by Paola-Ludovika Coriando [2002].
9. *Wegmarken* (1919–61). Edited by Friedrich-Wilhelm von Herrmann [2nd ed. 1996].
10. *Der Satz vom Grund* (1955–6). Edited by Petra Jaeger [1997].
11. *Identität and Differenz* (1955–7).
12. *Unterwegs zur Sprache* (1950–9). Edited by Friedrich-Wilhelm von Herrmann [1985].
13. *Aus der Erfahrung des Denkens* (1910–76). Edited by Hermann Heidegger [2nd ed., 2002].
14. *Zur Sache des Denkens* (1962–4).
15. *Seminare* (1951–73). Edited by Curd Ochwadt [1986].
16. *Reden und andere Zeugnisse eines Lebensweges* (1910–76). Edited by Hermann Heidegger [2000].

Division II

Marburg Lectures 1923–1928

17. *Der Beginn der neuzeitlichen Philosophie* (winter semester, 1923–4). Edited by Friedrich-Wilhelm von Herrmann [1994].
18. *Grundbegriffe der aristotelischen Philosophie* (summer semester, 1924). Edited by Mark Michalski [2002].
19. *Platon: "Sophistes"* (winter semester, 1924–5). Edited by Ingeborg Schüssler [1992].
20. *Prolegomena zur Geschichte des Zeitbegriffs* (summer semester, 1925). Edited by Petra Jaeger [2nd ed., 1988].
21. *Logik. Die Frage nach der Wahrheit* (winter semester, 1925–26). Edited by Walter Biemel [2nd ed., 1995].
22. *Die Grundbegriffe der antiken Philosophie* (summer semester, 1926). Edited by Franz-Karl Blust [2nd ed., 2004].
23. *Geschichte der Philosophie von Thomas v. Aquin bis Kant* (winter semester, 1926–7). Edited by Helmuth Vetter.
24. *Die Grundprobleme der Phänomenologie* (summer semester, 1927). Edited by Friedrich-Wilhelm von Herrmann [3rd ed., 1997].

25. *Phänomenologische Interpretation von Kants Kritik der reinen Venunft* (winter semester, 1927–8). Edited by Ingtraud Görland [3rd ed., 1997].

26. *Metaphysische Anfangsgründe der Logik im Ausgang von Leibniz* (summer semester, 1928). Edited by Klaus Held [2nd ed., 1990].

Freiburg Lectures 1928–1944

27. *Einleitung in die Philosophie* (winter semester, 1928–9). Edited by Otto Saame and Ina Saame-Speidel [2nd ed., 2001].

28. *Der deutsche Idealismus (Fichte, Hegel, Schelling) and die philosophische Problemlage der Gegenwart* (summer semester, 1929). Edited by Claudius Strabe [1997].

29/30. *Die Grundbegriffe der Metaphysik. Welt – Endlichkeit – Einsamkeit* (winter semester, 1929–30). Edited by Friedrich-Wilhelm von Herrmann [3rd ed., 2004].

31. *Vom Wesen der menschlichen Freiheit. Einleitung in die Philosophie* (summer semester, 1930). Edited by Hartmut Tietjen [2nd ed., 1994].

32. *Hegels Phänomenologie des Geistes* (winter semester, 1930–1). Edited by Ingtraud Görland [3rd ed., 1997].

33. *Aristoteles, Metaphysik Theta 1–3. Von Wesen und Wirklichkeit der Kraft* (summer semester, 1931). Edited by Heinrich Hüni [2nd ed., 1990].

34. *Vom Wesen der Wahrheit. Zu Platons Höhlengleichnis and Theätet* (winter semester, 1931–2). Edited by Hermann Morchen [2nd ed., 1997].

35. *Der Anfang der abendländischen Philosophie (Anaximander und Parmenides)* (summer semester, 1932). Edited by Heinrich Hüni.

36/37. *Sein und Wahrheit 1. Die Grundfrage der Philosophie* (summer semester, 1933); 2. *Von Wesen der Wahrheit* (winter semester, 1933–4). Edited by Hartmut Tietjen [2001].

38. *Logik als Frage nach dem Wesen der Sprache* (summer semester, 1934). Edited by Günther Seubold [1998].

39. *Hölderlins Hymnen "Germanien" und "Der Rhein"* (winter semester, 1934–5). Edited by Susanne Ziegler [3rd ed., 1999].

40. *Einführung in die Metaphysik* (summer semester, 1935). Edited by Petra Jaeger [1983].

41. *Die Frage nach dem Ding. Zu Kants Lehre von den transzenden-talen Grundsätzen* (winter semester, 1935–6). Edited by Petra Jaeger [1984].

42. *Schelling: Vom Wesen der menschlichen Freiheit (1809)* (summer semester, 1936). Edited by Ingrid Schüssler [1988].

43. *Nietzsche: Der Wille zur Macht als Kunst* (winter semester, 1936–7). Edited by Bernd Heimbüchel [1985].

44. *Nietzsches metaphysische Grundstellung im abendländischen Denken: Die ewige Wiederkehr des Gleichen* (summer semester, 1937). Edited by Marion Heinz [1986].

45. *Grundfragen der Philosophie. Ausgewählte "Probleme" der "Logik"* (winter semester, 1937–8). Edited by Friedrich Wilhelm von Herrmann [2nd ed., 1992].

46. *Zur Auslegung von Nietzsches II. Unzeitgemässer Betrachtung "Vom Nutzen und Nachteil der Historie für das Leben"* (winter semester, 1938–9). Edited by Hans-Joachim Friedrich [2003].

47. *Nietzsches Lehre vom Willen zur Macht als Erkenntnis* (summer semester, 1939). Edited by Eberhard Hanser [1989].

48. *Nietzsche: Der europäische Nihilismus* (second trimester, 1940). Edited by Petra Jaeger [1986].

49. *Die Metaphysik des deutschen Idealismus. Zur erneuten Auslegung von Schelling: Philosophische Untersuchungen über das Wesen der menschlichen Freiheit und die damit zusammenhangenden Gegenstände (1809).* (1st trimester, 1941). Edited by Günter Seubold [1991].

50. *Nietzsches Metaphysik* (1941–2). *Einleitung in die Philosophie–Denken und Dichten* (1944–5). Edited by Petra Jeager [2nd ed., 1990].

51. *Grundbegriffe* (summer semester, 1941). Edited by Petra Jaeger [2nd ed., 1991].

52. *Hölderlins Hymne "Andenken"* (winter semester, 1941–2). Edited by Curd Ochwadt [2nd ed., 1992].

53. *Hölderlins Hymne "Der Ister"* (summer semester, 1942). Edited by Walter Biemel [2nd ed., 1993].

54. *Parmenides* (winter semester, 1942–3). Edited by Manfred S. Frings [2nd ed., 1992].

55. *Heraklit. 1. Der Anfang des abendländischen Denkens* (summer semester, 1943); *2. Logik. Heraklits Lehre vom Logos* (summer semester, 1944). Edited by Manfred S. Frings [3rd ed., 1994].

Early Freiburg Lectures 1919–1923

56/57. *Zur Bestimmung der Philosophie*. 1. *Die Idee der Philosophie und das Weltanschauungsproblem* (war emergency semester, 1919); 2. *Phänomenologie und transzendentale Wertsphilosophie* (summer semester, 1919); 3. Anhang (summer semester, 1919). Edited by Bernd Heimbüchel [1987].

58. *Grundprobleme der Phänomenologie* (winter semester, 1919–20). Edited by Hans-Helmuth Gander [1992].

59. *Phänomenologie der Anschaung und des Ausdrucks. Theorie der philosophischen Begriffsbildung* (summer semester, 1920). Edited by Claudius Strube [1993].

60. *Phänomenologie des religiösen Lebens*. 1. *Einleitung in die Phänomenologie der Religion* (winter semester, 1920–1); 2. *Augustinus und der Neuplatonismus* (summer semester, 1921); 3. *Die philosophischen Grundlagen der mittelalterlichen Mystik* (notes for an undelivered lecture course 1918–9). Edited by Claudius Strube [1995].

61. *Phänomenologische Interpretationen zu Aristoteles. Einführung in die phänomenologische Forschung* (winter semester, 1921–2). Edited by Walter Bröcker and Käte Bröcker-Oltmanns [2nd ed., 1994].

62. *Phänomenologische Interpretationen ausgewählter Abhandlungen des Aristoteles zu Ontologie und Logik* (summer semester, 1922). Edited by Günther Neumann.

63. *Ontologie. Hermeneutik der Faktizität* (summer semester, 1923). Edited by Käte Bröcker-Oltmanns [2nd ed., 1995].

Division III

64. *Der Begriff der Zeit* (1924). Edited by Friedrich-Wilhelm von Herrmann [2005].

65. *Beiträge zur Philosophie (Vom Ereignis)* (1936–8). Edited by Friedrich-Wilhelm von Herrmann [3rd ed., 2003].

66. *Besinnung* (1938/9). Edited by Friedrich-Wilhelm von Herrmann.

67. *Metaphysik und Nihilismus*. 1. *Die Uberwindung der Metaphysik* (1938/39); 2. *Das Wesen des Nihilismus* (1946–8). Edited by Hans-Joachim Friedrich [1999].

68. *Hegel* (1938/39, 1942/43). Edited by Ingrid Schlüsser [1993].

69. *Die Geschichte des Seyns* (1938/40); *Koinôn. Aus der Geschichte des Seyns* (1939). Edited by Peter Trawny [1998].

70. *Über den Anfang* (1941). Edited by Paola-Ludovika Coriando.

71. *Das Ereignis* (1941–42). Edited by Friedrich-Wilhelm von Herrmann.

72. *Die Stege des Anfangs* (1944). Edited by Friedrich-Wilhelm von Herrmann.

73. *Zum Ereignis-Denken.*

74. *Zum Wesen der Sprache.* Edited by Thomas Regehly.

75. *Zu Hölderlin – Griechenlandreisen.* Edited by Curd Ochwalt [2000].

76. *Zur Metaphysik – Neuzeitlichen Wissenschaft – Technik.* Edited by Claudius Strube.

77. *Feldweg-Gespräche* (1944–5). Edited by Ingrid Schlüsser [1995].

78. *Der Spruch des Anaximander* (1946). Edited by Ingeborg Schüssler.

79. *Bremer und Freiburger Vorträge.* Edited by Petra Jaeger [1994].

80. *Vorträge.* Edited by Hartmut Tietjen.

81. *Gedachtes.* Edited by Paola-Ludovika Coriando.

Division IV

82. *Zu eignen Veröffentlichung.*

83. *Seminare: Platon – Aristoteles – Augustinus.* Edited by Mark Michalski.

84. *Seminare: Leibniz – Kant.* Edited by Hans-Helmuth Gander.

85. *Seminar: Vom Wesen der Sprache. Die Metaphysik der Sprache und die Wesung des Wortes. Zu Herders Abhandlung "Über den Ursprung der Sprache."* Edited by Ingrid Schüssler [1999].

86. *Seminare: Hegel Schelling.* Edited by Peter Trawny.

87. *Nietzsche Seminare 1937 und 1944. 1. Nietzsches metaphysische Grundstellung (Sein und Schein); 2. Skizzen zu Grundbegriffe des Denkens.* Edited by Peter von Ruckteschell [2004].

88. *Seminare: 1. Die metaphysischen Grundstellung des abendländischen Denkens; 2. Einübung in das philosophische Denken.* Edited by Alfred Denker.

89. *Zollikoner Seminare.* Edited by Claudius Strube.

90. *Zu Ernst Jünger.* Edited by Peter Trawny [2004].

91. *Ergänzungen und Denksplitter.*

92. *Ausgewählter Briefe: I.*

93. *Ausgewählter Briefe: II.*

94. *Überlegungen II–IV.*

95. *Überlegungen VII–XI.*
96. *Überlegungen XII–XV.*
97. *Anmerkungen II–V.*
98. *Anmerkungen VI–IX.*
99. *Vier Hefte I – Der Feldweg; Vier Hefte II – Durch Ereignis zu Ding und Welt.*
100. *Vigilae I, II.*
101. *Winke I, II.*
102. *Vorläufige I–IV.*

The *Collected Works* editions of previously published volumes contain the pagination for the earlier editions in the margins.

Some especially important works by Heidegger in German, which are available as individual volumes, are the following:

Gelassenheit. 2nd ed. Pfullingen: Günther Neske, 1960.
Holzwege. 5th ed. Frankfurt am Main: Vittorio Klostermann, 1972.
Kant und das Problem der Metaphysik. 2nd ed. Frankfurt am Main: Vittorio Klostermann, 1991.
Nietzsche. 2 vols. 2nd ed. Pfullingen: Günther Neske, 1961.
Der Satz vom Grund. 4th ed. Pfullingen: Günther Neske, 1971.
Sein and Zeit. 11th ed. Tübingen: Max Niemeyer, 1963.
Die Technik and die Kehre. Pfullingen: Günther Neske, 1962.
Unterwegs zur Sprache. 3rd ed. Pfullingen: Günther Neske, 1965.
Vorträge and Aufsätze. 3rd ed. Pfullingen: Günther Neske, 1967.
Was heist Denken? Tübingen: Max Niemeyer, 1954.
Wegmarken. Frankfurt am Main: Vittorio Klostermann, 1967.

ENGLISH TRANSLATIONS

Heidegger's collected works, letters, and other writings are rapidly being translated into English. A fine bibliography of Heidegger's works in English is found in Miles Groth, *Translating Heidegger* (Amherst, NY: Humanity, 2004) and on his Web site. Some especially valuable translations are the following:

Basic Problems of Phenomenology. Translated by Albert Hofstadter. Bloomington: Indiana University Press, 1982.
Basic Questions of Philosophy: Selected "Problems" of "Logic." Translated by Richard Rojcewicz and André Schuwer. Bloomington: Indiana University Press, 1994.

Basic Writings. Edited by David F. Krell. New York: Harper & Row, 1977. Revised and expanded, 1993.

Being and Time. Translated by John Macquarrie and Edward Robinson. New York: Harper & Row, 1962. Newly translated by Joan Stambaugh. Albany: State University of New York, 1996.

The Concept of Time. Translated by William McNeill. Oxford: Blackwell, 1992.

Contributions to Philosophy (From Enowning). Translated by Parvis Emad and Kenneth Maly. Bloomington: Indiana University Press, 1999.

Discourse on Thinking. Translated by John M. Anderson and E. Hans Freund. New York: Harper & Row, 1966.

"A Discussion between Ernst Cassirer and Martin Heidegger." Translated by Francis Slade. In *The Existentialist Tradition: Selected Writings*. Edited by Nino Langiulli. Garden City, NY: Doubleday, 1971.

Early Greek Thinking. Translated by David Farrell Krell and Frank Capuzzi. New York: Harper & Row, 1975.

Elucidations of Hölderlin's Poetry. Translated by Keith Hoeller. Amherst, NY: Humanity, 2000.

The End of Philosophy. Translated by Joan Stambaugh. New York: Harper & Row, 1973.

The Essence of Reasons. Translated by Terrence Malick. Evanston, IL: Northwestern University Press, 1969.

Existence and Being. Edited by Werner Brock. Chicago: Regnery, 1949.

The Fundamental Concepts of Metaphysics: World, Finitude, Solitude. Translated by William McNeill and Nicholas Walker. Bloomington: Indiana University Press, 1995.

Hegel's Concept of Experience. Translated by J. Glenn Gray. New York: Harper & Row, 1970.

History of the Concept of Time: Prolegomena. Translated by Theodore Kisiel. Bloomington: Indiana University Press. 1985.

Identity and Difference. Translated by Joan Stambaugh. New York: Harper & Row, 1969.

Introduction to Metaphysics. Translated by Ralph Manheim. New Haven, CT: Yale University Press, 1959. New translation by Gregory Fried and Richard Polt. New Haven, CT: Yale University Press, 2000.

Kant and the Problem of Metaphysics. Translated by James S. Churchill. Bloomington: Indiana University Press, 1962. Retranslated by Richard Taft. Bloomington: Indiana University Press, 1997.

Martin Heidegger and National Socialism: Questions and Answers. Edited by Gunther Neske and Emil Kettering. Translated by Lisa Harries. New York: Paragon House, 1990. (Contains "The Self Assertion of the German University" [the rectoral address], "The Rectorate 1933/34: Facts and

Thoughts," the *Spiegel* interview ["Only a God Can Save Us"], and "Martin Heidegger in Conversation" with Richard Wisser.)

The Metaphysical Foundations of Logic. Translated by Michael Heim. Bloomington: Indiana University Press, 1984.

Nietzsche I: The Will to Power as Art. Edited and translated by David F. Krell. New York: Harper & Row, 1979.

Nietzsche II: The Eternal Recurrence of the Same. Edited and translated by David F. Krell. New York: Harper & Row, 1984.

Nietzsche III: The Will to Power as Knowledge and Metaphysics. Edited by David F. Krell. Translated by Joan Stambaugh. New York: Harper & Row, 1987.

Nietzsche IV: Nihilism. Edited by David F. Krell. Translated by Frank A. Capuzzi. New York: Harper & Row, 1982.

Off the Beaten Path. Translated by Julian Young and Kenneth Hayes. Cambridge: Cambridge University Press, 2002.

On Time and Being. Translated by Joan Stambaugh. New York: Harper & Row, 1972.

On the Way to Language. Translated by Peter D. Hertz. New York: Harper & Row, 1971.

Ontology: The Hermeneutics of Facticity. Translated by John van Buren. Bloomington: Indiana University Press, 1999.

Parmenides. Translated by André Schuwer and Richard Rojcewicz. Bloomington: Indiana University Press, 1993.

Pathmarks. Edited by William McNeill. Cambridge: Cambridge University Press, 1998.

The Piety of Thinking. Translated by James Hart and John Maraldo. Bloomington: Indiana University Press, 1976.

"Plato's Doctrine of Truth." Translated by John Barlow. In *Philosophy in the Twentieth Century*. Vol. 3. Edited by William Barrett and Henry D. Aiken. New York: Random House, 1962.

Poetry, Language, Thought. Translated by Albert Hofstadter. New York: Harper & Row, 1971.

The Principle of Reason. Translated by Reginald Lilly. Bloomington: Indiana University Press, 1991.

The Question of Being. Translated by William Kluback and Jean T. Wilde. New York: Twayne, 1958.

The Question Concerning Technology and Other Essays. Translated by William Lovitt. New York: Harper & Row, 1977.

Schelling's Treatise on Human Freedom. Translated by Joan Stambaugh. Athens: Ohio University Press, 1985.

Supplements: From the Earliest Essays to "Being and Time" and Beyond. Edited by John van Buren. Albany: State University of New York, 2002.

Towards the Definition of Philosophy. Translated by Ted Sadler. London: Continuum, 2000.

"The Way Back into the Ground of Metaphysics" (Introduction to "What Is Metaphysics?"). Translated by Walter Kaufmann. In *Existentialism from Dostoyevsky to Sartre*. Edited by Walter Kaufmann. Cleveland: World, 1965.

What Is Called Thinking? Translated by Fred D. Wieck and J. Glenn Gray. New York: Harper & Row, 1968.

What Is Philosophy? Translated by William Kluback and Jean T. Wilde. New Haven, CT: College and University Press, 1958.

What Is a Thing? Translated by W. B. Barton and Vera Deutsch. Chicago: Regnery, 1969.

"Why Do I Stay in the Provinces?" Translated by Thomas Sheehan. In *Heidegger: The Man and the Thinker*. Edited by Thomas Sheehan. Chicago: Precedent, 1981.

Zollikon Seminars: Protocols – Conversations – Letters. Translated by Franz Mayr and Richard Askay. Evanston, IL: Northwestern, 2001.

BACKGROUND AND BIOGRAPHICAL

Arendt, Hannah, and Heidegger, Martin. *Letters: 1925–1975*. Translated by Andrew Shields. New York: Harcourt, 2003.

Bambach, Charles R. *Heidegger, Dilthey, and the Crisis of Historicism*. Ithaca, NY: Cornell University Press, 1995.

———. *Heidegger's Roots: Nietzsche, National Socialism, and the Greeks*. Ithaca, NY: Cornell University Press, 2003.

Clark, Timothy. *Martin Heidegger*. London: Routledge, 2001.

Elliott, Brian. *Phenomenology and Imagination in Husserl and Heidegger*. Routledge Studies in Twentieth Century Philosophy. New York: Routledge, 2004.

Friedman, Michael. *A Parting of the Ways: Carnap, Cassirer, and Heidegger*. Chicago: Open Court, 2000.

Gadamer, Hans-Georg. *Philosophical Hermeneutics*. Edited and translated by David E. Linge. Berkeley: University of California Press, 1976.

———. *Philosophical Apprenticeships*. Translated by Robert R. Sullivan. Cambridge, MA: The MIT Press, 1985.

———. *Heidegger's Ways*. Translated by John W. Stanley. Albany: State University of New York Press, 1994.

Gorner, Paul. *Twentieth-century German Philosophy*. Oxford: Oxford University Press, 2000.

Grondin, Jean. *Sources of Hermeneutics*. Albany: State University of New York Press, 1995.

Habermas, Jürgen. *Philosophical-Political Profiles.* Translated by Frederick G. Lawrence. Cambridge, MA: The MIT Press, 1983.

_____. *The Philosophical Discourse of Modernity: Twelve Lectures.* Translated by Frederick G. Lawrence. Cambridge, MA: The MIT Press, 1987.

Hopkins, Burt C. *Intentionality in Husserl and Heidegger: The Problem of the Original Method and Phenomenon of Phenomenology.* Dordrecht: Kluwer Academic Publishers, 1993.

Hoy, David Couzens. *The Critical Circle: Literature, History, and Philosophical Hermeneutics.* Berkeley: University of California Press, 1978.

Husserl, Edmund. *Psychological and Transcendental Phenomenology and the Confrontation with Heidegger (1927–1931): The Encyclopaedia Britannica Article, the Amsterdam Lectures, "Phenomenology and Anthropology," and Husserl's Marginal Notes in* Being and Time *and* Kant and the Problem of Metaphysics. Translated and edited by Richard E. Palmer and Thomas Sheehan. Dordrecht: Kluwer Academic Publishers, 1997.

Kisiel, Theodore. "On the Way to 'Being and Time': Introduction to the Translation of Heidegger's *Prolegomena zur Geschichte des Zeitbegriffs.*" *Research in Phenomenology,* 15 (1985): 193–226.

_____. "Why the First Draft of 'Being and Time' Was Never Published." *Journal of the British Society for Phenomenology,* 20 (January 1989): 3–22.

_____. *The Genesis of Heidegger's* Being and Time. Berkeley: University of California Press, 1993.

_____. *Heidegger's Way of Thought: Critical and Interpretative Signposts.* London: Continuum, 2002.

Kisiel, Theodore, and van Buren, John, eds. *Reading Heidegger from the Start.* Albany: State University of New York Press, 1994.

Löwith, Karl. *Martin Heidegger and European Nihilism.* Translated by Gary Steiner. New York: Columbia University Press, 1995.

May, Reinhard. *Heidegger's Hidden Sources: East Asian Influences on His Work.* Translated by Graham Parkes. New York: Routledge, 1996.

Megill, Allan. *Prophets of Extremity: Nietzsche, Heidegger, Foucault, Derrida.* Berkeley: University of California Press, 1985.

Misch, Georg. *Lebensphilosophie and Phänomenologie. Eine Auseinandersetzung der Diltheyschen Richtung mit Heidegger and Husserl.* 3rd ed. Darmstadt: Wissenschaftliche Buchgesellschaft, 1967.

Moran, Dermot. *Introduction to Phenomenology.* London: Routledge, 2000.

Noreña, Carlos G. "Heidegger on Suárez: The 1927 Marburg Lectures." *International Philosophical Quarterly,* 23 (December 1983): 407–24.

Ott, Hugo. *Martin Heidegger: Unterwegs zur seiner Biographie.* Frankfurt am Main: Campus, 1988. Translated as *Martin Heidegger: A Political Life* by Allan Blunden. New York: Basic Books, 1993.

Petzet, Heinrich Wiegand. *Auf einen Stern zugehen: Begegnungen and Gespräche mit Martin Heidegger, 1929–1976*. Frankfurt am Main: Societäts-Verlag, 1983. Translated as *Encounters and Dialogues with Martin Heidegger, 1929–1976*. By Parvis Emad and Kenneth Maly. Chicago: University of Chicago Press, 1993.

Pöggler, Otto. *Heidegger and die hermeneutische Philosophie*. Freiburg: Alber, 1983.

———. *The Paths of Heidegger's Life and Thought*. Atlantic Highlands, NJ: Humanities Press, 1997.

Risser, James. *Heidegger toward the Turn: Essays on the Work of the 1930s*. Albany: State University of New York Press, 1999.

Rockmore, Tom. *Heidegger, German Idealism and Neo-Kantianism*. Amherst, NY: Humanity Books, 2000.

Schnädelbach, Herbert. *Philosophy in Germany, 1831–1933*. Cambridge: Cambridge University Press, 1984.

Sheehan, Thomas. "The 'Original Form' of *Sein and Zeit*: Heidegger's *Der Begriff der Zeit* (1924)." *Journal of the British Society for Phenomenology*, 10 (May 1979): 78–83.

Sherover, Charles M. *Heidegger, Kant and Time*. Bloomington: Indiana University Press, 1971.

Solomon, Robert C. *From Rationalism to Existentialism: The Existentialists and Their Nineteenth-century Background*. New York: Harper & Row, 1972.

Spiegelberg, Herbert. *The Phenomenological Movement: An Historical Introduction*. 2 vols. The Hague: Nijhoff, 1969.

Stapleton, Timothy J. *Husserl and Heidegger: The Question of a Phenomenological Beginning*. Albany: State University of New York Press, 1983.

Taminiaux, Jacques. "Poiesis and Praxis in Fundamental Ontology." *Research in Phenomenology*, 17 (1987): 137–69.

———. "The Interpretation of Greek Philosophy in Heidegger's Fundamental Ontology." *Journal of the British Society for Phenomenology*, 19 (January 1988): 3–14.

GENERAL

Babich, Babette E., ed. *From Phenomenology to Thought, Errancy, and Desire*. Dordrecht: Kluwer Academic Publishers, 1995.

Barash, Jeffrey Andrew. *Martin Heidegger and the Problem of Historical Meaning*. Dordrecht: Nijhoff, 1985. Revised and expanded edition. New York: Fordham University Press, 2003.

Bernasconi, Robert. *The Question of Language in Heidegger's History of Being*. Atlantic Highlands, NJ: Humanities Press, 1985.

Blattner, William D. *Heidegger's Temporal Idealism*. Cambridge: Cambridge University Press, 1999.

Bourgeois, Patrick L., and Schalow, Frank. "The Integrity and Fallenness of Human Existence." *Southern Journal of Philosophy*, 25 (Spring 1987): 123–32.

Brandom, Robert. "Heidegger's Categories." *Monist*, 66 (July 1983): 387–409.

Buckley, R. Philip. *Husserl, Heidegger, and the Crisis of Philosophical Responsibility*. Dordrecht: Kluwer Academic Publishers, 1992.

Caputo, John D. *Radical Hermeneutics: Repetition, Deconstruction, and the Hermeneutic Project*. Bloomington: Indiana University Press, 1987.

———. *Demythologizing Heidegger*. Bloomington: Indiana University Press, 1993.

———, ed. *Heidegger*. American Catholic Philosophical Quarterly Expanded Special Edition, Vol. 69, No. 2 (Spring 1995). Published by American Catholic Philosophical Association, Washington, DC.

Carman, Taylor. *Heidegger's Analytic: Interpretation, Discourse, and Authenticity in* Being and Time. New York: Cambridge University Press, 2003.

Carr, David. *Time, Narrative, and History*. Bloomington: Indiana University Press, 1986.

Chanter, Tina. *Time, Death, and the Feminine: Levinas with Heidegger*. Stanford, CA: Stanford University Press, 2001.

Collins, Jeff, and Selina, Howard. *Introducing Heidegger*. New York: Totem Books, 1998.

Coltman, Rodney R. *The Language of Hermeneutics: Gadamer and Heidegger in Dialogue*. Albany: State University of New York Press, 1998.

Comay, Rebecca, and McCumber, John, eds. *Endings: Questions of Memory in Hegel and Heidegger*. Evanston, IL: Northwestern University Press, 1999.

Cooper, David E. *Heidegger*. London: Claridge Press, 1996.

Dahlstrom, Daniel. *Heidegger's Concept of Truth*. Cambridge: Cambridge University Press, 2001.

Dallmayr, Fred. *Between Freiburg and Frankfurt: Toward a Critical Ontology*. Amherst: University of Massachusetts Press, 1991.

Dastur, Françoise. *Heidegger and the Question of Time*. Translated by François Raffoul and David Pettigrew. Atlantic Highlands, NJ: Humanities Press, 1998.

De Boer, Karin. *Thinking in the Light of Time: Heidegger's Encounter with Hegel*. Albany: State University of New York Press, 2000.

Denker, Alfred. *Historical Dictionary of Heidegger's Philosophy*. Lanham, MD: Scarecrow Press, 2000.

Derrida, Jacques. *Margins of Philosophy*. Translated with additional notes by Alan Bass. Chicago: University of Chicago Press, 1982.

———. *The Gift of Death*. Translated by David Wills. Chicago: University of Chicago Press, 1995.

DiCenso, James. *Hermeneutics and the Disclosure of Truth: A Study in the Work of Heidegger, Gadamer, and Ricoeur*. Charlottesville: University of Virginia Press, 1990.

Dostal, Robert J. "The Problem of 'Indifferenz' in 'Sein and Zeit.'" *Philosophy and Phenomenological Research*, 43 (September 1982): 43–58.

Dreyfus, Hubert L. *Being-in-the-World: A Commentary on Heidegger's* Being and Time, *Division* I. Cambridge, MA: The MIT Press, 1991.

Dreyfus, Hubert L., and Hall, Harrison, eds. *Heidegger: A Critical Reader*. Oxford: Blackwell, 1992.

Dreyfus, Hubert L., and Wrathall, Mark A., eds. *Heidegger Reexamined* (4 vols.). New York: Routledge, 2002.

———. *A Companion to Heidegger*. Blackwell Companions to Philosophy. Oxford: Blackwell Publishers, 2005.

Faulconer, James E., and Wrathall, Mark A. *Appropriating Heidegger*. Cambridge: Cambridge University Press, 2000.

Fell, Joseph P. *Heidegger and Sartre: An Essay on Being and Place*. New York: Columbia University Press, 1979.

Føllesdal, Dagfinn. "Husserl and Heidegger on the Role of Actions in the Constitution of the World." In *Essays in Honor of Jaakko Hintikka*. Edited by Esa Saarinen, et al. Dordrecht: Reidel, 1979.

Frede, Dorothea. "Heidegger and the Scandal of Philosophy." In *Human Nature and Natural Knowledge*. Edited by A. Donagan, A. Perovich, and M. Wedin. Dordrecht: Reidel, 1986.

———. "Beyond Realism and Anti-Realism: Rorty on Heidegger and Davidson." *Review of Metaphysics*, 40 (June 1987): 733–57.

Fried, Gregory. *Heidegger's Polemos: From Being to Politics*. New Haven, CT: Yale University Press, 2000.

Fried, Gregory, and Polt, Richard, eds. *A Companion to Heidegger's* Introduction to Metaphysics. New Haven, CT: Yale University Press, 2001.

Fritsche, Johannes. *Historical Destiny and National Socialism in Heidegger's* Being and Time. Berkeley: University of California Press, 1999.

Fynsk, Christopher. *Heidegger, Thought and Historicity*. Ithaca, NY: Cornell University Press, 1993.

Gelven, Michael. *A Commentary of Heidegger's* Being and Time. 2nd ed. DeKalb, IL: Northern Illinois University Press, 1989.

Gillespie, Michael Allen. *Hegel, Heidegger, and the Ground of History*. Chicago: University of Chicago Press, 1984.

Golomb, Jacob. *In Search of Authenticity: From Kierkegaard to Camus*. New York: Routledge, 1995.

Grondin, Jean. *Le tournant dans la pensée de Martin Heidegger*. Paris: Presses universitaires de France, 1987.

Guignon, Charles B. *Heidegger and the Problem of Knowledge*. Indianapolis: Hackett, 1983.

_____. "Heidegger's 'Authenticity' Revisited." *Review of Metaphysics*, 38 (December 1984): 321–39.

_____. "Philosophy after Wittgenstein and Heidegger." *Philosophy and Phenomenological Research*, 50 (June 1990): 649–72.

Haar, Michel. *Martin Heidegger: Cahier a été dirige*. Paris: L'Heme, 1983.

_____. *Heidegger and the Essence of Man*. Albany: State University of New York Press, 1993.

_____. *The Song of the Earth: Heidegger and the Grounds of the History of Being*. Bloomington: Indiana University Press, 1993.

Hall, Harrison. "Love and Death: Kierkegaard and Heidegger on Authentic and Inauthentic Human Existence." *Inquiry*, 27 (July 1984): 179–97.

Harries, Karsten, and Jamme, Christoph, eds. *Martin Heidegger: Politics, Art and Technology*. New York: Holmes and Meier, 1994.

Haugeland, John. "Heidegger on Being a Person." *Nous*, 16 (March 1982): 6–26.

Heim, Michael. "The Finite Framework of Language." *Philosophy Today*, 31 (Spring 1987): 3–20.

Herrmann, Friedrich Wilhelm von. *Subjekt und Dasein: Interpretationen zu "Sein and Zeit."* Frankfurt am Main: Klostermann, 1985.

Hoffman, Piotr. *The Human Self and the Life and Death Struggle*. Gainesville: University Press of Florida, 1983.

_____. *Doubt, Time, Violence*. Chicago: University of Chicago Press, 1986.

Holland, Nancy J., and Huntington, Patricia J., eds. *Feminist Interpretations of Martin Heidegger*. University Park: Pennsylvania State University Press, 2001.

Huntington, Patricia J. *Ecstatic Subjects, Utopia, and Recognition: Kristeva, Heidegger, Irigaray*. Albany: State University of New York Press, 1998.

Inwood, Michael. *Heidegger*. Oxford: Oxford University Press, 1997.

Irigaray, Luce. *The Forgetting of Air in Martin Heidegger*. Austin: University of Texas Press, 1999.

Janicaud, Dominique, and Mattéi, Jean-François. *Heidegger from Metaphysics to Thought*. Translated by Michael Gendre. Albany: State University of New York Press, 1995.

Kearney, Richard. *Poetics of Imagining: Modern to Post-Modern*. New York: Fordham University Press, 1998.

Keller, Pierre. *Husserl and Heidegger on Human Experience*. Cambridge: Cambridge University Press, 1999.

King, Magda. *A Guide to Heidegger's Being and Time*. Edited by John Llewelyn. Albany: State University of New York Press, 2001.

Kockelmans, Joseph J. *On the Truth of Being: Reflections on Heidegger's Later Philosophy*. Bloomington: Indiana University Press, 1984.

———. *A Companion to Martin Heidegger's* Being and Time. Washington, DC: University Press of America, 1986.

Krell, David Farrell. *Intimations of Mortality: Time, Truth, and Finitude in Heidegger's Thinking of Being*. University Park: Pennsylvania State University Press, 1986.

Lafont, Christina. *Heidegger, Language, and World Disclosure*. Translated by Graham Harman. Cambridge: Cambridge University Press, 2000.

Levin, David Michael. *The Opening of Vision: Nihilism and the Postmodern Situation*. New York: Routledge & Kegan Paul, 1988.

Löwith, Karl. *Heidegger: Denker in dürftiger Zeit: Zur Stellung der Philosophie im 20. Jahrhundert*. Stuttgart: J. B. Metzler, 1984.

Macann, Christopher, ed. *Critical Heidegger*. London: Routledge, 1996.

Magnus, Bernd. "Heidegger's Metahistory of Philosophy Revisited." *Monist*, 64 (October 1981): 445–66.

Malpas, Jeff, and Wrathall, Mark, eds. *Heidegger, Authenticity, and Modernity: Essays in Honor of Hubert L. Dreyfus*. Vol. 1. Cambridge, MA: The MIT Press, 2000.

———. *Heidegger, Coping, and Cognitive Science: Essays in Honor of Hubert L. Dreyfus*. Vol. 2. Cambridge, MA: The MIT Press, 2000.

Maly, Kenneth, and Emad, Parvis, eds. *Heidegger on Heraclitus: A New Reading*. Lewiston, NY: Mellen Press, 1986.

Mansbach, Abraham. *Beyond Subjectivism: Heidegger on Language and the Human Being*. Westport, CT: Greenwood Press, 2002.

Marion, Jean-Luc. *Reduction and Givenness: Investigations of Husserl, Heidegger, and Phenomenology*. Evanston, IL: Northwestern University Press, 1998.

Marx, Werner. *Heidegger and the Tradition*. Translated by Theodore Kisiel and Murray Greene. Evanston, IL: Northwestern University Press, 1971.

———, ed. *Heidegger Memorial Lectures*. Translated by Steven W. Davis. Pittsburgh: Duquesne University Press, 1982.

McCumber, John. *Metaphysics and Oppression: Heidegger's Challenge to Western Philosophy*. Bloomington: Indiana University Press, 1999.

McNeill, William. *The Glance of the Eye: Heidegger, Aristotle, and the Ends of Theory*. Albany: State University of New York Press, 1999.

Mehta, Jarava Lal. *Martin Heidegger, the Way and the Vision*. Honolulu: University of Hawaii Press, 1976.

Milchman, Alan, and Rosenberg, Alan, eds. *Foucault and Heidegger: Critical Encounters*. Minneapolis: University of Minnesota Press, 2003.

Mohanty, J. N. *The Possibility of Transcendental Philosophy*. Dordrecht: Nijhoff, 1985.

Mugerauer, Robert. *Heidegger's Language and Thinking*. Atlantic Highlands, NJ: Humanities Press International, 1988.

Mulhall, Stephen. *On Being in the World: Wittgenstein and Heidegger on Seeing Aspects*. London: Routledge & Kegan Paul, 1990.

———. *Routledge Philosophy Guidebook to Heidegger and* Being and Time. London: Routledge, 1996.

———. *Inheritance and Originality: Wittgenstein, Heidegger, Kierkegaard*. Oxford: Oxford University Press, 2001.

Murray, Michael, ed. *Heidegger and Modern Philosophy: Critical Essays*. New Haven, CT: Yale University Press, 1978.

Nenon, Thomas J., ed. *Spindel Conference 1989: Heidegger and Praxis*. Memphis, TN: Memphis State University, 1990. *Southern Journal of Philosophy*, 28, suppl.

Nicholson, Graeme. *Illustrations of Being: Drawing upon Heidegger and upon Metaphysics*. Atlantic Highlands, NJ: Humanities Press, 1992.

Okrent, Mark. *Heidegger's Pragmatism: Understanding, Being, and the Critique of Metaphysics*. Ithaca, NY: Cornell University Press, 1992.

Olafson, Frederick A. *Heidegger and the Philosophy of Mind*. New Haven, CT: Yale University Press, 1987.

———. *What Is Human Being? A Heideggerian View*. Cambridge: Cambridge University Press, 1995.

Parkes, Graham, ed. *Heidegger and Asian Thought*. Honolulu: University of Hawaii Press, 1987.

Pietersma, Henry. *Phenomenological Epistemology*. Oxford: Oxford University Press, 2000.

Pippin, Robert B. *Idealism as Modernism: Hegelian Variations*. Cambridge: Cambridge University Press, 1997.

Pöggler, Otto. *Martin Heidegger's Path of Thinking*. Translated by Daniel Magurshak and Sigmund Barber. Atlantic Highlands, NJ: Humanities Press International, 1987.

———, ed. *Heidegger: Perspektiven zur Deutung seines Werks*. Köln: Kiepenheuer & Witsch, 1969.

Polt, Richard. *Heidegger: An Introduction*. Ithaca, NY: Cornell University Press, 1999.

———. *The Emergency of Being: On Heidegger's "Contributions to Philosophy."* Ithaca, NY: Cornell University Press, 2006.

Polt, Richard, ed. *Heidegger's* Being and Time: *Critical Essays*. Lanham, MD: Rowman & Littlefield, 2005.

Raffoul, François. *Heidegger and the Subject*. Translated by David Pettigrew and Gregory Recco. Atlantic Highlands, NJ: Humanities Press, 1998.

Raffoul, François, and Pettigrew, David, eds. *Heidegger and Practical Philosophy*. Albany: State University of New York, 2002.

Rée, Jonathan. *Heidegger*. New York: Routledge, 1999.

Richardson, John. *Existential Epistemology: A Heideggerian Critique of the Cartesian Project*. Oxford: Clarendon Press, 1986.

Richardson, William J. *Heidegger: Through Phenomenology to Thought*. 3rd ed. The Hague: Nijhoff, 1974.

Ricoeur, Paul. "Phenomenology and Hermeneutics." In *Hermeneutics and the Human Sciences*. Edited by John Thompson. Cambridge: Cambridge University Press, 1981.

———. *Time and Narrative*. 3 vols. Translated by K. McLaughlin and D. Pellaner. Chicago: University of Chicago Press, 1984–6.

Rockmore, Tom. *Heidegger and French Philosophy: Humanism, Antihumanism, and Being*. London: Routledge, 1995.

Rorty, Richard. *Philosophy and the Mirror of Nature*. Princeton, NJ: Princeton University Press, 1979.

———. *Consequences of Pragmatism*. Minneapolis: University of Minnesota Press, 1982.

———. *Essays on Heidegger and Others: Philosophical Papers*. Vol. 2. Cambridge: Cambridge University Press, 1991.

———, ed. *Heidegger and the History of Philosophy*. Special issue of *Monist*, 64 (October 1981).

Rosen, Stanley. *The Question of Being: A Reversal of Heidegger*. New Haven, CT: Yale University Press, 1993.

Ruin, Hans. *Enigmatic Origins: Tracing the Theme of Historicity through Heidegger's Works*. Stockholm: Almqvist & Wiksell, 1994.

Sallis, John. "End(s)." *Research in Phenomenology*, 13 (1983): 85–96.

———. "Heidegger/Derrida – Presence." *Journal of Philosophy*, 81 (October 1984): 594–601.

———. *Echoes: After Heidegger*. Bloomington: Indiana University Press, 1990.

———. *Reading Heidegger: Commemorations*. Bloomington: Indiana University Press, 1993.

Schalow, Frank. *The Renewal of the Heidegger-Kant Dialogue: Action, Thought, and Responsibility*. Albany: State University of New York Press, 1992.

Schmidt, Dennis J. "Between Hegel and Heidegger." *Man and World*, 15 (1982): 17–32.

———. *The Ubiquity of the Finite: Hegel, Heidegger, and the Entitlements of Philosophy*. Cambridge, MA: The MIT Press, 1988.

Schrift, Alan D. "Reading Derrida Reading Heidegger Reading Nietzsche." *Research in Phenomenology*, 14 (1984): 87–119.

Schürmann, Reiner. *Heidegger on Being and Acting: From Principles to Anarchy*. Translated by Christine-Marie Gros and Reiner Schurmann. Bloomington: Indiana University Press, 1987.

Scott, Charles E. *The Language of Difference*. Atlantic Highlands, NJ: Humanities Press, 1987.

Scott, Charles E., et al., eds. *Companion to Heidegger's* Contributions to Philosophy. Bloomington: Indiana University Press, 2001.

Seifert, Josef. "Is the Existence of Truth Dependent on Man?" *Review of Metaphysics*, 35 (1982): 461–82.

Seigfried, Hans. "Against Naturalizing Preconceptual Experience." *Philosophy and Phenomenological Research*, 48 (March 1988): 505–18.

Shahan, Robert W., and Mohanty, J. N., eds. *Thinking about Being: Aspects of Heidegger's Thought*. Norman: University of Oklahoma Press, 1984.

Silverman, Hugh J., et al., eds. *The Horizons of Continental Philosophy: Essays on Husserl, Heidegger, and Merleau-Ponty*. Dordrecht: Kluwer Academic, 1988.

Stewart, Roderick M. "Heidegger and the Intentionality of Language." *American Philosophical Quarterly*, 25 (April 1988): 153–62.

Taminiaux, Jacques. *Dialectic and Difference: Finitude in Modern Thought*. Atlantic Highlands, NJ: Humanities Press, 1985.

_____. *Heidegger and the Project of Fundamental Ontology*. Translated by Michael Gendre. Albany: State University of New York Press, 1991.

_____. *The Thracian Mind and the Professional Thinker: Arendt and Heidegger*. Albany: State University of New York Press, 1997.

Tanzer, Mark Besil. *Heidegger: Decisionism and Quietism*. Amherst, NY: Humanity Books, 2002.

Theunissen, Michael. *The Other: Studies in the Social Ontology of Husserl, Heidegger, Sartre, and Buber*. Translated by Christopher Macann. Cambridge, MA: The MIT Press, 1984.

Thiele, Leslie Paul. *Timely Meditations*. Princeton, NJ: Princeton University Press, 1995.

Thomä, Dieter, ed. *Heidegger Handbuch: Leben – Wirk – Wirkung*. Stuttgart: J. B. Metzler, 2003.

Thomson, Iain. *Heidegger on Ontotheology: Technology and the Politics of Education*. Cambridge: Cambridge University Press, 2005.

Tugendhat, Ernst. *Self-Consciousness and Self-Determination*. Translated by Paul Stern. Cambridge, MA: The MIT Press, 1986.

Tuttle, Howard N. *The Dawn of Historical Reason: The Historicality of Human Existence in the Thought of Dilthey, Heidegger and Ortega y Gasset*. New York: P. Lang, 1994.

_____. *The Crowd Is Untruth: The Existential Critique of Mass Society in the Thought of Kierkegaard, Nietzsche, Heidegger, and Ortega y Gasset*. New York: P. Lang, 1996.

Vallicella, William F. "Heidegger and the Problem of the Thing in Itself." *International Philosophical Quarterly*, 23 (March 1983): 35–44.

Van Buren, John. *The Young Heidegger: Rumor of the Hidden King*. Bloomington: Indiana University Press, 1994.

Vattimo, Gianni. *The Adventure of Difference: Philosophy after Nietzsche and Heidegger*. Baltimore: Johns Hopkins University Press, 1993.

White, Carol J. *Time and Death: Heidegger's Analysis of Finitude. Intersections of Continental and Analytic Philosophy*. Aldershot: Ashgate Publishing, 2005.

White, David A. *Logic and Ontology in Heidegger*. Columbus: Ohio State University Press, 1985.

Wood, David. *Of Derrida, Heidegger, and Spirit*. Evanston, IL: Northwestern University Press, 1993.

Wrathall, Mark. *How to Read Heidegger*. London: Granta, 2005.

Young, Julian. *Heidegger's Later Philosophy*. Cambridge: Cambridge University Press, 2002.

Zimmerman, Michael. "Heidegger's 'Existentialism' Revisited." *International Philosophical Quarterly*, 24 (September 1984): 219–36.

――――. *Eclipse of the Self. The Development of Heidegger's Concept of Authenticity*. Revised edition. Athens: Ohio University Press, 1986.

――――. *Heidegger's Confrontation with Modernity: Technology, Politics, and Art*. Bloomington: Indiana University Press, 1990.

――――, ed. *The Thought of Martin Heidegger. Tulane Studies in Philosophy*, Vol. 32. New Orleans: Tulane University, 1984.

ETHICS AND POLITICS

Beistegui, Miguel de. *Heidegger and the Political*. New York: Routledge, 1998.

Bernasconi, Robert L. "'The Double Concept of Philosophy' and the Place of Ethics in *Being and Time*." *Research in Phenomenology*, 18 (1988): 41–57.

Bernstein, Richard J. *The New Constellation: The Ethical-Political Horizons of Modernity/Postmodernity*. Cambridge, MA: The MIT Press, 1992.

Bourdieu, Pierre. *The Political Ontology of Martin Heidegger*. Cambridge: Polity Press, 1996.

Brainard, Marcus, Jacobs, David, and Lee, Rick, eds. *Heidegger and the Political*. Special Issue of the *Graduate Faculty of Philosophy Journal*, 14–15 (1991). (Includes an extensive bibliography by Pierre Adler.)

Collins, Jeff. *Heidegger and the Nazis*. New York: Totem Books, 2000.

Dallmayr, Fred R. "Heidegger, Hölderlin and Politics." *Heidegger Studies*, 2 (1986): 81–95.

――――. *The Other Heidegger*. Ithaca, NY: Cornell University Press, 1993.

Dauenhauer, Bernard P. "Heidegger's Contribution to Modern Political Thought." *Southern Journal of Philosophy*, 22 (Winter 1984): 481–86.

Derrida, Jacques. *Of Spirit: Heidegger and the Question*. Translated by Geoffrey Bennington and Rachel Bowlby. Chicago: University of Chicago Press, 1989.

Farias, Victor. *Heidegger and Nazism*. Edited by Joseph Margolis and Tom Rockmore. Translated by Paul Burrell, with the advice of Dominic Di Bernardi, and by Gabriel R. Ricci. Philadelphia: Temple University Press, 1989.

Ferry, Luc, and Renaut, Alain. *Heidegger and Modernity*. Translated by Franklin Philip. Chicago: University of Chicago Press, 1990.

Hatab, Lawrence J.: *Ethics and Finitude: Heideggerian Contributions to Moral Philosophy*. Lanham, MD: Rowman & Littlefield, 2000.

Hodge, Joanna. *Heidegger and Ethics*. London: Routledge, 1995.

Lacoue-Labarthe, Philippe. *Heidegger, Art, and Politics: The Fiction of the Political*. Translated by Chris Turner. Oxford: Blackwell, 1990.

Lang, Berel. *Heidegger's Silence*. Ithaca, NY: Cornell University Press, 1996.

Lyotard, Jean François. *Heidegger and "The Jews."* Translated by Andreas Michel and Mark S. Roberts. Foreword by David Carroll. Minneapolis: University of Minnesota Press, 1990.

Manning, Robert. *Interpreting Otherwise than Heidegger: Emmanuel Levinas's Ethics as First Philosophy*. Pittsburgh: Duquesne University Press, 1993.

Marcuse, Herbert, and Olafson, Frederick. "Heidegger's Politics." *Graduate Faculty Philosophy Journal*, 6 (Winter 1977): 28–40.

Marx, Werner. *Is There a Measure on Earth? Foundations for a Nonmetaphysical Ethics*. Translated by Thomas J. Nenon and Reginald Lilly. Chicago: University of Chicago Press, 1987.

Milchman, Alan, and Rosenberg, Alan, eds. *Heidegger and The Holocaust*. Atlantic Highlands, NJ: Humanities Press, 1996.

Nicholson, Graeme. "The Politics of Heidegger's Rectoral Address." *Man and World*, 20 (1987): 171–87.

Olafson, Frederick A. *Heidegger and the Ground of Ethics: A Study of Mitsein*. Cambridge: Cambridge University Press, 1998.

Pöggler, Otto. *Philosophie and Nationalsozialismus: Am Beispiel Heideggers*. Opladen: Westdeutscher, 1990.

Rockmore, Tom. *On Heidegger's Nazism and Philosophy*. Berkeley: University of California Press, 1992.

Rockmore, Tom, and Margolis, Joseph, eds. *The Heidegger Case: On Philosophy and Politics*. Philadelphia: Temple University Press, 1992.

Schalow, Frank. *Imagination and Existence: Heidegger's Retrieval of the Kantian Ethic*. Lanham, MD: University Press of America, 1986.

_____. *Language and Deed: Rediscovering Politics through Heidegger's Encounter with German Idealism*. Amsterdam: Rodopi, 1998.

Schürmann, Reiner. "Adventures of the Double Negation: On Richard Bernstein's Call for Anti-anti-humanism." *Praxis International*, 5 (October 1985): 283–91.

Scott, Charles E. The *Question of Ethics: Nietzsche, Foucault, Heidegger*. Bloomington: Indiana University Press, 1990.

Sheehan, Thomas. "Heidegger and the Nazis." *New York Review of Books*, June 16, 1988, pp. 38–47.

Tymieniecka, Anna-Teresa, and Schrag, Calvin O., eds. *Foundations of Morality*. Boston: Reidel, 1983.

Villa, Dana Richard. *Arendt and Heidegger: The Fate of the Political*. Princeton, NJ: Princeton University Press, 1996.

Vogel, Lawrence. *The Fragile "We": Ethical Implications of Heidegger's Being and Time*. Evanston, IL: Northwestern University Press, 1994.

Ward, James F. *Heidegger's Political Thinking*. Amherst: University of Massachusetts Press, 1995.

Wolin, Richard. *The Politics of Being: The Political Thought of Martin Heidegger*. New York: Columbia University Press, 1992.

————. *Heidegger's Children: Hannah Arendt, Karl Löwith, Hans Jonas, and Herbert Marcuse*. Princeton, NJ: Princeton University Press, 2001.

————, ed. *The Heidegger Controversy: A Critical Reader*. Cambridge, MA: The MIT Press, 1993.

Young, Julian. *Heidegger, Philosophy, Nazism*. Cambridge: Cambridge University Press, 1997.

Zimmerman, Michael E. "Karel Kosik's Heideggerian Marxism." *Philosophical Forum*, 15 (Spring 1984): 209–33.

————. "Philosophy and Politics: The Case of Heidegger." *Philosophy Today*, 33 (Spring 1989): 3–20.

————. "The Thorn in Heidegger's Side: The Question of National Socialism." *Philosophical Forum*, 20 (Summer 1989): 326–65.

AESTHETICS AND LITERARY THEORY

Brogan, Walter. "The Battle between Art and Truth." *Philosophy Today*, 28 (Winter 1984): 349–57.

Bruns, Gerald L. *Heidegger's Estrangements: Language, Truth, and Poetry in the Later Writings*. New Haven, CT: Yale University Press, 1989.

Fóti, Véronique M. *Poiesis-Sophia-Techne: Between Heidegger and the Poets*. Atlantic Highlands, NJ: Humanities Press, 1991.

Gosetti-Ferencei, Jennifer A. *Heidegger, Hölderlin, and the Subject of Poetic Language: Toward a New Poetics of Dasein. Perspectives in Continental Philosophy*. New York: Fordham University Press, 2004.

Harries, Karsten. *The Ethical Function of Architecture.* Cambridge, MA: The MIT Press, 1997.

Kockelmans, Joseph J. *Heidegger on Art and Art Works.* Dordrecht: Nijhoff, 1985.

Schaeffer, Jean-Marie. *Art of the Modern Age: Philosophy of Art from Kant to Heidegger.* Princeton, NJ: Princeton University Press, 2000.

Schrift, Alan D. *Nietzsche and the Question of Interpretation: Between Hermeneutics and Deconstruction.* New York: Routledge & Kegan Paul, 1990.

Tymieniecka, Anna-Teresa. *The Poetry of Life in Literature.* Dordrecht: Kluwer Academic Publishers, 2000.

Tymieniecka, Anna-Teresa, ed. *The Philosophical Reflection of Man in Literature.* Boston: Reidel, 1982.

Vattimo, Gianni. "Aesthetics and the End of Epistemology." In *The Reasons of Art.* Edited by Peter McCormick. Ottawa: University of Ottawa Press, 1985.

Wood, Robert E. *Placing Aesthetics: Reflections on the Philosophic Tradition.* Athens: Ohio University Press, 1999.

Wright, Kathleen. "The Place of the Work of Art in the Age of Technology." *Southern Journal of Philosophy,* 22 (Winter 1984): 565–82.

Young, Julian. *Heidegger's Philosophy of Art.* Cambridge, UK: Cambridge University Press, 2001.

SCIENCE AND TECHNOLOGY

Borgmann, Albert. *Technology and the Character of Everyday Life: A Philosophical Inquiry.* Chicago: University of Chicago Press, 1984.

Borgmann, Albert, and Mitcham, Carl. "The Question of Heidegger and Technology: A Critical Review of the Literature." *Philosophy Today,* 31 (Summer 1987): 99–194.

Bourgeois, Patrick L. "Fundamental Ontology, Scientific Methods, and Epistemic Foundations." *New Scholasticism,* 56 (Fall 1982): 471–9.

Emad, Parvis. "Technology as Presence: Heidegger's View." *Listening,* 16 (Spring 1981): 131–44.

Fandozzi, Phillip R. *Nihilism and Technology: A Heideggerian Investigation.* Washington, DC: University Press of America, 1982.

Feenberg, Andrew, *Heidegger and Marcuse: The Catastrophe and Redemption of History.* New York: Routledge, 2004.

Feenberg, Andrew, and Hannay, Alastair, eds. *Technology and the Politics of Knowledge.* Bloomington: Indiana University Press, 1995.

Glazebrook, Trish. *Heidegger's Philosophy of Science.* New York: Fordham University Press, 2000.

Kelly, Michael. "On Hermeneutics and Science: Why Hermeneutics is not Anti-Science." *Southern Journal of Philosophy*, 25 (Winter 1987): 481–500.

Kockelmans, Joseph J. *Heidegger and Science*. Washington DC: University Press of America, 1985.

Kolb, David A. "Heidegger on the Limits of Science." *Journal of the British Society for Phenomenology*, 14 (January 1983): 50–64.

Loscerbo, John. *Being and Technology: A Study in the Philosophy of Martin Heidegger*. The Hague: Nijhoff, 1981.

Lovitt, Harriet Brundage, and Lovitt, William. *Modern Technology in the Heideggerian Perspective*. Lewiston, NY: Mellen Press, 1995.

Rouse, Joseph. "Kuhn, Heidegger, and Scientific Realism." *Man and World*, 14 (1981): 269–90.

———. "Heidegger's Later Philosophy of Science." *Southern Journal of Philosophy*, 23 (Spring 1985): 75–92.

THEOLOGY AND RELIGIOUS STUDIES

Ballard, Bruce W. *The Role of Mood in Heidegger's Ontology*. Lanham, MD: University Press of America, 1991.

Bonsor, Jack Arthur. *Rahner, Heidegger, and Truth*. Lanham, MD: University Press of America, 1987.

Caputo, John D. *Heidegger and Aquinas: An Essay on Overcoming Metaphysics*. New York: Fordham University Press, 1982.

———. *The Mystical Element in Heidegger's Thought*. New York: Fordham University Press, 1986.

Crowe, Benjamin. *Heidegger's Religious Origins: Destruction and Authenticity*. Bloomington: Indiana University Press, 2006.

Gall, Robert S. *Beyond Theism and Atheism: Heidegger's Significance for Religious Thinking*. Dordrecht: Nijhoff, 1987.

Hemming, Laurence Paul. *Heidegger's Atheism: The Refusal of a Theological Voice*. Notre Dame, IN: University of Notre Dame Press, 2002.

Kovacs, George. *The Question of God in Heidegger's Phenomenology*. Evanston, IL: Northwestern University Press, 1990.

Macquarrie, John. *An Existentialist Theology: A Comparison of Heidegger and Bultmann*. New York: Macmillan, 1955.

———. *Heidegger and Christianity: The Hensley Henson Lectures, 1993–94*. New York: Continuum, 1999.

Schalow, Frank. *Heidegger and the Quest for the Sacred: From Thought to the Sanctuary of Faith*. Dordrecht: Kluwer Academic Publishers, 2001.

Sheehan, Thomas. "Metaphysics and Bivalence: On Karl Rahner's 'Geist in Welt.'" *Modern Schoolman*, 63 (November 1985): 21–43.

Sikka, Sonya. *Forms of Transcendence: Heidegger and Medieval Mystical Theology.* Albany: State University of New York Press, 1997.

Westphal, Merold. *Postmodern Philosophy and Christian Thought.* Bloomington: Indiana University Press, 1999.

Zimmerman, Michael E. "Heidegger and Bultmann: Egoism, Sinfulness, and Inauthenticity." *Modern Schoolman,* 57 (November 1980): 1–20.

PSYCHOLOGY AND PSYCHOTHERAPY

Cohn, Hans. *Heidegger and the Roots of Existential Psychotherapy.* London: Continuum, 2002.

Condrau, Gion. *Martin Heidegger's Impact on Psychotherapy.* New York: Mosaic, 1998.

Faulconer, James E., ed. *Reconsidering Psychology: Perspectives from Continental Philosophy.* Pittsburgh: Duquesne University Press, 1990.

Hoeller, Keith, ed. *Heidegger and Psychology.* Special Issue of the *Review of Existential Psychology and Psychiatry.* Seattle, 1988.

McCall, Raymond J. *Phenomenological Psychology: An Introduction, with a Glossary of Some Key Heideggerian Terms.* Madison: University of Wisconsin Press, 1983.

Medina, Angel. "Heidegger, Lacan and the Boundaries of Existence: Whole and Partial Subjects in Psychoanalysis." *Man and World,* 18 (1985): 389–403.

Messer, Stanley B., Sass, Louis A., and Woolfolk, Robert L. *Hermeneutics and Psychological Theory: Interpretive Perspectives on Personality, Psychotherapy, and Psychopathology.* New Brunswick, NJ: Rutgers University Press, 1988.

Oliver, Kelly, and Edwin, Steve, eds. *Between the Psyche and the Social: Psychoanalytic Social Theory.* Lanham, MD: Rowman & Littlefield, 2002.

Thompson, M. Guy. *The Truth about Freud's Technique: The Encounter with the Real.* New York: New York University Press, 1994.

INDEX

Lightning Source UK Ltd.
Milton Keynes UK
UKOW02f1020290116

267378UK00002BA/301/P